'How refreshing to read a biography in which the author is half in love with her subject. There are none of the usual patronising putdowns, envious backbiting or mean-spirited cavilling in Anne de Courcy's portrait of the Earl of Snowdon'
Richard Davenport-Hines, *Sunday Times*

'An onslaught of revelation, a dizzyingly switchback ride of mixed emotions, pomp and sleaze ... very true to life'
Duncan Fallowell, *Daily Telegraph*

'[A] juicy biography ... it is impossible here to convey the combination of high society and low morals, of frightfully good taste and awful cheese that de Courcy has managed to dish up'
Observer

'Step forward, Snowdon. You're nicked ... Full of eye-popping revelations' *Mail on Sunday*

'Has anyone not slept with Lord Snowdon? The priapic Earl's multi-layered love life is the dominant theme of this chatty and penetrating biography, packed as it is with love affairs, love-children ... and love-struck mistresses, often several at one time ... Snowdon makes a glamorous, capricious, selfish and surprisingly philanthropic subject for this lively account of a man and his era'
Daily Mail summer reading

Anne de Courcy is a well-known writer with a long career in journalism, most recently with the *Daily Mail* for whom she did interviews, historical features and book reviews, as well as editing a page on readers' dilemmas. She has written eleven books, including *The English in Love*; *1939: The Last Season*; *Society's Queen*; *The Viceroy's Daughters*; *Diana Mosley* and *Debs at War*. She lives in London and Gloucestershire.

By Anne de Courcy

The English in Love
1939: The Last Season
Society's Queen
The Viceroy's Daughters
Diana Mosley
Debs at War
Snowdon: The Biography

Snowdon

THE BIOGRAPHY

✣

Anne de Courcy

PHOENIX

A PHOENIX PAPERBACK

First published in Great Britain in 2008
by Weidenfeld & Nicolson
This paperback edition published in 2009
by Phoenix,
an imprint of Orion Books Ltd,
Orion House, 5 Upper St Martin's Lane,
London, WC2H 9EA

An Hachette UK company

1 3 5 7 9 10 8 6 4 2

A CIP catalogue record for this book
is available from the British Library.

ISBN 978-0-7538-2587-7

Typeset by Input Data Services Ltd, Bridgwater, Somerset

Printed and bound in Great Britain by
CPI Mackays, Chatham, Kent

The Orion Publishing Group's policy is to use papers that
are natural, renewable and recyclable products and
made from wood grown in sustainable forests. The logging
and manufacturing processes are expected to conform to
the environmental regulations of the country of origin.

www.orionbooks.co.uk

Contents

CONTENTS

List of Illustrations

The author and publishers would like to thank the following for their very kind permission to reproduce photographs: Lord Snowdon, 1, 2, 4, 8, 9, 12, 21, 22, 31, 34, 35, 39, 41, 42, 54, 55, 58, 59, 60, 62, 63, 67, 68; Bryan Adams, 78; Anthony Barton, 10; Robert Belton, 6, 18, 19, 20, 23, 24, 30, 36, 37; Melanie Cable-Alexander, 70, 71; Princess Caracciolo, 47, 48; Michael Dover, 77; Andrew Farquhar and the Snowdon Award Scheme, 64, 65; Andy Garnett, 13, 14; Milton Gendel, 43, 61; Polly Higson, 16, 17, 72; Elliot Philipp, 66; Veronica Keeling, 11; Peter Saunders, 15; Marjorie Wallace, 76; Camera Press London: 26 (Tom Blau), 27 (Snowdon), 33 (Cecil Beaton), 40 (IMS), 45 (Tom Blau), 46 (Snowdon), 50 (Penny Tweedie), 56 (Snowdon), 74 (Stewart Mark), 75 (Mark Stewart); Country Life, 5, 7; Getty Images: 3, 28, 32, 44, 49, 51, 52, 29 (AFP), 57 (Tim Graham); Peter Keen, 25; NI Syndication, 53; PA Photos, 73.

Acknowledgements

I would like to express my great gratitude to Lord Snowdon. He was the perfect biographical subject, not only because of his brilliant talent, campaigning work for others, colourful life, complex and interesting personality, and kindness giving up hours of his time to lengthy taped interviews but because he never once attempted to influence what I wrote. It only remains to add not only my admiration but also my affection.

*

The material in this book is primarily based on many hours of talk with Lord Snowdon, who also gave me full and unfettered access to his files and archives.

It is supplemented by conversations with the following, to whom I would like to express my profound thanks for their kindness in talking to me at such length and so freely: the Countess of Airlie (Lady of the Bedchamber to HM the Queen), Lady Elizabeth Anson, Peregrine Armstrong-Jones, the late Robin Banks, Anthony Barton, Robert Belton, Lorenzo Berni, Stephen Bradshaw, Gyles Brandreth, Peter Brandt, Marigold Bridgeman, Julian Broad, Lt-Col. Frederick Burnaby-Atkins, Melanie Cable-Alexander, Dame Frances Campbell-Preston (Woman of the Bedchamber to Queen Elizabeth the Queen Mother), Princess Judy Caracciolo, Robert Carey-Evans, Sir Edward Cazalet, Victoria Charlton, Felicity Clark, Justin de Blank, Lord de Vesci, Sholto Douglas-Home, Michael Dover, Meredith Etherington-Smith, Andrew Farquhar, Leslie Field, Andy Garnett, Milton Gendel, Mary Gilliatt, Lady Glenconner (Extra Lady-in-Waiting to Princess Margaret from 1971), Janet Goodwin, Lady Grade, Elizabeth Greenfield (dresser to Princess Margaret), David Griffin (chauffeur to Princess Margaret from 1977), Jill Duchess of Hamilton, Pamela Lady Harlech, Nicholas Haslam, Malcolm Higgins (footman and then butler in Kensington Palace), Polly Higson, Emily Hirst, Evelyn Humphries, Angela Huth, Derek Jackson, Anthony Johnson, Veronica

Keeling, John Larkin (chauffeur to Princess Margaret 1964–77), Betty Lawson, the late Earl of Lichfield, Viscount Linley, Sir Dai Llewellyn, Peter Lyster Todd, Anna Massey, Lord McColl, the late George Melly and Diana Melly, Thomas Messel (first cousin to Lord Snowdon), Lord Napier and Ettrick (Private Secretary to Princess Margaret 1973–98 and then her Treasurer until her death in 2002), Sue Odell, Terry O'Neill, Tom Parr, Pat Paxton, Lady Penn (wife of the late Lt-Col. Sir Eric Penn, Comptroller of the Lord Chamberlain's Office 1960–81), Dr Elliot Philipp, Graham Pigott, Anthony Powell, Margaret Purcell, the Marchioness of Reading, John Rendall, Luba and Richard Rhodes, Helen Robinson, Kenneth Rose, the Earl of Rosse (half-brother to Lord Snowdon), Lady Jaqueline Rufus-Isaacs, the late Simon Sainsbury, Raymond Salisbury-Jones, Ingrid Seward, Tom Stacey, Graham Stark, Jane Stevens, Tim Symonds, the late Dr Frank Tait, the late William Tallon (page to the Queen Mother), the late John Timbers, Bernard Thomas, Dylan Thomas, Lady Juliet Townsend (Lady-in-Waiting to Princess Margaret 1965–71), the Hon. Gina Tritton, Hugo Vickers, Dame Gillian Wagner, Marjorie Wallace, Christopher Warwick, the Hon. Annabel Whitehead (Lady-in-Waiting to Princess Margaret 1971–4), Lynne Wilson, Richard Wood and Francis Wyndham.

I am most grateful to Her Majesty Queen Elizabeth II for permission to quote the letter from Queen Elizabeth the Queen Mother which appears on pages 280–1.

My thanks are due to the Royal Archives for permission to use material from their files. I am most grateful to Justin de Blank for permission to use his contemporary record of the engagement ball at Buckingham Palace and to Andy Garnett for the extract from his memoir Lucky Dog, to Sholto Douglas-Home for allowing me to use extracts from his father's commonplace book, and to Brian Hoey for donating to me his seven sacks and four box files of press cuttings on Lord Snowdon, which were an invaluable source of publicly recorded material. I would like to thank Alexandra Shulman, editor of Vogue, for her kindness in letting me rummage through the magazine's archives, the staff of the Daily Mail library and the London Library for their help and assistance, and of course my nonpareil editor Benjamin Buchan.

Princess Margaret's ladies-in-waiting and Private Secretaries and the servants at Kensington Palace were illuminating about the Snowdons' life there and the relationship between them – here I should perhaps say that nowhere did Lord Snowdon himself describe this. I am indebted to the late William Tallon for descriptions of life at Clarence House, Royal Lodge and Princess Margaret's relationship with the Queen Mother. I have, incidentally, used the term 'Queen Mother' throughout (rather than the more correct 'Queen Elizabeth'), chiefly because that is how most people think of her and also to avoid possible confusion with the Queen.

ACKNOWLEDGEMENTS

I would also specially like to thank Christopher Warwick, Princess Margaret's chosen biographer, who knew her for twenty years, for insights and anecdotes – many hitherto untold – as well as information; and Leslie Field, author of *The Queen's Jewels*, for her expert assistance on Princess Margaret's jewellery.

I am very grateful to Spike Milligan Productions for permission to print a letter to Lord Snowdon, to Roy Strong and Weidenfeld & Nicolson Ltd for permission to reproduce material from *The Roy Strong Diaries 1967–1987*, and to Michael Bloch, the estate of James-Lees Milne and Michael Russell Publishing for permission to reprint extracts from the diaries of the late James-Lees Milne.

For the loan of photographs from their private collections I am greatly indebted to Bryan Adams, Anthony Barton, Robert Belton, Melanie Cable-Alexander, Princess Caracciolo, Michael Dover, Andy Garnett, Milton Gendel, Polly Higson, Veronia Keeling, Peter Saunders, Lord Snowdon and Marjorie Wallace.

Anne de Courcy
January 2008

I

The Other Son

-*|*-

On 6 May 1960 Antony Armstrong-Jones stood on the balcony of Buckingham Palace, his new bride by his side and a cheering mass of over 30,000 spectators below. It was an extraordinary, intoxicating moment, so overwhelming that at the time his mind was a blank. He was thirty years old, he was at the peak of his profession, and he had just married the sister of the Queen of England. What else was there left to do, or conquer?

For some people, power is the ultimate aphrodisiac. For others, it is fame, money or social success. The twin motivating forces in the life of Antony Armstrong-Jones were work and sex, both backed by immense, charismatic charm and a drive and determination unfettered by many of the usual constraints. The relationships this complex, inflammable mix involved were shaped not only by his own nature but, as with so many of us, by the attitudes of those who surrounded him in his early life. This is his story.

Antony Charles Robert Armstrong-Jones, always known as Tony, was born on 7 March 1930. Although there were brains and talent on both sides of his family, and considerable wealth on one, there was nothing to indicate the extraordinary life that he himself would lead.

His parentage was a mingling of Welsh, Jewish and English. His father, Ronald Owen Armstrong-Jones, born on 18 May 1899, and called to the Bar of the Middle Temple in 1922, was Welsh to his fingertips. Ronnie, as he was always known, was the son of the brilliant surgeon, Robert Jones:* their antecedents included Welsh farmers, shipowners, a High Sheriff of Caernarvonshire and, it is believed, King Edward I of England. Ronnie's mother Margaret, who brought the Caernarvonshire estate of Plas Dinas into the family, was the daughter of Sir Owen Roberts (who also owned the Surrey estate of Henley Park), but by the time Ronnie inherited it in 1943 the original 800 acres had shrunk to extensive grounds and fourteen acres of parkland.

Tony's mother Anne Messel, daughter of the wealthy banker Leonard Messel and his wife Maud, had a more exotic heritage. The originator of the Messel family fortune was the banker Aaron Messel, of Darmstadt, whose grandson Ludwig Messel, also a banker in the family firm, settled in London soon after the Franco-Prussian war of 1870–71, converting from Judaism to Christianity when he married. Alfred Messel, Ludwig's brother, who remained in Germany, became so famous that he was known as 'the Kaiser's architect'; he designed the Berlin National Gallery as well as various opulent private palaces and was the first architect to use steel and glass through several floors – later, his great-nephew Tony was to show the same innovative streak. Berlin's Messelplatz and Messelstrasse were named after Alfred.

By 1890 Ludwig had prospered to such an extent that he was able to buy the beautiful 900-acre Nymans estate, at Handcross in West Sussex, inherited by his son Leonard after his death. From the outset, much of his time was spent in creating the famous Nymans gardens (now the property of the National Trust). Five years after leaving Oxford, Leonard Messel married Maud, the daughter of the famous *Punch* artist Linley Sambourne (whose London house in Kensington, 18 Stafford Terrace, remained in the family until 1980, when it was sold to the Greater London Council). Their two sons, Linley and Oliver, were born in 1899 and 1904 respectively, their daughter Anne on 8 February 1902.

Anne, educated at home and presented at Court in June 1922, grew up to become one of London's reigning beauties, known throughout society not only for her lovely face and slender figure

---

* In 1913, to avoid confusion with another medical Jones, he hyphenated Armstrong, the surname of the father of a relative of his wife, to his own by deed poll.

but for her exquisite, Art Deco-inspired clothes, made for her in London and Paris. Her costumes at the fancy dress balls so popular in the twenties were famous, designed by her younger brother Oliver, who had emerged as a celebrated creator of stage sets and costumes, most notably for the popular series of Cochran revues. The two were close: Oliver, short, dark-haired, extrovert, giggly – though he could also cry at will – was an enchanting companion of immaculate taste.

When Anne met the young barrister Ronald Armstrong-Jones, through her brother Linley who had rowed in the same crew at Magdalen College, Oxford, it was for Ronnie love at first sight. Soon Anne, too, found that she was in love and a few months after their meeting they were engaged. When they married on 22 July 1925, Ronnie was twenty-six and Anne twenty-three. It was a glittering society wedding at St Margaret's, Westminster, and on the surface there appeared to be all the omens for a long, happy and fruitful union: the bride was young, beautiful and rich, the groom good-looking and charismatic with the promise of a brilliant career at the Bar.

They settled in the house given by Leonard Messel to his daughter as a wedding present, 25 Eaton Terrace, in Belgravia; its baroque decoration, tempered by Syrie-Maugham white, owed much to Oliver. Here the young couple's first child, Susan Mary, was born on 12 February 1927 and their second, Tony, three years later. All seemed set fair.

But within the next year the marriage had begun to unravel. Ronnie needed to focus on his work to establish himself in his career at the Bar; the mondaine Anne found her deepest satisfaction in the world of clothes and parties and the theatrical milieu of her brother Oliver. She was metropolitan and image-conscious to her fingertips; Ronnie was flamboyant, unpunctual and fond of outdoor sports such as shooting and fishing. Among the mirrored glass witch balls and febrile chatter of friends like Cecil Beaton he felt like a fish out of water; conversely, Bar gossip or serious discussion of cases were the last things that interested the glittering Anne. As she observed, Ronnie 'loved going out and girls,' adding crisply 'but not my type of either'.

Although the marriage broke down irrevocably in 1931, appearances were kept up for another two years and it was not until 1933 that they separated. Ronnie hoped that the separation would not be permanent but, as Anne pointed out, 'Actually, he was well rooted in another romp by this time.'

For him, it was the beginning of a gypsy-like existence that led from house to house and woman to woman. That winter, he acquired the lease of 6 Trevor Square, Knightsbridge, conveniently near Hyde Park for the children and their nanny, Laura Gunner – Anne and Ronnie had agreed to share the children equally between them. Their decree nisi was granted on 22 February 1935, the decree absolute on 28 August.

Three weeks later, on 19 September 1935, Anne married Michael Parsons, who had succeeded to the earldom of Rosse at the age of twelve when his father was killed in action in 1918. He was four years younger than Anne and in every worldly sense a catch, a kind, generous and good-looking man who had inherited the romantic Birr Castle, in County Offaly, Ireland, set in its estate of 26,500 acres, and Womersley Park in West Yorkshire (the family fortune had been founded on nearby coalmines).

As the wife of a rich man and châtelaine of two grand estates, Anne was in her element, her innate talents exactly fitting her new role. She was not Oliver's sister for nothing: her houses were always splendidly decorated and she took immense trouble over every detail of their running. She could sew beautifully, she often designed and made her own Christmas cards, interleaving them with a piece of dark green tissue paper to protect and preserve the reproduction and she was a knowledgeable and creative gardener. Their life followed a pattern, moving according to the seasons from house to house. She and Michael would progress in their chauffeur-driven cars (neither of them could drive) from Birr to her house in Eaton Terrace to Nymans and then to Womersley, often taking in 18 Stafford Terrace, which her mother had persuaded her to use as a pied-à-terre.

Her social career went from strength to strength – as did her image of herself as the most beautiful and spectacular woman in any gathering. Dressed in dramatic silks and velvets in jewel colours from Molyneux, Schiaparelli or Victor Stiebel, wearing the famous Rosse emeralds or the five Womersley diamond stars, she would pause as if for applause when she entered a theatre, opera house or ball. Hugely socially ambitious, she became known as Tugboat Annie ('because she goes from peer to peer' ran the joke)* and her earlier marriage and everything connected with it were quickly consigned to oblivion.

The children could not be so dismissed but when, on 21 October 1936 and 23 December 1938, William Clere Leonard Brendan Wilmer Parsons (Viscount Oxmantown) and his brother the Hon. Desmond Oliver Martin Parsons were born, without question her Armstrong-Jones offspring took second place. As both Tony and Susan resembled their father rather than her, in colouring as well as in appearance, there may have been some unconscious wish to push everything connected with the divorce into the background of her mind. What maternal attention she had – and this was in the days when a brief morning encounter and an hour after tea was considered normal for upper-class parents and children – was lavished on her two Parsons sons. On both Tony and Susan – although, of course, neither realised it at the time – the effect of this downgrading was damaging in the extreme.

Tony was only five when his parents divorced. It was an era when divorce was rare, conspicuous and poorly regarded, its traces marking those it touched even peripherally. For Tony and Susan, it meant primarily both isolation and shuttling between two different and opposed worlds: the formal, nanny-led ambience of Birr Castle, their mother's new domain, and the life favoured by Ronnie, the carefree atmosphere of Plas Dinas and the small terrace house in First Street, Chelsea, full of theatrical friends – in 1936 he had married a vivacious, athletic Australian actress from Perth, Carol Coombe. 'Wednesday 18 June. Daddy and Carol married,' wrote the six-year-old Tony in his small pocket diary, going on to list his daily intake of sweets.

The divorce had been acrimonious and resentment still hung like a cloud over the children's lives, discernible to them by the

---

* To Waugh and the Mitfords, she quickly became Tuggie, as in 'Tuggie came to lunch.'

crossness their arrival seemed to produce in the other parent, each of whom had them for half the school holidays. Anne, who admired the romantic Little Lord Fauntleroy look, would send Tony back to his father in pale blue velvet, his blond locks down to his shoulders. Ronnie, after a holiday at Plas Dinas, with its beach barbecues and boating, would return Tony in battered grey flannel shorts with his hair, cut on the last day before his return, as short as possible. The children were sent off from London by train to Holyhead and then on the mail boat to Dun Laoghaire, where the Rosses' chauffeur, Hoisted, would meet them and drive them to Birr in the Humber. Sometimes in the summer Hoisted would take all the children on a day-long picnic to Connemara to look for amethysts on the beach, or to Galway to bathe.

Letters and affidavits passed snappishly between the two parents. Anne Rosse aimed much of her venom at Ronnie's breezy new wife, Carol: 'I am compelled to say that the condition and mental attitude of the children each time they return to me, apart from specific instances, have led me to consider that Mrs Armstrong-Jones is not a responsible person to have charge of the upbringing of my daughter ... In the case of my son there have been occasions illustrating Mrs Armstrong-Jones' complete irresponsibility with regard to matters of health which show, in my opinion, that she is not capable of ever having complete charge of children.'

Ronnie responded that his wife, the daughter of the respected Sir Thomas and Lady Coombe, was very fond of the children and that Anne's demand that a governess accompany them even if they were with their parents was unreasonable ('I submit that the provision that the children shall while with me always be accompanied by a governess is neither fair nor necessary,' wrote Ronnie).

When Anne proposed in February 1937 that Susan should be made to rest every afternoon in a darkened room Ronnie's response a month later began 'I can only say that I am amazed at the contents of your letter ...' But he reserved his real broadside for her contention that Susan remain with her during term time ('personal care by someone she loves and trusts is essential for Susan's health and happiness') by pointing out that after Susan had been ill at Nymans 'you did not hesitate to let her undertake the long and tiring journey to Ireland. I also see by your address that at present you are in London while they are still in Ireland so it doesn't seem that they are enjoying at the moment your personal supervision which you consider so necessary.'

For both Tony and Susan, the contrast between their two lives was enormous. If their genial, asthmatic father was down on his luck, they would return from the grandeur of Birr to a small cottage somewhere; if he had had a run of successful cases, it would be to a large and lavishly run house. Discussions about finances were frequent. Ronnie depended on his fees and, although sometimes extravagant, he was extremely aware of, and careful with, money, a trait inherited by his son. Carol was a warm and uninhibited person, but compared to his mother's cool, impeccable style, Tony began to find her brash and even vulgar. (Much later, the divergence in the two parents' lifestyles and the enmity between them was reflected in Tony's alternating attitudes to them. 'He was always non-speaks with one or other,' said Princess Margaret.)

Always close, the two children became still closer: Susan the sweet-natured, protective older sister; Tony the naughty little brother whom she adored, supported and frequently got out of trouble, in a pattern that would be repeated throughout their lives. For a long time the central figure in their lives was their nanny, Laura Gunner, who loved both of them dearly and as a consequence felt keenly the subordinate position they held in their mother's affections vis-à-vis her two Rosse sons.

Because of the children's peripatetic lifestyle, the lack of contact with their mother was accentuated. When they went to stay with their maternal grandparents – whether or not their mother was there – it was not even in the same house. Instead, it was in a much smaller establishment on the other side of the road in the village, where they lived together with Nanny Gunner and Susan's governess Miss Martin ('Marty'). From here, six-year-old Tony and Susan, aged nine, went across to see their grandparents after lunch. Tony was later to describe his grandfather as 'a grumpy little bugger, very self-important, very Jewish' but both children adored their serene, beautiful grandmother and respected her wisdom.

It was at Nymans that Tony first became conscious of the house that was to mean more to him than any other – and to which he would remain faithful for far longer than to any of the women who would later figure in his life. For him, Old House, as it was called, would always represent the magic, the happiness and the sense of a private world in which anything is possible, evoking the childhood, secure and happy with his sister and Nanny, that in many ways he never outgrew.

This small dwelling, tucked away in the Nymans woods, was just under two miles away from the big house and its thirty-acre gardens down the bumpy Nymans drive and a mile from the village of Staplefield Green. It was originally an ironmaster's house dating back to 1471, then two Tudor workmen's cottages which were knocked into one and a Georgian façade added. The cottage windows still retained the original leaded lights, the oldest walls were hung with red tiles, the roof was tiled and the great beam above the hall fireplace bore the date 1672. It had no lighting or heating, and a sandpit sufficed for plumbing.

The children adored it. On summer afternoons they would walk through the woods with Nanny Gunner, to find a tea of cucumber sandwiches, bread and butter and honey laid out ready for them. Sometimes, when they went to draw the pure spring water from the well in the garden, they would be greeted by the call of a cuckoo – one of the gardeners could mimic the bird exactly. At other times there would be Easter egg hunts round the Old House garden, and fishing in the nearby lake for pike.

Although the Armstrong-Jones children were in the same house as their mother when they went to her at Birr there was, if possible, even more formality than at Nymans. All the children lived on the top floor, the domain of Nanny Gunner, and the rooms they could enter – and by which door – were severely regulated. The Georgian Gothick saloon, with its beautiful eighteenth-century Waterford chandelier and 1870 flock wallpaper, was out of bounds, as was the drawing room and the small library. Dining room lunch was governed by strict protocol. While adults – the Rosses and their many guests – entered by the main door from the hall to eat five or six courses in this imposing room with its dark red wallpaper hung densely with family portraits, the children were forbidden to use any but the 'children's door'. Through this, at the other side of the room, they would file in decorously after the first course or two, to sit with Nanny and any visiting governess or tutor at a small round table near the window. After they had eaten their two courses Anne Rosse, sitting at the near end of the long mahogany dining table that could seat sixteen, would give them their signal for dismissal by turning her chair round and enquiring: 'And what are the children doing this afternoon?'

In the nursery, a sunny room with a brass fender, rocking horse and cupboard full of toys, the boys as well as Susan would play with a dolls' house. This was made by the estate carpenter, Willy Eades – with whom Tony spent as much time as possible – and was a model of the Georgian houses that later caused Birr to be listed as a Georgian heritage town. Sometimes, when they knew adults were out of the way, the boys would slide down the polished yew-wood banisters surrounding the square stairwell that rose from the hall. For more freedom, they would retreat to a room in the tower, where they were amply forewarned of Nanny Gunner's approach by the creaking of her knees as she slowly mounted the stairs. Outside, there was the endless game of pushing each other down the rough, grassy sides of the moat or, on wet days, pulling each other along in the trolleys that ran along under the ceiling of the 100-foot 'turf house', where the 1,600 donkey-loads of peat that was the year's supply of fuel for Birr was stacked.

The template of Tony's subsequent life was largely laid down in these early years. Moving between school, two sets of parents and often to a house different from the one in which he had stayed on the previous holiday – in all, Ronnie moved twenty-seven times during his lifetime – inculcated his habit of compartmentalising not only the different aspects of his life but also the people in them. Later on, a wife might suddenly discover that someone she thought was a stranger to her husband had known him well for twenty years, or there would be a sudden, mysterious dis-appearance that remained unexplained.

His childhood feelings for his mother were, in turn, responsible for much of the complexity of his later relationships with women. He was simultaneously dazzled by this glittering figure and resent-ful of a lack of attention that amounted to rejection; and it is a psychological truth that a child who has not had proper mothering often not only cannot form a relationship with a woman in later life, but also cannot trust women – sometimes to the extent of wanting to be the first to strike a blow. Or as the psychologist Perry London has observed: 'Parent-child interactions are the main area from which individual adjustment patterns develop.'

As a parent Anne was distant and aloof – even when there was too much noise from the nursery floor, she would not mount the stairs herself to demand quietness but sent her husband up instead to remonstrate. Her preferred style was to be worshipped rather than to hug and kiss, while like all little boys Tony longed for her love and approval. His schoolboy diary is full of remarks about 'Mummy'. Nor did it help that she often referred to him as her 'ugly son', or that she would introduce the Parsons boys as 'my sons', forgetting Tony hovering in the background. 'Oh, and this is my other son,' she would say on these occasions if a visitor asked who he was. The pattern of enthralment to her glamour and simultaneous, albeit unconscious, anger at being either ignored or passed over in favour of his younger siblings manifested itself later in, among other things, an attraction to the beautiful and a destructive urge to push against the boundaries of a relationship until the hapless partner finally conceded defeat.

With his mother's affection not forthcoming, Tony sought the next best thing, attention. This was most easily achieved by naughtiness. The awareness that her Parsons children, in particular the heir, William, were his mother's focus added a certain childish malice to such mischievousness; later this would surface in the touch of cruelty with which many of his jokes and repartee were edged. With others, he quickly learned that as a golden-haired, blue-eyed, smiling little boy charm was an infallible weapon to use on grown-ups; this, too, was to prove irresistible in adult life.

His sister Susan suffered as much if not more from their mother's dismissiveness. Anne was devoted to her niece Victoria Messel (the daughter of her brother Linley) and when Victoria was staying would often say fondly: 'She's my daughter,' adding, if Susan were there, 'Oh, and that's my other daughter.' Susan, shy and sensitive, felt this deeply but her reaction was the opposite of Tony's: to gain the longed-for approval by being as good as possible.

From early on Tony was a tease. An agile child, he would climb the tallest trees at Birr and then scream that he was stuck and could not get down. As his wails became ever more terrified and pathetic the devoted Nanny Gunner, risking life and limb, would climb up to help him. As she neared him, he would shin quickly down the other side of the tree, leaving her helplessly aloft, and stroll nonchalantly in to lunch as if nothing had happened. Once, driven beyond endurance, she chastised him with an ivory hair-brush. But as usual his luck held and the brush broke.

There was further bickering between his parents when Tony went to his preparatory school, Sandroyd (then near Cobham, Surrey). Both Anne and Ronnie accepted that as Tony had only had a 'governess education' thus far (apart from a brief spell at the all-girls Francis Holland School in Graham Terrace, London, after which he became their only Old Boy), he would initially find the work difficult and be backward compared with boys who had attended pre-prep schools. His father organised his school clothes, chiefly grey shorts, white shirts and the purple school cap with the letters S.S. on the front. Nanny sewed on the name tapes and Tony began at Sandroyd in the autumn term of 1938, 'too early', thought Anne, who took her eight-year-old son there for his first term but who, unlike his father, seldom visited him there again.

The following year there was disagreement over a boarding school for Susan: her mother thought that Susan was too delicate for one; Ronnie put forward the opinion of his eminent doctor father that she was perfectly healthy and that he himself believed it would give her life some much-needed stability. Ronnie won. 'Susan went back to Scool erly in the morning 8 am,' wrote Tony in his pocket diary on 1 May 1939 (the school chosen was Downham). Ronnie concluded his letter by submitting that if either himself or Anne should visit Sandroyd, forty-eight hours notice should be given so that the headmaster had time to warn the other parent in case the two of them accidentally met. 'I have just heard from the Headmaster at Sandroyd that you are going to see him at 3 p.m. on Sunday. As you no doubt know I am going to Chapel that morning but will have left the School by lunch time.'

Sandroyd's headmaster, Hugh ('Tizzy') Ozanne, was a man of

powerful personality, emphasised by his piercing gaze and smooth black hair, who ran the school well. The year after Tony's arrival war broke out (on 3 September 1939); from then on the sixty-odd boys would gather at 8 a.m. in the big wooden hall to listen to the BBC news, transmitted via the school radiogram, so that all of them were aware of what was going on in the war in which so many of their fathers and brothers were engaged. In their fertile imagination one of their schoolfellows, called Schreiber, was whispered to be a German spy; the response of Tony and his friends was to make dummy automatic guns and keep them under their pillows in case of attack by the unfortunate Schreiber.

During music lessons, which passed over the tone-deaf Tony's head, Wagner's *Tannhäuser* music would reverberate to the rafters. After lessons in the morning and lunch everyone had to sit in the library for three-quarters of an hour, reading a book of their choice – the school library contained blameless volumes, chiefly of adventure tales, such as those by John Buchan and the *Scarlet Pimpernel* series by Baroness Orczy. Detective thrillers, though not exactly forbidden, were frowned on. At bedtime in the senior dormitory (The Chintz) excerpts from Ruritanian tales such as *The Prisoner of Zenda* were read to its inmates by the headmaster, who told them that they should go to bed 'weary, content and undishonoured'.

This insistence on moral rectitude caused at least one former fellow pupil of Tony's to wonder later if a certain latent homosexuality lay beneath the headmaster's urbane appearance. 'His addresses to a large audience of senior boys – he had a gift for oratory – would often include declamations against friendships that trespassed into forbidden regions, while his habit of lurking round the school's outdoor lavatories on the pretext of intercepting illicit activities also caused speculation.' Tony, however, was usually too busy chattering to another small boy at the end of the queue to notice his headmaster's presence. Even then, it was noted by fellow pupils that Tony, though small in stature, was physically well endowed – although it was the young Prince Andrew of Yugoslavia who won the clandestine school peeing competition.

Air raids soon prompted the removal of Sandroyd from Cobham to Rushmore House (formerly owned by the Pitt-Rivers family) in

Tollard Royal, Wiltshire, about twelve miles from Shaftesbury, where the boys could build tree hides, toboggan, learn to shoot on a .22 range or collect firewood. Although, because of his small size, Tony did not excel at games, he was a good and plucky boxer, becoming the school's featherweight champion at eleven, boxing at what was called extra-special weight – five stone six and under. Among his fellow pupils at Sandroyd were two who were to be among his closest friends, Jocelyn Stevens and Simon Sainsbury.

School did nothing to suppress Tony's natural high spirits and sense of mischief – typically, in a form photograph he is the only one with his hands behind his back rather than at attention. Nor, except in mathematics, in which he usually came near the top of the form, did it teach him very much. 'Rules red out. Have two lessons and Prep. Very Dull KNOW interesting thing,' runs the entry for Tuesday 6 May 1941.

He was much more interested in pitting his wits against the masters, usually provoking them in seemingly innocent fashion. The Latin master, Mr Hughes – known as Huffer – had a habit of repeating himself and was easy to work into a state of excitement and exasperation at which Tony, with his sharp mind and intuitive grasp of a situation, excelled. 'Utor governs the ablative case, the ablative case,' Huffer would intone. Then came silence and a long look at Tony, whose small figure, alert and smiling, waited for the next move.

'Armstrong-Jones, decline bellum,' Huffer would say ominously. 'Bellum, bellum, bellum, belli, bello, bello,' Tony would respond – but so fast that it sounded liked 'Blum, blum, blum ...'. 'Armstrong-Jones, remember you are here *on sufferance, on sufferance,*' Huffer would explode, but there was little he could do in the face of accuracy. Once again, Tony had got away with it. Yet despite his lack of academic prowess ('Armstrong-Jones may be interested in something, but it is not anything we teach here,' wrote his headmaster) he managed to pass the Eton Common Entrance.

Before leaving Sandroyd, each boy visited Tizzy Ozanne in his study, supposedly to be warned against the dark possibilities that so occupied the headmaster's mind. As Tony recalled: 'You had to go and have a Leaver's Lecture, and you weren't to tell anybody about it. You were alone with him in his study, which you'd never been to before. He said: "You're going on now to Eton. And you'll find that sometimes another boy might ... put his hand on your thigh." And that was as far as it got. He never told me what to do. But I knew about the facts of life anyway.'

Inventions had begun early. At six he had constructed a submarine for his bath. It was made of shaped wood and weighted in the centre with drawing pins. A bit of lead from an old toothpaste tube was stuck on at the front, which allowed it to glide in a shallow dive to the bottom of the bath; on hitting this, the lead fell off and it glided up again. If launched in a swimming pool at the right angle it could cover the whole length.

In whatever he made he was encouraged and helped by his uncle Oliver, a frequent visitor to Birr. Kind, charming, brilliant, infinitely ingenious and a committed homosexual, throughout his life Oliver Messel was Tony's adored mentor and a major influence. The camp atmosphere in which Oliver lived and moved rubbed off on his nephew, as did his attitude to creativity and work. As Carl Toms, the designer who worked with both of them and knew them both intimately, later said of Oliver: 'When he was engaged in work only the best would do from himself and his workforce. He found it vital to achieve the highest possible standard and it had to be higher than anyone else's. Nor did he like competition. He hated the thought of being put on one side or forgotten. He had a faultless instinct [over work].' When Tony grew up, exactly the same could be said of him.

As Tony's own creativity flowered, he adopted one room at Birr as a workroom. Its position in the castle may have had a subliminal influence on his life: to reach his workroom, he had to pass through a shrine to photography, Mary Rosse's darkroom. Mary, the third Countess of Rosse (1813–1885), was one of the earliest photographers, taking portraits, still lifes and other compositions and leaving behind her the oldest fully equipped darkroom in the world. She was the first woman to win the silver medal award of the Royal Photographic Society of Ireland, for her work in the 1850s.

In 1983, the laboratory where she worked was rediscovered and the equipment and chemicals used by Mary, and many of her negatives and stereoscopic prints, were found on shelves and in wooden boxes. For anyone as curious as Tony, they would have been something to investigate and, if possible, make use of. Certainly, his schoolboy diary records the taking of photographs.

He went to Eton in the Michaelmas half of 1943, to the same house, Upcott's, as Simon Sainsbury, then emerging as a gifted pianist and sportsman (in one epic Eton and Harrow match at Lord's in 1947, in front of the royal family, in which he was the opening bowler, he also scored a century. Later he became President of Pop.)*

Despite the exigencies of wartime, the school uniform of tailcoat (for boys of five foot four inches and over) was still worn. Smaller boys wore short Eton jackets, known as bumfreezers; Tony remained in his until his last year at the school. The only relaxation concerned top hats: these were no longer worn outdoors every day and all day as in the pre-war years, but only on Sundays, Eton holidays and if a boy should go further than the parish church, halfway down Eton High Street. Because of clothes rationing (coupons were needed to buy all new ones), second-hand clothes could be bought from Eton tailors Denman & Goddard and Welsh & Jeffries.

For the first two weeks, each new boy was looked after by an older boy. Then came the nerve-racking colours test – by now each new boy had to know all the Eton houses and the special colours of every house and sporting rank.

Nor did the war affect the rich vein of eccentricity that ran through the school, often epitomised in the masters – or their wives. One of these was the legendary Grizel Hartley, whose husband, a housemaster, was on active service. An unmistakable figure with her trousers and long hair, she called everyone 'darling' and was known for her sharp wit. When another housemaster, Oliver Van Oss, had secured for his house the young Lord Chelsea (originally destined for the house of Grizel's husband Hubert

---

* The Eton Society, known as Pop, is a self-elected body of boys deemed to stand head and shoulders above their peers. Many were the school's leading athletes. To be asked to join was a mark of the highest approbation.

Hartley) and was proudly extolling the virtues of this aristocratic acquisition, Grizel responded briskly: 'I suppose you've checked that he has an anchor on his bottom?'

In such a climate Tony's inventiveness caused admiration rather than the mockery or disapproval with which adolescents often greet something outside the expected norm. He spent a lot of time in the school of mechanics, where only wood could be used – all metal was needed for the war effort. He made tiny crystal wireless sets (the boys were forbidden radios) that he sold for half a crown (12.5p) each. His own radio, strictly forbidden, was kept under the floorboards of his room, to be switched off whenever he heard the footsteps of his housemaster John Upcott (later the house became that of Denis Wilkinson). He fixed up a series of buttons under the linoleum which were wired to bells or lights inside his room so that he could hear or see any approach and rigged up another bell that would ring if someone tried to remove the key to his sock (tuck) box.

Then came a gadget for rolling cigarettes, a photographic enlarger from empty tomato soup cans and an electric toaster. This last item was primarily to help him in his duties as a fag, one of which was to make toast for his fagmaster, on which would be spread potted meat, jam or honey for tea. With so many small boys crowded round holding out toasting forks (there were no toasters), the fire was often difficult to get near to – and woe betide the boy who did not produce his toast in time. (Ingenious though Tony's toaster was, he did not escape censure: its wires left a pattern of burns on each piece of toast, for which he was beaten by the captain of the house, Hargreaves major.) Food was a constant preoccupation for all of them; one of Tony's favourites was a 'tunny' – a piece of fried bread spread with a creamy tuna mousse that cost 4d from the school shop, Rolands. Sometimes he would vary this with cream cheese, made by allowing his daily pint of milk to go sour and then straining it through a handkerchief.

Eton's closeness to London meant that many of these activities were interrupted by air raids, or warnings of them. If the siren went after 11 p.m., next morning's Early School (7.30, pre-breakfast) lesson was cancelled. With V-1 and V-2 rockets there was no chance to get to the shelter so boys would crouch under their desks and hope for the best, but by the end of Tony's second year the war in Europe had ended.

His work improved, his boxing career flourished – by 1946 he was boxing for Eton. 'We had a terrible thing called the Quadrangle. You used to fight in the morning and then, if you won, you had another fight in the afternoon, which was pretty nasty. The toughest school was people like Oundle. There was Oundle, Bedford, Haileybury,' he recalled. Because he could not swim he spent his first year as a 'slack bob' then, after passing his swimming test, became a 'wet bob' (a rower) as his father had been, from then on spending a considerable time on the river.

His interest in photography was growing steadily and in his second year he swapped an excellent microscope he had been given by his grandfather for a cheap camera belonging to another boy; and made a primitive enlarger out of old biscuit and tomato soup tins. These various pieces of equipment left only enough space in his seven-foot room for the bed and dishes of chemicals – and once led to a nasty shock. 'I shall never forget sitting up in the middle of the night and reaching out for a tooth glass of water – only to find I was drinking hypo [developing fluid].' The following year he revived the moribund Eton Photographic Society.

There was only one visit from his mother during his school career and she did not even attend the highly social Fourth of June, an event few parents missed. The reason given was that she was looking after the Officers' Mess at Womersley Park; this had been requisitioned by the Army (the family still retained one wing which the officers would visit to dine with Anne). The message this behaviour conveyed clearly was that she did not regard her son as a priority. His father came once a half (all that was then allowed), driving down in his second-hand Mercury, a large American car, with a grille at the back so that his whippets could breathe and, once, his Messel grandmother came in a huge Daimler, stone hot-water jars in the back to warm her feet under a large rug.

In the summer holidays of 1946 at Plas Dinas there was a new toy: his father gave him a small but powerful motorbike, a 250 BSA, on which he would whiz along the mountain roads of North

Wales. It was often hard to start and one day when Tony had been kick-starting it for some time he felt a terrible pain in his leg. At first he thought he had sprained it but as he straightened up he noticed a pain in his back. When he got back his stepmother Carol rubbed his back with embrocation. This did no good and, headachy and feeling ill, he went to bed early – but not before Carol had taken his temperature. It was 102°F (38.9°C) and his father called the doctor who, mercifully, realised that his young patient was seriously ill and performed a lumbar puncture.*

Next morning Tony's temperature soared to 105°. The initial diagnosis of the fluid taken from his spine indicated that he was suffering from either tubercular meningitis or poliomyelitis.† It was virtually a death sentence. If the former, Tony would soon sink into an irreversible coma and die. Recovery had never been known. The second (before a protective vaccine was developed) did offer a chance of survival but was often fatal and, if not, usually meant severe crippling, since much about the disease was not then known. 'I remember everyone coming in to see me, my mother came over from Ireland and Nanny was there crying,' Tony recalled. Later, his father wrote that he could never have imagined praying that his son would have polio.

1946 was, in fact, the year of a polio epidemic. Contaminated water was supposed to be one channel by which the virus was spread and many swimming pools were closed. Tony, as a wet bob, had spent much time on the river at Eton and had often bathed at Cuckoo Weir. 'Once when my father Ronald was rowing there during his time at Eton, his oar encountered an obstacle. He thought it was a branch or something and pushed hard – and up came a bookie, still in his bowler hat, his face covered with green slime, who had lost all his money at Windsor races the week before.'

Once polio was diagnosed, Anne Rosse believed her son should

---

* The drawing-off of spinal fluid for testing.

† Polio is a viraemia – a virus in the bloodstream that can settle anywhere, almost always where there has been severe strain or trauma of a muscle. In Tony's case, the energetic kick-starting of his motorbike for a lengthy period and the consequent strain on that muscle would have caused the virus to settle in the muscles of his leg (the limb later afflicted).

be sent to hospital rather than nursed at home. Backed in this opinion by the senior physician of the Liverpool Royal Infirmary, Dr Henry (later Lord) Cohen, she carried the day and Tony was sent to the Infirmary by ambulance. It was a terrible time. He was bored and miserable at being confined to bed, depressed by a future that looked bleak, and lonely – his only family visits were from his sister Susan, for whom he knitted an immensely long scarf while lying on his back. His uncle Oliver, designing for Covent Garden and Glyndebourne, was as ever thoughtful, sending instructions for model-making and getting friends like Noël Coward and the cabaret star Beatrice ('Bea') Lillie (whose son had just been killed and who said that Tony reminded her of him) to visit him, and sing for him, when they were playing at the Liverpool Adelphi.

Gradually his paralysed legs came back to life and, with intense determination but agonising slowness, he learned to walk again. Finally, after six months, he emerged from the Infirmary with a withered left leg that was an inch shorter than the right one, a knowledge of deaf and dumb language learned from a fellow patient and the realisation that, apart from his sister, the only person on whom he could truly rely was himself.

2

On His Way

※

The six months he spent in Liverpool Infirmary honed Tony's already strong will into a powerful weapon that would aid him in his future career – one of the secrets of his early success was never taking no for an answer. He needed every ounce of determination he could muster to work through the regime of learning first to move and then to walk again. Encouragement came from the nurses, doctors and other patients, but chiefly from his own positive attitude (today well known to benefit the immune system).

His convalescence was spent at Womersley. Nanny Gunner, to whom he was, and remained, devoted, was with him to look after him, a comforting presence in this difficult time. He was – just – able to put one foot in front of the other when he arrived and at first spent much of the time being wheeled about or sitting in a chair, being tutored under a cherry tree by a pink-trousered young man called Anthony Le Hoghton. Gradually, his muscles improved and, first with crutches, then with a stick and finally unaided, by his seventeenth birthday he was walking again and able to return to Eton, where photography began to occupy more and more of his time.

Just before this birthday, there was a family disaster. The winter of 1946/7 was one of the coldest on record and during one freezing night of February 1947, the Nymans fires were heaped so high that heat percolated through the chimney into a timbered attic. At 3 a.m. Colonel Messel was woken by the smell of burning. The family and their servants escaped the fire that was soon blazing, but half the house and all the treasures therein were reduced to ashes. One of the most disastrous losses was the wonderful botanical library, an irreplaceable collection. The house burned for three days: the intense cold had frozen its lake, water from which might have saved it. It was never rebuilt, although the family maintained the remaining part of the 'Tudor' wing as their focal point for running the gardens, buying a nearby Victorian house to live in. Several years later Colonel Messel gave the property to the National Trust.

Back at school at the beginning of the summer half of 1947 there were a few concessions because of his condition: he was allowed a bicycle instead of having to walk everywhere, and in the morning could leave the fold-up bed in his room down. The inventing went on. When his new housemaster, Mr Wilkinson, somewhat rashly said: 'You can have anything in your room so long as you've made it yourself,' the challenge was irresistible. Gramophones were forbidden though records were not, so, sticking to the letter of the law, Tony built a radiogram. Soon there was a stream of visitors and his only record, 'Chiquita Banana', was played endlessly. One of the boys who came to hear it was his prep-school acquaintance, Simon Sainsbury; their lifelong friendship was formed during that last year.

Unable to do National Service because of his leg, Tony went from Eton straight to Jesus College, Cambridge, in October 1949, to study architecture. It was hoped that he would follow in the footsteps of his distinguished architect great-uncle Alfred Messel. His impact on his fellow undergraduates was immediate. 'Tony is one of those strange figures who, over the last fifty years, has hardly changed in appearance, still slim and slightly built with a slight limp and a fine display of gleaming white teeth in his sunny smile,' wrote Justin de Blank, who sat at the desk in front of him and became a friend.

Tony was one of the younger undergraduates, since most of those of his age opted to do their National Service before rather than after university and many others had fought throughout the war – sitting nearby, in the Cambridge School of Architecture in Scroope Terrace, was just such a character, a former Air Force pilot known as 'Spud' Murphy, who had joined up from Dublin in 1939 and ended the war as personal pilot to a senior general. But Tony's youthfulness did not stop him from keeping the room entertained with a fund of stories and jokes – many filthy – all told, thanks to his excellence at mimicry, in suitable accents.

The day after arriving he made another great friend. Anthony Barton was a tall, extremely good-looking young man of Irish extraction who lived in France, where his family owned the famous Château Leoville Barton vineyard in Bordeaux and a thriving wine export business. He arrived the same term as Tony and the two met almost at once, at the Jesus boathouse. Tony had gone there because he wanted to continue with his rowing and Anthony because he wanted to begin – his older brother was a great oarsman. They were the same age (Anthony, who lived in France at the family château, was not subject to British National Service), which made an immediate bond when surrounded by so many older people.

Sometimes there were parties in Tony's rooms overlooking Chapel Quad, everyone drinking South African sherry because of its cheapness. Rules were strict, everyone having to be back in their own college by midnight. Jesus, with its double row of railings and spikes, was especially difficult to climb into, a problem easily circumvented by Tony, who with his usual ingenuity quickly made a copy of the key to the dustmen's lift, thenceforward used for unofficial comings and goings by himself and his visitors. On one occasion, this lift was used as the entrance to one of his sherry parties, a uniformed footman (hired by Tony for the evening) standing inside to conduct guests to his rooms in dignified fashion.

One consequence of Tony's very individual approach was that he aroused strong feelings: great affection or extreme resentment or annoyance, often because if he himself did not like someone this was made perfectly obvious, generally with the quick-witted sarcastic remarks or the mockery of which he was a master.

His interest in photography was maintained through his friend Jocelyn Stevens who had started a small Cambridge magazine called *Cameo*, for which Tony was commissioned to take pictures. But rowing was occupying more and more of his time and after being awarded his Trial Cap in his first year, he rowed for his college. As Jesus was then a very strong rowing college, his ability as a cox was soon noted and he was picked early in 1950 to cox the Cambridge Eight in that year's Boat Race (his own explanation for being picked so early in his university career was that he was 'prettier' than his only rival).

Training intensified and with it the need to be as light as possible. To lose weight, he would pull on two sweaters and spend hours shovelling grain into the lorry of a friendly contractor (on the day of the Boat Race, he weighed eight stone nine pounds). He also devised a series of exercises for himself as well as training with the Eight.

During the months before the race the crew's day began with a cold shower and then a drive to Ely for twelve miles on the river, usually with an icy wind straight from the North Sea whipping over them. To protect themselves from the cold they wore trousers made of blanket material so dense and heavy that if they had capsized the weight of the saturated fabric would have put them in serious danger of drowning. The wooden boat (it was before the age of fibreglass) known as the 'Banham Bombshell' would give the cox a hefty kick to the base of the spine at each stroke. Here too, Tony's combination of inventiveness and lateral thinking was brought into play with a useful piece of gadgetry, a wind-up calibrated clock adapted from a darkroom timer, with which he measured the stroke rate. This he wired up with a bell, which could be heard only by himself and Bow – Harry Almond, who weighed in at ten stone eight pounds. No one except the American crews then used a microphone, considered a bit infra dig; Tony was able to make his voice, clear but not loud in ordinary conversation, carry effortlessly across the water. The real work of art was the boat's rudder, which he designed and made from aluminium and laminated mahogany.

The day of the race, 1 April 1950, was dry although rain threatened and there were strong winds of around eighteen to twenty knots from the west, making the temperature of 14°C (57°F) seem much lower on the open water. The $4\frac{1}{2}$ mile marathon began punctually at 12.30, the crews more or less evenly matched until they reached Hammersmith, when their oars touched. There followed an unprintable conversation between Tony and the Oxford cox as the latter had to jam on his rudder. This slowed Oxford down, and Cambridge won triumphantly by three and a half lengths.

Since it was one of the first races to be televised* and there were enormous crowds, their victory attracted great publicity. There was no throwing of the cox into the river then; instead, Tony took the crew to drink to their victory at his uncle Oliver's house in Pelham Crescent. Here Cambridge muscle and the illusionism of the stage came into curious juxtaposition when Alistair McLeod, number three in the Cambridge crew and the august President of the University Boat Club, leant languidly against a marble pillar only to have it wobble perilously – it was made of papier-mâché. Later, still in their pale blue blazers, the Eight went to dinner at the Empress Club in Dover Street, and then on to the Astor nightclub.

Tony's rowing triumph came at a price. The hours he had spent on the river were at the cost of work and although he had been awarded his Rowing Blue he was to fail his architecture exams. Meanwhile, there was pleasure to be pursued. This chiefly involved dashing up and down to London on his much-loved Matchless 350 motorbike, generally with a friend on the pillion. With only four women's colleges (and none mixed), there were few girls in Cambridge, so that except for the May Balls all the best parties took place in the capital. Together, Tony and Anthony Barton went to one of the May Balls, successfully gatecrashed two more, then, on the fourth night, still in party mood but with no ball to go to, decided to look for action elsewhere. They set off to London on the bike to take out two girls who shared a flat, only to find they had been stood up.

They consoled themselves as best they could with a certain amount of alcoholic refreshment, then roared off back to Cambridge. At 3 a.m., the roads were virtually empty; racing down a hill and through a red light, Tony was taken unawares by a sharp bend to the right. Anthony had just time to say to himself: 'He's never going to make it at this speed,' when the bike went straight on and into a ditch. Anthony sailed over his friend's head and landed in a field of cabbages, his only ill effect the loss of a shoe.

---

* The Boat Race was first televised in 1936 but then not again until 1949.

Scrambling to his feet, he ran back to the road. Tony, overcome by drink and profound weariness, had passed out and was lying on his back, snoring – a noise mistaken by the worried Anthony for a death rattle.

The situation was saved by a lorry driver on his way to London, who stopped when he saw the pair, then chivalrously turned round and drove them back to Cambridge. The Matchless was irreparably damaged and Tony's love affair with motorbikes temporarily suspended. Instead, he bought a 1927 open two-seater motor car for £20, in which he and a friend – usually Anthony – would dash round the countryside or up to London. It was in this car that he drove up to London to see his sister Susan, in a wedding dress designed and made by their mother, married on 20 May 1950 to John Vesey (later the 6th Viscount de Vesci). The reception was held at their grandmother's house, 104 Lancaster Gate. Shortly after their marriage, to Anne's horror, Susan was received into her husband's Catholic faith.

As usual, there were holidays at Birr as well as with his father. By now, of course, Tony took all meals with the adults, though he would usually call in to the nursery where his younger half-brothers were eating their supper to help himself to the simple nursery food he would prefer all his life – sausages, scrambled egg, rice pudding, fish cakes – before going downstairs to pick at the elaborate six-course dinners Lady Rosse served to her guests.

If there were young house parties, there was dancing to the radiogram in the saloon, drinks of gin and orange, and tennis, for which Tony acted as ball boy. When girlfriends came to Birr they too would be put to stay on the top floor, with its solitary bathroom down the passage. This offered an almost irresistible temptation to those who, like Tony and his brothers, were in the know. Above the bath was a window that sloped slightly (now painted over), opposite which was a mirror. By climbing up on a chair in the next room anyone looking through this window could see the occupant of the bath reflected in the mirror. Fortunately, none of the unsuspecting female visitors ever realised this.

Some of the other tricks that Tony played on women at this stage had a slightly sadistic edge. Girlfriends would be invited to row on the lake at Birr in a birchbark canoe brought back by a

Rosse forebear from British Columbia. What they did not know was that the only way to maintain balance in this craft was to sit cross-legged so that, invariably, they fell in, upon which Tony would let them splutter and thrash around until, gallantly, rescuing them. One occasional trick was to catch a pike in the lake, make the chosen girl an apple pie bed and put the pike between the sheets. As the girl's toes touched its cold, slimy mass she would scream in pure horror – an added frisson was given by the fact that after death a pike's jaws can snap shut if touched and – who knows? – might have trapped a toe.

After failing his architecture exams Tony was 'rusticated' – that is, asked to leave the University for a year during which, the College authorities assumed, he would study the work he had missed and then, contrite and refocused, return to work diligently for his degree. His tutor, sending him down, said: 'We would have thought differently if you had done more for College rowing rather than for the University.'

To someone of Tony's naturally impatient temperament, with a boredom threshold so low as to be almost invisible and a hatred of what he saw as wasting time, the idea of postponing his degree had nothing to recommend it. The photography that had been gradually becoming ever more important to him seemed to offer something at which he could work hard – and enjoy. He told his parents that instead of returning to Cambridge at the end of the year he wanted to become a professional photographer.

His mother's reaction was instantaneous and negative. Photography then was not a career for anyone who could be described as a gentleman. Photographers were tradesmen, who came to the tradesmen's entrance, and were treated as such, and for Anne, to whom social considerations were all-important, the idea of her son embarking on such a life was not only a black mark against him but, vicariously, against her too. She sent an anguished telegram. 'Do not agree suggestion changing career. Telephone this evening. Fondest love. Mummy.'

The telephone call resulted in the decision that Tony should wait to discuss his future with Michael Rosse and the sympathetic

Oliver when he came to Ireland that summer. By the time Oliver arrived in August 1950, Anne had been part-persuaded by Michael Rosse that Tony should do what made him happy. Oliver supported Tony wholeheartedly. Nevertheless, Tony was told he ought to seek his father's approval.

Largely thanks to Tony's stepmother Carol, Ronnie had been persuaded to rent (for £500 p.a.) a handsome flint and brick house called Coombe Court at the end of a long drive in a secluded valley near Lewes. Coombe Court was a paradise for the young. Tony and Susan rode ('she was always much keener than me'), on horses looked after by a German prisoner of war who had decided to stay on in England. At weekends or during the vacation Tony would often take friends to stay at Coombe. Ronnie, always convivial, would sometimes arrange for them to be brought down en masse in a bus on which drinks were served freely; once there, friends like Andy Garnett (from Eton) and Anthony Barton enjoyed the impromptu parties instigated by Carol, when the carpet was rolled back and everyone danced to the radiogram.

During the week Ronnie and Carol lived at a set of ground-floor chambers in Albany, with a large, sunny drawing room, where they gave parties constantly, their main feature a steady supply of the pretty girls, often Australian friends of Carol, by whom Ronnie loved to be surrounded.

By now Ronnie was doing extremely well at the Bar. His speciality was 'running down' cases,* in which he generally appeared for those seeking damages through their insurance companies. A brilliant advocate, he would put across irrefutable points in his somewhat high-pitched voice which, if he were under exceptional stress, would tend to 'disappear' owing to his asthma. His skill at handling expert witnesses in court and assessing damages made him the leading junior in this field, with a place in his chambers at 5 Essex Court in the Middle Temple eagerly sought. Gregarious, warm-hearted, kind, a keen party-goer and giver and one who loved the fun of life, he was a popular Master in Chambers, so much so that his exceptional frugality in other matters ('tight as a drum', said one colleague) was simply treated as a joke.

---

* Cases involving people or vehicles knocked over or 'run down' by another vehicle.

When tackled about the idea of photography as a career Ronnie, too, agreed that Tony should do a more 'suitable' job and approached various contacts in the City, the wine trade and the tobacco business. But Tony's obvious lack of enthusiasm was such that none of these friends of his father was inclined to offer him anything. Tony himself knew that although he had an entrée into the family stockbroking firm founded by his grandfather, City life was not for him.

Another abortive 'lead' into a business career was, however, to prove fruitful: that autumn his father started him off in a car hire firm, Owen Lloyd (Hire Services) Ltd, where he met the company secretary, solicitor John Humphries. Humphries was to become hugely important to Tony, working for him throughout his life, without charge, with legal advice of the highest quality.

Staying with his father in Albany Tony did not have to worry about rent, but earning money was essential. For a brief spell he worked for Searchers, an agency that let flats and bedsits. Their method was simple. Tony, on his motorbike, would scour London for advertisements for flats or rooms to let in newsagents' windows, note them down and take them back to Searchers, who would add on £1 to the weekly rent mentioned on the newsagents' cards before offering the list to clients.

Finally, in November 1950, when Ronnie realised that Tony was absolutely serious about the idea of photography, he decided to help. A small flatlet was found in Albany for Tony on the mezzanine floor above the porter's lodge. Here he blacked out the bathroom to serve as a darkroom, kept chemicals in the bath, and built a special bed in an alcove in the small bedsitting room to leave space for the clients he hoped would soon arrive.

His first serious commission was from Lady Hardwicke (the former actress Pixie Pickard), who asked him to photograph her at home, with her Alsatian, her Siamese cat and her black kitten. What Tony did not realise at the time was that she would like his pictures so much that she would order 500, to use as her Christmas card. As well as printing and developing all of them he had to trim each with nail scissors – all he had to hand – stick them onto their mounts with Grip Fix and then press them until dry by standing them between books.

Just before Christmas that year he joined the studio of the society photographer Baron – his father had paid £100 to have him taken on for three years – working in the darkrooms and finishing rooms and assisting in the studio. Baron – his real name was Sterling Henry Nahum – came from a family of Italian Jews from Tripoli, who had settled in Manchester and made a success in the cotton trade. Baron and his twin brother Jack moved to London in the 1930s. Baron himself had learned his trade as an Army photographer but quickly realised that the fastest way to succeed in his profession was to photograph the well-known looking as glamorous as possible. Soon he had established a reputation for portraiture and when he began to photograph royalty he became a friend of the Duke of Edinburgh and, like him, a member of the Thursday Club, an all-male dining club.

Baron's success meant that he needed a large staff. His bread and butter work was photographing débutantes and captains of industry at thirty guineas a time – then an astronomical sum.* With his average of five sittings a day he needed thirty people to work in his Brick Street, Park Lane studio. A Baron portrait followed a recognised pattern. 'There was a standard arrangement of spotlights,' said Tony later. 'The main light was high above the camera to thin the face and give a sharp shadow under the nose, four back lights – two for the hair and two for the hands – and a small spot near the camera to fill in shadows and make the eyes sparkle. Oh, and a fifth to light the tapestry background he often used.' Tony was paid £2 15s 1d a week.

It was while Tony was working for Baron that Oliver Messel, whose role in Tony's life was quasi-paternal, gave Tony his twenty first birthday party, a dinner for forty people, seated at four round tables of ten each, with a cabaret of three black song and dance men from New York's West Side (Baron arrived in a smart grey Prince of Wales check suit, only to find that everyone else was wearing dinner jackets; he dashed home and reappeared in his).

But most of Tony's time was spent in the basement darkroom,

---

* A guinea was worth £1 1s.

feeding prints into a rotary drying machine. Its likeness to a mangle prompted him to use it to press his trousers before setting off for parties. One day Baron came downstairs unexpectedly with a party of VIPs when the trousers were only halfway round the drum and Tony was caught in his underpants. This, and the boredom of the routine, served to speed him on his way after a mere six months. When David Sim, another of the Baron apprentices, set up a small basement studio at 59 Shaftesbury Avenue, Tony joined him in August 1951.

Both worked extremely hard, with little time for going out, in an attempt to establish themselves. Tony churned out bad copies of Baron portraits at six guineas each, snapping away at parties on most evenings and at weddings on Saturdays. As an Old Etonian, a former Cambridge man, the son of a successful barrister* and the stepson of an earl he had many contacts on the Old Boy network. Already his style was emerging: wedding photographs were then formal and posed, with everyone carefully grouped, and taken with a plate camera; Tony treated his as reportage, using available light and a small hand-held camera, moving around freely among the guests and snapping constantly. When it came to selling their photographs, Tony would get Sim to represent him because he looked the more grown-up of the two. One of the jobs acquired this way was with the *Tatler*, so impressed by the young photographer's portfolio that early in 1951 they sent him to Madeira to stay at Reid's Hotel, then a favourite for those who wanted to winter somewhere warm.

Already the chutzpah and determination never to be thwarted in pursuit of a photographic goal, no matter how much those in his own world disapproved, were making themselves felt.

When pictures of boys going back to Eton were wanted by another glossy, Tony went down to his old school at the beginning of one half and photographed everything from luggage being unloaded to embarrassed farewells from parents before going to the room of his half-brother Martin Parsons and taking more photographs there – all without seeking the necessary written permission. Not surprisingly, the headmaster, Robert Birley, was

---

* Ronald Armstrong-Jones took silk in 1954.

furious at this unheard-of invasion of privacy by someone who should know exactly how heinous an offence this was. 'I think you should know', he wrote to Tony, 'that I am writing to the parents of those boys whose photographs appeared with their names to let them know that this was done without my knowledge.'

Soon Tony began to contribute to *Picture Post* and the weekly society magazine the *Sketch*. At home, in Albany, he took pictures of girlfriends, using them as models and sending the results to one of the glossies. Some were débutantes whom he had met at the various dances he was invited to or had gatecrashed – usually in the company of his friend Anthony Barton. Their ploy when gatecrashing was to choose a party that had joint hostesses, so that each woman would think the other had invited these unknown guests. Once, driving away from such a party with a magnum of champagne, they ran into a traffic bollard. Almost at once a policeman appeared and they improvised a story about a green Jaguar hurtling so fast round the corner that the accident happened while they tried to avoid it. Impressed by their youthful open faces, the policeman swallowed the tale.

Tony had always intended to set up on his own and again his father helped implement this plan. Ronnie, through his involvement with a firm called Greencoat Properties, found a former ironmonger's shop for sale in the Pimlico Road, a street not then regarded as fashionable. There was an amicable parting from David Sim and on 29 September 1952 Tony took over the ground floor of 20 Pimlico Road (a plumber called Perks still occupied the basement). Its rateable value was a mere £21 a year.

He furnished and decorated it himself, making a bookcase on top of which was his bunk bed, and covered the walls with Regency-striped paper, with an ivy leaf pattern over the entrance. Junk shop buys of gilded lamps and framed Audubon bird prints added atmosphere. Outside, he whitewashed the walls of the small back yard (later useful for unseen entries and exits) and installed a park bench and a stone cupid. Lastly came the front door, discreetly impressive with a lion's head knocker, grey paint picked out in white and a Georgian-style portico (made, naturally, by himself) overhead. He was on his way.

3

Pimlico Road

From the start, Tony displayed characteristics that would remain salient throughout his life: meticulous attention to detail, impeccable organisation, persistence, compartmentalism in both his private life and his work, and the ability to exploit, often ruthlessly, some potentially rewarding or lucrative situation, often from information gleaned from a chance remark or encounter.

Beneath the gaiety, the seeming insouciance and the general high-spirited, happy-go-lucky atmosphere lay a steely professionalism and a sharp eye for the finances of the little studio. Names and dates were indexed in a sittings book, together with a job number that was cross-referenced in the relevant files, prints, interviews and press cuttings in annual scrap-books (later handsomely bound in red leather with gold date and title lettering), so that even thirty or forty years later finding a particular negative was a matter of minutes.

His belief that there was nothing to beat natural light was there from the beginning. To simulate daylight he made a large aluminium box, six foot by three foot, filled it with sixty 100–watt lightbulbs and covered the whole thing with white tissue paper; it could be moved about the ceiling or folded up and put in a car. The last thing he wanted, he felt, was to appear to copy the Baron technique of posed shots with carefully placed spotlights.

The first step was to tell a waiting world that Antony Armstrong-Jones was now ready to take its photograph. In those days, acquiring a telephone line was often a matter for protracted negotiation: there was invariably a queue for the more popular exchanges. The installation of his nearly suffered an extra delay, thanks to one of his more recherché ideas. When the telephone engineer finally arrived, Tony was in the midst of composing his own Christmas card, depicting himself playing the part of three generations. First, he was dressed as a nineteenth-century paterfamilias, in braided jacket, drainpipe trousers, mutton-chop whiskers and gold watch chain, a get-up that elicited only a passing glance from the engineer. When he returned dressed in a child's sailor suit with round straw hat the man looked less happy; the third incarnation – as an elderly lady in a high-necked Edwardian dress with cameo brooch, bewigged hair on top of his head and a huge feathered hat – sent the engineer flying. Finally another was persuaded to come, the job was completed, and Tony put an advertisement in *The Times*. 'Mr Antony Armstrong-Jones has just opened a new photographic studio at 20 Pimlico Road, SW1, Tel: Slo 5324,' it read. He also sent postcards and a map showing how to reach the studio to all his friends and possible clients.

Once installed in Pimlico Road, Tony's social and professional life began to take off. The two were deeply intertwined: he would take a camera to the débutante parties he was asked to, sending the results to one of the society magazines – by 1951 he had achieved his first *Tatler* photograph – and meet girls through his work. One of his methods was to pick out the prettiest girls at a party, offer them a studio photograph, give them a print or two and sell the pictures to a magazine. Often the girls or their mothers would then recommend him to friends, who would in turn book a sitting. Always, though, even from his earliest days, he kept the copyright.

The little studio hummed with activity, with young men and women rushing in and out, working, chatting, teasing, listening to Tony tell jokes or laughing at the mimicry of people or voices at which he excelled. Always at the centre of things, he was mercurial, charming, lithe and fit, startlingly good-looking with white teeth and vivid blue eyes in a tanned face – whenever he got the chance, he would sunbathe on the roof, preferably with a girlfriend, both lying on reflective silver foil to mop up every last ray.

At lunchtime bottles of wine would be opened although in general and even in those days, his spending habits were frugal. Friends remember that he seldom had ready cash on him if a visit to a pub was entailed, yet he was generous with invitations to stay. Friends like Anthony Barton or the designer Tom Parr would come down to Sussex with him or, sometimes, to Birr. Both noted independently that his mother's attitude to Tony, despite his efforts, was far cooler than to her Rosse sons (although his stepfather, Michael Rosse, treated all the boys exactly the same).

Often this coolness extended to his guests. When Tony and Simon Sainsbury returned at six in the morning from a hunt ball two hours' drive away, neither of them made breakfast at nine. Sainsbury was one of the guests who surfaced later, to be berated soundly by Anne; for him, the change in mood was a startling volte-face from the charming, slightly gushing hostess of the night before. Once, when Tony and Parr went to her room while she was breakfasting to say good morning, they found her sitting up in bed drawing the pudding for lunch to show the chef how she wished it to look. It was made clear that she did not wish to be distracted from this important task and that greeting her son and his guest very much took second place. She behaved in exactly the same way to Tony's sister Susan, still the person he was closest to. Her attitude was so painful to them both that the only way they could deal with it was by treating it as a shared joke.

By contrast, Oliver had never been less than kind, loving and generous and in turn Tony's devotion to him never wavered. Tony's need to treat his relationship with his mother at a surface level fused with his natural bent towards the theatre and stagecraft, so fostered and influenced by Oliver, to create a glittering outward persona, like one of Oliver's famous masks. Years later, he was to say: 'I like magic. I like illusion. I like defying gravity.' With a mask, you can be who or what you want to be, picking up, discarding or changing the outward persona at will; nor is there any need to confront the reality behind it. All his life, if reality in personal relationships was painful, Tony would shy away from confronting it.

In addition to his deep affection for his uncle, Tony's own creativity followed roughly the same lines, and he enjoyed nothing more than designing and making objects, usually alongside Oliver, at the Pelham Crescent house where Oliver lived with a large, kindly and foul-mouthed Danish man called Vagn Riis Hanson, always known as the Great Dane, who had left his wife Zoe and their children to live with Oliver. In 1953, as a sign of their total commitment, Oliver and Vagn made wills leaving everything to each other. Vagn, though accepted by everyone in Oliver's life, found more favour with some than with others. After Oliver had taken him to stay with his sweet-natured mother Maud Messel (Tony's grandmother), Mrs Messel remarked gently but truthfully: 'It's so easy to love one's loved ones – but not so easy to love one's loved ones' loved ones ...'

Often Tony would spend summer holidays staying with Oliver, whose custom it was to rent an apartment in Venice for the months of August and September, perhaps taking a friend like Tom Parr or Simon Sainsbury. By day Oliver would sunbathe on the Lido while Vagn sat in St Mark's Square sipping Pernod; by night he and Tony would wander through Venice, Oliver pointing out detail after exquisite detail of the buildings and squares through which they passed to his enthralled nephew until, as Tony said: 'We would end up in some gay bar at five in the morning.'

For here, as in Oliver's professional milieu of stage and theatre, homosexuality was taken for granted, a camp manner seemed as natural as breathing and promiscuity was an accepted fact in a world where intense relationships often lasted only as long as each production. In this febrile atmosphere, surrounded by decorative and glossy people – Oliver had a wide acquaintance in the acting and dance worlds – few could escape the drenching aura of homo-eroticism. When taken to Oliver's house for dinner, for instance, Barton was surprised to find he was expected to kiss the waiters and staff.

With its Aubusson carpets, marvellous collection of Crown Derby, Rockingham and Meissen china, papier-mâché busts wearing wigs, massive gilt looking-glasses, chairs and sofas over-flowing with books, feathers, gauzes, the house exuded a hothouse atmosphere in which Tony, fascinated by the beautiful, the exotic and the erotic, felt at home. Small, appealing, attractive, his eyes sparkling with energy and the desire for fun, he employed his natural flirtatiousness with men as well as women and was in consequence a target for them.

It was a predilection that caused his father great alarm – as a barrister, of course, no one was more aware than Ronnie that homosexuality was against the law and a criminal offence.* Deeply prejudiced against it – perhaps because fearful for his son – he would warn him against certain individuals with the words: 'He's a bu-ugger! He's a bu-ugger!' delivered in his hoarse, asthmatic voice with its customary repetitions. This did not influence Tony, many of whose closest friends were homosexual or had homo-sexual leanings, from choreographer and ballet director John Cranko and Simon Sainsbury to the designer Carl Toms (with whom Tony later shared a flat in New York). As for Oliver, Ronnie always referred to his brother-in-law by the pejorative single word 'Messel', uttered in condemnatory tones. This view was so firmly held that after Ronnie died Tony's young half-brother Peregrine was forbidden by his mother (Ronnie's third wife) to spend any time with gay men until he was eighteen for fear that he would be 'turned', the idea presumably being that by eighteen the 'right' sexual preference would be firmly established.

Ronnie would have been even more alarmed had he known of the advent of a new friend in his son's life, a man who had received a conviction at Marlborough Magistrates Court, London, in 1952, for importuning (he pleaded guilty to a 'minor offence', and was fined £2). Jeremy Fry, whom Tony had met through an Oxford friend, Peter Saunders, was a tall, extremely good-looking man with compelling green eyes, a charismatic presence and an over-whelming, magnetic attraction – and taste – for men and women alike. He was a scion of the Fry chocolate family and, especially appealing to Tony, was a brilliant engineer with a number of inventions to his credit. He was born in 1924, so was six years older than Tony, and had already founded (and was Chairman of) the Rotork Engineering Company. Like Tony, he had enormous energy. Soon the two had formed a deep and abiding friendship.

---

* It is perhaps worth noting that half a century ago the Kinsey reports on human sexuality suggested that while around ten per cent of people (of both genders) were totally heterosexual or totally homosexual, the eighty per cent majority lay on a continuum somewhere in between.

They were so close that their voices eventually began to sound alike.

To most of the girls who worked in the Pimlico Road studio, there seemed little doubt that Tony was gay, especially when they saw him kiss friends like John Cranko on the lips. Then there was the camp manner he had absorbed from Oliver and his penchant for the slightly malicious joke, often wounding to the person at whose expense it was made. When one of his young assistants returned to the studio after a visit to the dentist she was greeted, to her huge embarrassment, with the words: 'I hope they fit all right,' in front of clients; and when his stepmother Carol let on that she had been frightened by a silent heavy breather at the end of the telephone one night, he would ring her up in the small hours and pant heavily and lasciviously into the mouthpiece. 'So funny to hear her reaction,' he would tell the friend who tried to dissuade him.

But there were also, and increasingly, girls. 'If it moves, he'll have it,' was the summing-up of one close friend. For in truth, the twin motors that drove him throughout his life were work and sex; and a day without either was considered wasted. Men friends were those who could amuse him, who were fun to do things with; he said later: 'I didn't fall in love with boys,' adding thoughtfully a moment later, 'but a few men have been in love with me.'

To women, his attitude was more complex. During those early years it was a sudden infatuation that could strike in a matter of minutes, and the chosen girl would find herself wooed with a romantic concentration that was irresistible – all the more so because, at the time, it was perfectly genuine. She was the adored one, she was the most beautiful creature he had ever seen, she was the perfect companion he had been seeking all his life. When the dazzled eighteen-year-old fell into his arms – many of his inamoratas were the beautiful débutantes he photographed – it became even more of a challenge to see if he could get this virginal creature into bed, something infinitely more difficult in those pre-pill days when the fear of pregnancy was every girl's worst nightmare. Usually, he succeeded. One friend who often stayed with him remembers that 'every now and then a new face would appear. Some of them lasted two or three days, others two or three weeks.'

These affairs were conducted with great discretion and, thanks to his habit of compartmentalising his life, often simultaneously. One of the most important, which continued throughout his life, began on 26 September 1951, at the twenty-first birthday party of his friend Andy Garnett. Here he met a ravishing blonde eighteen-year-old and although next day he went to the Rosse Yorkshire estate of Womersley for the weekend, their affair was soon in full swing.* She was a girl with whom he would found an enduring friendship. Another was with a second blonde beauty, Camilla Grinling, who lived in nearby Bourne Street (although if he could be said to have a type, it was girls who reminded him of Leslie Caron, the dark, gamine French actress best known for her role as Gigi). Camilla had come into his orbit through Peter Saunders, whose girlfriend she had been when Tony originally ran into both on the ski slopes. When Tony had a supper party Camilla would cook the dinner in her more sizeable kitchen and carry it round to the studio.

On other nights he would go out, sometimes with a man friend like Anthony Barton or Andy Garnett. What he hated was committing himself in advance; while the others agreed dates to meet for a film, dinner or drinks Tony would never enter into such plans, preferring to ring up at the last minute, after the studio was shut, to go out with whoever was free. Invariably there was someone: such was his magnetism that many of his conquests simply kept their diaries open.

Another girl who figured largely in his life was his assistant, Robin Banks. The daughter of a distinguished airman, Air Commodore Banks, Robin was not only a talented painter but efficient and uncomplainingly hardworking. She had begun by painting backgrounds but soon found herself doing everything from keeping the accounts, making bookings and developing photographs to sweeping the floor and cooking on the primitive stove the baked-potato-with-an-egg-in-it lunch that Tony favoured, with working hours that went on until the various jobs were finished – this sometimes meant camping in the studio as by midnight or the small hours she was too tired to travel home to her parents in

---

* Disclosing the name at present would cause personal difficulties.

Weybridge. Described as 'marvellously nubile, fair, with straw-coloured hair, bursting out all over,' by one admiring friend, she was an inevitable target for Tony – unfortunately for him, though, she was in love with someone else. In those early days, with money tight, his father often took the pair of them out to dinner at Peter's, the café across the road where lunch could be had for half a crown. Tony's favourite trick was to put Robin off her lunch with remarks like 'I've just seen the sweat from that waitress's armpit dropping into your soup,' or 'Did you notice she had nits?' until total revulsion caused her to push her lunch away – which he would then devour.

To earn a living, he was photographing dance after dance, usually for the *Tatler*, sometimes for the *Sketch*. As it was the custom to affect a distaste for publicity, however secretly flattered one might feel, it was also the custom to regard the photographers at these parties as pests. Again and again, it was made clear that photography was on a par with, say, waiting at tables, not least by *Tatler*'s legendary social columnist, 'Jennifer', in private life Mrs Betty Kenward.

Mrs Kenward prided herself on her personal friendships with those about whom she wrote her gushing, popular lists describing who had attended various balls, parties, race meetings or luncheons. Carefully coded adjectives could be translated by those in the know: 'beautiful' meant 'pretty', 'attractive' meant 'plain' and a semicolon often separated the sheep from the goats – and photographers, in Mrs Kenward's eyes, were definitely goats. When Tony asked her politely one evening what angle she would like on a particular shot she hissed back: 'Don't ever dare speak to me! I *never* speak to photographers!'

Sometimes there was even physical violence. Various young hearties were offended by Tony's determination to get whatever picture he was after, largely because they felt he was using his social contacts to infiltrate somewhere he might not be welcome in order to make a profit out of it, partly because one of their own sort was doing something they considered 'impossible'.

At a party for débutante April Brunner in 1954 he was pushed into a goldfish pond in white tie and tails, to emerge dripping with mud; at another in early June, for Sarah Chester Beatty, he was debagged by two Old Etonians – ironically, in view of his later marriage into the family, the leader was the Hon. Fergus Bowes-Lyon,* nephew of Queen Elizabeth the Queen Mother – while two more sat on his head, leaving him almost unconscious in the bushes in the Savoy garden. 'It may have been funny to some,' he said later. 'But to me it was unforgivable. It seems that it is infra dig to be in society and a photographer at the same time.' But next day, with typical courage, he turned up looking smart in a grey morning coat in the Royal Enclosure at Ascot, his face covered in cuts and bruises.

When Tony's grandfather, old Colonel Messel, died in 1953 the remains of Nymans – the wing left standing after the fire of 1947 and the 600-acre estate, including the superb gardens – were left to the National Trust with the proviso that members of the family could live in properties on it at a peppercorn rent for the next three generations. One of these dwellings, Tony's beloved Old House, was taken on by his uncle Oliver. For Tony himself there was an expansion of territory: two years after he had moved to the Pimlico Road studio the basement beneath became vacant and he snapped it up.

Soon it was his living quarters, with an all-white sitting room and a bedroom with violet-coloured wallpaper, reached by a spiral staircase of wooden treads round a polished copper pillar, made by Tony from some unwanted copper plumbing. Much of the hard work was done by the long-suffering Robin, under the direction of Anne Rosse, who would arrive at the studio bejewelled and dressed up to the nines. Waving her arms languidly, she would describe how to cut and swathe elaborate curtains while a resentful Robin ('I had been hired for *photographic* work, not for decorating someone's sitting room') crawled about on the floor with scissors and pins.

The room was furnished by Tony: blessed with a discerning and eclectic eye, he was able to pick up vivid and attractive junk shop finds. Every room was wired for music, a stuffed bird with a

---

* Later the 17th Earl of Strathmore.

hidden mechanism moved continually in a gilded cage and guests were invited to scratch their names on a large Regency mirror with a diamond kept especially for the purpose. Tony, in black sweater and black leather jacket, would usher clients down to the little sitting room and give them a drink. He would chat away, while pacing up and down in his crêpe-soled boots, a glass of whisky heavily diluted with water in his hand, all the while watching for characteristic poses, mannerisms or expressions.

He was meticulous about politeness, both to clients (unless he took a sudden dislike to one) and from clients to his own staff. When the Kabaka of Buganda booked a sitting, Tony carefully explained to his then assistant, a cheerful cockney, that although the Kabaka was black, he was royal and to be treated with great respect. Unfortunately, the Kabaka failed to keep his appointment that day. When he turned up unannounced two weeks later, everyone had forgotten about him and to Tony's horror his arrival was announced with the cry of 'Tony, there's a nigger outside to see you!'

Other than in his attitude to these early clients, his lifelong need to run counter to established customs expressed itself in anything from a highly charged individualism to simple provocation that concealed an outright rebelliousness. Even his favourite games – 'teases', he would have called them – were designed to discomfit. One was played with his friend Andy Garnett, owner of a high-powered motorbike, on sunny evenings in London. With Tony on the pillion, the pair would draw up alongside the car of a glossy couple obviously on their way to an elegant evening's entertainment, as Garnett recalled in his memoir, *Lucky Dog:*

> I especially remember Tony Armstrong-Jones, who could be marvellously brazen. The beautiful, glamorous XK120 Jaguar open two-seater car had just been introduced and on sunny summer evenings smart young men in dinner jackets with their flopsies at their side, dressed to the nines in cocktail or long dresses, drove these beautiful cars to deb dances or parties. The cars had their rear-view mirrors fitted to the front wings, seemingly yards forward from the open cockpit. We used to squeeze between the traffic stopped behind a red light and chose the front end of a Jag with a particularly odious-looking young man at the wheel. Tony would

turn the adjacent mirror 90 degrees so that it became a looking-glass for him. Then with his nose a couple of inches from the mirror, he would squeeze an imaginary spot. That ritual complete, he would stare at the mirror with music-hall concentration and adjust the parting of his hair, occasionally wiggling the mirror as if to get a better view. It was good spectator sport for the waiting drivers and pedestrians. Sometimes the driver would join in the fun but often he got into a noisy rage, especially if his girl was laughing at him as well as at the charade. With a green 'go' light the bike, with its high power/weight ratio, shot away before the car started to move.

Another favourite game took the form of a competition. Each of them had to get into an occupied taxi as it paused at Knightsbridge or Sloane Square and see who could get to Piccadilly first, by sweet-talking the people in the taxi. 'I beg your pardon, I'm so sorry to intrude but I'm just desperate to get to Swallow Street. Driver, where are you going, towards Piccadilly? Very kind, I'm so grateful to you.' To avoid being turned out of the taxi by the occupants or having to escape before the cab driver stopped the cab and rolled up his sleeves meant keeping up a convincing patter. Invariably, the game was won by Tony, deploying his charm at full blast and quite unabashed at any inconvenience he might be causing. For what Tony wanted he was determined to get – if possible at a bargain price.

This meant that the studio curtains were not the only sewing Robin had to do. Drainpipe trousers were then the fashion and Tony, always a style leader, liked his ultra-narrow; whenever he bought new jeans or trousers Robin had to take in the side seams until it was only just possible to pull them on over his feet. Worse still was a tailoring job for his Fiat Topolino. When he decided he wanted a sunshine roof, he cut the little car in half laterally and detailed Robin to make the hood out of thick rubberised canvas that could only be stitched with an industrial sewing machine. This was then fitted on a frame made by Tony.

Yet for staff, the frustrations and moods that he would take out on them were more than counterbalanced by the fun, the excitement of watching how he put one of his superb and original shots together and above all by the feeling of being included. 'There was never any Us and Them,' said one. 'If he was asked to stay to a meal by a client, he wouldn't sit down at the table unless I was included too. Once, when we were photographing Field Marshal Lord Montgomery's grandchildren, Monty said to Tony: "Oh, you'll stay for a spot of lunch? Your man can get a bite at the pub up the road." And Tony said at once: "No, I'm terribly sorry, we've got to go back to London." He simply wasn't going to have it.'

There were, naturally, occasional mistakes on the path towards success. Once, photographing a charity event, the Birdcage Ball, he had the bright idea of asking everyone to stick their head in a gilded birdcage he had had made specially, for £1 a shot. 'When I came to develop the rolls of film there was nothing on them,' he recalled when discussing the fear he felt before every photographic session. 'So I had to spend days sending everyone their £1 back. I remember the agony. But if you don't have dread [of something going wrong] you might as well give up.' Another major fiasco was caused by Robin who, exhausted by hours of developing late into the night (there were only two small developing tanks), put water that was several degrees too hot onto one set of films, thus boiling all the emulsion off. Unfortunately, it was of a wedding and thus the pictures could not be repeated.

Drawn naturally to the ambience of the theatre and, to a lesser extent, the ballet, through the work of his uncle Oliver, Tony began taking theatrical photographs, at first for the nearby Royal Court theatre (later, his work here was described by fellow photographer and rival Patrick Lichfield as 'absolutely ground-breaking'). It was then a tradition set in stone that such pictures should portray the stars at their glossy best, whether in costume or in some becoming outfit. Hollywood stills showed female stars as icons of glamour, all carefully set hair, luscious dark lips and shaded cheekbones, the men broodingly handsome with a thrilling aura of barely restrained virility; and the photographs displayed several at a time in glass frames outside the Shaftesbury Avenue theatres followed the same pattern. At that time, the king of theatre photography was Angus McBean. Stars loved him because his posed and often heavily retouched photographs allowed them to appear as impossibly beautiful as, secretly, many of them believed themselves to be. McBean's pre-eminence in the field meant that rising young photographers did their best to emulate his style. 'He was a wonderful photographer,' said Tony, 'but his photographs had little to do with reality.'

At first Tony was content to follow in McBean's footsteps. Soon, however, he would change theatre photographs for ever. One day, realising that even a sharply defined McBean photograph could not be seen from across the street and that when you did look at it, the glossy portrait did little to convey either the character of the actor or the essence of the part he or she was playing, Tony decided on a different approach. This could be summed up in a phrase he used to describe his work. 'All photography is about really is snapshots. It's capturing a moment that is typical.'

Today the idea of a photographer using a small hand-held camera and moving around as opposed to posing his subject motionless in front of a prepared background may sound commonplace but then, especially in the theatre, it was revolutionary. Only someone whose originality of mind was untrammelled by preconception and whose belief in himself was sufficient to go against the prevailing ethos despite his comparative lack of experience could have achieved such a masterstroke. For a young man of twenty-four it was extraordinary.

The first of these new-style photographs was for Terence Rattigan's hit play *Separate Tables* in September 1954 and from then on an Armstrong Jones photograph* was instantly recognisable. Nor did he hesitate to take the occasional liberty even with his own brand of realism: his 1956 photograph of Alec Guinness in *Hotel Paradiso*, for instance, enlarged the head and emphasised the whites of his eyes. Not everyone, however, was happy with these grainy, often harshly realistic shots: the veteran actress Gwen Ffrangcon-Davies was so enraged that she once climbed a stepladder, tore down his picture of her and demanded that it be replaced by 'something flattering by dear Angus'.

With Oliver's name as an Open Sesame, Tony was able to

---

* For his photographic work Tony dropped the hyphen in his surname.

persuade directors to let him attend rehearsals, where he would creep about quietly on crêpe-soled shoes, an anonymous figure in sweater and trousers with a small hand-held camera, snapping away discreetly as the actors worked their way into parts. Once, dressed in an electrician's overalls, he infiltrated rehearsals at the Vienna State Opera without a single singer being aware of his presence. The best of the shots, dramatic and full of action, were blown up poster-size and, when displayed outside the theatre or used as life-size standing cut-outs in the foyer, were immediate eye-catchers.

As with the débutantes, Tony would offer a rising young actor or actress or, sometimes, an established personality a free photograph and a couple of prints – if they wanted more they had to pay ten guineas each. With his custom of retaining the copyright, he could then sell such a portrait to a magazine. One of the girls he photographed in this way (in March 1955) was a tiny, exquisite eighteen-year-old dancer of largely Chinese descent called Jacqui Chan, then appearing in the hit play *Teahouse of the August Moon*.

Jacqui, with her porcelain looks and exotic charm, was Tony's first real love. They would meet whenever they could, chiefly at the Pimlico Road studio where Jacqui, running round after Tony, fetching, carrying and attentive to his every word, soon became known as resident girlfriend. From the start there was no question of marriage and neither discussed it: Jacqui was very young and just beginning to achieve real notice as a dancer and Tony believed that thirty was a good age for a man to marry. Not even the marriage of his dear friend Jeremy Fry to his former girlfriend Camilla Grinling in 1955 shook this resolve.

Instead, he took up a new enthusiasm, designing an underwater camera (it must be remembered that such devices were then unknown) and persuading *Tatler* to send him to the Riviera to photograph social notables as – hopefully – they dived and cavorted underwater. With Tom Parr he drove to the Côte d'Azur in a Humber, which Tom, working at the car company Rootes, could get at a discount. The day before they left the Côte Tony discovered that, owing to something wrong with the camera, none of the underwater photographs of the various peers and celebrities he had taken had come out. Nothing daunted, he photographed Tom and a woman met on the beach whom he had persuaded to join in, captioning them with the names of those in the failed photographs. As every outline was blurred and indistinct, *Tatler* printed the results in happy ignorance. The two of them then went on to Venice, where Princess Chavchavadze, also met on the beach, lent them her elegant gondola, with its liveried gondoliers, for sightseeing. At night they returned to their hotel, the cheapest they could find.

At home, Old House at Nymans still exerted its magnetic pull. Chatting one day to a great friend, the witty and kind-hearted photographer Bob Belton, Tony began to describe it. 'Oliver hasn't done anything to it so it's pretty basic,' he said, 'but we could go there for the weekend, if you like.' After this, going down on fine weekends became a habit. The two of them would drive down with sleeping bags, portable radio and oil lamps – there was still no electricity or sanitation and although Oliver had installed a bath it was not connected up. They would set a log fire blazing, near which they would sleep, pump water from the well by the front door, nip into the overgrown garden for calls of nature, go to the local pub for meals and swim in the nearby lake.

Work was flowing in – so much so that Robin could take it no more. Although the drive home was easier after she had bought Tony's small Fiat when he began to need a vehicle that could take equipment and be securely locked, the cumulative fatigue of late nights spent developing and long days on her feet had become intolerable. She gave notice.

When Anne Rosse heard about this, she took action. Robin was far too useful to be allowed to go. She summoned the exhausted young woman to see her at 18 Stafford Terrace, where Robin arrived at 8 a.m. – the only time possible in her long working day. There she was greeted by Anne, whose head was draped in a shawl ('this is far too early an hour for me – I cannot be seen until ten o'clock') and the peremptory demand that she stay with Tony. 'You cannot leave him,' insisted Anne. But Robin stood her ground. 'I'm sorry but I must,' she replied. 'My legs are giving way and, quite simply, I'm too tired to go on.'

4

'Tony Snapshot'

>|<

With Robin gone, Tony had to look for a new assistant. He took the most practical step he could think of, writing out a postcard saying: 'Theatrical photographer urgently requires assistant,' with his telephone number below. This he put on the Jobs Vacant notice-board at the best-known school of photography, the Poly – fortunately it was the end of the summer term (of 1955), and also of the school year.

Here it attracted the attention of a young man of twenty-two called John Timbers, who had begun by working for a photographer, then done his National Service followed by two years at the Poly. As he did not want to work for his original employer again he telephoned Tony. 'Come down and have a spot of lunch,' suggested Tony. Although Tony's friend Peter Saunders, notably blond and handsome, was there, it was Tony whom Timbers perceived as 'startlingly good-looking'. The occasion was memorable for another reason: it was the first time Timbers had eaten avocado vinaigrette. After some discussion, Tony asked: 'Can you start tomorrow?' Timbers thought for a moment and said: 'Why not?'

Work of all kinds was building up. In January 1956 Tony wrote an article in the *Sketch* about taking photographs out hunting, for which he equipped himself with hunting clothes from secondhand shops, breeches bought for twenty-five shillings and a pair of non-matching boots ('well, you only see one at a time,' he commented) for ten shillings. There were stage pictures of Dirk Bogarde, photographs in Vienna and the entire cast of a comedy at the Apollo, quickly followed by more pictures for society magazines of the smartest skiers at Gstaad for a fee of £6 a page.

Soon afterwards he achieved his first picture in the *Daily Express* – then the newspaper all photographers aspired to. His shots were of the secret wedding of Leslie Caron and Peter Hall, in Marylebone Register Office – Tony, a friend of Leslie's after his pictures of her as Gigi, doubled as witness. After the wedding Leslie dashed off to the theatre and Tony to the black *Express* building in Fleet Street to hand his pictures to the night editor so that they would be in time for the next day's edition. When he asked for a credit (a byline) the night editor gave them back to him with the words: 'We never give photographic credits.' But Caron was news and there were no other pictures – so Tony got his credit as well as the £30 fee.

Yet even in 1956 and despite his growing fame the view of photographer as tradesman was still very much in evidence. When on 21 April he took the wedding photographs of Lady Anne Coke, 23-year-old daughter of the Earl of Leicester, at Holkham Hall in Norfolk, her father dubbed him 'Tony Snapshot'. Nor was there any question of him joining the guests – many of whom he knew – for lunch. More bruisingly, her bridegroom, the Hon. Colin Tennant (former escort of Princess Margaret), whom he knew perfectly well, made him use the servants' entrance. It was the start of a lifelong bitter enmity towards Tennant, whom he seldom later referred to even in print without the epithet 's–t'. At the time he merely said: 'I'll get even with you for that,' adding more prophetically than he knew, 'I'll marry your best friend!'

With other clients, he would joke about this treatment. To the débutantes he met at parties, both socially and from behind the camera, he would describe snubs he thought amusing, making the best possible story out of them while setting the girls, often rather shy, at their ease. There would be unusual backgrounds: he photographed one of them, Angela Huth, down by the Thames; she found something 'very inspiring' about his zest for life, his way of suddenly taking her off to look at a church or a house. 'He had an eye for the extraordinary in the ordinary,' she recalled. 'He brought a very original and special eye to the everyday which made it scintillate, so he was huge fun to do things with.'

Soon the social *de haut en bas* attitude to Tony's profession would change – and it was Tony who did much to change it. When he realised the young Duke of Kent would be twenty-one on 9 October 1956, he wrote to him offering to do his coming-of-age pictures. The Duke, who had perhaps heard of him through their mutual friend Jane Sheffield, decided that he would like to be photographed by someone nearer his own age than by any of the well-known photographers of the day and the photographs, taken on 1 August and released to coincide with the Duke's birthday, went round the world.

In the theatre, notable camera coups were Paul Scofield, Eartha Kitt and Marlene Dietrich. Dietrich was notoriously particular where her image was concerned, so Tony was determined to create the aura of heavy-lidded, smoke-filled sensual promise evoked by such songs as 'The Boys in the Back Room'. To produce it he put three people under the piano, all puffing furiously at their cig-arettes, so that Dietrich was surrounded by wisps of curling smoke. But when he returned at three in the morning with the contacts – which had to go to press at nine – she examined them closely and then rasped at him huskily: 'Dear boy, I like zis one. But I like ze smoke on zat one. Will you put zem togezzer?' 'But, Miss Dietrich, it's terribly difficult ....' 'No, it's not,' replied the diva, giving him a technical explanation of how it should be done ('You just put my face in the enlarger and shade zis part with your hand, so ...'). When she had finished, she handed him the prints. 'Oll right? Now you run along and do that.' He did, and the resultant pictures added to his reputation.

More personal to Tony was his first published photograph of his love Jacqui Chan, now a principal dancer in *The King and I*. It appeared under the headline 'The Face I Love' – Harold Keble, the editor of the *Express*, had wanted to print it under 'The Girl I Love' but Tony, conscious this was perfectly true, felt it might be indiscreet.

Jacqui, now accepted as Tony's girlfriend, stayed at the Pimlico studio whenever she was not touring. She was a great favourite with Tony's father Ronnie. If Tony was out for the evening, he would take her out to dinner, sometimes raiding the petty cash to do so, which drove Tony to a frenzy of irritation. Yet though two other friends, Jocelyn Stevens and Jane Sheffield, got married in July – the wedding pictures taken by Tony – and contemporaries all around him were marrying, Tony felt no urge to follow their example. Establishing himself beyond doubt was still his priority.

The chance to do this came quickly, with the commission that every photographer dreamed of – a request from the Queen to photograph herself, Prince Philip and their two children, Prince Charles and Princess Anne. When staying with her great friends, Lord and Lady Rupert Nevill, the Queen had seen Tony's photographs of their children, taken in silhouette, had been struck by them, and had asked who had taken them. Some weeks before Prince Charles's eighth birthday on 14 November 1956 the Palace got in touch with Tony.

He was determined to make the most of this amazing opportunity that had suddenly dropped into his lap. For him, this meant producing something different from the then stereotyped royal picture. He wanted a natural setting – and, of course, the natural light by which he always worked – and he wanted the two children to be at their ease.

The gardens of the Palace, with their trees, stream and odd pieces of classical statuary, seemed to provide such a background. The spot he chose – a stone bridge on which the Queen and Prince Philip would stand, looking at their children on the bank of the stream below – was reminiscent of late-eighteenth-century romanticism, while the grouping of the figures expressed an altogether modern informality. The children, he planned, would be fishing in the stream; this, he thought, would amuse them both and cause them to relax. To make sure that all the figures would be posed against the setting as he wished he did a reference sketch beforehand; then hired a rod and bought two trout from a fishmonger. All was now ready.

On the morning of the great day his daily, Mrs Peabody, brought him his breakfast as usual. 'I thought you should have a good breakfast today,' she said, 'so I've cooked those two trout ....' Hastily Tony rushed out and bought a book instead. Later he recalled: 'I was so nervous doing that photograph that I remember having to pee behind a tree just before the royal party arrived. Luckily there are a lot of trees in the Palace gardens.'

When the photographs came out, of the two children reading a book by the stream, with their parents, in clothes that any well-to-do country couple might have worn, smiling down on them from above, his reputation and his fees rose exponentially. 'The Queen is quite delighted with the photographs of the children,' wrote her Assistant Private Secretary, Martin Charteris,* on 26 October 1956, adding that a number of copies had been ordered for the press as well as some for herself.

One person to whom his success was upsetting rather than a pleasure was Cecil Beaton, until then the acknowledged royal photographer. 'I don't think A.A. Jones's pictures are at all interesting,' he wrote sniffily in his diary, 'but his publicity value is terrific. It pays to be new in the field.' Beaton's sense of bitter rivalry was augmented by the fact that he was extremely jealous of Tony's uncle. Oliver Messel lived next door to Beaton in Pelham Crescent – but in a much larger house with a double rather than a single frontage. Once, hearing (mistakenly) that Oliver was very ill, he arrived at the house dressed in black and carrying a sheaf of lilies. When the door was opened by Oliver himself, Beaton's expression changed. Saying, 'Oh, they told me you were dying,' he turned on his heel – taking the lilies with him.

It was an enmity that Beaton extended to Oliver's sister Anne, for whom his hatred became legendary. His watercolour caricatures depicting her as an arch-snob (a bit rich coming from Beaton) were shown freely around his circle. They were beautifully done but, as Lady Anne Tree remarked: 'I don't think Cecil would have got his knighthood if the royal family had seen these.'

Tony's reputation had already soared. That June his first exhibition, 'Photocall', was opened by Leslie Caron at Kodak House, Kingsway. For the time it was unorthodox in the extreme, including a nineteen-foot-high picture of the ballerina Anya Linden leaping, landscapes, slum photographs and triple life-size portraits of the

---

* Martin Charteris was Assistant Private Secretary 1952–72, then Private Secretary 1972–77, to the Queen. He was created a life peer, Lord Charteris of Amisfield, in 1978 and he died in 1999.

fashion designer Dior, the painter Annigoni and actors Edith Evans, Ingrid Bergman and Laurence Olivier in his role as Archie Rice in John Osborne's *The Entertainer* – for this, Tony had retouched the natural slight gap between Olivier's front teeth to enlarge it, thus almost imperceptibly heightening the character's aura of desperation and seediness. Equally unconventional was the picture of film impresario Mike Todd, face frozen in an aghast rictus and arm outstretched with open palm upwards – caught by Tony at the moment Todd feared a door would slam and waken his wife Elizabeth Taylor, sleeping next door.

After his royal success *Vogue*, with whom Tony had been trying to negotiate a contract for some time, immediately offered him one but, now aware of his worth, he drove a hard bargain. On 28 June 1957 Sadruddin Aga Khan wrote to ask if Tony could attend his marriage in Geneva (to the exotic Anglo-Indian fashion model Nina Dyer) as his personal photographer. 'All expenses will be taken care of and you must feel free to decide your personal fee.' Two hundred guineas is scribbled on the letter – worth well over £3,000 now. His fees were always the highest the market could bear and sometimes more. A letter from *Vogue* complains of an invoice of nine guineas for three prints. 'It's miles more than the studio charges and even a good bit more than Parkinson [Norman Parkinson was an already legendary photographer].'

Further royal photographs followed: the Queen and Princess Anne in August 1957, a ninth birthday one of Prince Charles in which – another first for royal children – he stood with his hand in his pocket. This time, the Queen bought both the copyright and the negative for five guineas – the only person who would have been allowed to do so. 'Charles pictures absolutely terrific you have set a new standard,' ran the telegram sent by Harold Keble of the *Daily Express*, on 10 November 1957. This too was wormwood to Beaton: as Penny Gilliatt gleefully telegraphed Tony: 'Cecil's nose reported unjointed unmendable, super love Penny.'

There was so much work that Tony's assistant John Timbers was finding the combination of late hours and journey times exhausting. 'If you want to move nearer I'm sure Pa can speed things up,' said Tony. Ronnie, a director of the Greencoat Company which owned blocks of flats in Ebury Street and the Coleshill Buildings, directly behind Tony's studio, duly found the delighted Timbers a place to live.

This was a cold-water walk-up on the top floor of the Coleshill Buildings consisting of bedroom, sitting room, kitchen and a lavatory on the balcony. The rent was £8 a month, just under half of Timbers' monthly earnings (Tony paid him £5 a week). Timbers put a shower in the kitchen to provide washing facilities – previously there had been none – and Tony rigged up a telephone line from the studio, across the courtyard and up to Timbers' balcony. Eventually this was disconnected by Timbers to avoid late-night calls from Tony saying that he had lost some vital address or piece of film and could Timbers come over and help him look for it.

In September 1957 Tony was in Malta, taking photographs for Sacheverell Sitwell's book on the island and getting up at five in the morning to catch the right light. And just before Christmas there was a coming-of-age photograph of Princess Alexandra (whose twenty-first birthday was on Christmas Day 1957). It was a time of frenzied work. There were still the commercially successful débutante portraits on which, now established, he could stamp his own style. His February 1958 cover of Lola Wigan for *Queen* magazine broke with the usual format: instead of a girl shot full-face and smiling with pearls around the neck, this was a three-quarter face, unsmiling portrait in which the eyes are cast down above a suggestively naked shoulder.

As well as theatre portraits there was the highly prestigious request to photograph the Prime Minister, Harold Macmillan, to whom he had been introduced by Lady Elizabeth Cavendish (Macmillan was her uncle by marriage). His fee was twenty guineas; on 29 October 1957 a letter from Downing Street asked for 'a hundred of the small photographs of the Prime Minister'.

He was also working on designs for the sets and costumes of a musical for John Cranko, *Keep Your Hair On*, for which he was paid a total of £250, with £3 a day living expenses for every day he had to spend out of London, photographic expenses up to £200 and first-class return fares for any necessary journey; all bills, posters and programmes were to carry the sentence 'scenery and costumes designed by Tony Armstrong Jones'.

Work, however, was no impediment to the starting of one of his more serious love affairs. This began when he photographed the beautiful young actress Gina Ward, whose father had wanted some photographs taken for her débutante season the following year.* Tony was now so sought after for débutante photographs that bookings had to be made months in advance. Gina arrived at Tony's Pimlico studio at nine in the morning on Boxing Day 1957. Their mutual infatuation was immediate and blazing.

After the session, he asked her if she had seen the great married American actors Alfred Lunt and Lynne Fontaine, who were starring in a pre-London run of Dürrenmatt's *The Visit* in Brighton's Theatre Royal, which had opened two days earlier, on Christmas Eve. 'Why don't we go and see them this afternoon?' he suggested. They held hands all the way through; watching one romantic scene, where the stage couple were alone on a bench in the woods at dusk, Tony squeezed Gina's hand so tightly she thought it was going to bleed, but their feelings were so strong she never thought of withdrawing it.

Even at the time, though, and even caught up in the thrilling ecstasy of first love, Gina realised that she could not expect fidelity. 'He couldn't buy a packet of cigarettes without flirting with the man or woman behind the counter.' Aware of this, Gina became desperately jealous, particularly of a ballet dancer called Gilbert Norman.

Keep Your Hair On opened at the Apollo Theatre on 13 February 1958. 'Darling don't panic it is going to be a tremendous success I am thinking of you always bless you Georgina' telegraphed Gina Ward from Paris, where she was studying; from Womersley came a telegram from Nanny Gunner, 'Heartfelt wishes for tonight' and from his father a short, loving note: 'Darling Tony, I wish you so deeply a personal triumph tonight. You deserve it and let's pray it comes.'

---

* Georgina Ward's father, George Reginald Ward, the son of the 2nd Earl of Dudley, was a Conservative politician who became Secretary of State for Air and was created Viscount Ward of Witley in 1960.

KYHO was a dismal flop. From the moment a gallery first-nighter yelled the word 'Encore!' very slowly after the thirteenth verse of a song called 'Never be a Bore' it galloped downhill and the last twenty minutes were inaudible through the catcalls and caterwauling of the audience. It was so savagely mauled by the critics that it came off after less than twenty performances. Tony got off lightly compared with the show's authors. 'I saw it last night and frankly it was made for me by your absolutely brilliant sets,' wrote the designer David Hicks who summed up, albeit in more flowery language, the general view. 'I almost cried when I realised how poor was the music and general lack of style and chic which alas accompanies the enormously elegant and original background which you have dreamed up.'

A fortnight after the show's disastrous launch Tony was invited to the most momentous dinner party of his life. Two years earlier, he had met Lady Elizabeth Cavendish, extra lady-in-waiting to Princess Margaret, through John Cranko, whose successful revue *Cranks* ran until the autumn of 1956. Lady Elizabeth was closely involved in it and when, one evening after the show, John Cranko gave a supper party, Tony and Lady Elizabeth were among the guests.

Lady Elizabeth had already heard of Tony through her lifelong companion, the poet John Betjeman, who knew Tony's mother Anne quite well (in 1957, at a Guy Fawkes party, they decided to found the Victorian Society together, supported by Nikolaus Pevsner); and on 20 February 1958 she invited the young photographer to a small dinner party in the Cheyne Walk house of her mother, the Dowager Duchess of Devonshire. The party was given for her friend and employer Princess Margaret, and she thought that Tony's originality, sense of fun and high spirits would appeal to the Princess. At table she placed them next to each other, with their backs to the window, its heavy curtains excluding the light from the street lamps outside and creating an atmosphere of warmth and intimacy.

The two hit it off at once. The Princess was immediately intrigued by Tony, so completely unlike her normal escorts in every way yet from a similar background and with many friends in common. Quickly they established their mutual interest in the arts and ballet; his high spirits and sense of fun gave their conversation sparkle and enjoyment, though like many of the women who had worked for him or passed through his studio she thought that he was homosexual. 'I enjoyed his company very much but I didn't take a lot of notice of him because I thought he was queer,' she told her authorised biographer Christopher Warwick.

In any case, Tony appeared bound up in work. Less than a month after that first dinner party he was photographing the sensational Tennessee Williams play *Cat on a Hot Tin Roof*. There were well-paid though anonymous advertising photo sessions and pictures of businessmen and stars like Beatrice Lillie for *Queen* magazine.

At the same time he was designing ski wear – orange balloon jackets of waterproof silk over tight knickerbockers – and a trapeze coat of leather with a fur collar, praised by Audrey Withers, the Editor of British *Vogue* as 'beautiful, elegant and exciting'. They were sold at the Walton Street boutique of Jacqui Chan's friend Kiki Byrne. He was also working on what would become his book, *London*.

His habit of photographing, without fee, those he thought might be useful continued. One of these was the débutante Henrietta Tiarks, of whom he took the first picture. Henrietta, who later married the future Duke of Bedford, was nominated Deb of the Year (1958) and the appearance of her picture triggered another rush of débutantes and their mothers to the Pimlico Road studio.

Contacts and friends were an additional route to professional success. Andy Garnett lived in the East End in a flat that was originally an eighteenth-century sailmaker's loft in Limehouse, its eighty-foot main room overhanging the water. From this, he would take Tony on the back of his motorbike to small courtyards and narrow alleys impassable to a car, introducing him to louche or little-known spots, many of which were to appear later in Tony's book (for which he got an advance of £250 in November 1958 from Weidenfeld and Nicolson). Soon after this, Garnett himself went off to Paris, where Tony and his sister Susan came to stay with him, zipping round the beautiful city in one of the first of the new Minis.

Before he left, Garnett made another introduction that was to have a more significant outcome. For some time, Tony had been looking for a hideaway that he could keep completely secret and late in 1956 he spotted what he wanted.

One of Garnett's acquaintances, Bill Glenton, a journalist specialising in waterfront reporting, had established himself at 59 Rotherhithe Street in 1954. It was an old building that had once been a pub, overlooking the river. On the ground floor was a spare room, with a dented concrete floor, chipped plaster and flaking paint. Glenton used this when he held a party for his Fleet Street friends, who sat around on coils of rope and orange boxes while they drank. He had also acquired an old piano, often played while they talked. Garnett had met Glenton in a Limehouse pub one Sunday lunchtime and had mentioned that a friend of his was looking for a room. A few months later, when Garnett next went to see Glenton, Glenton said: 'A pal of yours has really been bugging the hell out of me to let him have a room here.' It was, of course, Tony, applying his usual persuasive charm in his pursuit of what he wanted – and, as usual, getting it.

First, Tony persuaded Glenton to take him round the neighbourhood in his Morris 1000, looking at place after place. A view of the river, said Tony, was essential. None was suitable. Then, suddenly, he asked if he could have Glenton's ground-floor room and, once Glenton had agreed, asked him to not to tell anyone – not even his friend Andy Garnett, through whom he had originally met Glenton. With his habit of keeping every aspect of his life separate, Tony did not tell Garnett either that he had installed himself in No. 59 or that he was using in *London* many of the places that Garnett had shown him on his motorbike. When Garnett discovered this he was, understandably, irked that someone he regarded as one of his oldest friends had not told him about either of these projects, neither of which would have been possible without him; it led to a certain coolness for some time.

A fortnight after Glenton had said he could have the room rent-free, Tony turned up with his assistant, carrying planks of wood, tools, a hamper of food and several bottles of burgundy. Together they set to work, making cupboards from the deal planks both to hide pipes and serve as storage space, and painted the walls a gleaming white, Tony smoking pungent 'Disque Bleu' cigarettes almost incessantly and taking swigs from one of the wine bottles. A stove and washbasin were installed behind one set of doors, a larder behind a second and the third devoted to clothes. For the floor, he bought squares of cheap rush matting, made in Hong Kong. Most of the stitching-together of these squares, a job hard and painful on the fingers, was done by the faithful Jacqui, sitting cross-legged on the floor.

Once these basics were done he hung a floor-to-ceiling painting of a choleric eighteenth-century admiral – bought for thirty shillings in a Chelsea antique shop – on one wall, with a brass telescope on a stand and a hammock adding further nautical touches. Later, finding the admiral's presence overwhelming, he pushed an old upright piano in front of him. He also installed a round table, some chairs and a tiny gas cooker and added a large mirror, a golden cage with three stuffed lovebirds, a chiming wall clock and various glasses, plates and ornaments of carved ivory. A bronze bust of Jacqui Chan's head stood in a place of honour.

By now, his feelings for Jacqui were such that although he had originally had no plans to marry her he did once ask his closest friend, Anthony Barton, if he should. 'I don't think that would be a good idea,' said Barton, aware both that Tony was not ready for marriage and that the worlds Tony and Jacqui came from were too dissimilar. 'No, I suppose not,' replied Tony.

At the same time, he was continuing his liaison with Gina. For her, their affair was magic. He visited her in Paris and took her to *Irma La Douce*, which impressed him so much he told Peter Brook about it; the next day Brook went over and decided to put it on in London (it was staged at the Lyric, Hammersmith in 1959).

At the ball given for Gina on Tuesday 27 May 1958 at the Dorchester by her uncle Eric, the Earl of Dudley, in a setting reminiscent of the Royal Pavilion at Brighton, Tony was the first guest to arrive. It was a party full of the grand and the smart – there were five dukes, one of whom, the Duke of Kent, was royal.

Yet while the Duke of Kent necessarily sat at her right hand, on her left sat not one of the numerous other aristocrats there but Tony. After the ball, they crept away together to the Pimlico Road studio.

At 9 a.m. the doorbell went. Tony, who had consumed a good deal of champagne, groaned and said: 'I can't – you go.' She put on his dressing gown and opened the door. There stood Anne Rosse, immaculately dressed as usual, but clearly angry. Well aware, from everything Tony had told her, that he felt constantly rejected by his mother, Gina was as welcoming as she could be. 'Lady Rosse, how lovely to see you,' she said. But Anne, turning her profile towards the girl, only asked in an icy voice: 'Where's my son?' 'Still in bed,' replied a subdued Gina, upon which Anne walked off at once without a word.

For Tony, the Rotherhithe room had the same sense of apartness, almost of magic, possessed by Old House – a place to be alone or to work, and to entertain chosen, but only chosen, friends. On his motorbike the journey took a mere ten minutes; sometimes he would take a friend to spend the night there, both of them sleeping on straw-filled palliasses on the floor. At low tide, anyone reasonably agile could climb out of the window and walk about on the foreshore; high tide might see a swan or two floating past. Near the window was a telescope, to study passing craft and the life of the river.

The sole drawback to this idyllic hideaway – apart from the roughness of an area where any stranger was viewed with a deep suspicion that sometimes boiled over into violence – was the inadequacy of the sanitary arrangements. The only lavatory in Glenton's house was high up at the top of the stairs under the glass roof over the balcony, 'rather like an outside lavatory indoors' wrote Glenton later. Even the chain with which it was flushed was rusty and insecure.

Gradually Tony began to bring other friends there. One of these was Lady Elizabeth and when, in the autumn of 1958, severe fire damage forced her lover John Betjeman to move out of his flat in Cloth Fair, Smithfield, Tony, away for most of the autumn and after obtaining Glenton's permission, was able to offer Betjeman the Rotherhithe room. When Betjeman, accompanied by Lady Elizabeth, arrived, he looked round delightedly and exclaimed at once: 'Oh, how jolly! This *is* going to be fun! I shan't want to go back to my own place.' He was there for six weeks in all, writing (on 13 January 1959) when he left: 'No words of mine can thank you enough for Rotherhithe. I used to lie in bed listening to the plop-plop at high tide and the swish of waves at low tide and thank God for being alive. I don't exaggerate when I say it is the nicest room in the nicest part of London.'

Tony himself was off to New York. The Features Editor of *Vogue*, Penelope Gilliatt, with whom he had had a brief affair and who had become a fast friend, had suggested that he come to New York to do some work for American *Vogue*. There followed a letter from Alexander Liberman, then General Art Director for all the Condé Nast titles and a man of immense influence, asking him to fly to New York in mid-November for a month for *Vogue*. 'Please let me know when and if you can come. We will of course pay all expenses.'

Liberman, an artist to his fingertips, was not always the easiest person to work for. 'Dear Friend,' he would begin, when he had some particularly harsh criticism to dole out. 'You curled up in your boots whenever you heard those two words,' remembered Tony. 'They might take the following form – "Dear Friend, you know how deeply I admire you but those last photographs of yours were a total disaster ...."' In addition, although the most prestigious of magazines to work for, *Vogue* was notorious for its low fees and for stinting on expenses wherever possible. Tony, accordingly, was put in a cold-water flat without a telephone. He could do little about comments by the great Liberman, but he managed to organise better living conditions for himself through a typical piece of quick-wittedness.

One day he was asked by the sittings editor for his telephone number so that she could arrange photo sessions at short notice. Without hesitation he gave her that of the Santa Claus in Macy's department store (as a Christmas one-off it was not recognisable). When she rang she was answered with: 'Ho, ho, ho and what do you want for Christmas, little girl?' She replied with some asperity:

'Mr Armstrong-Jones, I do hope you sober up in time for our photography session tomorrow morning.' Tony soon got his telephone – and hot water.

From then on, Tony was paid enough to acquire a flat with a telephone. He returned from New York in the New Year of 1959 with a suitcase stuffed with presents for Jacqui, having spent most evenings after work prowling Bloomingdale's basement in search of them. Friends had already noted that he was seldom unkind to her, while other girls, especially if they became too clinging, could be treated with a certain casual cruelty. 'Oh, were we supposed to be going out to dinner? I'd quite forgotten.'

At home, his portraits had become famous. That spring and summer he photographed grandees from Oxford and Cambridge like Lord David Cecil, F.R. Leavis and Hugh Trevor-Roper (later Lord Dacre), the surrealist artist Dali and the cast of the musical *Candide* at the Saville Theatre. There were thirty of his pictures in an exhibition of contemporary photography at the Gallery of Modern Art in New York, and when the *Daily Express* polled its readers on which official portraits they liked best, Tony won with his balcony portrait of the royal family.

One Saturday afternoon early in 1959 he paid his first visit to Royal Lodge, Windsor, to find that its large drawing room, or saloon, was extraordinarily similar to the one at Birr Castle with which he was so familiar. Princess Margaret, listening to Tony's stories of New York, asked him if he had seen the Bernstein musical *West Side Story* and put on her record of its songs. When she went to see it again in February, with the Queen and Lady Elizabeth Cavendish, Tony accompanied them.

As 1959 progressed, even Jacqui found herself treated differently. One evening at dinner with her and two friends Tony suddenly got up from the table at 8.30 and left. 'Where have you been?' she said when he finally returned. 'Mind your own business,' replied Tony shortly, and said no more. Sometimes he would disappear for an evening without explanation, refusing any when he returned. When evenings became weekends, and all he would offer was: 'I'll be back on Monday morning,' it was too much even for the long-suffering Jacqui. There was a flaming row and Jacqui, who was in any case about to go on tour in Europe in a show called *Moon over the Rainbow Shore*, went off for good.

For anyone who had known about it, one telling incident would have provided a clue to a secret aspect of Tony's life, as well as illustrating his determination to hit back at anyone who offended him. In November 1959 he was commissioned to photograph the writer Kingsley Amis for a beer advertisement, during which Amis remarked of Princess Margaret: 'The woman obviously has no mind at all. You remember that crap of hers about it not being any good our sending the products of our minds up into space while our souls remained stuck down below in the dives and the espresso bars – schoolgirl essay stuff.' 'I can assure you you're quite wrong,' replied Tony. 'She is in fact an extremely intelligent and well-informed woman.' When Amis asked if he knew the Princess the answer was: 'I have met her on several occasions.' And that, in Amis's eyes, though unfortunately for Amis not in Tony's, was the end of the matter.

When it came to the end of the session Tony said that as he was driving down to Bath he could give Amis and his wife a lift to the friends they were going to visit in Staines, to save them getting the taxi and train they had planned. At Slough, he said he felt thirsty and would like to visit a pub. All three had a drink. After it, Tony turned to the Amises, said what fun the day had been, hopped into his car – and drove off, leaving the Amises standing on the pavement. Eventually, after finding a bus going in the right direction, they arrived at their destination an hour and a half later than if they had left when and how they had originally intended.

The absent Jacqui Chan was still much in Tony's mind, although he had assured his lover Gina that the affair was over. Once, while he and Gina were standing in a theatre foyer waiting to go to their seats, Tony turned white. 'What is it?' asked Gina. Turning her head, she saw a Chinese girl, at first sight rather like Jacqui.

Tony had now acquired a host of friends from the arts, theatre and films as well as those in society. One of the closest of the new ones was the actor Peter Sellers, then a star of *The Goon Show* (originally entitled The Go-On Show). Sellers, five years older than Tony, was brilliantly talented, mercurial, imaginative and superstitious – he consulted fortune tellers and astrologers and once called a halt to filming when a secretary appeared in a purple sweater as he had heard that purple was the colour of bad luck. Like Tony, he adored gadgets and efficient pieces of machinery (though unlike Tony, he could never make them work); he was also subject to crippling bouts of depression so black they could shadow everyone around him – Tony included. Characteristically, one of his letters to Tony begins simply: 'Random depressed thoughts jotted down at random ....'

On good form, however, no one could be a more entertaining companion. One evening Sellers took Tony to a tiny one-room restaurant run by a young Italian couple, Lorenzo and Mara Berni, who would also become friends. Later their establishment, greatly expanded, would become known as the chic and sophisticated San Lorenzo, of Beauchamp Place in Knightsbridge.

Professionally, Tony was at the top of the tree. With success, however, had come a certain degree of angst. He confided to one friend how boring it was that he had scaled the summit in photography and all that stretched ahead of him was the tediousness of a life of getting people to smile into the camera. Whereas Oliver, he continued, with a greater variety of talents and therefore more breadth, had a much richer, fuller life. What no one yet knew was that in one aspect of his life predictability could not be more distant: he had embarked on a courtship so extraordinary that it would turn accepted tradition on its head.

5

Margaret

❊

On 19 February 1948, Duff Cooper, the former British Ambassador to France and a noted appraiser of women, went with his wife Lady Diana to a luncheon at Buckingham Palace with the King, Queen and their two daughters, the Princesses Elizabeth and Margaret Rose (as Princess Margaret was then called). Afterwards he wrote in his diary: 'We enjoyed it enormously. Conversation never flagged and was really amusing. Margaret Rose is a most attractive girl – lovely skin, lovely eyes, lovely mouth, very sure of herself and full of humour.' He added presciently: 'She might get into trouble before she's finished.'

It was not long before she did. The Princess, then seventeen (she was born on 21 August 1930) was already in love with one of her father's courtiers, a love that would blaze across headlines and almost cause a constitutional crisis. Like her uncle David, the Duke of Windsor, she had become besotted with someone else's spouse. But in Margaret's case it was, with hindsight, almost inevitable.

Group Captain Peter Townsend, DSO, DFC and bar, the King's Extra Equerry, was a glamorous war hero who had been selected for royal service in 1944 under an 'equerries of honour' scheme. Born in 1915, he was fifteen years older than the Princess, whom he met for the first time when she was a fourteen-year-old in ankle socks. He came from a family that had served King (or Queen) and country for several generations and for him any demand, hint or barely expressed wish from the royal family was regarded as an inflexible command. When the King asked him to escort his daughters riding, or to the theatre, keep a watchful eye while they danced with friends or accompany them on picnics at Balmoral, he regarded it not so much as a duty as an expression of devotion. The King, in turn, thought of him in some measure as the son he never had.

As Margaret grew older, nearing the age at which first love strikes with all its force, the man she saw most of was the handsome, attentive Townsend, a ready-made hero figure who was, quite plainly, devoted to her and her family. Despite his record as a deadly and courageous fighter ace, he was gentle, sensitive and intuitive, qualities that appealed to the vulnerable core hidden beneath Margaret's wilful, confident, coquettish exterior. When Townsend accompanied the royal family on their February–April 1947 tour of South Africa, the two were in each other's company every day and almost all day. 'We rode together every morning in that wonderful country, in marvellous weather,' the Princess told a confidante. 'That's when I really fell in love with him.'

Margaret herself was enough to tempt any man. A pocket Venus (she was five foot one) with a voluptuous hourglass figure, she had a tiny waist, the superb complexion she had inherited from her mother and huge dark-fringed eyes that in some lights looked violet, in others a deep sapphire blue. She was intelligent, capricious, wilful, often flirtatious, sometimes freezing, easily bored but witty, sparkling and gay when with those whose company she enjoyed. In the drab post-war years, and at a time when royalty commanded a respect akin to awe, this beautiful young princess was an object of intense interest to the general public – and of fascination to many of the young men with whom she came in contact.

But she was not interested in any of them. At first Townsend, married and with a family, did not realise quite how fond of him the Princess had become. The whole Court was preoccupied with the declining health of the King, a heavy smoker, and for those close to him this was the matter of pre-eminent concern. Although there were mutterings in the Household about the growing closeness of the Princess and her father's equerry they did not reach the ailing King – who had he been well would surely have noticed and taken gentle but effective steps to stop the affair before it went too far. At the same time, Townsend's marriage was falling apart: as his absences from home grew even more prolonged, unsurprisingly his wife Rosemary drifted into an affair.

Then, on 6 February 1952, King George VI died of lung cancer. At a stroke, the Princess's world was turned upside down. Apart from the immensity of her grief, every dynamic of her life changed. Although always her father's special delight, she had got to know him much better, and to love him even more, as she neared adulthood. So close were they that one of the big problems of Margaret's future life would be that no one would, or could, ever measure up to her father.

At that moment, though, all she knew was that she had suddenly lost the person who meant more to her than anyone in the world; she had to leave her home (difficult though it may be for most people to think of Buckingham Palace as a home, to the Princess it *was* home); her mother had withdrawn into a state of almost cataleptic shock, distancing herself from all those around her; and her sister, with whom she had shared virtually every aspect of her life, was now on a different plane, suddenly a sovereign hedged about by the constant demands of her position. She felt herself to be utterly alone, except for Peter Townsend – by now the pair had admitted their love for each other.

The last years of the King's life had meant that Townsend was busier than ever as he strove to do everything possible to support the King, the Queen and the Princesses. When the King died, Queen Elizabeth and her younger daughter moved into Clarence House and Townsend went with them as Comptroller; a few months later the Townsend marriage was dissolved.

It was far easier for Margaret and Townsend to conduct a full-blown love affair within Clarence House as the Princess had her own apartments – a sitting room on the ground floor, a bedroom on the second floor. As the Queen Mother's apartments were on the first floor, the two might pass whole days without seeing each other – although they always met for lunch – so that the Queen Mother could ostensibly be unaware of the situation. Even when the Princess told her mother of her feelings for Townsend, the Queen Mother merely employed her well-known 'ostrich' technique of burying her head in the sand and hoping this difficult situation would go away.

At this stage it was still known only to a few. But when, at the Queen's Coronation on 2 June 1953, the Princess lovingly picked a piece of real or imaginary fluff from the lapel of her lover's tunic under the eyes of the television cameras perched high in Westminster Abbey, the secret was out, the rumours confirmed.

It was a love affair beset with difficulties from the start. The Royal Marriages Act of 1772 stated that a Royal Personage (as defined in the Act) could not marry without consent until he or she reached the age of twenty-five; thereupon, after serving twelve months' notice on the Privy Council, marriage without consent was possible. As Townsend was divorced, it was impossible for the Queen, as head of the Church of England (which forbade marriages between divorced persons) to give her consent to someone so high in the line of succession. At twenty-five, though, the Princess would not need this consent. But, and in Margaret's case it was an enormous But, even then it was not possible both to marry and to remain royal – if the person she was marrying was divorced. It was one or the other. It is not clear whether or not this last point was explained to the Princess.

It was decided that the best plan on all counts would be for Townsend to leave the country for a year (at the end of which they were asked to wait another year) and then, on his return, the couple could make their decision. Both Townsend and the Princess realised that he would have not only to leave the Royal Household but that they should part for the time being. On 30 June 1953 Margaret and the Queen Mother left for a sixteen-day tour of Rhodesia. Townsend was given the post of Air Attaché in Brussels – announced before he had had time to tell his sons – and, cruelly, made to leave before rather than after the Princess's return on 10 July. For those two years they wrote – Townsend's letters were always addressed to Miss Iris Peake, the Princess's lady-in-waiting – they spoke on the telephone, they went through all the tortures of a long absence from the beloved.

When Townsend returned, the moment of truth was upon them; but their decision was far from instantaneous or easy. Friends offered them safe houses to which they were pursued by the press; headlines urged the Princess to make up her mind; both of them had to consider not only whether they wanted to spend the rest of their lives together but also whether the Princess could adjust to life as an ordinary housewife (Townsend was not rich and she knew nothing of life outside a palace) – and whether, after all, with the example of her uncle David in mind, she could face the prospect of defying the Church's teaching.

Few could have guessed how much her religion really meant to Princess Margaret. For several years, she had belonged to a small prayer group under the leadership of the Dean of Westminster, Eric Abbott, which she had joined during her misery after her father's death. She had come to it through Marigold Bridgeman, who had met the Princess soon after the war when both were staying with the Elphinstones, cousins of the royal family. Meetings of this group took place sometimes at Marigold's flat or at the Bridgeman family place, Dowdeswell Park, in Gloucestershire, where the group often went for weekends, or at the Dean's home in Westminster.

If the latter, they would often be followed by breakfast in the Jerusalem Chamber;* if, as more usual, they took place in the evening – because most of the men worked – they would begin around seven and continue until ten or ten-thirty, with a break for a simple supper in the middle. There were prayers – if anyone wanted the group to pray especially for someone, they would say so – and sometimes a talk by the Dean or a discussion of a book they had read.

Townsend and Margaret saw each other again for the first time on 12 October 1955. Less than three agonising weeks later, the two of them came to the conclusion that their love could have no happy ending. The Princess was advised that she would lose her royal status, something which she found impossible to imagine and she knew that, privately sympathetic though the Queen was to her sister, as sovereign and head of the Church she could not give her consent. With Townsend's help, a statement was drafted in the Princess's name.

---

* This part of the deanery was originally the abbot's parlour and dates from the late fourteenth century. It derives its name probably from the tapestries of the history of Jerusalem that once adorned it. In 1413, Henry IV died in this room, thus fulfilling the prophecy that 'he would die in Jerusalem'. The chamber, which contains outstanding mid-thirteenth-century stained glass, was restored in 1624.

'I would like it to be known that I have decided not to marry Group Captain Peter Townsend,' ran the renunciation that was flashed around the world on 31 October 1955. 'I have been aware that, subject to my renouncing my rights of succession, it might have been possible for me to contract a civil marriage. But mindful of the Church's teachings that Christian marriage is indissoluble, and conscious of my duty to the Commonwealth, I have resolved to put these considerations before others. I have reached this decision entirely alone, and in doing so I have been strengthened by the unfailing support and devotion of Group Captain Townsend. I am deeply grateful for the concern of all those who have constantly prayed for my happiness.'

When the Townsend affair was over, the Princess put it resolutely behind her. Inside Clarence House it was hardly, if ever, mentioned. As the beautiful, tragic heroine of a star-crossed love, she aroused both chivalry and sympathy and the country speculated eagerly about the men in her circle – would it be the Duke of Marlborough's heir, Sunny Blandford, the Hon. Dominic Elliot, son of the 5th Earl of Minto or perhaps the rich and generous Billy Wallace who eventually won her? One of the closest of all, Colin Tennant, had put himself out of the running when he married Lady Anne Coke. The Princess was giving no clues. Night after night, usually in a party of six or eight, she would visit theatres, restaurants and nightclubs, smoking cigarettes through a long holder between courses and sipping whisky.

Her life developed a routine. She would stay in bed until eleven – she never appeared before lunch unless she had an engagement – breakfasting off a pot of weak china tea and what she picked from a plate of fruit. She would then get up and have her bath, with the aid of Ruby Gordon, her dresser* (sister of the Queen's dresser, Bobo Macdonald) and select her clothes and jewellery.

As with the Queen, clothes had to conform to the needs of 'the job'. Pencil skirts were out because they made walking up steps and getting in and out of cars difficult without showing too much

---

* As the Royal Family always called lady's maids.

royal leg, sleeves of coats and suits had to allow for the royal wave, hat brims could not conceal the face, black could not be worn except for mourning and, of course, she had to be perfectly groomed at all times in case of the unexpected photograph. This meant everything had to look as good from the back as the front and be as crease-free as possible – all skirts, jackets and coats were fully lined. Footwear had to be comfortable enough to stand in for long periods at a time, yet because of her lack of height she could never wear flat shoes. Often the solution was a solid, clumpy heel.

Her shoes and cigarette lighters were cleaned every morning, and her hairdresser, René, called on her regularly. Sometimes she would play with her dogs, two Sealyhams called Pippin and Johnny and her favourite, a King Charles spaniel called Rowley. At 12.30 she would appear looking groomed and fresh and go to her desk, on which sat a large glass of fresh orange juice and her mail – when her friends wrote to her they put their initials discreetly on the bottom left-hand corner of the envelope, so that their letters could be placed directly on her desk. Then came lunch, with the Queen Mother and members of the Household.

With them, she was not always popular, in part because of her frequent rudeness to her mother. 'Why do you dress in those ridiculous clothes?' she would ask as the Queen Mother stopped to discuss something with a lady-in-waiting. She would become furious that drinks before lunch (notorious for their potency) would sometimes go on for an hour, so that lunch would not be served until two. 'Oh, for goodness' sake, Mum,* let's go in,' she would complain. 'We can't go on like this.' The television set at Royal Lodge was another cause of trouble: Princess Margaret would simply switch it to another channel without a word if she did not like what the Queen Mother was watching, regardless of the latter's expostulations. Yet the Queen Mother never lost her temper. Only by her hands could those who had served her for a long time tell that she was annoyed. 'It was the way she moved a book, a piece of furniture or a glass,' recalled her page William Tallon.

---

* According to staff at Clarence House, the Princess always called her mother 'Mum'.

Margaret was equally inconsiderate to her mother's staff. If there was a Christmas party at Buckingham Palace, to which the staff of Clarence House were invited, the Queen Mother would invariably dine out with a lady-in-waiting or have something light so that her servants could get to the party, whereas Princess Margaret would deliberately have a dinner party that evening. It was a perversity that can perhaps be explained by the fact that, unlike the Queen Mother and the Queen, who had successively been the first lady in the land, Princess Margaret, always number two, was determined to insist on her royal status.

Several of those close to her, including at least two of her ladies-in-waiting and the historian Kenneth Rose, concluded that this insistence was not entirely due to the wilfulness inherent in her own nature but owed much to two other factors. The first was that although she knew from childhood that she would always remain in second place vis-à-vis her sister, with her father she had been number one. As he famously said: 'Elizabeth is my pride but Margaret is my joy.' She had adored him; and with his death she had lost the person who had meant most to her in the world.

Secondly she believed herself to have been 'hard done by' scholastically. The early education of the Princesses was left in the hands of their nursery governess. 'Queen Mary tried to beef up the lessons but Queen Elizabeth didn't think education [for women] necessary,' said Rose. The story goes that Queen Mary, herself extremely cultured and well versed in the fine arts, was deeply concerned about how little the Princesses were being taught and remarked to the Queen: 'I really do think the girls should be getting a better education.' Her words fell on stony ground. The Queen canvassed all her friends, saying: 'I don't know what she's going on about. My sisters and myself were all educated by a governess and we all married very well. In fact, you might say one of us married very well indeed.'

When it became clear that Princess Elizabeth would one day inherit the throne, she was taught constitutional history by Henry (later Sir Henry) Marten, the Vice-Provost of Eton, lessons that began when she was thirteen. Margaret was not allowed to accompany her sister. 'She never got over not being allowed to have lessons with the Vice-Provost like the Queen did. She wanted to accompany her sister but wasn't allowed to. She was very virulent on that,' commented Rose. Later, another 'second place' difference was to appear: at eighteen Elizabeth was allowed to serve on a Council of State; Margaret, like other members of the royal family, had to wait until she was twenty-one.

As someone intelligent, quick, passionately interested in the arts – she became an avid visitor of museums and galleries – Margaret not only later bitterly regretted her lack of formal education, but the intellectual discipline it imposes would no doubt have gone some way to curbing her self-willed approach to life. As it was, one of the contradictions at the heart of her personality was that she could never really decide what she wanted to be: party girl or regal princess – and her voltes-face as she switched from one mode to the other sometimes bewildered even those close to her. Naturally bohemian and a rebel, she had been brought up by a mother who was the last Queen-Empress and whose lifestyle reflected this – even when the Queen Mother went into the garden of Clarence House to walk her dogs two footmen were standing by to open the doors for her. That said, one of Margaret's greatest qualities was loyalty in friendship.

At twenty-eight she was at the height of her beauty and charisma, poised, stylish, and groomed to perfection. In one of the long and elegant evening dresses that made the most of her petite, feminine figure, swathed in furs and glittering with diamonds, she was an icon of glamour, exuding an aura of sophisticated, challenging sexuality, with a glance that could turn from melting to icy in a moment. She was imperious, wilful and, if she was bored, showed it – at one small buffet supper dance given in her honour, when her host asked her: 'Ma'am, will you start the dancing?' she replied: 'Yes – but not with you'.

At these times, friends learned to keep their distance, though few could resist the flattery of being asked to drive her home. 'Honk three times,' she would say, and after three blasts of the horn the electric gates to Clarence House would swing open. Sometimes all the aspiring gallant would hear as the front doors swung open was: 'Thank you so much – it's been a lovely evening', as she stepped inside; at other times there would be an invitation to come in and 'finish the evening'.

When one of Princess Margaret's dazzled admirers asked her in the spring of 1958 if she would sit for a photograph for him – he knew just the right photographer – she agreed. The chosen photographer was Tony, whom she had met a month or two earlier with Lady Elizabeth Cavendish. Immediately, Tony took charge of the sitting in his usual way. With the utmost politeness, he made her change her clothes, her jewellery and her pose as if she were any other sitter, at the same time chatting away with his mixture of jokes, gossip about mutual friends and stories of the theatrical luminaries he had photographed.

Margaret, accustomed to unquestioning deference, had never met anyone like him. It was at this point that their real rapport began. She decided that she wanted Tony in her circle and, after a while, his face could be seen among the parties of six or eight people in which the Princess went to the theatre or dined out. As he was not a known escort, no one paid any attention to the appearance of an extra man in her wide and varied acquaintance.

Nor did anyone notice when he came to his first luncheon party at Clarence House on 11 November 1958. ('It will be too sad if you cannot come!' Margaret had written a fortnight earlier in her letter of invitation. 'If you do, I must warn you immediately that I will bore you by forcing you to look at my photograph of Mamma in the heather, which has blown up very nicely.' She ended: 'Yours very sincerely'.) Such luncheons were an event for staff as well as guests: although the Queen Mother preferred plain food such as roast beef, game or salmon, everything else was elaborate and splendid – up to thirty people could sit at the dining table on the gilded chairs with red plush seats, there were at least five courses, silver and crystal glittered beside crested porcelain, in front of the Queen Mother stood her flask of ice with silver tongs and a silver swizzle stick for her champagne. Tony was seated beside Margaret, with Princess Alexandra on his other side.

Secret visits to his Pimlico studio began, the Princess's car dropping her unobtrusively in the adjacent, parallel road. Dressed as anonymously as possible in tweed skirt, sweater and headscarf, she would slip down a small alleyway that led to the studio's backyard – at the back, the basement was at ground level – and down the spiral staircase into the small sitting room where Tony would cook them a simple supper. Once she asked if she too could sign her name on the large mirror there with the diamond he kept for this purpose. But he would not allow it, saying that too many of his friends worked in or for the media. Sometimes they would sunbathe together on his flat roof, invisible to anyone below.

Occasionally he would whisk her off to the room in Rotherhithe. Bill Glenton had noticed that Lady Elizabeth Cavendish had become a frequent visitor and that Tony himself was being not only uncharacteristically secretive about any guests but also scrupulous about preparing the room for them. When he sprayed the entrance hall with an air purifier and replaced Glenton's run-of-the-mill lavatory paper with soft, violet-tinted toilet tissue it could have served as a hint that a special visitor was expected.

When Margaret did come – at first kept out of sight of Glenton – it was usually in the company of friends, but sometimes, later in the year, they would meet there alone. Other meetings were at the houses of a very few close friends like Lady Elizabeth and Penelope Gilliatt – but none of those in the so-called 'Margaret Set' – and at weekends, when the Princess joined her mother at Royal Lodge, Tony would drive down to Windsor to see her there. It was known that he was building an aviary there, chiefly for budgerigars, and the assumption – by the few who noticed – was that this was for the Queen Mother. As the year drew on, another excellent excuse for visits was his commission to take the twenty-ninth birthday portraits of the Princess. In any case, so outré was the idea that the Queen of England's sister was conducting a secret love affair with a photographer that this was the greatest protection of all against discovery.

For Tony it was all overwhelming. He was used to pretty girls, from unsophisticated débutantes to models and actresses of varying degrees of experience, and he was aware of the effect his own well-honed sexual expertise had on women. But Margaret was something different. She was beautiful, charismatic and voluptuous; she was also intelligent, witty and deeply interested in the arts. If all this was not enough, she was gilded with the mysterious, mythic aura of royalty, as revered, precious and unattainable as a jewel locked in a velvet-lined box.

Everything around her spoke of this. For a simple weekend country house visit the names of fellow guests had first to be submitted to her lady-in-waiting, accompanied by a dossier on each one. At every meal the Princess was always served first and no one could speak to her without first being addressed by her. In some houses, if she did not help herself to, say, potatoes, no one else could. At smart dinner parties, where it was the norm to wear long evening dresses, the formality was still greater, with jewels brought out from the bank and sometimes long white gloves.

She was a challenge like no other – even to take the Queen's sister on the back of a motorbike was something almost unbelievable and the thought of a relationship overwhelming. When she made her interest plain, for once he was not the one controlling the situation. Tremendously impressed by the Princess and all her qualities, he was also enormously proud of himself for becoming her lover.

Each was a person of extraordinary sexual magnetism, with a libido to match. When they entered each other's force field of attraction their mutual gravitational pull was irresistible and soon they were sexually besotted. Everything they discovered about each other, from their interest in the arts and the theatre to the people they liked meeting and their private badinage, enhanced their feelings. That their passionate love affair was completely secret added to its intensity, emphasising their feeling of being enclosed in a magic, invisible bubble.

Yet although by the summer of 1959 they were deeply in love and conducting an affair, he was still leading his busy private life at full throttle. Girls still came and went at the studio, and although Jacqui Chan was less in evidence, he was still carrying on his affair with Gina Ward.

There was, too, another development that would return later to haunt him. At weekends he often went to visit Jeremy and Camilla Fry, the couple who had become, together, his two closest friends. Naturally, he took the Princess to see them at their house, Widcombe Manor, near Bath; and on weekends when she had engagements or he could not see her, he often went down there by himself.

It was the end of the decade. Though aristocrats and the rich had always behaved more or less as they wanted, moral and social constraints had confined most others within a recognised code of behaviour. Now, just over the horizon, was the liberation of the sixties, with its explosive mixture of sexual freedom, the breaking down of taboos and the steady dismantling of class barriers. Tony, with his urge to challenge accepted boundaries, was at the forefront of this new age. In the sophisticated world in which he and the Frys moved, where relationships of every kind flourished and where it was implicit that sexual orientation was a matter of preference, it was inevitable not only that they would be in the avant-garde of any such attitude but also that their behaviour would represent it.

All three knew each other intimately; Jeremy's passion for Camilla had waned and, awakened but frustrated, she found it easy to encourage a charming former boyfriend; while Jeremy and Tony were highly sexed. Alcohol and 'poppers' helped them all shed any remaining inhibitions. As one friend put it later: 'it was a pretty good free-for-all there'. During one of these romps in early September 1959 a child was conceived; soon afterwards, in October, Tony went to stay at Balmoral for the first time.

Again, no one attached any significance to his visit, thinking – if at all – that he was there in a professional capacity. Although he did not blend into the heathery, tweedy ambience of the Castle in the way that most visitors did – the thin socks and suede shoes he wore with his tweed shooting suit and his polo-neck sweaters were one example – thanks to early outings with his father he was a good shot and, for Princess Margaret, who had been missing him badly, the best of companions.

While he was staying there the Princess received a letter from Peter Townsend telling her that he was going to marry a Belgian girl of nineteen named Marie-Luce Jamagne. The Princess, stunned by this piece of news, told Tony of the letter as they were out walking together on the last day of his visit – but warned him not to ask her to marry him. Although he is popularly supposed to have proposed to her while they walked in the Balmoral heather, the letter she wrote to him on 9 October, after his return to London, does not sound like that of a fiancée: 'I don't know when I've enjoyed having someone to stay here so much as when you came,' is the phrase that best sums up its tone. She ended: 'I feel I really ought to thank *you* for coming. It was such fun and you were so nice to be with. Darling, best love from Margaret.'

She was determined to show the world what was in fact the truth: that she was no longer in love with Townsend and that his marriage would not wound her. On her return from Balmoral she went to stay with Lord and Lady Abergavenny at Eridge, in Kent, in a large house party, fortuitously on the weekend that the papers carried the news of Townsend's engagement.

As one of the party, Raymond Salisbury-Jones (son of Sir Guy Salisbury-Jones, Marshal of the Diplomatic Corps) who arrived late to find he was sitting beside her at dinner, recalled: 'The next morning a message came round to every room in the house that the Princess absolutely was not to see the papers. I get quite a lump in my throat when I think about this as it must have been a very difficult moment for her. So we all talked about all sorts of other things.' Later she asked Salisbury-Jones if he would take her for a drive in his Silver Cloud Rolls-Royce; on their return an hour and a half later the rest of the party had gone for a walk. Knowing that he played the piano, she said: 'Shall we make music? I'd like to sing.' They went into the empty drawing room and Salisbury-Jones sat down at the piano. 'All she wanted to sing were hymns, melancholy hymns like "Abide with Me". We played and sang for about forty minutes.'

The bond between Tony and the Princess was steadily increasing, a fact acknowledged by the Queen Mother who, unlike many others in the royal family, had no reservations about Tony. She approved of him wholeheartedly, so much so that she determined to give a party for her daughter and the man Margaret now clearly loved. Ostensibly this dance, at the end of October 1959, was to welcome Princess Alexandra (another favourite) home from Australia. There were 250 guests, who danced until 3 a.m. Tony and Margaret, scarcely able to hide their feelings for one another, were finally asked by the Queen Mother to lead a conga up and down the staircases and through the rooms of Clarence House.

At the same time, the private life of Tony's father was giving both him and Susan concern. Ronnie, who had begun a relationship with an air hostess called Jenifer Unite, had been drifting apart from his Australian wife Carol. To a colleague at the Bar he confessed: 'I can't stand her near me any more.' He was preparing himself to broach the question of a parting when Carol returned from holiday in Ischia to say that she had met a handsome Italian called Pepe Lopez in the mud baths there – when their hands had touched accidentally under the mud, it caused an immediate attraction.

'Ghastly dramas,' wrote Susan from Ireland, 'Daddy telephoned last night in a terrible state, *madly* upset and really desperate – anyway the saga is that he said his piece to Carol who said she wanted to marry this Italian. Poor Dad had visualised saying he wanted to be rid of Carol but had never even thought she might be the one to want a divorce. She made the Italian come round to First Street and then she packed her things and left. I was frightfully worried when he rang off as he sounded in utter despair, saying things like "if two wives leave me there must be something very wrong with me". You can imagine. Anyway he rang me last night having been out to dinner at the Garrick and sounded calmer.'

On 11 November 1959 Ronnie, who hated to be on his own, wrote to his son: 'Jenifer and I have decided that we can't let things go on drifting any more and so we are going to get married. I want you to know at once so that you don't suddenly see it in the gossip columns. We haven't decided whether it will be before or after Christmas. You and I have always been very dear to each other and this won't make the least difference. All love my dear boy. PS I have of course told Carol and she is delighted.'

By Christmas Margaret and Tony had also decided on marriage. Only one or two people knew of this, in particular Jeremy and Camilla Fry, who had offered a 'safe house' where they could be alone together during this last part of their courtship. 'Was the second weekend you stayed much easier than the first?' wrote Camilla Fry after one visit. 'I am sure PM enjoyed it more this time. She seemed so much easier to talk to.' It was, in fact, while staying at Widcombe Manor with the Frys that they became engaged. Apart from the Frys, no one suspected this, although the sharp-eyed Bill Glenton noticed that Tony's style was changing: the tight, faded jeans and desert boots were giving way to well-cut dark suits and crisp white shirts and Tony's assistant John Timbers, who knew that Tony and the Princess would sometimes meet in the Rotherhithe room, was aware that 'something was going on'.

The Queen's consent naturally had to be sought and during the royal family's Christmas sojourn at Sandringham Tony came down to visit – he had not been asked to stay as this might have given the game away. With her consent given the Queen, who was pregnant with Prince Andrew, asked if they would refrain from announcing their engagement until after the birth of her child. This was naturally agreed, although Margaret mystified the friends who asked her to stay by her lengthy private telephone calls every evening.

Tony, aware that the longer such an explosive secret was kept the greater the likelihood of its emerging into the public domain, decided to spend a few weeks with his sister Susan in Ireland. (It was during this visit that he photographed Brendan Behan, who afterwards took them to a Dublin pub where a memorable conversation took place when a priest known to Behan bicycled past. 'D'ye know what that fockin' priest said to me the other fockin' day?' said Brendan. 'No,' said Susan, who had never met anyone like him before. Brendan, turning to Tony, said: 'He said: "I want to fock my fockin' sister-in-law." So I said to him: "Well, it's a lot better than fockin' your fockin' brother-in-law."' Stunned, Susan, who was almost teetotal, asked for a large glass of gin and tonic.)

Back at his studio, Tony told his staff that he 'might soon be doing something else'. Most of them thought he meant films. Possibly, if they had known about his conversation two months earlier with the young interior designer David Hicks, they might have picked up a hint. 'I'm going to make a very grand marriage,' said Hicks. 'Oh, really?' said Tony. 'Who to?' 'Lady Pamela Mountbatten,' replied Hicks proudly. 'Oh, I don't call that grand,' responded Tony.

Knowing that his engagement would soon be announced, he was aghast when Ronnie told him that his own marriage was just about to take place: both he and Susan, aware that a three-times-married father-in-law for the Princess would make a juicy morsel for the press, begged Ronnie to postpone it for a few months. But Ronnie was adamant (or 'bolshy', as his children saw it), saying to Tony: 'Why can't you change the date of *your* wedding?' Useless to explain that dates involving the Queen could not be changed at a whim; neither Tony nor Susan could shift him. On 11 February Ronnie, now fifty, was married for the third time, to the 31-year-old Jenifer in Kensington Register Office. It was not exactly an auspicious omen.

When the Queen gave birth to Prince Andrew, on 19 February 1960, the long wait was nearly over. Margaret had told one or two of her closest friends, swearing them to secrecy. One was Marigold Bridgeman, to whom she broke the news as they sat in Marigold's sister's bedroom, always used by Margaret when she came to stay at Dowdeswell, but as Marigold had never heard of Tony this did not have quite the impact it might have done.

There were a certain number of loose ends to be tidied up. Tom Parr got a call from Tony one evening asking if he could come round and have a drink. Once in Parr's flat he said: 'I long to look at your photograph albums.' 'Certainly,' said Parr, 'but there's nothing you don't know because whenever we were on holiday together you wielded the camera.' But Tony insisted, examining all three volumes minutely. Three days later the engagement was announced – and Parr realised that Tony had been frightened that some of Parr's pictures might be in some way compromising. For someone who had been as close to Tony as Parr, the implication that Tony did not really trust him not to reveal a putative cause of scandal was wounding.

The strain of keeping the secret and ensuring that nothing discreditable leaked out began to show. Telephoning his friend the writer and journalist Francis Wyndham, his voice shaking, Tony said he thought he might be having a nervous breakdown, adding almost immediately 'What is a nervous breakdown?' Francis, who had known Tony since they both worked on *Queen* magazine, was confused by this sudden change in someone he had always known as sparkling company and suggested that Tony went away for a while. 'But I'd only have to come back.'

On Wednesday 24 February, five days after Prince Andrew's arrival, Tony was at last able to tell his assistants that in two days' time there would be 'an announcement'. His Princess would soon be able openly to wear the engagement ring he had given her – a rose-like ruby surrounded by a marguerite of diamonds that he had found at the jeweller S.J. Philips for £250.

Other disclosures would be more difficult. On Thursday night he telephoned Gina Ward, the gorgeous young actress with whom he had been having an affair. At first she was too staggered by his news to feel anything but shock and disbelief, simply saying over and over again: 'Tony, you *can't* take this on.' 'But I can, I can,' he said in the eager way so familiar to her. 'And anyway,' she cried, 'you're in love with me! You'll have an awful life.' Only after the call was over and she realised that he had no doubts or second thoughts, did the pain of her own loss strike home, with the feeling that she had been 'broken into a hundred pieces' (nevertheless, she was to remain an adoring and lifelong friend).

On the morning of Friday 26 February 1960 Tony's great friend and fellow photographer Robert Belton, then renting a room in John Cranko's Pimlico house, was told by Cranko's housekeeper that Tony Armstrong-Jones was on the telephone for him. 'Can I come and see you?' asked Tony. 'Yes, sure,' said Belton. When Tony arrived he asked Belton to get in the car, then drove it 400 yards away. 'I'm getting married to Princess Margaret and they're announcing it tonight after the six o'clock news,' he told Belton, who could hardly believe his ears ('I knew he saw her but I'd no idea they were so close'), before asking him if he would tell Jacqui Chan before the announcement. She was filming at Pinewood so Belton rang and left a message that he would come and pick her up after work. He drove down to Pinewood through pouring rain, sent in a note to tell Jacqui he had come to collect her and at ten to six she scrambled into the car. With only minutes to go Belton wasted no time in telling her. There was a long silence and then she said: 'Well, I hope she can cope better than I could.'

At Clarence House the Treasurer, Sir Arthur Penn, told the staff that all leave was cancelled for the following weekend. When those who normally accompanied the Queen Mother, like her page William Tallon,* arrived at Royal Lodge that Friday, the staff were called into the canteen, where Sir Arthur told them that Princess Margaret was engaged. 'Who to?' was the immediate response. 'Well, a photographer – called Armstrong-Jones,' said Sir Arthur.

From the assembled staff, few of whom had heard of Tony, there was a long-drawn-out 'ooh!' of disappointment. Most of them had thought it would be the immensely wealthy Billy Wallace, one of her most favoured escorts. Then the Princess herself told them, adding that Tony would be arriving 'with all his goods and chattels' that night. Not many miles away, driving back to London with rain thrumming on the windscreen, Jacqui Chan and Belton heard on the car radio the words: 'It is with the greatest pleasure that Queen Elizabeth the Queen Mother announces the betrothal of her beloved daughter the Princess Margaret to Mr Antony Charles Armstrong-Jones, son of Mr R.O.L. Armstrong-Jones QC, and the Countess of Rosse, to which union the Queen has gladly given her consent.'

---

* In 1978 William Tallon became Page of the Backstairs and Steward, giving rise to his nickname 'Backstairs Billy'.

6

Engagement

-}|<-

Never has a royal love affair leading to an engagement been kept so secret. Although Tony's best friends were aware, in the words of one of them, that 'something was up', none of them had any idea of the seriousness of the couple's feelings for each other.

Andy Garnett, Tony's close friend since their schooldays, opened a newspaper while enjoying a leisurely Saturday morning breakfast with an Italian painter friend at a café in Shepherd Market, Mayfair, 'and found myself as staggered as everyone else'. But the shock, thought another friend, Justin de Blank, then living in France, was nothing to the horror the Editor of *France Dimanche* must have felt as his paper, at that moment being printed and distributed, appeared with the headline 'La Princesse Margaret a décidée enfin d'entrer dans un couvent.'

As soon as the engagement was announced, warnings flew thick and fast amid the stream of congratulations. Those closest to the couple were the most distressed. Lady Elizabeth Cavendish asked the Princess if she was quite sure about her feelings 'because you won't always know where he is and he won't always want to tell you'. Tony's brother-in-law, Lord de Vesci, who knew the Princess very well, advised: 'Tony, for God's sake don't.' Jocelyn Stevens cabled from Lyford Cay, his estate in the Bahamas: 'Never was there a more ill-fated assignment.' Anthony Barton felt Tony was making a terrible mistake, 'especially when he suddenly changed, wearing smart clothes and giving up smoking Gauloises and smoking other cigarettes instead – he was too strong-willed to give in to all that'. Peter Saunders, who did not like the Princess, thought Tony would put himself into a very difficult position.

'These people aren't for you, Tony,' he warned. 'They will chew you up and spit you out. I know it's a physical thing at the moment but at the end of the day for goodness sake don't do it.'

Others felt the Princess was the one who should be warned off. When the Queen Mother telephoned Cecil Beaton and told him of the engagement, Beaton said: 'Oh, how wonderful, you must be thrilled ma'am, how simply marvellous, he's terribly clever and talented.' When he put the telephone down he said in tones of disgust: 'Silly girl!' Even Noël Coward, a fervent royalist, noted in his diary: 'He [Tony] looks quite pretty but whether or not the marriage is entirely suitable remains to be seen.'

Kingsley Amis, perhaps to get his own back after the trick Tony had earlier played on him when he had been rude about the Princess (whom he had never met), reacted by badmouthing both of them, calling the Princess 'famed for her devotion to all that is most vapid and mindless in the world of entertainment . . . and her appalling taste in clothes' and describing Tony as a 'dog-faced tight-jeaned fotog of fruitarian tastes'.

To the ancient aristocracy and those close to the throne, the shock was immense. Here was the daughter of the last King-Emperor, brought up amid scenes of immense grandeur at a time when half the map of the world was red, about to marry not, as might have been expected, the eldest son of a duke with vast estates in the offing, but a man who, as they saw it, was not even in a 'respectable' profession but took snaps for a living. Even using the name Tony, rather than the more formal Antony, caused a slight sniffiness. When Cecil Beaton told his Wiltshire neighbour, Lord Pembroke, of the engagement, Pembroke exclaimed: 'Then I'll go and live in Tibet!'

For Anne Rosse, Tony's engagement to Princess Margaret was the culmination of all her social ambitions. She had been fearful that he would marry Jacqui Chan, whom she disliked on purely social grounds. 'She wanted me to make an upwardly mobile marriage,' said Tony. From being 'my ugly son', he was now her pet and the approval he had always craved was at last forth-coming – but for all the wrong reasons. Ronnie, on the other hand, was deeply upset. 'When he was cross he would sign his letters "RAJ" and not "Your loving father",' recalled Tony. 'Now I got

Ronald Armstrong-Jones, Tony's barrister father, was gregarious, popular and successful.

Tony's mother Anne, here seen with Tony, was a noted society beauty.

Tony, aged three, on his mother's lap.

Susan Armstrong-Jones, Tony's sister, aged nine.

Nymans, the home of Tony's Messel grandparents, in the 1930s.

Oliver Messel, Tony's uncle, at the height of his fame in the 1930s.

Birr Castle, in County Offaly, west of Dublin, became the home of
Tony's mother in 1935 when she married Michael, Earl of Rosse. It had been
lived in by the Parsons (the family name of the Earls of Rosse) since 1620.

Tony (seated on ground) with the Cambridge Eight
of 1950 that he coxed to victory.

The victorious cox signing autographs after the race.

Anthony Barton, a fellow Cambridge undergraduate who became a close friend.

Tony and Anthony Barton, with Tony's Fiat sports car.

Tony's 1952 montage Christmas card, in which he models a Victorian paterfamilias, an Edwardian *grande dame* and a small boy in a sailor suit.

Emmy Hirst (*centre*) aged eighteen, at the twenty-first birthday party of Andy Garnett, where she met Tony.

(*right*) Andy Garnett met Tony at Eton and became a close and lifelong friend.

Peter Saunders, a friend of Tony's whom he had first met on the ski slopes.

Jeremy Fry, brilliant inventor and charismatic personality, in 1955.

Camilla Fry (née Grinling), who married Jeremy Fry in 1955.

one saying "Boy, you would be mad to marry Princess Margaret –
it will ruin your career." My father loved Jacqui Chan and would
have liked me to marry her,' but not even this parental reaction
caused Tony any qualms. Equally upset were his employers, the
Daily Express, who were furious that he had not at least given
them a head start on rival newspapers.

A frisson of horror ran through many of the courtiers. Sir Alan
Lascelles (who had done much to destroy the Princess's romance
with Peter Townsend)* was equally unhappy about this one,
lamenting to Harold Nicolson that 'the boy Jones has led a very
diversified and sometimes a wild life and the danger of scandal
and slander is never far off'. Nicolson himself noted in his diary:
'At least Mr Jones is not a homo, which is rare these days.'
Meanwhile a story circulated that a Cambridge rowing coach,
who had been in love with Tony in his university days, had
committed suicide when he heard the news of the engagement (by
swimming out to sea from the island of Jersey).

Tony went into hiding at once, first staying at the house of his
friend Simon Sainsbury's brother John in Eaton Terrace, then
moving into Buckingham Palace on Monday 29 February. Here
he had a bedroom and sitting room on the first floor, reached by
a lift. There were net curtains, so if he wanted to he could look
out down the Mall without being seen. It was, he thought, rather
like a service flat, with its heavy mahogany furniture, plain décor –
white walls with touches of gilt – his meals served on a tray and a
footman looking after him. He would enter with his own latchkey
by the Privy Purse door; both at the Palace and Royal Lodge his
arrival would be heralded with the code words based on his initials
'The Taj Mahal is coming.' His secretary Dorothy Everard came
to work for him in the next room, chiefly answering engagement
letters. As the press did not know he was there, he could often nip
out in his car when the road was comparatively empty.

---

* Sir Alan ('Tommy') Lascelles, a courtier who served four monarchs, lastly as
Private Secretary to the Queen in 1952–3. He strongly disapproved of Townsend's
relationship with Margaret, telling him: 'You must be either mad or bad.'

To move from relative anonymity to royal life, even with the comparative restraint then shown by the media, meant an immense amount of adjustment. He had to learn to walk two paces behind the Princess, to look attentive and smiling at all times, to say nothing controversial and (in public) always to wait until the Princess had finished speaking so as to be sure never to interrupt her. Then there were such minor but important points as clapping with raised hands so that he could be seen to be clapping, to say nothing of the complications of precedence. Usually these were strictly observed, but at lunchtime in royal households, for instance, everyone sat where they wanted, and while fiancés could be placed together, married couples never were.

One enormous advantage was his natural discretion. Although he made light of it, the strain of the extraordinary, hermetic atmosphere of the Palace, the feeling that the very walls had ears, sometimes showed. 'They're very powerful,' he told one friend in a shaking voice. 'They listen to everything. I don't care. One just has to speak as though it's not happening. They're probably listening now.'

Press attention was unremitting – even their first engagement photograph, taken for *The Times*, had been interrupted by a helicopter buzzing overhead and he and the Princess had had to dart for cover under the rhododendrons of the Royal Lodge gardens. For friends, it took a long time to overcome the seeming unreality of the situation. Robert Belton, receiving a telephone call from Tony at Buckingham Palace, with the noise of music in the background, said: 'I can't hear you very well – could you turn the radio down?' 'That's not the radio,' responded Tony, 'it's the band – they're changing the guard. Do you want a favourite played?' After a week he asked John Timbers to go and see if there was any mail at the Pimlico studio. It was piled so high that Timbers could barely get through the door.

He would sometimes escape in the evening to see friends, bringing Princess Margaret, in tweed skirt, twin-set and pearls, her face obscured by headscarf and dark glasses, in his little Mini. One evening, after a friend who lived on Cranko's ground floor had taken Jacqui Chan, just back from a round-the-world tour, out to dinner, Jacqui said she would love to see her old friend Bob Belton, who was sharing Cranko's house. It was after eleven and Belton had gone to bed so the two of them went up to Belton's room. Jacqui, perched on the edge of the bed, was chatting merrily when the doorbell went. Her friend answered it, to find Tony and Margaret there, also come to see Belton. He managed to whisper to Tony that Jacqui was up there. Instantly, Tony turned to Margaret and asked her to watch the car. When he came upstairs he told Belton to put his fingers in his ears so that he and Jacqui could have a private chat. Next morning Princess Margaret telephoned and when told what had happened laughed and said, 'I realise now why I wasn't allowed to come up!'

On another occasion Tony arrived with his sister Susan at Belton's Thurloe Place studio. 'If I can arrange it,' he said, 'would you like Old House? Oliver has the lease and he doesn't use it and of course I can't now.' Belton, who had earlier lamented that the fun they had had going down to Old House in Tony's single days was now over, was amazed at the generosity of the offer and accepted delightedly (he would have it for seven years in all). The rent was £5 a year; Belton had the roof completely redone at a cost of £1,000 and plumbing, a gas oven and a fridge installed.

Once officially engaged, the celebratory dinners began. One was with the Hon. Colin and Lady Anne Tennant (whose wedding Tony had photographed four years earlier). Both the Tennants knew the Princess well. Anne's mother, the Countess of Leicester, was a lady-in-waiting to the Queen, Anne herself had carried the Queen's train at the Coronation; her husband Colin was a great friend of the Princess and before his marriage a frequent escort. As Princess Margaret loved the Caribbean, neither of the Tennants was surprised when they learned over dinner that the couple would be spending their honeymoon there. 'Why don't you stop off at Mustique?' said Colin, who had bought this beautiful little island in 1957 for £45,000. 'It's very primitive but it has magical beaches. Anne and I will be there, living in our hut, and we won't bother you at all.' It was an idea that would have far-reaching consequences that no one could have foretold.

Tony's uncle Oliver was one of the first to give a luncheon party for them. When he asked the Princess if there were anyone special she would like to meet, she replied that she had always admired the witty revue star Beatrice Lillie and would love to meet her. The luncheon began successfully, but what no one knew was that Beatrice Lillie (in private life Lady Peel) was an alcoholic – and every single course, from the sherry in the soup to the flambéed main dish and the brandy in the pudding, contained alcohol. At the end of the meal she quietly slid off her chair and under the table. She was carried upstairs, still out cold, and laid on a chaise-longue in the first-floor drawing room, where she was left to recover.

Oliver, who was working extremely hard on fittings with Elizabeth Taylor for the film *Cleopatra*, rushed back to work as soon as Tony and the Princess had gone, his guest forgotten. At about 3.30 the fitting room telephone rang and his assistant Anthony Powell answered it. 'This is the South Kensington Police Station,' said the voice at the other end. 'Mr Messel is rather busy, could I take a message?' asked Powell politely. 'Well,' said the voice, 'we just wanted to tell him that there's a naked woman on his balcony throwing bottles at everybody who goes past.' History does not record how Miss Lillie eventually arrived home.

Tony was, of course, constantly invited to Clarence House. His future mother-in-law, the Queen Mother, had become extremely fond of him, although some of her Household took the same attitude to him as the Palace courtiers. To observant eyes, this slight frostiness could be discerned in the simple matter of pre-lunch drinks. These were served from a trolley, usually martinis or gin and Dubonnet, while in the corner an old-fashioned radiogram quietly played 1930s tunes like 'Smoke Gets in Your Eyes.' The Queen Mother, who did not want footmen in the drawing room before lunch, left the serving of drinks to her private secretaries and equerries, most of them former soldiers, who quietly and efficiently poured them out for Elizabeth, the Princess and their guests. But for Tony, neither royal nor by now really a guest, they resented performing this service – yet to help himself would have looked a trifle presumptuous. He felt the same hesitation when Kenneth Rose came to see him at Clarence House at teatime. 'I'm told I can ring for tea,' said Tony diffidently. When it arrived on a huge tray, both of them saw a 'real Clarence House tea' for the first time – boiled eggs, potted shrimps and three cakes beside the usual array of jams and scones.

The day of the wedding was to be 6 May 1960, seven weeks after the Queen in Council had given her formal consent to the marriage. To celebrate, the Queen gave an engagement ball at Buckingham Palace. Tony's Cambridge friend Justin de Blank, asked to escort Lady Mary Strachey, lady-in-waiting to the Queen when she was Princess Elizabeth, provides a vivid description of it:

The traffic was chaotic but the cars with golden Xs were ushered by the police up the wrong side of the road into the palace in a trice. We arrived with some of the Commonwealth Prime Ministers and in fact I drew up immediately behind our own Prime Minister's car. The inner courtyard was quite dark except for the entrance, ablaze with colour and lights. Cars drew up in fives and sixes and the liveried footmen in their gold and red coats, powdered wigs, black bows and silk stockings opened the nearside doors and helped the girls out. We parked our cars in the Great Courtyard and followed the girls in.

Up the stairs, along a gallery and into the ballroom. How wonderfully the chandeliers twinkle! Look, there's the Queen and the Duke and there's Tony and PM. They circle the floor and then with a gesture wave their guests to dance. Animated conversation everywhere. The duchesses looking magnificent in their tiaras, the Commonwealth premiers fabulous in their exotic dress clothes, Cabinet Ministers in Court dress, Noël Coward looking like a prehistoric exhibit straight out of the Natural History Museum, Cecil Beaton quite beautiful. How much prettier Princess Alexandra is than she appears in her photographs.

The bishops waltz divinely. The service was perfect, the lights, the people, the girls. Where did they come from? English girls with fabulous complexions, magnificent shoulders rising out of those flowing ball dresses. 'Look at that one over there on the right – did you ever see such perfection? No, there's one even better over there.' Where can they be kept until they are released to go to parties such as these?

Here come Tony and PM. 'Hello, Tony. Well, er, congratulations!' I was talking to him when one of these marvellous creatures came up. 'Lucy darling, meet an old friend, Justin de Blank. Do you know I received I suppose about 1,000 letters from all and sundry but one of those that was very special was the one from Justin.' But she soon loses interest and wanders off.

Instead I chat to Joyce Grenfell, David Cecil, Simon Phipps and others. The amusing little man in our party with a foreign accent turns out to be a prince of Prussia. I am taken to see the pictures. Although the names on the frames are all pretty famous, the pictures themselves look somewhat dusty and unloved [this was before the days of cleaning pictures to bring them back to their original brightness]. Later on, find ourselves sitting around chatting to Tony and PM until suddenly they start playing The Queen. It's three o'clock!

There were one or two hiccups on the road to the altar but none caused major problems. The plan was for Tony and Margaret to travel to the Caribbean on the royal yacht *Britannia*, which would serve as their base there, and questions were asked in Parliament about the expense of using her for their honeymoon. The Queen Mother offered to pay the £60,000 it cost herself but in the event the Macmillan government voted the money through. The choice of a best man also caused a last-minute flurry.

Anne Rosse had been anxious that Tony should have his eldest half-brother, Lord Oxmantown, as best man. But his underlying resentment at what he saw as his mother's lifelong neglect, only emphasised by her volte-face when he got engaged to the Princess, put that idea out of court. Instead, as Buckingham Palace announced on 19 March 1960, he intended to have his best friend Jeremy Fry. Just over two weeks later (on 6 April) it was revealed that Fry had stood down owing to a recurrence of jaundice. The real reason, discovered but not stated by the press, was that Fry had been convicted at Marlborough Street Magistrates Court, London, in 1952 for a minor homosexual offence for which he had been fined £2 (this was, of course, at a time when homosexual behaviour was still a criminal offence).

Jeremy Thorpe, a close friend of Tony's since their Eton days, was briefly considered but a discreet enquiry by the Chief Constable of Devon discovered that he also was thought to have homosexual tendencies. In the end Tony settled for a man of irreproachable reputation, Dr Roger Gilliatt – the husband of his great friend Penelope Gilliatt – who was not only the son of the Queen's gynaecologist but also Consultant Neurologist at the National Hospital for Nervous Diseases in Bloomsbury. They had known each other for about six years.

The public enthusiasm for the wedding was immense. It was wonderful and romantic, the beautiful young princess finding happiness again with a magnetically attractive young photographer after sacrificing a great love. When they went to the opera with the Queen Mother in March, the whole audience stood and cheered.

Wedding presents poured in. The near-200 Tony received personally included a pair of matched Purdey shotguns from the Queen, on which Tony put his own imprint by asking Carl Toms, brilliant designer and great friend, to engrave the silver mounting on the stocks; the resultant chasing was reminiscent of exquisite eighteenth-century Spanish silverwork. (Later the Queen gave him a black Labrador called Doon from her Sandringham kennels, so famous for the superb gun dogs they produced that an untrained Sandringham puppy cost £1,600 – a huge sum then – if you were lucky enough to be able to get hold of one.)

Anne Rosse gave a large and splendid mahogany four-poster bed, an antique walnut chest of drawers and several other pieces of furniture; the Eton schoolmate with whom Tony had swapped his grandfather's microscope for a camera wrote sending it back as a wedding present; cigarette lighters, decorative boxes and photograph frames arrived by the score; the staff at Womersley gave some silver; a Kentish firm sent in a case of their own wine and 6d ($2\frac{1}{2}$p) was deducted from the pay of every serviceman towards a wedding present.* From the four regiments of which the Princess was Colonel-in-Chief came a dining room table that could be enlarged with flaps.

In the heady excitement of being able to be together openly, with the prospect of marriage only weeks away, neither Margaret

---

* The one chosen was a small marble-topped commode, with the surplus funds distributed between King George's Fund for Sailors and the British Commonwealth Ex-Services League.

nor Tony realised what difficulties could lie ahead. She was fascinated by his haut Bohemian world, peopled by vivid, amusing characters from the stage, journalism and the arts, so different from those among whom she had been brought up. He believed absolutely that he could cope with the pressures of living within the protocol and values of a Court life that, despite two world wars, had hardly changed since Victorian days; and the friendliness with which he was treated by the royal family did nothing to dispel this conviction. From their point of view, his intelligence, natural finesse, excellent manners and obvious devotion to Margaret spoke heavily in his favour. He was the first commoner for 400 years to marry the daughter of a monarch;* for the more far-sighted members of 'the firm', to include someone who had worked for his living all his adult life added a welcome contemporary note to an institution often accused of living in the past.

Deeply in love, seeing each other at their best, happiest and most unselfish, neither Tony nor Margaret realised that they were each, *au fond*, accustomed to getting their own way – and making life extraordinarily unpleasant for anyone who prevented them. As one friend put it sadly: 'They were both centre-stage people – and only one person can occupy the centre at any given moment.'

On 6 May 1960 the omens could not have been happier – clear blue sky, bright sunshine. From the flagposts along the Mall hung white silk banners with the initials T and M entwined on red Tudor roses, with a sixty-foot arch of pink and red roses outside Clarence House. There was a grandstand outside Westminster Abbey and discreetly hidden television cameras inside (it was the first royal wedding to be televised).

Among the two thousand guests were not only the expected array of statesmen, peers, ministers and close friends of the bride and groom, but also the three living wives of the bridegroom's father – including, of course, his mother Anne Rosse, dressed to the nines for the occasion in a Victor Stiebel suit of gold brocade with mink collar (of which she later commented in satisfied tones: 'This was acclaimed by the world as the smartest'); Jacqui Chan, escorted by Bob Belton, arrived in a car

---

* Cecily, daughter of Edward IV, had married Thomas Kymbe in 1503.

sent by Tony and slipped through a side door; another guest was his daily, Mrs Peabody and the village postman from his father's home in Wales, Plas Dinas.

The bride, by contrast, did not ask any of the Clarence House staff who had cared for her for years. Margaret had not made herself popular with them, treating those who looked after her inconsiderately and with maddening demands that often caused endless extra work (it is only fair to add that when she had her own household at Kensington Palace her staff were devoted to her). Lord Adam Gordon, the Comptroller of the Household, summed up the feelings of many of them in a remark heard by William Tallon, standing close by. As Margaret passed him where he stood on the top step as the glass coach waited to take her to the Abbey, he bowed and said, 'Goodbye, Your Royal Highness,' adding as the coach drew away, 'and we hope for ever.'

Margaret made an exquisite bride. Her dress, largely designed by Tony and his friend Carl Toms though ostensibly by Hartnell, had three layers of organza over tulle. It was simple and elegant, making the most of her tiny waist and sumptuous bosom. With it she wore her magnificent Poltimore tiara (known to her intimates as 'me second-best tarara'), high and regal-looking with its stylised diamond leaves and flowers scintillating against her dark hair. Her wedding ring was of Welsh gold – some of the gold from which the Queen's wedding ring had been made had been set aside for Margaret – her high-heeled shoes were white and she carried a bouquet of white orchids.

Tony was a slight, elegant figure in his wedding morning coat, by the tailors who had made for him since he was an Eton schoolboy, Denman & Goddard of Sackville Street. Gina Ward, sitting on the aisle, watched him as he came carefully down it, his slight limp barely noticeable. Outside the Abbey and down the Mall, with its roses, golden domes, gleaming coronets and fluttering flags, there were packed crowds of onlookers – over 1,200 fainted and had to be treated by members of the St John Ambulance Brigade. As Tony led Princess Margaret onto the Buckingham Palace balcony soon after one o'clock, to stand there with the

Queen, Prince Philip and the royal children, the cheering rose to a crescendo.

At the wedding breakfast for 120 afterwards, with the band of the Grenadier Guards outside playing Princess Margaret's favourite tunes from *Oklahoma*, Prince Philip made a short speech welcoming Tony as the newest member of the royal family, to which Tony replied before he and the Princess cut the six-foot wedding cake.* After the wedding breakfast, Tony and the Princess, this time in yellow silk, drove in an open-topped Rolls to Battle Bridge Pier on the Thames (near London Bridge) where *Britannia* was waiting. The crowds' enthusiasm was such that the car had to slow to a walking pace and they arrived twenty minutes late. As the Princess stepped on board her personal standard was flown and five minutes later *Britannia* set off downstream with the band of the Royal Marines playing on deck and a cacophony of sirens, bells and cheers from the river and its banks, Tony and the Princess waving from the bridge.

The outward voyage was full of the formality to which the Princess was used but which was, if not unfamiliar, alien to Tony. At dinner she wore a long dress every night, with jewels and a tiara; he put on a dinner jacket. They stayed in their own apartments and were rarely seen by the crew, who in any case had been ordered to avert their eyes as they served coffee or drinks by the pool, used increasingly as they neared the warmth of the Caribbean – for at first, as Tony wrote to his new mother-in-law, they had both felt exhausted and had 'spent the first three days flat out'. His letter of 19 May, written on the last of the three nights they spent anchored off Tobago (where the millionaire Fred Latour had lent them the use of a private beach and a bungalow built on it), begins: 'Madam, I wish I knew where to begin to thank you for everything, for this wonderful feeling of warmth and welcome that you have shown me over the past months. I have never in my life been as happy as I have been during the restful weekends at Royal Lodge.'

---

* Later, slices of this cake and several others were distributed to the staffs of the various royal palaces, the officers and crew of the royal yacht, the regiments of which the Princess was Colonel-in-Chief and officials of the charities, hospitals and schools of which she was patron. In all, 1,089 pounds of cake, approximating at two ounces per person, were sent out.

His sentiment might have sounded exaggerated but it was exactly how he felt: all his life he would remain devoted to the Queen Mother and happy and at ease in her company.

Early one evening, as the Tennants sat by their house on Mustique, looking out to sea, they saw *Britannia* arrive, and lower a boat. From it stepped a smart, white-clad young officer to ask if they would like to come aboard for dinner. 'I sent a message back saying we'd love to,' said Anne Tennant, 'but that as we hadn't had a bath for a month could we possibly have a bath first? Our hut was very primitive – no hot water, electric light or anything like that.' They were given a cabin and a bath and during the course of dinner Colin Tennant told them of the beautiful empty beaches of white sand, suggesting they chose a different one every day. There were eight of these on the three-mile-by-one-mile island.

From then on, each morning sailors from *Britannia* would go to the chosen beach, set up a miniature camp with a small tent for shade and lay out a picnic lunch and drinks before departing to leave the couple entirely alone. With photographers haunting them, the tent often became a refuge. When *Paris Match* hired a light aircraft that appeared while Tony and Margaret were having lunch, they had to get under the table and reach their hands up and over for food.

In the evenings they would join the Tennants for drinks. They seemed, thought Anne Tennant, very much in love and very happy. During one of these evenings Colin, realising that he and Anne had not given them a wedding present, said to his old friend Margaret: 'Look, Ma'am, would you like something in a little box or ...' – waving his arm about – 'a piece of land?' 'A piece of land,' replied Margaret, looking at Tony, who smiled in agreement although, inwardly, it confirmed his growing dislike of Colin: wedding presents, felt Tony, should be given to a couple jointly, rather than to one person only, as Colin clearly intended.

A spot on a small peninsula, then covered with dense, thorny vegetation over its steep downward slope overlooking Gelliceaux Bay, was chosen for its privacy and its views. Perhaps, with hindsight, something in a box might have been better.

7

A Glittering Couple

※

While the Armstrong-Joneses were on honeymoon, a baby daughter was born to Camilla Fry (on 28 May 1960). The little girl, delivered in the same four-poster bed slept in by Princess Margaret on her visits, was christened Polly; Tony was one of her godparents.

Three weeks later, on 18 June, the Armstrong-Joneses arrived back in England. On their return, they moved into No. 10 Kensington Palace, a smallish, detached eighteenth-century house on the north side of the Palace, while the apartment designated for them, No. 1A, was being restored.

Tony's new life meant a complete change of outward persona, from (in public) switching to British cigarettes to a shorter haircut and a completely new wardrobe. The tight jeans, chukka boots and leather jackets that he had worn as a working photographer would not do to accompany the Princess to official engagements or to semi-public events like the ballet or theatre. For these, well-cut suits were essential – and a considerable expense. He was helped at first by an allowance of £1,000 a year.

Margaret herself was always perfectly groomed, even down to the false nails she frequently wore over her own small square ones, helped by her dresser Ruby Gordon who came with her to Kensington Palace. The only person outside her family allowed to call the Princess 'Margaret', Ruby, like a number of the 'old' courtiers and servants who had expected Margaret to make the grandest of marriages, disapproved heartily of Tony and had no hesitation in showing it.

She did this by ignoring his presence and any orders he might give and by various gestures that could – just – be put down to accident or forgetfulness. Margaret kept a photograph of Tony under the glass of her dressing table and Ruby would carefully put the Princess's silver-backed dressing table mirror on top of it to hide it. When she called the Princess in the morning, she would bring one cup of tea only, setting it down firmly on the Princess's side of the bed. Margaret who, like the Queen, had been virtually brought up by Ruby and her sister Bobo Macdonald, could not bring herself to speak sharply to her maid.

By 10.30 the Princess was in the drawing room, waiting for the menus – usually consisting of a main dish, salad and savoury – to be sent up by Mrs Miles, the cook. For formal meals, Margaret was naturally punctual – 'I was brought up to respect a soufflé', she would say – and at Clarence House had often expressed her irritation when she thought pre-lunch drinks had lasted too long at one of the Queen Mother's luncheon parties. Their first dining room held only ten, so that guests were very much the inner circle: Oliver Messel, Jeremy Fry, Roger and Penelope Gilliatt, Billy Wallace, and Barton and his wife, over from France – Anthony stayed with them so often, as he frequently came on business trips on his own, that he had his own room. If they were going to the theatre with close friends, the cook would often leave something simple, like steak and washed salad leaves, so that Margaret could quickly prepare a meal when they came home. Their drawing room had a greenish chintz on the sofas, a bust of the Princess's father George VI on a writing desk in the corner, a grand piano, a trolley with drinks and a beautiful clock.

Tony quickly adapted to royal protocol, at first adhering to it enthusiastically. He was the perfect consort for the Princess on her official visits, decorously following her close behind and always saying the right thing. Sometimes this received an unexpected answer. One of their first visits together was to Sandhurst, where the Princess was presenting the Sword of Honour. This was for the year's most outstanding officer cadet. The second prize was a telescope, but no explanation was forthcoming for this. Tony, making conversation to one of the wives at the reception later, said: 'Look, everyone knows what the Sword of Honour is, but what's the telescope for?' She did not know, so the question was passed right down the line of those waiting to be presented. Finally

Tony came to a junior cadet, to whom he said: 'Do tell me, I'm so frightfully ignorant, I should know what the telescope's for.' 'Oh, I can tell you what it's for,' said the boy, concealing his aston- ishment that anyone should ask such a question. 'It's for looking at things a long way away.'

The Queen quickly became fond of her brother-in-law. He was meticulous about following the correct etiquette, always calling her Ma'am (his children were to know her as Aunt Lilibet), bowing before kissing her on the cheek and enquiring through an equerry when it would be convenient to telephone Her Majesty (although if she rang him, she would say: 'Oh, Tony, it's Lilibet'). He got on surprisingly well with Prince Philip – one of Philip's early letters has an arrow pointing to his signature 'Philip' with the words 'Try and bring yourself to call me this!' He had a particular rapport with Prince Charles, to whose opinions and enthusiasms he listened seriously and sympathetically; the Prince, too, enjoyed Tony's wit and sharp sense of humour.

Within the family, he learned that his wife – always 'M' to him – had several different names: a few people, like the Queen and her cousin Margaret Rhodes, called her Margaret, to the Queen Mother she was usually Darling and to the younger generation like Prince Charles she was Margot or Aunt Margot.

He participated in some of his new family's customs, such as their private race on Gold Cup Day at Royal Ascot, which took place on the course before the start of that day's racing. The party would ride out of Royal Lodge and line up together to be started by Lt-Col. (later Sir) John Miller, the Crown Equerry. 'We went like the clappers,' recalled Tony. 'Princess Margaret always won. I was last every time. I couldn't grip because of my leg [affected by polio at sixteen] so I was always put on the safest horse, which not unnaturally was the slowest. Once when the others had to stop I couldn't. I was headed straight for the Queen so all I could do was yell and she just got out of the way in time.' The race was followed by drinks in the paddock, after which the party would go back to change and appear in their finery to drive demurely down the same course along which they had recently galloped as hard as they could.

The prayer meetings that the Princess had attended before her marriage continued, either at the Westminster home of Eric Abbott, the Dean of Westminster, who had officiated at their wedding and who meant a great deal to both of them, or in the drawing room of their small apartment at No. 10 Kensington Palace. These small gatherings took place on Thursdays at either drinks or teatime when, ironically in view of the future, they would pray chiefly for those whose marriages were not going smoothly. Tony regularly made part of the group and could be relied on to bring a few laughs to their proceedings. He was a favourite with the Dean who, realising that such meetings were not his natural habitat, would often give him a surreptitious wink. When the group went to stay at Marigold Bridgeman's home in Gloucestershire for a 'prayer weekend', where Tony would rather have spent the time on something practical like clearing the overgrown churchyard, he was notable for his consideration and good manners. 'We must go and say goodbye to the staff,' he would always quietly remind the Princess if she had forgotten or was in a hurry.

Their love was unmistakable and both found it difficult, as one friend put it, 'to keep their hands off each other'. There are touching vignettes of their delight in each other's company – Margaret flying down early after an official appointment in Scotland in order to be with her husband sooner, the couple walking hand in hand down Cheval Place to Tony's car after a party at Lord and Lady Grade's Montpelier Walk penthouse, where the Princess had persuaded Lew Grade to do his famous Charleston.

They would also return frequently to the little room in Rotherhithe for an evening completely to themselves, without the formality that surrounded their daily lives. They would arrive unobtrusively, darting through the door when the street was clear – once, Glenton, on the lookout for their arrival, had to move one of the courting couples who took refuge in doorways on dark nights, receiving a mouthful of abuse as he did so.

For both Margaret and Tony, this whitewashed room in the East End brought back the romantic atmosphere of their courting days. Tony did the cooking – almost always steaks, salad and (for him) potatoes, followed by cheese, with both of them drinking red wine and smoking constantly – Tony his favourite Gauloises, Margaret pulling her Chesterfields out of the gold Cartier cigarette case her father had given her two years before he died. Afterwards, the Princess would don a pair of rubber gloves and wash up in a small basin in the sink. Occasionally a friend or two would join them – in June 1961 Noël Coward recorded a dinner party *à quatre* with Tony and Margaret and Margaret Leighton at Kensington Palace 'and after dinner drove secretly to Tony's place or "studio" in Rotherhithe, where we banged the piano and threw empty Cointreau bottles into the river.... They were both very sweet and obviously happy.' Once they arrived with friends for an after-theatre supper, in a gleaming Rolls-Royce, an anomaly in that neighbourhood but fortunately regarded by the locals as the advance guard of a funeral. Nevertheless, when they emerged, a child had chalked the message 'Carol is a dirty biuch [*sic*]' on one side of the car.

After their marriage, Tony introduced the Princess to many more people from the outside world. One selection was the current Cambridge Eight. Princess Margaret, whose idea of rowing men was of people who were large, tough and drank a lot, put away her precious Fabergé *objets*. But as she said later, she had never had a nicer, more well-mannered set of guests – who drank only orange juice.

He also, in a move that foreshadowed his much greater personal involvement, set up a fund for helping disabled people, putting into it the £10,000 he had earned from royal photographs. Later he was to comment:* 'If something in your private life changes and you get money for doing certain things then that money should go to charity and not to you.'

To the delight of Anne Rosse, they spent the New Year of 1961 at Birr Castle. Margaret asked her old beau, Billy Wallace, Tony invited Jeremy and Camilla Fry – a clear signal that although he had been unable to have Jeremy as best man, the friendship was still as strong. His sister Susan and Lord and Lady Rupert Nevill were also there. The visit was not altogether sunshine and light. Margaret disliked what she thought of as Anne's 'posing' and deliberately did not tell Anne by what name to call her; Anne, who did not dare risk a snub, did what she

---

* To the author.

could to rectify this lack of intimacy by calling her new daughter-in-law 'Darling'.

The visit gave Anne Rosse full scope for her penchant for grand dressing and theatrical entrances, with dinner invariably an elaborate affair, and even the moment of departure an opportunity for creating an effect. The Snowdons, who had to leave early, said goodbye to Michael Rosse but did not want to wake Anne, who always rose late. Suddenly a voice came from the top of the stairs. 'My darlings, you're not going without saying goodbye!' There stood Anne Rosse, in a moss green velvet housecoat, fully made-up and coiffed. Slowly and theatrically, she walked down the wide staircase with its carved ceiling and banners hanging down, arms outstretched, the green velvet train of her gown flowing behind her. As an entrance, it could not have been bettered, but for those about to leave, it was a trifle overdone.

Further scope for Margaret's irritation came later on a visit to Abbey Leix (the home of Tony's sister Susan, Lady de Vesci), after a dinner party that ended at 2 a.m. Half an hour later, there came a telephone call from Anne Rosse, proclaiming in anguished tones that she had lost one of her diamond stud earrings. Susan, her husband, Margaret, Tony and all the servants were roused and set to search for it. Next morning Anne Rosse telephoned. 'Darlings, I'm sorry I put you to all this trouble. I found it in the car.'

At the top of his profession before his marriage, Tony had never envisaged giving up work, although he knew that the commercial photography he had done previously was no longer a viable option. One day when he and Margaret were staying with Jeremy and Camilla Fry, Cecil Beaton came over for a drink before lunch. When Beaton fulsomely congratulated the Princess on her marriage, adding: 'May I thank you Ma'am, for removing my most dangerous rival,' Margaret replied, poker-faced: 'What makes you think Tony is going to give up work?' Beaton paled.

On 23 January 1961, Tony joined the Council of Industrial Design as an unpaid adviser. It was work for which he was eminently suited, with his faultless eye for design and capacity for taking endless trouble to achieve the desired end. But it was at best part-time and, as he would soon discover, was not enough to mop up his fizzing energy.

That autumn Tony was elevated to the peerage. One of the reasons he accepted a title, he later said, was for the sake of his son. Highly unlikely though it was that the new baby should ever succeed, if it were a boy it was then close in line to the throne – and would it have done to have a former Mr Jones as king? On 3 October 1961 Tony became the Earl of Snowdon, with the courtesy title of Viscount Linley of Nymans.* He had originally wished to be called Earl of Caernarvon, the county of his family, but there was an Earl of Caernarvon already. The second choice was Arvon, the part of Wales he came from, but when Anthony Eden was created Earl of Avon the similar-sounding names might have created complications. Finally he settled on the euphonious and historic Snowdon.

At the end of October the Princess moved back into Clarence House (well equipped for any form of medical intervention) to await the birth of their first child. The question of children had never been discussed before their marriage; once married, Tony found that he desperately wanted them and the Princess lovingly agreed.

On 3 November 1961, their son David Albert Charles was born by caesarean section. Twelve days later, on 15 November, Tony's half-brother, Peregrine, was born to his father Ronnie's third wife Jenifer, who herself was only a year older than Tony.

Princess Alice of Athlone, who came to lunch to see the Snowdon baby, remarked when she came down from visiting Princess Margaret: 'Almost anyone could be that boy's mother – he's so like his father.' The Snowdons' child was named after the Queen Mother's favourite brother, the Hon. Sir David Bowes-Lyon, who had died three months earlier at the age of fifty-nine when staying with her at Birkhall.

David was to be christened in December, at Buckingham Palace – which naturally meant a christening photograph. Bec-

---

* He did not take his seat in the House of Lords until 28 February 1962, when he was introduced in both his titles. Princess Margaret, with his father, mother and stepmother, watched from the Commonwealth Gallery.

ause Tony had given up his photographic studio on marriage, he no longer had an assistant. He still, however, photographed members of the royal family for their private albums and to record special family moments. As he himself necessarily had to be in many of the wedding or christening groups, he needed someone of proven experience and absolute discretion to help him, both in the setting-up of the picture and to click the shutter once he had dashed into the group. The obvious person was his old friend and fellow photographer Bob Belton, invariably there when it came to the many photographs he took of the Princess – holding a reflector shade, pulling up a piece of jewellery at the back to Tony's shouted command because it was dangling too low.

At his first royal group photograph, of the six-week-old David Linley at Buckingham Palace, Belton was terrified. He and Tony had set up their equipment in the White Drawing Room and then Tony had gone to join the christening party of about 200, leaving Belton alone with his nerves. Just before the royal family were due to enter, he went to check the cameras. As he did so, the door opened and a two-year-old child ran in, followed by a woman. 'I'm sorry,' she said, as she chased the child. 'At this age they get their fingers into everything.' Belton looked up – to see the Queen, who smiled and said: 'You're Tony's friend.' Her manner was so relaxed and friendly that all his terror left him – though there were still occasional pitfalls. Tony had reassured him that the royal family were very easy to 'direct' and that if you wanted the Queen to turn her head, say, slightly to the left, you simply said: 'Ma'am, please could you look to the left.' What he had not reckoned on was that in the large christening group photograph there were seven women entitled to be called 'Ma'am', so that as he uttered the fateful sentence seven heads swivelled as one.

Tony was immediately besotted with his son, so much so that two months after David's birth he did not want to leave him and fly with his wife for their planned three-week winter holiday in Antigua. But as Margaret, who had been largely brought up by nannies and governesses, pointed out, provided little David got his four-hourly bottle on time, he would not mind whether it was his mother or the new, very experienced nanny Verona Sumner who gave it to him (unlike the Queen, Margaret did not feed her children herself).

Miss Sumner, an excellent nanny, was another who disliked Tony, mainly because he wanted too much to do with 'her' baby. Tony, who had been largely brought up by his own very loving nanny, had always resented the distance at which his mother had held him during his own childhood, and was determined there would be none between him and any children he might have; consequently he visited the nursery far more than the Princess – visits that were fiercely resented by Nanny Sumner.

No. 1A Kensington Palace, one of two habitations in a beautiful Wren building and the largest of the grace-and-favour apartments in the Kensington Palace complex, had for many years been allowed to run down and decay and was so dilapidated when it was proposed for the Snowdons that they were unable to move into it until mid-March 1963. It had suffered such extensive damage from an incendiary bomb during World War II that the basement floor could be seen from the first floor and it had then remained untouched and structurally deteriorating. Maintaining it was the responsibility of the Ministry of Works but, where a private building would have been listed and the owner obliged to keep it up, the Ministry had neglected to do anything about it until forced to by the prospect of new tenants.

This did not stop Willie Hamilton, the Labour MP for West Fife, known for his stringent questioning on all things royal, from raising in Parliament again and again the question of the increased expenditure on grace-and-favour residences, with particular reference to No. 1A (by the end of 1961 he had written 112 letters to the Ministry of Works on the subject).

Both Tony and the Princess were worried at the implication that large sums were being spent out of the public purse simply in order to provide them with a home when most of the money spent went on the structural repairs – basic plumbing and drainage, rewiring, electricity and heating – that were in any case the responsibility of the Ministry. Tony, much more media-savvy than the Princess thanks to his contacts in the press, believed that they should instantly refute the idea that their first home was being paid for largely by the taxpayer. For the composition of such an important letter, to be sent to the Minister of Works, Lord John Hope, he sought the advice of his old Eton friend Kenneth Rose, who had been a 'beak' (master) while he was there. Rose's draft formed the basis of the letter later sent. Its main points were contained in the following two paragraphs:

> As you know, it was simultaneously announced in March (a) that the Queen had offered Princess Margaret and myself the use of 1A Kensington Palace as a permanent home, and (b) that the restoration and adaptation of the property would cost £70,000, of which £50,000 would be charged to the Royal Palace Vote by your Ministry.
>
> These two statements seem to have become so confused in the public mind that nearly everybody believes that this large sum of money is being spent only to provide us with a new home. Whereas the truth of the matter is that your Ministry would have had to spend £50,000 on the building whoever went to live there; and that the only alternative to spending such a sum is to let a magnificent example of Wren architecture crumble to ruins.

After suggesting that a press conference should be held in No. 1A so that journalists and photographers could see for themselves exactly how parlous a state the building was in, he concluded by saying: 'You will not, I hope, think that we wish to put your Ministry in the pillory! But we shall certainly be there ourselves unless the matter is presented to the public in its true form.'

Lord John, however, refused to allow the media into the house to see for themselves the parlous state it was in, contenting himself with a written reply to Willie Hamilton's questions without setting out the position in full, so that the fact that the money spent on No. 1A was mainly due to refurbishment and restoration was not generally grasped and would resurface from time to time, notably when the Public Record Office released documents after forty years that claimed that over £300,000 had been spent on special marble floors and that the Queen Mother had donated cupboards. Not only Tony but the Ministry of Works architect, Harold Yexley, in charge of the renovation works then, refuted these claims. 'I do not recall insisting on a marble floor. The very beautiful slate floor was provided by Lord Snowdon,' wrote Yexley. 'The Strawberry Hill Gothick panelling was bought by the Princess. The Queen Mother's cupboard is more likely to be a handsome bookcase designed by Lord Snowdon's uncle, Oliver Messel [it was].'

The house suited them admirably. Tony's imagination and skill at using *objets trouvés* were put to good use. The first room entered on the ground floor was a wide hall, paved in a design by Tony of diamond-shaped black Welsh slate from the North Wales quarry of his godfather, Michael Duff. The hall led directly to the large drawing room with its kingfisher-blue walls, pale grey curtains and a specially made blue, grey, apricot and gold Spanish carpet, a wedding present from the City of London. In the centre, at right angles to the fireplace, were two large blue and gold sofas. At one end were the Princess's desk and a pair of Regency blackamoors holding torches aloft. At the other, facing those who entered, was a baby grand piano – a present from Anne and Michael Rosse – on which stood framed family photographs. The fireplace, like the one in the dining room, came from a Victorian house near London Bridge that was being demolished; Tony bought both for £250. On one wall hung a collage of souvenirs – first night tickets, a restaurant bill, a lock of hair. From the window there was a peaceful view of the garden and, beyond, Kensington Gardens. Tony's study was next door. Tony cut a hole between this room and the drawing room that emerged through a china cabinet, so that films could be projected from his study onto the drawing room wall.

Also on the ground floor were the dining room, with apricot walls and a John Piper over the mantelpiece, conservatory and kitchen. The eggshell colour of the units was chosen by Margaret when she saw Tony boiling an egg; this was carefully wrapped up and sent to the paint manufacturers.

On the first floor were Tony and Margaret's bedrooms, separated by the Princess's bathroom, and three rooms for David (and, later, Sarah) and their nanny, with staff rooms on the floor above. The servants' sitting rooms were in the basement, as were Tony's darkroom, a store room, a room where his secretary, Dorothy Everard, worked and a small kitchen where she prepared

106

lunch for him when he was on his own. The basement had its own entrance, through which friends and sometimes clients would come, leading directly into Tony's office with its green corduroy sofa and green canvas chairs.

Tony was determined to use his flair for design and craftsmanship to the utmost in their new home. He made mahogany panels to veneer the plain doors so that they looked heavy and suitably impressive (many of the panels were glued on by the Princess), designed louvred cupboards in his dressing room with its dark green carpet, tan cork walls and gilded Napoleonic day bed, given him by Princess Margaret, and used slate from Michael Duff's quarries in the high-tech kitchen with its beige Marley tile floor. No detail was too small to escape his attention, from the shape of the taps to the colour of the sealer used over the wood floors.

Margaret's bedroom was also large, with pale green walls, a beige carpet, yellow furnishings and a huge double bed covered with an exquisite embroidered bedspread made by the School of Needlework. Her bathroom was perhaps the *chef d'oeuvre*, with its pink walls and carpet, decorative white Gothic arches (found during a weekend with the Frys) and ingenious octagonal towel rail-cum-radiators over which hung thick pink bath towels. In the centre of the octagon was a glass case holding some of her collection of exotic shells, while from the bath there was a splendid view of Hyde Park.

It was in this bathroom that Tony took one of the most beautiful of the many photographs he took of his wife, piquant in its contrast between intimacy and formality, the obvious if unseen nakedness of the subject and the elaborate and expensive gown waiting in the wings. Margaret, with her make-up and hair already done and the Poltimore tiara in place, is bathing before what Tony described as a 'posh dinner' when he snapped her, head and neck alone visible above the rim of the bath.

On Tony's first day at the Haymarket offices of the Council of Industrial Design in January 1961 he had met James Cousins, then ensconced in a small office at the rear of the building overlooking Leicester Square. Cousins, formerly on the architectural staff of Imperial College, became one of the many people to help Tony –

who always liked to have someone working with him – co-opted through Tony's well-honed blend of charm and determination.

It was Cousins who helped the Snowdons move from No. 10 to their new home, No. 1A, driving a van between the two filled with the smaller and more fragile objects. On the first of these short trips Princess Margaret sat in the back of the van with her precious china collection and their new dinner service; Cousins, who had never driven the van before, put his foot on the brake instead of the accelerator, sending the Princess flat on her face amid the china – fortunately, nothing was broken and the Princess merely laughed. It was also Cousins who managed the construction of the huge extractor hood, designed by Tony to fit above the island cooking unit in the Snowdons' kitchen. Knowing that it would be complicated and difficult to make, Cousins persuaded a friend from his Imperial College days, the Professor of Engineering, to have it constructed by the College's Engineering Department (eventually the College wrote off the considerable expense of its making). Designed by Tony, this hood later inspired a hood over an open fire in the James Bond film *Goldfinger*.

More servants were needed to run the larger establishment – No. 1A, a large house on four floors, had about twenty rooms. The Princess, who had never done anything for herself in her life except wash her King Charles spaniel Rowley in the bath, drying him with her hairdryer, would not have contemplated even the lightest task, such as arranging flowers. The Comptroller of their House-hold, Major the Hon. Francis Legh (nephew of Sir Piers ('Joey') Legh, equerry to King George VI) had been Private Secretary since 1959. The male staff – chef, chauffeur, butler, under-butler and footman – were Tony's province; the female – housekeeper, nanny, nursemaid, kitchen maid and her dresser – were engaged by the Princess. Ruby Gordon, the Princess's original dresser, had shown her hostility to Tony once too often, and had been replaced by Miss Isobel Mathieson.

For the Snowdons' servants, life was hard work. A schedule shows that the Household routine ran to the minute, with entries like: '12.00 Drinks tray to Drawing Room. 12.00–12.30 Lunch (staff), 12.35–2.45. Complete preparing Dining Room, Serve lunch, Wash up lunch.' The average working day for the butler and under-butler began at 7.30 with the laying-up of calling (early morning tea) trays and breakfast trays and ended at 10.30 after dinner had been washed up. From Monday to Thursday each had off an alternate afternoon, from two till six, and evening from six – provided there was no luncheon or dinner party. There was a similar timetable for the housemaids and daily helps.

Margaret's new chauffeur, John Larkin, a former bus driver, was another essential: Margaret had never driven in London (although she sometimes essayed an automatic off-road in Windsor Great Park) and indeed did not have a driving licence. In London, her cars included the big black official Phantom IV Rolls-Royce, a smaller black one and a Silver Cloud II.* Larkin, who started at £16 a week, also looked after Tony's labrador, Doon, taking him back at night to his home in Bounds Green, north London – Tony, not an animal-lover, saw the dog only when shooting.

The butler, Malcolm Higgins, who joined as a footman in 1962 after two butlers had already left because of the strain, began at £7 10s, a weekly wage that later rose to £9 10s, with hours as long as his employers wanted – sometimes from six in the morning to midnight. At his interview with Tony – in Tony's bedroom, as he was recovering from 'flu – Higgins found that he and Tony, who believed that employees should be congenial and interesting as well as efficient, talked about the theatre, ballet, photography and the visual arts generally – everything, in fact, except the job. When Tony decided, after the lengthy talk, to take Higgins on, he simply said that there was a temporary butler who would instruct him in his duties.

Tony's day would begin around 7.30 or eight. He would leave a note in the pantry the night before to say when he wanted to be

---

* Later in the sixties, the Phantom was replaced by a green Silver Shadow, with a long wheelbase, customised by Tony with such things as pearlised door handles instead of chrome. One object that did not make the transition was the number plate, PM 6450 – the initials, of course, referring to the Princess and the number to a date: 6 April 1950. When Larkin asked her if she wanted it transferred she replied: 'No – it refers to an incident in my past best forgotten about. I want something that doesn't mean anything.' The number chosen was CGXM.

called. At the precise time, the under-butler, Richard Wood, who valeted him, came into his room and drew the curtains; while running the bath he would lay out Tony's clothes and put cufflinks in his shirt. Cleaning his shoes and washing out his cigarette holder would have been done beforehand. Richard would then bring in breakfast, usually featuring scrambled eggs, sausages or bacon, before going to the pantry to clean the silver, do the flowers and prepare for one of the luncheon parties held on most days of the week. After serving at table he would wash up (dishwashers were virtually unknown at that time) helped by the footman, who would later serve tea. Richard's duties began again in the evening with dinner or, on film premiere or theatre evenings, a dozen or so people to wine and smoked salmon at seven, followed by serving a three-course dinner to the company at anything up to midnight – followed, of course, by the washing-up, this time on his own.

As the popular Snowdons were asked away every weekend they cared to go, this meant weekends on duty for both the Princess's maid and Richard, who would pack for their mistress and master respectively, before Richard drove them in advance with the luggage in a small Volkswagen to the weekend destination. There they would unpack, hang or press the clothes ready for the arrival of Tony and the Princess, before Richard helped that night at their hosts' dinner table.

On Royal Lodge shooting weekends, Richard would call Tony, lay out his shooting clothes, put on his own shooting clothes – he also acted as Tony's loader – and collect cherry brandy, coffee and fruit cake from the kitchen to serve to the guns at eleven. After the last morning drive, he would go quickly back to Royal Lodge, pick up the shooting lunch, bring it back and serve it. Sunday night meant the whole process in reverse with perhaps a dinner party to prepare for at Kensington Palace that night. Afternoons were free but there were no days off; his wages were £7 a week (when he left after seven years they had risen to £12 per week).

Hard though the terms sound today, there was much competition for a place in the Snowdon household: nowhere else could such a large and interesting collection of the best-known faces in the land be seen at close quarters; to work there meant kudos and the best possible reference for a job anywhere else; as with other royal households, No. 1A was a safe haven for anyone homosexual in those more difficult days; and the Snowdons themselves – particularly Tony – were kind and noticing employers.

Although trying with their autocratic demands and disregard of how these might conflict with routine or much-needed rest, both Snowdons understood the need for occasional large dollops of praise and encouragement. Richard, unable to go into the drawing room to do the flowers for a large party the following day because the Princess was still sitting there, finally managed it after the couple had gone out to a late dinner. Next morning he found a note from Tony: 'Dear Richard, I've just seen the flowers in the drawing room. They are an absolute masterpiece.' Above all, life with the Snowdons was never dull.

Once installed, Tony set up a welding shop in the Kensington Palace stables – later to become refuge as well as workroom – and there he and Cousins would work on furniture designed by Tony. As Cousins could only join him after his work at the Design Council had finished for the day, this usually meant a late night for him, sometimes until 3 a.m. if Tony was particularly en-thused about a project. On such nights, Tony would lend him his Mini Cooper, with its number plate MWL (Margaret With Love) to drive back through the empty streets to his Hampstead home. Cousins would have to return it the following morning before going on to the office. This Mini Cooper, dark green and bought for £500, was one of the first ever made. Tony had literally been in at its birth, having met its designer, Sir Alec Issigonis, when skiing in Davos; sitting beside Sir Alec in a mountain-top restaurant, he watched the designer sketch his ideas for a small, new, light car on a napkin. When Tony took delivery he had had Sir Alec's original side-to-side windows changed to up-and-down ones, but both Sir Alec and Margaret remonstrated, saying that the former would be more protective of the Princess's coiffure. Tony changed them back again.

Pottering about at Kensington Palace and the necessarily spor-adic demands of the Design Council was not enough for Tony's surging flow of creative energy. He was not only used to hard work, he needed it. Any newspaper or magazine in the world would have leapt at the chance of employing him but great care had to be taken both to avoid the taint of commercialism and of exploiting the royal connection.

Although the Princess had ample private funds – the income both from a trust fund set up by her father King George VI and the £20,000 (the equivalent of £1 million today) left her in 1942 by the society hostess Mrs Ronnie Greville – the idea of being in any way a 'kept' man appalled him. Both he and Princess Margaret were anxious that he should find something suitable, and both were responsible for finding the job that eventually ensued and that proved to be one of the happiest and most creative of his life.

The Princess asked Jocelyn Stevens, who had married her long-time close friend and lady-in-waiting Jane Sheffield in 1956, to make it known discreetly to the Editor of the *Sunday Times*, Denis Hamilton, that Tony would be interested in a job there if a suitable position could be found. Tony said the same thing to a great friend of his, Mark Boxer (the cartoonist Marc), who was working on the paper. The result was that he signed a contract with the *Sunday Times* (which launched its magazine on 4 February 1962) to become an 'Artistic Adviser' for a fee of £5,000 a year, for three months of which he would not be available. He would be responsible directly to Hamilton, he would never take royal pictures and there would be no publicity – apart from the bare initial announcement – over any features he was required to do. In practice, this meant that his byline, then 'Lord Snowdon' rather than the simple 'Snowdon' of later days, was exactly the same size as the rest of the *Sunday Times* photographers, and that no one knew in advance that it was he who was coming to take a particular shot. He attended his first conference of the *Sunday Times* editorial board on 6 February 1962 – rushing off afterwards to the family lunch at Buckingham Palace that commemorated the tenth anniversary of the Queen's accession.

On features that he organised, on such subjects as the theatre or architecture, the contract specified that he could spend up to £500 a time on expenses and travel or extra help. Once again, he shrewdly retained the copyright in all the photographs he took after their initial publication in the *Sunday Times* (most were to appear in the magazine). He was also able to work for glossy magazines such as *Vogue*, where the Features Editor, Pamela Colin (later Lady Harlech), became a close friend of both Snowdons.

When the appointment was announced rival newspapers were predictably outraged, partly because the yearly salary he was reputedly earning was believed to be the huge sum of £10,000, but largely because they assumed that owing to his position he would be able to photograph those who would refuse any other photographer. More germane to this new career was the row that blew up over whether or not he should join a trades union, then mandatory for any working reporter or photographer though not for an executive. His contract gave him an executive position, but as he intended to take photographs the union rule applied and he eventually joined the NUJ (National Union of Journalists).

Quickly it became apparent that he had left the frivolity of his earlier 'social' photographs far behind. His first piece for the *Sunday Times Magazine* (on 25 February 1962) was on the incomparable partnership of Britain's prima ballerina, Margot Fonteyn, and Rudolf Nureyev, the latter newly escaped from behind the Iron Curtain, as they rehearsed at Covent Garden – one spectacular shot shows Nureyev, apparently defying the force of gravity, flying diagonally upwards, straight as an arrow, in one of his gigantic leaps.

Emotionally, too, his work took on a new depth: the photographs he took for a feature on the old showed a compassion that was almost reverence, treating them with dignity and understanding. It was the same in real life: he sent his old char Mrs Peabody an invitation 'to come and see the baby', and flowers and photographs when she was in hospital. 'I am able to sit in a wheelchair for three hours each day with my leg propped up,' she wrote from Queen Mary's Hospital, Roehampton, to thank him.

The Snowdons still retreated from time to time to the little room in Rotherhithe. Here one day in May 1962 the Queen Mother spent an evening with them, after careful preparations by Tony's secretary, who brought down cold meats, salad, fresh fruit, champagne, gin, table wines, whisky, new candles and clean tea towels and covered the sagging divan with a thick coloured throw, after first cleaning the place to within an inch of its life.

Tony's chief worry during those halcyon years was his father, in and out of hospital with mysterious pains. These were, in fact, the first signs of the cancer that later killed him. On 14 January 1963, Ronnie wrote from the Metabolic Ward in St Mary's Hospital, Paddington: 'Don't be surprised [at the address] I told you that I was coming here for three weeks to have every check and test under the sun and that is what has happened.' Three weeks later he was thanking his son for his promise to send him by car to Bath, where an operation was planned. After it, he returned to Plas Dinas, from which he wrote sadly on 4 April: 'I am afraid I am only making slow progress. The doctors *will* give me so many pills and yesterday I was in bed all day being violently sick because two of the prescribed pills clashed. That makes it impossible to gain weight.'

He recuperated in a flat in Brighton, welcomed there by a large bunch of roses and tulips from Tony, but by June was in such pain that he went to see his surgeon again, who sent him to the King Edward VII's Hospital for Officers in London's Beaumont Street for a full examination under general anaesthetic. Eventually, much weaker, he was able to return to Wales.

The informal and familiar atmosphere of a studio, with its democratic, Christian-name approach, could not have been more of a contrast to the splendours of the life Tony had entered on less than two years earlier, such as the ball at Windsor to celebrate Princess Alexandra's marriage, with the Castle floodlit, pink, amber and deep coral azaleas ten feet high in full bloom, the women ablaze with spectacular jewels, in one case a parure of sapphires that had belonged to Marie Antoinette.

There was a sitting with the Queen, intended partly to produce a portrait, partly to serve as a model for new coinage. Neither she nor Tony thought his photographs were particularly flattering. 'I have been staring at myself in the glass since I have been doing my fittings over the past two days here and I think the likeness is unfortunately very accurate!!', she wrote to Tony in her letter of thanks on 9 January 1963. But her approval of him was signified by the bestowal of an honour that would fit him for one of the most important ceremonies of her reign: she appointed him

Constable of Caernarvon Castle. The first intimation of this was a letter from the Prime Minister, Harold Macmillan, on 19 March 1963 telling him that 'it is my duty to recommend to The Queen the name of a successor to Lord Harlech as Constable of Caernarvon Castle,' and asking if Tony would be willing for his name to be submitted to Her Majesty for this appointment. Tony was naturally delighted, and on 3 April 1963 he heard that the Queen had approved his appointment.

Later in the year (on 14 November 1963), at a charity reception at St James's Palace, Cynthia Gladwyn, wife of the British Ambassador in Paris, noted that 'Princess Margaret looked very pretty in a turquoise blue dress, with a beautiful turquoise and diamond tiara and necklace to match,* and was fortunately in a good mood. Tony had a sun-lamp burnt brown complexion and his hair had been tinted a curious new colour. Sachy Sitwell afterwards described it as peach but I would say apricot.'

The new shade so tartly described by Cynthia Gladwyn was the result of Tony and the Princess attempting to achieve the same hair colour as an outward expression of their deep love for each other. Fortunately, it was a phase that did not endure – but then, less happily, nor did their personalities remain in step for very much longer.

There were a few clouds in Tony's life. He felt distress when the Gilliatts' marriage broke up, although both remarried quickly: Penelope Gilliatt to the playwright John Osborne, Roger to interior designer Mary Green. Peter Sellers, to whom he was exceptionally close, also remarried (in February 1964), to the beautiful Swedish actress Britt Ekland. The first time Sellers brought her to lunch at Kensington Palace Tony seized the chance to photograph her, using the wide hall of No.1A, with the front door open to allow full play of the natural light on which he insisted. Other friends seemed to be out of circulation or in difficulties. 'Carl [Toms] has

---

* These were the wedding present of George V to the Queen Mother when she married the Duke of York. She in turn gave them to Margaret for her twenty-first birthday. Other jewels frequently worn by Margaret were a five-string necklace of pearls, a three-string pearl necklace with a diamond clasp, a diamond and drop pearl necklace and earrings (now in the possession of her daughter Lady Sarah Chatto) and a single-row diamond necklace given by Queen Mary.

disappeared to Tangier, saying he will return when the spirit moves him. I hope he is not referring to the spirit he went with,' Tony wrote to Oliver Messel from Royal Lodge at Easter 1964.

While the Snowdons were still in complete, loving accord, Kensington Palace became the most enjoyable place in the country to be asked to. Tony and the Princess were undoubtedly the nation's most popular and glamorous couple. As good-looking, photogenic, romantic, exciting and deeply in love as the hero and heroine of a fairy story, their glamour was irresistible. They were highly visible and they were royal at a time when being invited to a royal palace was the ultimate social accolade.

Their salon became a place where the arts and the Establishment were mixed with absolute conviction in a way that no other couple could have managed: unlike any previous royal spouse, Tony knew the worlds of the stage, design and the arts intimately. Their parties were gatherings of the beautiful, the famous and those who would contribute – Dudley Moore would play the piano, Cleo Laine and her husband John Dankworth would sing, Peter Sellers would 'become' different comic characters, Spike Milligan and Richard Stilgoe would spark off each other, John Betjeman would tell stories.

Anyone who was asked to spend an evening 'en famille', often with the Princess playing the piano and singing songs from one of the musicals she loved, felt especially honoured. Even such hardened sophisticates as Noël Coward, accustomed to meeting everyone from the Mountbattens to Hollywood's finest, invariably recorded these soirées as 'charming', also confiding to his diary that when she sang his songs, accompanying herself on the piano, 'Princess Margaret surprisingly good. She has an impeccable ear, her piano playing is simple but has perfect rhythm, and her method of singing is really very funny.' For dinner parties, always black tie, women would buy new long dresses and borrow jewellery or get it out of the bank. (For the Princess, these evenings held an echo of the man whom she had loved more than any other, her father; on the dining table stood the small, inch-long gold clock made by Cartier that had belonged to him. Later she gave it to

Tony.) In the summer there would be parties for thirty or forty in the garden, with guests from the worlds both moved in: beautiful starlets, glamorous society girls, musicians, artists, politicians, movie stars, writers and designers.

The close bond between the couple, expressing itself in witty but affectionate banter, encouraged sparkling conversation while the aura of royalty made every evening memorable, if at the same time unnervingly awe-inspiring. One guest entertained there remembers the cartoonist Osbert Lancaster's hand shaking as he held his gin and tonic, while his wife, Anne Scott-James, the cool and sophisticated former Editor of *Harper's Bazaar*, blushed when addressed by the Princess. Such was the respect for royalty that when the waxwork model of Tony was stolen from Madame Tussaud's and dumped in a telephone box with the receiver to its ear, no one dared tap on the window of the telephone box. Nevertheless, Mrs Betty Kenward ('Jennifer' of the *Tatler*), possibly still bristling at Tony's attempting to talk to her when he worked as her photographer, invariably referred to him as 'Princess Margaret's husband' in her social column; and in her memoirs there are only two, unavoidable, references to him, both conspicuously lacking the usual flowery adjectives.

Even without their immense social cachet, their looks, wit, talent and charisma would have made the Snowdons the most desirable of guests or hosts – for those who had the nerve to ask them back. One was Angela Huth, who lived with her first husband Quentin Crewe in a flat in Wilton Crescent with a dining room that would seat eight and a drawing room of outsize length, so that much of the Crewes' entertaining consisted of giving a dinner party and asking other friends to join them after dinner. After Angie Huth (later to blossom as a novelist) and Quentin Crewe, a friend of Tony's from their days together on *Queen* magazine, had been invited to lunch at Kensington Palace, she thought of asking the Snowdons back to one of her after-dinner parties. 'We always had the people of those days – the Rolling Stones, George Melly, the Tynans – so we thought they might enjoy it. I rang up Princess Margaret and asked her if she'd like to come and she said she'd love to. I remember Anthony Blond being very drunk, Sandie Shaw standing there with bare feet as usual, Elaine Dundy [Mrs Tynan] sitting under the piano and Shirley Maclaine holding hands with Edna O'Brien. Princess Margaret absolutely adored it and they stayed until 7 a.m. From then on we were tremendously good friends.'

There was much of this kind of entertaining. The drama critic Ken Tynan, a great party-giver, would ask the Snowdons with such people as the actress Jean Marsh, the playwright Peter Shaffer, the poet Christopher Logue and the polymathic Dr Jonathan Miller along with Spike Milligan, Peter Brook, Alan Sillitoe, Peter Cook and their respective wives.

For the Princess especially these gatherings were diverting, as when she found that she was expecting her second child she cancelled virtually all her public engagements (pregnancy was a much more private affair then) and, to fill in her days, saw as many friends as she could. As Angie Huth was pregnant at the same time and had been ordered by her doctor to stay in bed for six months, Princess Margaret and Tony would often come round with a projector, screen and a film, set up the screen at the end of the bed and watch a film together. Often, if the Crewes had no one to cook for them, complete meals for four would be sent round on trays to Wilton Crescent from Kensington Palace.

Yet already cracks had begun to appear in the Snowdon marriage, though at this stage only visible to those closest to them. The trouble was that both were stars, accustomed to centre-stage, to being the focus of attention, and a certain competitiveness was almost inevitable. The Princess was royal but Tony was magnetic, and wittier. There were arguments and, more ominously, the beginning of the put-downs, then usually disguised as a joke, that were later so to unnerve the Princess. In the late summer of 1963, invited to stay by the rich Greek shipowner Stavros Niarchos on his private island of Spetsopoula, friends on a nearby island held a party to celebrate Princess Margaret's birthday (on August 21). Tony arrived, bringing with him a present for everyone except his wife. Later a barbecue was planned and the Princess, upstairs, shouted down to Tony: 'Oh, darling, what shall I wear?' 'Oh, I think that ballgown you wore last week,' he replied. Margaret, knowing it was a celebration, aware of the grand Niarchos style and brought up in ballgown culture, suspected nothing and arrived downstairs dressed to the hilt to find everyone else in jeans and sand shoes.

Back at home, pregnant, bored and aware that her husband was steadily immersing himself more and more in his work and the coterie of those with whom he worked closely, she became more rather than less possessive, trying to track him down by telephone or turning up unexpectedly at restaurant or studio. Tony would return later and later, usually to disappear immediately to his basement workroom or to the office next door, where he would go through paperwork with the faithful Dorothy. His low boredom threshold, solipsistic view of the world, need to be surrounded by the witty, the beautiful or the entertaining, his instinct to push away a woman if he felt hemmed in by possessiveness or 'clinginess', and his scarcely conscious determination to do something or meet someone only when he wanted to, meant that he would often refuse Princess Margaret's demands that he 'come and meet X'. On these occasions, he would shut the door and refuse to come out, leaving Margaret, naturally imperious and brought up to believe that everyone would obey her slightest whim, at a loss.

Although the Princess had less to do than usual, Tony, conversely, had never been busier. There were still portraits – Charlie Chaplin laughing at lunch in a restaurant in Vevey, his napkin held up to his face, David Hockney in a Paddington street carrying a huge gold handbag (in an era when even a satchel worn by a man would have been looked at askance), Sophia Loren in an ornamental bath, her small naked son in the crook of one arm, the other stretched bare under a waterfall of dark hair, and the painter Lucien Freud. 'He couldn't have been nicer but I found him very frightening – he scared the shit out of me,' recalled Tony later. More importantly, there was the opening in October 1964 of the Snowdon Aviary at London Zoo, a 150-foot-long by 80-foot-high tour de force of gauzy metal net held up in pyramidical shapes by aluminium poles. Designed by Tony and two colleagues, it looked almost as weightless as the birds flying about inside it, yet the filmy mesh used 118 miles of wire.

To everyone's surprise, the difficulty was not keeping the Zoo's rare birds inside this futuristic structure but keeping the London sparrows out. Tony, who had been dreading that one of the birds inside would fly into the mesh, one day spotted a small bird in a corner with its beak bent back. He rushed off at once to speak to the curator, Mr Yelland, saying: 'It's happened – a bird has flown into the mesh and seriously damaged its beak.' Mr Yelland ran down, exclaiming 'Where, Tony, where?' When Tony pointed to the bird Yelland laughed and said: 'Tony, you fool – that's the bent-beaked flycatcher.'

The birth of their second child, Sarah Frances Elizabeth, in the nursery (converted to a delivery room) of 1A Kensington Palace on 1 May 1964, brought the Snowdons together again temporarily. Immediately, Tony sent Richard to the flower shop Feltons in the Brompton Road for a huge bouquet of flowers for his wife and, anxious not to go against the protocol that decreed that the Queen must be the first to know of the baby's birth and sex, instructed him: 'If they do it up in pink ribbon hide it, otherwise the press'll know that it's a girl.' An hour after the birth he was allowed to see Margaret and his daughter, then he telephoned the Queen, the Queen Mother, his own mother and his sister Susan. He sent the chauffeur, Avery, round to his father's latest dwelling, 61 Prince's Gate Mews, with a note. 'It was sweet of you to send Avery round with the note so early in the morning,' wrote Ronnie, 'and Jenifer and I were delighted to go round on Sunday and see her.'

Mother and baby were soon visited by the Queen Mother, sparkling with diamonds but clad in deepest black with black osprey feathers in her hat, as the Court was in mourning for the King of Greece. She was followed by Princess Alice, who came down the stairs remarking: 'This must be a very happy day for you, Elizabeth.' 'Well, it is, Alice,' responded the Queen Mother, 'but I find it so difficult to look convincingly happy in black.' Unfortunately, 'convincingly happy' would soon be a phrase that could not be applied to the Snowdon marriage.

8

Married Life

※

What struck everyone about the Snowdons during the first years of their marriage was the way in which their ideas and behaviour meshed. They worked as a team and their conversation, witty, funny, lighthearted and easy, each sparking off the other, reflected this. If the Princess was to make a speech, Tony would help her with ideas which she, quick to grasp anything new, would transmute into words and approach, so that the final draft was their joint work. When she spoke, he never took his eyes off her.

When they went on a royal visit to Copenhagen to mark British Week in Denmark it was as a team. Day by day they helicoptered to different Danish cities from the Fredensborg Palace of King Frederik and Queen Ingrid, whose guests they were, visiting stores and attending fashion shows and military tattoos. They were so effective that on 10 October 1964 the Ambassador wrote to say that he was 'lost in admiration of all you did,' adding, 'I do not myself see how any visit could have been a more complete success. The Danes loved you both; were flattered that you seemed to appreciate them and their country so much and were deeply impressed by your interest, energy and enthusiasm. If it's not cheek to say so, I think that you both managed to put over the picture of a modern and interesting Britain much better by what you said and did than any amount of preaching on our part.' Proof of this was the fact that there was a £6 million rise that year in sales of British goods to Denmark.

Margaret for her part, learning that Tony did not like animals, sent her two Sealyhams to Windsor, keeping only Rowley, the King Charles spaniel, but arranging for him to be exercised by the butler.

As the focus of attention herself, she would not always notice those small details by which an impression is made; Tony, intuitively quick in personal relations, would quietly remind her that a handshake in the kitchen of whatever house or embassy in which she had been staying would 'make the day' for the staff.

Nor did he forget those who had looked after him earlier. Nanny Gunner, the one constant presence in his life as a small boy, wrote to him on 20 July 1964 to thank 'My darling Tony' for his 'great generosity' in giving her a large cheque for her holiday and for asking her to Kensington Palace to see his children. 'I spent such a happy day with your little ones, and think Sarah is so sweet, a perfect baby, and David is just wonderful, he is already a good little host, and so like you were at that age,' she wrote fondly. And at the Docklands Settlement Ball at the Savoy on 30 November 1964, typically it was Tony who spotted that the young singer Julie Rogers's act had been cut out because the cabaret was running late and that she was holding back tears as the cast lined up to be presented. When Tony asked her why she had not appeared and she told him, he said: 'Couldn't you please come and sing for us upstairs?' Miss Rogers did so (and later wrote him a thank-you letter).

Although tensions had begun to show between the couple at times, there was no sign of these during the holiday they took in August 1964 as guest of Karim (always known as 'K'), the Aga Khan, taking with them numerous presents – a camera, telescope, cufflinks and some beautiful cutlery. K was in the process of launching an £80 million holiday complex on the Costa Smeralda, Sardinia, that he hoped would become a glamorous and elegant resort for the rich and stylish. He put the Snowdons up at the Hotel Pitrizza. For both of them it was a dream holiday, with its waterskiing, swimming in the clear, unpolluted waters around the island, and lazy days spent aboard K's yacht *Amaloun*, sailing to deserted bays, where they would anchor and picnic.

From Sardinia they went on to Venice, where they stayed with Janie and Jocelyn Stevens at the famous Palladian Villa Malcontenta. All of them had the impression it was haunted. In the evenings, if they were not going out, they would all sit very close together, with bedtime always bringing, in Janie Stevens's words, 'a slightly nervous feeling'. Princess Margaret would plan what they would do each day in the way of sightseeing, writing up her notes in the evening and questioning the others as to what they had seen.

The two couples would often go to Rome, where they would meet Judy and Milton Gendel, who lived in an elegant flat in the ancient Jewish quarter. Judy, formerly Judy Montagu and a great friend of the Princess, had sold her house in Walton Street at the beginning of 1958 and moved to Rome, marrying the art historian Milton Gendel in New York in April 1962. These Italian holidays became an idyllic summer pattern, full of jokes and laughing, sunshine and the wonderful sights of Italy. When they moved on somewhere, outriders rushed down small side streets, blowing their horns, the speed and dash appealing to the Italian love of fast cars. At first they were pursued everywhere by the Italian press; as one of them said to Janie, 'You have to remember that Princess Margaret and Elizabeth Taylor are the two most wanted women in the world.'

For Princess Margaret, Balmoral had always been a large part of her year. Tony had stayed there as her guest in their courtship days; now, as a fully fledged member of the royal family, he was, as it were, on the inside looking out, and for several weeks at a time – over the previous ten years, he had seldom had a holiday that had lasted longer than a fortnight and the need for hard, constant work had become etched into his psyche. The first summer he spent at the Scottish castle he arrived with numerous cameras; and some of the shots – notably landscapes – still hang on a corridor wall.

At first the novelty of life in the Castle, surrounded by members of his new family, was not only fascinating but meant paying attention to its customs and mores. In those early days there was a sense of being on trial: a few of the servants were not very polite (although never in front of the senior royals) and Prince Philip's habit of sitting down to a silent breakfast with the newspaper was somewhat unnerving. Then, too, although for the Queen, her sister and her mother Balmoral was the place where they felt most secure and relaxed, life there was hedged about with just as much protocol as at Buckingham Palace or Windsor Castle. Its picnics and barbecues, masterminded by Prince Philip, with the Queen making the salad or doing the washing-up in a small cottage on the estate, had faint overtones of the Petit Trianon while dinner at the Castle itself was formal. Black tie and long dresses were invariably worn even if it was just 'family', with numerous footmen in evidence. The Queen, who kept a silver box of dog biscuits on the table in front of her to feed the corgis from time to time, usually wore long-sleeved dresses, it was said to hide the scars on her arms from nips as a corgi tried to snatch a biscuit offered to one of its fellows.

Much etiquette surrounded the shooting for which Balmoral was famous. Punctuality for the nine o'clock start was essential, with the guns gathering near the line of beautifully polished dark green Land Rovers. Dress was tweed plus-fours or plus-twos with matching waistcoat, check shirt and tie, all in sludgy, dull green-brown shades that would blend into the heather, a tweed cap and coloured socks with flashes. Only Tony, with his constant urge to be somehow 'different', broke the code, with polo-neck sweaters and his own-designed baggy plus-fours or knickerbockers and, when shooting from Birkhall, sometimes a black umbrella. While shopping with the Princess in Ballater, he would sport knee-length leather boots and a jacket cut rather like an artist's smock. Another tease was to sit on a small stool on the Balmoral lawn pretending to cast when learning to fish.

But he was determined not to show up badly with the guns – the Duke of Edinburgh was a crack shot, as were many of the young officers from Scottish regiments such as the Gordon High-landers who were in attendance on the sovereign while she was in Scotland, and a number of the guests. It was not an ambience where someone known only as a photographer was expected to shine, but Tony was about to prove the doubters wrong.

Already a good shot from days spent shooting with his father, he polished up his skill by going for lessons to the West London Shooting School, where experts gave personal tuition, using clay pigeons – two in quick succession in front, then two behind, with his second gun handed to him by a loader. Tony's excellent eye, natural quickness of reaction and determination easily com-pensated for any handicap caused by his weak leg – here the Duke, with whom he got on well, always showed thoughtfulness in suggesting that Tony was driven to a stand or butt, rather than walk with the others. His bad leg also meant that he could not go stalking, as this meant walking, often miles, on the hill, with a ghillie to find the deer, followed by the actual stalk – sometimes hundreds of yards wriggling along flat on one's stomach through rough heather – to get close enough for an accurate shot (to the heart).

There was more shooting in late autumn at Windsor, where the Duke had generously given Tony five days – days on which he could ask friends like Jocelyn Stevens and Peter Sellers. When Sellers married Britt Ekland, she came down too. Neither the former Goon nor the glamorous Swedish actress fitted the usual pattern of Royal Lodge shooting guests, although they did their best to adapt to the general ambience of well-worn tweeds and well-trained gun dogs.

Sellers, who spent money like water on anything mechanical, from cameras to cars (and then usually tired of them), would come down equipped with wonderful guns – one purchase was a £1,200 12-bore from Purdeys – and togged out, as Britt recounted, in 'padded hacking jacket, boots, breeches and a Sherlock Holmes deerstalker. He also engaged an instructor who would shadow him, and shout "fire" every time pheasants flew overhead.' Unfortunately he was such a poor shot that he missed every bird. Eventually Tony and Jocelyn, one on each side of Sellers, took to standing a pace or two to the rear of his line of sight, crying 'Yours, Peter!' as a pheasant came over. As Peter shot – and invariably missed – so did Tony and Jocelyn, crying 'Yours, Peter! Well done!' as the bird tumbled from the sky. Sellers would beam with pride at his skill.

On these days, Tony managed to secure one democratic advance. The shooting party's luncheon consisted of excellent hot stews brought out in Thermos flasks to one of the buildings in the Park. The keepers did not share in these but were given, in Tony's words, 'any old thing'. As in his single days, when any attempt to treat his assistants as somehow inferior was icily rebuffed, this made him angry. 'I thought that we must all have the same food – it always made me frightfully left-wing if we didn't,' he said. 'So we got huge round Thermos flasks that you could put a lot in and we all had the same. It was a bit of an uphill struggle but gradually everything got better, after quite a long time.'

*

Sellers and Tony were also responsible for a fifteen-minute home movie made specifically for the Queen's thirty-ninth birthday in April 1965, paid for by Sellers to the tune of £6,000. It shows Sellers declaring that he is a quick-change artist and will now give his impression of Princess Margaret. 'I will now do, in what I can safely say is the world record time of six and one quarter seconds, my celebrated impression of Her Royal Highness the Princess Margaret!' He disappears behind a screen, flings various articles of clothing over it and then, a few seconds later, the real Princess Margaret emerges, curtseying and smiling. Britt played Queen Victoria (as a silent-movie vamp) and Tony alternated as a one-legged golfer and a homosexual gangster.

Royal Lodge, pink among its tall trees, was a constant weekend destination, varied by visits to Tony's mother at Birr or, for shooting weekends, Womersley. Princess Margaret, whose 'take' on her mother-in-law's theatricality was somewhat acerbic, would occasionally allow this to show. At one Womersley dinner, where grouse was on the menu, Anne Rosse pressed the Princess to indulge herself by emphasising the freshness and desirability of what was being served. 'Oh, Ma'am do take plenty – it's all shot on the estate.' 'Oh, Ma'am, do have some vegetables – they're all from the garden.' Then came the game chips – from which, unfortunately, a corner of blue salt packet appeared. It was too much for the Princess. 'From the garden, Anne?' she enquired dryly.

Tony's much-loved Old House, now rented by his friend Bob Belton, was just under two miles away from the Messel family house Nymans, where Anne Rosse often stayed in the small part of the building that had escaped the flames in the 1947 fire. Sometimes Margaret and Tony too would go down. While Belton was making Old House habitable – among other things, it had a virtually new roof – he would often stay with them at Nymans and the three would go to church at Staplefield the next morning, with visits to the Lanes in Brighton later. Although the Princess wore casual clothes, usually with a headscarf and dark glasses, she and Tony were the most recognisable couple in the kingdom and 'double-takes' were frequent. If they wanted to buy, this could be an embarrassment as when, in one antique shop, the owner asked nervously: 'Are you Princess Margaret?' When she replied, smiling,

'Yes,' he said, 'Can I offer you something?' As she remarked afterwards to Belton: 'That often happens and you can't say no, it would seem so rude, so you just have to find the cheapest thing you possibly can.'

At Nymans, they would often visit Lord and Lady Reading and their children, Simon, Anthony, Jackie and Alexander, born respectively in 1942, 1943, 1946 and 1957, who lived a scant quarter-mile from Old House. Belton had known the Marquis and Marchioness of Reading since long before the Snowdons' marriage when Jackie, a leggy teenager, already gave promise of great beauty.

In those days Belton, a dog-lover, would go over simply to walk with the Readings, their dogs, and his own. Once, when Margot Reading asked the Rosses, the Snowdons and Belton over for a drink, the youngest Reading son, aged seven, and in his pyjamas and dressing gown, had been told he would meet a real live princess before going to bed and had been carefully instructed what to do when he met her. As the party entered, he took one look at the two women – and marched straight up to Anne Rosse, dressed as usual as if off to a smart dinner party and glittering with diamonds, and solemnly bowed deeply. Much to Princess Margaret's amusement she, in her casual country tweed skirt, stood by completely ignored.

With Jocelyn and Janie Stevens, the Snowdons were the first visitors to their friends the Crewes' new house, Wootton House, five miles west of Bedford (to which the Crewes had moved soon after the birth of their daughter), arriving unexpectedly in the helicopter of their friend Tommy Sopwith.* It was the Crewes' first weekend in the house and it had not yet been done up. Princess Margaret spent the afternoon with Angie Crewe, tearing off old wallpaper from the drawing room wall.

There were holidays with the Aga Khan at the Costa Smeralda, with Harold Acton at the Villa La Pietra near Florence, and with the Stevenses in Rome and Venice. Sometimes they would visit friends like Andy Garnett, often back from France for weekends, when he would stay in his old flat in Limehouse, on the first floor

---

* Son of Sir Thomas ('Tommy') Sopwith, ace pilot and aircraft designer who founded the Hawker Siddeley Group.

with a steep staircase straight down to the pavement. When Tony and the Princess came to dinner Andy would get the local Chinese restaurant to send in food, the waiters walking along the nearby canal towpath holding dishes of their speciality, jellied fish. On one disastrous evening Garnett, leading the way downstairs to open the door for the Princess, stepped onto the pavement to see a car parked there with condoms filled with water hanging like balloons from the door handles, windscreen wipers and mud-guards. He drew back hastily, with Princess Margaret at his shoulder asking innocently, 'Andy, what are those?' while the embarrassed Andy groped for words. Tony, following behind, realised at once and told his wife while ushering her away. Garnett discovered later that it was the work of a neighbour from the next-door building.

One evening the Sellerses took Tony and Margaret to the little Beauchamp Place restaurant run by Lorenzo and Mara Berni. There were only nine tables in the single small basement room that led into a minute courtyard, the tablecloths were paper and prices were so low that it was not granted the credit card facilities then coming in. So venerated was royalty at that time, and so acknowledged were Tony and Margaret as the country's most glamorous couple, that when they first went there a party of Italian women from the Consulate, the Embassy and the media instantly rose to their feet and stood respectfully waiting until the Snowdons had taken their seats.

San Lorenzo quickly became a favourite haunt of Tony's, to escape to with friends from boring parties or to call into for a late meal or numerous glasses of wine and chat until three or four in the morning. Tony, proud of the strength acquired during his determined rehabilitation from polio, would arm-wrestle all comers, from the waiters to other customers – and always win. 'You have no idea how strong he was,' said Lorenzo later. 'I called him Fortebraccio – after all, his name is Arm-strong.'

After the Snowdons had been married for four years the demolition of the houses in Rotherhithe Street was scheduled, including the one that had seen so much of Tony and Margaret's courtship.

Sentimental reasons apart, it was something Tony disapproved of on both aesthetic and ethical grounds, fighting valiantly against it (or as the Chairman of the London County Council put it in a letter of 24 July 1964, 'we did not see eye to eye on the question'), writing in February 1964 that 'this row of houses is I believe unique; it is the only surviving relic of Canaletto's waterfront (comparable rows in Limehouse and elsewhere are of later date) ... this type of humble housing is particularly English but has now almost disappeared – the enclosed Canaletto book will show you what I mean'.

He continued – as he invariably did in such disputes – with constructive suggestions:

> Could not these houses be saved for their obvious charm, and adapted to a semi-public use so that their spectacular view of the river life would be widely enjoyed? One possibility that naturally interests me would be craft workshops, something like Williamsburg in the USA, Aarhus in Denmark or Digswell at Welwyn. London is the great centre of high-quality handwork, and most craftsmen are increasingly perplexed to find workshop accommodation. To adapt these houses as workshops would not be too difficult, and they would be a self-contained tourist attraction.
>
> Another possibility which might interest the British Council might be to adapt the houses to accommodate visitors from overseas. This area has very much more character than, for instance, north Kensington where so many of our friends from the Commonwealth and elsewhere make their one and only acquaintanceship with London.

But the LCC was unshakeable. They wanted it as an 'open space' in the planned Bermondsey Comprehensive Development Area. The Snowdons lost their romantic bolt-hole and that aspect of the river much of its charm.

Giving up the room at Rotherhithe brought into sharper focus something they had been thinking of in a desultory way for some time. Both agreed that what they needed, especially for the children, was somewhere in the country that actually belonged to them (their Kensington Palace apartment was, of course, the property of the Queen).

Tony was fortunate in that he had his work to escape to – and work for Tony was as much a need as food. It was stimulation, relaxation, fulfilment, it was the essential antidote to boredom – and, quite soon, it became a means of escape. He was not the type of person to spend the rest of his life walking two paces behind the Princess (nor would she have wished him to). Unlike the Duke of Edinburgh, who knew when he married the future Queen that one day he would have to abandon his profession and take on the secondary role of consort, and who poured his energy and enthusiasm into causes like the Duke of Edinburgh's Award and the World Wildlife Fund, Tony was determined to remain his own person, with his own career as far as possible intact.

Nor was he about to change his method of working. He had always put in long hours, driving himself with a ferocious energy and expecting those around him to do the same. His preferred ambience was workroom or studio, preferably with one other person there with whom he enjoyed a work-related intimacy – a photographic assistant whom he knew and liked, a fellow designer off whom to bounce ideas for a project or its completion, or simply someone who enjoyed making things as much as he did.

As the first years passed so did the intoxication of newly-wed life. The strangeness of being whisked to the theatre in mere minutes, flanked by outriders, of being stared at and admired, became everyday. His nature, full of enthusiasms, craving constant stimulation, his determination to do everything his way, his urge to break down or break free of barriers coupled with a constant, almost subliminal instinct to irritate, to scratch, to push at boundaries, reasserted itself.

The Princess had quite a different idea of marriage formed, not unnaturally, by those she had seen at the closest of quarters: her parents' and her sister's. In these, though both spouses had their own offices and areas of duty, togetherness was the general theme. Margaret spoke to her sister and her mother on the telephone constantly, she had never had lunch alone in her life and, after the closeness of their early times together, she expected that she would see Tony often during the day – and hers started much later than his. While she enjoyed partying late and seldom rose before at least eleven, Tony would get up early, breakfast in his dressing room and set off for his office at the Design Centre or the *Sunday Times*.

She found herself inventing things to do: washing the coral she had collected, sticking the sides of matchboxes on tumblers so that she would have something to strike a match on if she wanted to smoke while drinking whisky, and shampooing her spaniel Rowley in the bath ('I've told them I have to wash Rowley because he wouldn't like it if anyone else did') and then drying him with her hairdryer. As time passed, their different hours would be another of those discrepancies that drove a wedge between them. 'Darling, when you were in Scotland and I was here working in London I missed you very much indeed and longed for you to be with me,' runs one letter from Tony to his wife. 'But I managed to get a lot of work done mainly by going to bed at a reasonable hour and getting up early in the morning.'

Tony was determined to contribute to their considerable household expenses. Although the rates, heating and lighting, the costs of the official car, and the staff, secretarial and office costs needed to fulfil the Princess's official obligations came out of her annual Civil List allowance of £15,000, everything else had to be paid for. For Tony to do his share he needed to work; and to work he needed his sleep. To return home for lunch, sometimes breaking off arbitrarily in the middle of a job, would be difficult and time-consuming – more, it might smack of special privilege.

Brought to accept this, Margaret then had to face a husband absent for much of the evening: once home, Tony would usually dive into his office or workroom in the basement to deal with his numerous letters or, more likely, to spend time crafting something in the congenial company of a fellow designer. Usually this was James Cousins, who spent evening after evening making furniture – including the desk that Tony uses to this day – and being taught welding by him. Cousins was often asked to lunch or dinner and sometimes taken down to Royal Lodge – once, he had the unnerving experience of sitting between Princess Margaret and the Queen Mother on a sofa watching a television programme in which two teams of participants argued about whether the monarchy should be retained or abolished, after which there was a vote – won by the abolitionists. As he wondered what to say the Queen Mother sprang up. 'What do they know about being royal?' she exclaimed. 'I'm going to bed!'

Cousins was also cajoled into helping Anne Rosse with the Nymans garden – once falling out of a tree when cutting off a branch; taken to Abbey Leix, the home of Tony's sister Susan and her husband Lord de Vesci, he found himself involved in redesigning the kitchen along with other projects. He travelled with Tony on Design Council assignments, returning to Kensington Palace in a helicopter, flying in past the top-floor Hilton restaurant, its customers open-mouthed as they passed. One trip was to Northern Ireland, where Tony made his usual impact. 'I could eat him!' said one girl of Tony as they passed; with another, a deaf mute, Tony communicated in the sign language he had learned when a boy with polio; in Wales he made his first public speech on matters of design, aided by the faithful Cousins. He shone on these visits, of which the aim was to try and persuade manufacturers to come up with better-designed products.

His work for the Council was something Tony took extremely seriously and his views on design were trenchant, extending to the buildings he had studied as an architectural student – including why so many bad buildings are passed by planners. 'If you look at London from a helicopter it doesn't look half-bad. It's the same looking down on models of buildings and that's why a lot of things get passed. What you should do when looking at the model of a new development is to shove a handbag mirror inside the model so that you can see what the buildings will look like at ground level.'

Just as a city only 'works', he believes, if people of all incomes can live cheek by jowl, so good design, that functions well, is of the greatest importance. In pursuit of this aim, he never hesitated to express himself freely to the head of the Council of Industrial Design, Paul Reilly. 'I am writing to you today not as an old friend but because you are an old friend I feel I must be able to communicate with you as Director of the Council of Industrial Design in the frankest possible way,' begins one letter, written on Christmas Eve 1964. 'As you know, without sounding pompous or silly about it, I do mind desperately about the image of the COID ... and with the best intentions in the world I do not see how any editor can make an exciting story or pictures of those things that have won awards this year.' He went on to point out the faults in two award-winning chairs ('sharp corners that rub on your cuffs,' 'collapsible chair is totally unstable') and an electric convector heater that could be fused by any child pushing something into one of its openings. 'Paul, I do hope you do not mind me writing in this way but I felt there was no point in my seeing the design awards if I do not really say what I think of them,' he concluded. His genuine interest was much appreciated.

As Tony worked himself into his two new jobs the demands on his time increased, with correspondingly less for the Princess. It became noticeable that she was less and less welcome 'downstairs' – once, when they were making a bookcase with which she wanted to help, Tony simply told her to go away. Cousins, usually invited by the Princess to lunch or dinner when she knew he was working there, saw that Tony absented himself from these meals more and more.

During the day, her attempts to join him also met with rebuffs. Margaret, often with little to do and fascinated by Tony's world of writers, actors, painters and the generally well known, wanted to accompany him on his photography sessions for the *Sunday Times*, whereas he wanted these to be as anonymous as possible consistent with his new status – he would, for instance, always insist on going with his assistants in the same bus or train rather than in the car that was now usually sent for him. In any case, for a wife to accompany a husband during his work was something quite outside normal practice for any photographer; for Tony, already the focus of attention because of his quasi-royal status, it would have made life impossible – although himself famous, his professionalism, charm and gift of empathy ensured that he could quickly get rid of any feeling of constraint or self-consciousness, make his sitters relax, and thus capture the shot he wanted.

As it was, he was in a state of acute nervous tension before any important photograph. One colleague remembers him arriving very late at the flat of the great actress Edith Evans, something unusual for Tony, for whom punctuality was of prime importance. 'How could you do that to Edith Evans?' he was asked afterwards. 'I was actually early,' replied Tony, 'but I was sitting in my car outside shaking, asking myself: "How *do* you photograph Edith Evans?"'

For Margaret, accustomed to having her own way and still besottedly in love with her husband, Tony's explanations of the need for her to stay behind carried little weight and she would regularly telephone the studio or house where she knew he was working. To Tony, used to leading his life on his own terms, this devotion was stifling and increasingly he refused to take her calls. As Tony distanced himself so she became increasingly possessive. She would try and find out where he was lunching that day, several times turning up unannounced at the restaurant, its staff thrown into turmoil by her arrival. At a studio, an embarrassed assistant, aware from Tony's shaken head that he refused to speak to her, would say he was in mid-shot and could not be disturbed.

During the months leading to Sarah's arrival and their aftermath, she could hardly bear him out of her sight. When she heard the car return, she expected him to come straight to her – instead of which he went downstairs to where his secretary Dorothy Everard was waiting. She would ring for the butler, Malcolm, and say: 'Oh, Malcolm, I think Lord Snowdon's in – will you tell him I'm in the drawing room.' Tactfully Malcolm would respond, 'I think I'll just check, Your Royal Highness. It may be just Avery [the chauffeur].' Malcolm would tell Tony that the Princess wanted to see him, to which Tony would reply 'I'm not coming up – I can't. Tell her I've got work to do.' Malcolm would say: 'I can't say that, my lord. I'll have to tell her you'll be up when you can.'

Margaret's next ploy would be to tell Nanny Sumner to bring David down. In would come David in crisp white garments, Malcolm would be sent down again and this time Tony would, somewhat unwillingly, emerge. They would go into the garden, for tea on the lawn and games with David, Nanny Sumner interrupting frequently to say: 'Careful, my lord, you'll get him dirty.' 'Dirty, Nanny?' replied Tony one day. 'Look at this.' And he rolled David, squealing with delight, down the slope, soiling his immaculate white shorts and shirt.

When Tony travelled, Margaret hated it. After Richard, the under-butler, had returned from taking Tony to the airport, he would be called into the drawing room to find the Princess in tears, asking: 'Is Lord Snowdon on the plane?' When Richard replied: 'Yes, your Royal Highness,' there would be fresh tears.

Tony, of course, did not see the tears but only the behaviour that followed, which had the effect of making him yet more desirous of his old, wide-ranging freedom. Margaret, brought up by parents who never reprimanded her, unfamiliar with the word No and indulged by a father who adored her, was now in the grip of an all-consuming love that demanded constant proximity to its object while Tony, at the best of times, needed space – and could turn on those who threatened it too drastically. The result was that in the close-knit circle of his *Sunday Times* colleagues there was a tacit awareness that their star photographer welcomed ideas that led to trips abroad. What they did not know was that almost never, once abroad, did he write to or telephone his wife – who grew correspondingly more frantic in her efforts to track him down or at least to maintain contact.

One such trip was to Venice, with Bob Belton, to photograph Fonteyn and Nureyev. Here, too, there were telephone calls from Margaret. When she could not get through to her husband she would ask to speak to Belton, who was then forced into excuses ('I'm afraid he's on the stage, Ma'am'). 'Will you ask him to ring me?' the Princess would say. If Belton had to ring to find out that all was well at home the Princess would think that the call coming through from Venice was from her husband – only to find that it was his friend. 'Where *is* he?' she would cry unhappily. Only when Dorothy Everard managed to speak to him and said: 'I think you should ring. The clouds are very dark,' did he do so. For Dorothy, as for Belton, both of whom liked the Princess greatly but whose loyalty was to Tony, this position 'in the middle' was both unpleasant and embarrassing.

Margaret's almost hysterical possessiveness was partly based on the feeling that while he was away from her Tony would not necessarily be faithful. He went out without her to the sort of party where meeting beautiful girls was inevitable, he saw old girlfriends and, as she knew, his sexual appetite was demanding and constant.

The Snowdons were, of course, together when they entertained and then usually at their best. Their party at Kensington Palace given four days after *Private View* was published on 14 October 1965 was a spectacular success. Two years earlier, Tony had photographed Francis Bacon, Victor Passmore, Robert Madeley, William Coldstream, Frank Auerbach, William Scott and David Hockney for a *Sunday Times Magazine* feature, 'British Painting Now', and many of those included in the book came to the party, along with a crowd of Snowdon friends. It was noted how Princess Margaret went round talking to everyone, remembering all the names, often after a fleeting introduction, and the feeling of warmth in the air. Even the rivalrous Cecil Beaton, usually ready to find fault with one or other of the couple, was moved to write in his diary that night: 'I went to the KP party given to all the painters and sculptors by the Snowdons and enjoyed myself so much that when after a day's interval from the studio I returned there, it was with fresh strength and impatience to get started again.' The book was a huge success and there were many letters of congratulation, most of them on the lines written by Peter Sellers: 'A unique collection of the most vividly impressive photographs I have ever seen in one album. Love from P and B.'

In January 1965 Tony and the Princess went to stay with his sister Susan at Abbey Leix House in County Waterford, he wearing a suede overcoat that set a new fashion. Here there was an anti-British demonstration against them. A gang of nine men, who later appeared in court, had fused power lines, sawn down trees to block the roads, cut telephone wires and attacked a policeman with a petrol bomb before fleeing. Nothing daunted, Tony and Margaret drove out next day in an MG 1100, with escort, to the cheers of local people.

At the beginning of February there was a visit to Royal Lodge, where every year the Queen Mother spent the anniversary of her husband's death (6 February 1952) attending Holy Communion at nine in St George's Chapel, Windsor. Here tempers flared again. Margaret was determined to remain at Royal Lodge and Tony wanted to go to Nymans and Old House; they marched up and down the drawing room shouting at each other before setting off for church, where they sat side by side in the front pew. As the chaplain intoned the familiar sentences of the Communion service the words 'love and fellowship' seemed curiously inappropriate to those sitting behind the two rigid backs.

Increasingly, the activities Tony threw himself into seldom

involved the Princess. Later in February he went skiing again at Klosters with friends – without her. In March he flew to Dublin to spend the weekend with his sister Susan, whose eighteen-month-old daughter had died some weeks earlier.

Unsurprisingly, rumours that there was a rift in the marriage began to trickle out, so strongly that when Tony went to Venice, to stay at the Villa Malcontenta, taking with him his friend Bob Belton, the only time the pair could see Venice – Tony with his hat pulled down, a scarf hiding most of his face and dark glasses – was in the early morning or late evening, such was the pursuit of the pack of press photographers. At the same time, he was zealous in trying to help his friends through their own marital troubles: 'Darling Tony,' wrote Camilla Fry from Widcombe, 'We were both so grateful to you the other night, slogging all that way down – it is very comforting to know that someone minds so much about one's happiness but it seems so awful that you only come down here now to sort out disasters.'

The chatter about the Snowdon marriage stopped for a while when they went on an official visit to Uganda on 13 March 1965, but they were only briefly together; almost immediately on their return Tony went to stay again with Susan.

It was a time when he flung himself into physical activities. In July he lapped the 37-mile Grand Prix course on the Isle of Man on a Triumph 650cc Twin with a friend, Dennis Craine. The first time round, on open roads, took forty-four minutes; the second time, with the roads closed, he achieved a lap record of twenty-one minutes. He took up waterskiing and Princess Margaret, realising that this was a sport in which she could successfully join him, also took it up and soon did very well. Both enjoyed it so much that it became a favourite activity, and with Simon Sainsbury they shared a speedboat on one of the lakes in Windsor Great Park – a flooded former gravel pit – with tuition from the English National Water Ski Champion, until the paparazzi got wind of it and hovered about, waiting for shots of the Princess in her wetsuit or, better still, the possibility of her crashing into the water.

This harassment, especially by a photographer called Ray Bellisario, got so bad that the Queen's Press Secretary, Commander Richard Colville, wrote to the Press Council about it. His letter included a vivid description of two of these pests, one from the *Daily Express* and one a freelance, who were discovered lying hidden in the undergrowth around the lake, cameras trained on the hut where the Princess was changing and who were, in Colville's words, 'escorted off the property'. Thereafter their privacy was more respected and the waterskiing continued for a time. Sometimes they would invite friends like Pamela Colin,* taking them back to Royal Lodge afterwards for lunch, where the Queen Mother might join them ('You don't know what it's like to curtsey in a wetsuit,' said Pamela).

In the summer of 1965 Jeremy Fry bought Le Grand Banc, a small hamlet in the Luberon, Provence – a group of seven old, half-ruined houses built of the local silver-coloured stone and set in lavender fields above a deep gorge known as the Canyon of Oppedette. He planned it as a community where friends could stay or those with a 'cultural problem' to work out could live, with a communal kitchen and dining room in one house and a hi-fi system in the converted stables for dancing. Later, it would provide a reunion setting for Tony, his family and old friends.

At home, Tony had taken a photograph (in May 1965) that was to prove iconic. It was for a feature on children, showing the dreadful conditions in which many grew up. One of the 700–odd shots Tony took shows both his compassion and instant perception of misery. The subject, a small, filthy, two-year-old boy,† is wearing an outsize shirt buttoned in an attempt to hide the bruises on his legs; Tony saw at once that they were there and adjusted the shirt to let them show. The feature, called 'Some of our Children', was published on 29 August in the *Sunday Times Colour Magazine*, with Tony's shot on the cover. Later the NSPCC used it in their fundraising campaign.

Along with the harrowing subject matter of some of these 'social realism' features came lighter moments. 'David, do you spend a

---

* London Editor of American *Vogue* from 1963 until 1969, when she married Lord Harlech.

† The boy, Peter Roche, later wrote of his experiences in *Unloved: The True Story of a Stolen Childhood*, published by Penguin in 2007.

lot of time thinking about young girls?' Tony asked the noted art critic of the *Sunday Times*, David Sylvester, as they left Brighton to drive to Cambridge. Sylvester looked out of the window, remaining so deep in thought that Tony gave up the idea of conversation. Finally, as they neared Cambridge, he turned to Tony and said simply 'Yes'.

That summer Tony and Margaret went to Italy together, first to the south, then to Rome, to which they drove, smiling and tanned, Tony stripped to the waist in the heat. Their car was a custom-built blue and silver open-topped Aston Martin that Tony had bought for £3,000 (a fraction of its market value) from Peter Sellers. Sellers, anxious to keep in with the royal couple, would give, or sell to Tony for almost nothing, any of the gadgets and machinery he bought so freely that Tony admired, from camera lenses to stereo equipment. Tony passionately loved the car, which had only done 5,000 miles; once, at 4 a.m., he drove from Kensington Palace to Windsor in it in twelve minutes.

The car immediately caused press interest; whatever the Snowdons did was the subject of speculation or comment. 'I am extremely upset and depressed, as I know you are,' wrote Sellers to Tony on 17 September 1965, 'about the general position with the press. It seems there is no way for us to carry on our friendship without some t—t misconstruing something or other, somewhere, some time. ... As you know, with the Aston Martin, they phoned me in Ischia and asked me if I had sold it to you. I said the car was still in my possession and I had not sold it. Fortunately, nobody followed that up, but they could easily have done by checking the registration ... maybe the best thing is to find some set piece to trot out to press people.'

In Rome, where they went to stay with Judy Montagu and her husband Milton Gendel, there was a scene, culminating in Tony climbing out of a window and up onto the roof. 'It's the only place I can get away from her,' he said of his wife. And on the roof he remained until persuaded down by Jocelyn Stevens, who had been rung by the frantic Margaret when her own pleas to come down had met with no response – Jocelyn and Janie Stevens had come out to Rome to join the Snowdons. When they went to Balmoral that year Tony lopped a good fortnight off his visit.

*

On 4 November they flew to the United States for a hectic three-week five-city tour. Like all royal visits, it had entailed an exhaustive amount of detailed planning (there are four large boxes on this trip alone in the Royal Archives), first involving an earlier investigative visit by the Princess's Treasurer and Private Secretary, Major the Hon. Francis Legh,* that July during which he sorted out queries ranging from whether or not the Princess would express her delight at being on the West Coast for the first time when she arrived in San Francisco (she would) to laying down ground rules for photographers – 'no flashbulbs nearer than twelve or fifteen feet and no pictures to be taken during a meal'.

The couple were besieged with invitations, ninety-seven of which had to be turned down with a charming note ('Time will not permit her Royal Highness's meeting you on this visit but she wanted you to know how greatly she appreciated your thought in writing'). Presents were bought to bestow, chiefly photograph frames and silver or gold hexagonal pencils, timetables and outfits for each day worked out and brief biographies of each person they would meet typed up: 'Alice Longworth – Mrs Longworth is eighty-one and the daughter of President Roosevelt. She is the widow of a distinguished speaker of the House. Mrs Longworth has for many years been active in the social life of Washington.'

Although Tony had been to the United States before, Margaret had not and her excitement was intense. With them went the Princess's friend and lady-in-waiting Lady Elizabeth Cavendish, to whom Tony also was devoted. Whether it was Lady Elizabeth's healing presence, the pleasure of new sights, the great success of the trip or a mixture of all three, it brought them back to the days when they worked as a partnership, joking, laughing and loving instead of fighting. The only sour note was the implication (in the British press) that they spent their time at parties and that the trip, which cost the Foreign Office £30,000, was a barely disguised promotional tour for Tony's book *Private View*.

Tony, who realised the importance of impressions disseminated by the press, immediately sought to put the matter straight. He

---

* Three years later he was awarded the KCVO.

pointed out one unassailable fact: that only evening occasions had been covered and their official appointments – they had two days off in two weeks – were ignored. His book, he added, had sold 45,000 copies in the US, all the profits from which were given to charity. In the House of Commons, the President of the Board of Trade was able to tell Willie Hamilton, the constant scourge of the royals, that Margaret's visits to British fashion shows and promotions of British goods in New York and Los Angeles had neither been arranged nor subsidised by the Board of Trade.

That winter of 1965/6, when Tony planned to go skiing with the Frys, Stevenses and Bartons, Margaret insisted on coming too. 'She's fucked up my holiday,' muttered Tony crossly. Although, in ordinary life, it would be perfectly normal for a wife who wanted to accompany her husband on a skiing holiday to expect to do so, and to be made welcome by everyone else, there was some justification in Tony's remark.

Apart from the press photographers – then just beginning to be known as paparazzi – who surrounded them whenever she and Tony were together, Margaret brought both her ordinary routine and her imperious ways to what should have been the hard exercise and informality of the ski slopes. She spent all morning in bed while Tony, who adored skiing, got up early. Just before lunch she would emerge fresh from her bathroom to drink several glasses of gin before lunch. In the evening when the others, physically tired after a day on the slopes, felt like bed, Margaret wanted to stay up late drinking whisky and being entertained. One evening the others came back from skiing to find Barton's wife Eva with an odd-looking coiffure, half-curly and half-straight – she had been having her hair done when a frantic message came through that Her Royal Highness wanted some company, so Eva had to leave the salon with her hair half-done.

Tony did not make things easier. He and Barton skied together, since they were the weakest skiers. 'Make sure he gets to our meeting place at the right time,' the others told Barton, 'because if she's kept waiting things will go wrong.' Tony, well aware of this, would either ski down very fast and then claim innocently that there was time for another run, which would of course cause them to be late or, foiled, suggest: 'Well, we'll stop and have a drink', with the same result. It made for a heavily unpleasant atmosphere.

Home again, both slipped into their old habits, the Princess bored and unhappy, Tony escaping as much as possible from the confines of royal duties and routine. In January 1966, the *Sunday Times* proposed an assignment in India. As both the Queen and Prince Philip knew, the relationship between Britain and India then needed handling with great care, and Prince Philip wrote to warn Tony that the Indian government were 'very sensitive and touchy about poverty' at that moment but that if Tony treated it in a way that showed they were trying to improve things, as a sympathetic observer, he would be very welcome. It was excellent advice and Tony took it.

At the time, Anthony Barton, handsome, engaging and Sarah's godfather, was staying with the Snowdons as he always did on his visits from France on business. This time it was to be more prolonged than usual. 'If you're going to be away I'd better go,' remarked Barton to Tony as they sat at dinner. 'No, no,' said Princess Margaret, 'if you do you'll go off and find some girlfriend – much better stay here.' Tony added his voice and Barton agreed. Tony left for India on 4 February. Then, one evening, with no preliminaries, Margaret said to Barton: 'Let's go to bed.' Startled, he replied: 'No, I think our relationship's not that.' She edged closer and said: 'Well, I think you could be a bit more cuddly.' Few men could have resisted her, and Barton did not.

Their affair was spread over several months, dependent on Barton's visits. But his conscience was troubling him and he had no intention of endangering his marriage – and even at the time he felt that there was more than a hint of revenge in her enthusiasm for him. An affair with one of her husband's oldest and closest friends was, after all, a classic way for a lonely and neglected wife to strike back. 'No one need ever know,' said the Princess. And for a while, they did not.

The year 1966 had begun badly. On 27 January Ronnie died of cancer at Plas Dinas. He was only sixty-six. Tony and Princess Margaret attended his funeral at the nearby ancient church of Llanwnda, along with local farmers, neighbours and tenants.

To Tony's annoyed surprise the family property did not pass to him as Ronnie's eldest son. Instead, the Plas Dinas estate – the house, a collection of cottages and farmland – was left to his young half-brother, Peregrine, who would come into it at the age of twenty-five. The main farm, by the house, was sold to pay death duties. Ronnie made his motives clear in a letter, dated 5 June 1963, to his executors:

> My object was to provide primarily for those of my family who most need financial support and also to ensure as far as possible that Plas Dinas should be retained in my family.
>
> Both my daughter Susan and my son Tony are well provided for and I have therefore given to each of them in my will such a sum as I thought my Estate could afford as a mark of my great affection for them. I also gave them each a substantial monetary present during my lifetime.
>
> I have provided in my Settlement that my Plas Dinas property and the settled funds should go to my son Peregrine on his attaining the age of twenty-five or if he dies before that age leaving children, to his eldest son or daughter.
>
> If these trusts fail then the property and the settled funds will go to my son Tony.
>
> I am anxious that the property, particularly Plas Dinas house and garden, should stay in the family. If Tony is unable to retain it I earnestly hope that he will either transfer it or make it available for some other member of our family who is able to make reasonable use of it.
>
> I should like this letter to be shown by you to Tony as soon as possible after my death.

Ronnie left various bequests. The family silver – and Ronnie's fishing tackle – went to Peregrine, each of his grandchildren was left £500, and Susan and Tony each got £2,500.

Tony also inherited certain personal effects, among them his father's elegant dress studs, onyx with a diamond in the centre. By now he had enough jewellery to fill a brown leather box, lined with brown velvet, that he designed for it. There were numerous cufflinks – his favourites, garnet with a diamond star centrepiece, were a present from Princess Margaret; several of the fashionable tie or cravat stickpins, some with diamond crescents or motifs, one favourite one in ruby and gold; the small, flat gold lighter that he usually carried and another, larger, handmade gold one; and a gold watch given to him as a wedding present by Tom Blau, the head of Camera Press, the agency that syndicated his photographs.

The little watch was a reminder of earlier, carefree days. He was finding the difficulties of being a working photographer and, to put it bluntly, accessory to a public personage, difficult to reconcile – especially with the added discrepancies of their very different ways of life and hours of sleeping. Although nobody enjoyed the grand elements of being royal more than Tony, the straitjacket of protocol was beginning to irk him. His natural instinct towards perversity ('he always likes to come in through a different door,' as one friend put it) reasserted itself, in everything from his clothes to his behaviour. Sometimes it took the form of simple rudeness, as Cecil Beaton recorded in his diary on 5 July 1966. 'Once Sellers was having lighting for some sculpture installed in the garden and asked Tony's advice which he was giving when Princess Margaret, sucking at a long cigarette holder, sidled up and said, "Don't you think it would be better if ... " to which Tony answered her by telling her to piss off.'

Added to this there were his inborn restlessness and his unstoppable urge towards new sexual conquests. Both he and Margaret were people for whom sex was important and their marriage had been one in which physical passion played, and continued to play, a large part. Tony, however, resisted few of the opportunities that came his way, as well as maintaining contact with old girlfriends, as he would do all his life. His world was one in which both long relationships and casual encounters coexisted. One account of him at a party given by Kenneth Tynan describes Princess Margaret telephoning to find out if her husband was there and Tony, with a beautiful black model on his lap, making negative signs. To the embarrassment of many at the party Princess Margaret, sitting alone in Kensington Palace, asked innocently who was there, and then asked to have a chat with those she knew.

There were, of course, still many occasions when they entertained or went out together – such as a July dinner with Anthony Barton, his wife Eva and others at the new and exciting Post Office

Tower restaurant which, high above London, revolved slowly above the glittering panorama of lights. But beneath the surface there were painful misunderstandings, communicated to each other by long handwritten letters, Tony's often delivered the night before he left on a trip to avoid a confrontation. One read:

> I am so looking forward to coming home, but I am somewhat saddened that you yet again choose to ignore my advice about going to bed at a reasonable time, instead staying up till 5.30 and 3.30 insensitively with Anthony .... it really isn't good for you continuously to stay up so late drinking and so on.... If things are not going very well at the moment, then please darling do discuss things with me and I'm sure we can straighten it out. I was rather shocked that you took such pride in telling me that you had had only three half-hearted affairs this time and it was much better when I was in India. All I ask is not to make it too obvious.

His letter concluded: 'I love you very much, darling, and everything can be all right if you want it to be. Maybe we both have made a lot of mistakes. Everyone does, but let's try, not only for the children's sake but also because you are such a marvellous person and I love you, to just get together and work and have fun.'

Margaret pointed out that when she asked him about his work he did not answer, but when she did not he accused her of taking no interest. What she found difficult to bear, she said, was 'the silent treatment, the dreaded fed-up sighs, the flouncing out'. Her letter, written on 3 July 1966, was pleading and loving – 'you are such bliss to be with when you're sweet and laughing and clever so I'll try all in my power to please you if you'll give me some nice cosy affection'.

In an effort to sort out their difficulties, Tony suggested that Margaret visit a psychiatrist (she had earlier suffered from a mild degree of post-natal depression), the well-known Dr Peter Dally. It was not a success. 'Tony sent me to him,' Margaret confided to a friend later. 'He said it would be the answer. But I only lasted one session – I didn't like it at all. Perfectly useless!'

Both agreed they needed a place of their own. They looked at houses together in the hope of finding a suitable one to buy, but what Princess Margaret did not realise was that Tony had not given up hope of Old House. Their search was chiefly in the West Country, near their friends the Frys, a factor discounted when in 1966 the Frys' marriage finally broke up. For Tony this was a devastating blow. To him the Frys were the golden couple, their beautiful eighteenth-century house was almost a second home, it was here that he and these two people whom he loved, and was loved by, had spent hours of fun, warmth and joyousness.

On the Frys, the ethos of the sixties had taken its toll: there had been too many infidelities, too much blurring of moral certitudes, for the marriage to survive. Camilla struggled against Jeremy's sexual indifference and lack of jealousy, Jeremy chose novelty in the shape of sculptor Lynn Chadwick's wife Frances. When Camilla discovered Jeremy's affair with Frances, she had petitioned for divorce, although she later withdrew the claim and there was a reconciliation. But for the Chadwicks it was too late: Chadwick decided to bring his own petition for adultery, naming Jeremy Fry as co-respondent. Before Chadwick's petition came to court, there was tragedy. Frances realised that she had left her husband and children for a man whose feelings, as he told her when questioned, were not the equal of hers. In the ensuing emotional turmoil of misery and guilt, she killed herself. She was found in her Paddington flat on 3 November 1964 with the gas turned on and newspapers at the door and windows. The Fry marriage had lingered on for another two years.

Then came another blow. At home in France, Barton had left one of Margaret's letters lying about – and his wife Eva picked it up and read it. It meant the end of the affair, which, despite the fallout, was to Barton a relief. The only problem was that the couple were just about to go and stay with the Snowdons again. Eva Barton felt that as nothing had come into the open they might as well pretend that nothing had happened. But this course of action proved impossible for her to sustain – and one evening she went to Tony and told him what had gone on. It cannot have been a total surprise, as Margaret had confided in several people; while others must have noticed those minute, seemingly insignificant but tell-tale signals that pass between two people with a sexual link.

It was what Tony had suspected – and indeed, he had almost thrown his wife and his friend together – but preferred to ignore. Earlier still, when the couples were staying together at Royal Lodge, he had said to Barton: 'I wish to hell she'd take a lover and leave me in peace.' Nevertheless, when faced with incontrovertible proof of Margaret's unfaithfulness he was deeply upset. He went to Barton in tears, but tried to cover his red eyes and sniffs by explaining: 'I've got a terrible cold.' There was no serious acrimony but the Bartons left straightaway. 'I'm sure we'll see each other again,' said the Princess to Barton as he said goodbye. 'I wonder,' he replied. It was not until many years later, at Sarah's confirmation, that the couples met again (the Princess wrote to ask both of them). A tentative relationship was resumed. Then, when the Bartons' son, who was Tony's godson, died, all Tony's former warmth and affection for his old friend came rushing back. Generously, he told him: 'I forget what that thing in the past was – it's all forgotten now.'

An invitation from the Aga Khan to stay on the Costa Smeralda in Sardinia again helped tighten the bonds of the Snowdons marriage: sunshine and sea always had a beneficial effect on them both. Tony arrived loaded with presents for K – well-designed knives and forks, a camera, a telescope, photographs of their friends and cufflinks. 'I cannot thank you enough, dear Tony,' wrote K on 6 September 1966, 'for having given me a wonderful holiday on the Costa Smeralda because it is thanks to you that I was able to get away from time to time, and for having spoilt me in such a really wonderful way.'

The happy memories of the holiday were shattered by a shock on 5 October, when Tony learned that his former stepmother, now Carol Lopez, had been killed in a car crash. He flew out straightaway to attend her funeral in Rome on 7 October.

Only a fortnight later, on 21 October 1966, came news of one of the greatest peacetime disasters in British history. At 9.15 a.m. the children of Pantglas Junior School in the Welsh mining village of Aberfan, in South Glamorgan, had just finished prayers and returned to their classrooms after singing 'All Things Bright and

Beautiful' when, in the words of one survivor, 'there was a roar like the end of the world'.

Invisible through the fog that shrouded the village, an avalanche of pit waste had begun its slide down the mountainside from the tip 500 yards above. Less than thirty seconds later millions of tons of mine waste, boulders, rock, sludge and water crashed down to engulf the school, first destroying a farm cottage above it and killing all the occupants, and then enveloping about twenty houses in the village below. Fifty-six children (there were 254 on the register) and two teachers were saved then or later; mercifully, a number from a nearby village, delayed by the fog, had never reached the school. The total number of deaths proved to be 144, 116 of them schoolchildren.

Tony learned of the disaster when telephoned by a friend he had made on one of his Design Council tours, Mervyn Jones, head of the Gas Board, who lived in Cardiff ('we called him Jones the Gas'). Every drop of Welsh blood in his veins rushed to the fore and he knew he had to go to Aberfan at once. Normally so meticulous about protocols and permissions, for once he did not consult the Palace as to whether he should do this. When Princess Margaret asked him why he had to dash down straightaway he simply replied: 'Because I'm Welsh.' Richard Wood packed his case, including a shovel, and took him to Paddington to catch the overnight train, so that he could be there as early as possible. He arrived at Cardiff at 2 a.m., where Mervyn Jones met him and they drove to Aberfan.

The scene of grief and desolation that confronted them was terrible – parents attempting to dig, often with their bare hands, stunned survivors standing around, some with possessions because they had been told to evacuate their houses. Tony was taken straight to the mortuary at Bethania Chapel, where a queue of about fifty, mostly fathers, were waiting outside to identify the bodies of their children; when he emerged, he looked grey and shattered. He was taken to the nearby house of the Lord Lieutenant for some sleep but could not rest and returned at 6.30 a.m. to the village.

Attempting to help would have been no good. Tony, like the others who had arrived armed with shovels, quickly realised

Tony in the 1950s outside a bric-a-brac shop in the Portobello Road. He relied heavily on such shops for furnishing his studio.

Jacqui Chan, the beautiful 18-year-old actress and dancer who in the mid-1950s became Tony's regular girlfriend.

Jacqui and Tony on Tony's motorbike.

Old House as it was when Tony took friends down in the 1950s.

The front hall of Old House, furnished by Oliver Messel, in the early days. The large kettle in which water was heated for baths can be seen ready for use on the log fire.

The plumbing at Old House was non-existent. Tony's friend Bob Belton takes an alfresco bath in water drawn from the well outside the front door.

Tony beginning the remodelling of the garden at Old House.

The back of Rotherhithe Street as it was when Tony had his room there. Number 59 is the house nearest the camera. Tony's ground-floor room, beneath the bay window, had five narrow windows looking out onto the Thames.

The photographer conducting a sitting, 1958.

The official portrait of Princess Margaret for her twenty-ninth birthday in August 1959, taken by Tony during their secret courtship. Bob Belton, acting as photographer's assistant, had wound an elastic band round the far side of her pearls to shorten them into a choker.

Crowds in the Mall
on their wedding day,
6 May 1960.

The newly married Tony and Margaret wave from the balcony
of Buckingham Palace.

David's christening at Buckingham Palace. *Left to right standing*: Tony, Lady Rosse, Princess Marie Louise (hidden behind the Queen Mother), Princess Alice, the Duchess of Kent, Prince Charles, Prince Philip, Ronald Armstrong-Jones, the Duke of Gloucester. *Seated*: Queen Elizabeth the Queen Mother, the Queen with Prince Andrew, Princess Margaret holding David, Princess Anne seated on floor.

Princess Margaret with the Snowdons' first child, their son David,
Viscount Linley.

that he would only have got in the way of the trained rescue teams. Instead he listened to those who wanted to pour out their feelings, went into houses and made cups of tea for weeping men and women or tried to comfort them in silence. All the compassion in his nature, veiled from those close to him by a wall of emotional inarticulacy and flippancy, bubbled up like magma in the presence of this awful, awesome tragedy peopled by the figures of those trying to rescue the children. He was the first member of the royal family there and his presence was appreciated by the sorrowing community; his gift for empathy made him instinctively choose the right words or remain silent when words were inappropriate.

As the Prime Minister, Harold Wilson, wrote in his diary:

> The highest praise was for Lord Snowdon. He had gone spontaneously and instead of inspecting the site, he made it his job to visit the bereaved relatives, sitting holding the hands of a distraught father, sitting with the head of a mother on his shoulder for half an hour in silence.
>
> In another house he comforted an older couple who had lost thirteen grandchildren – in another where they were terribly upset he offered to make a cup of tea, went into the kitchen and returned with a tray with cups for them all. He helped an older man persuade his son, who was clutching something in his tightly clenched fist, to open his hand. It was a prefect's badge, the only thing by which he had been able to identify his child ...

Holding back his own feelings was difficult for Tony, but as he said later:* 'You couldn't cry. It's showing your emotions too much and you shouldn't if you're down to help. It's a bit like a doctor crying. Also, crying when they have lost their children is almost impertinent.'

He also managed to visit the hospitals, talk there to the nurses and those who had been saved. One of these, nine-year-old Bernard Thomas, who had been reading a book when the disaster happened, was taken to St Tydfil's Hospital with his younger brother Andrew. There, Tony sat on his bed and helped the two boys colour in a picture of a steamship. The day was so long that he

---

* To the author.

could not return that night; the following morning Prince Philip arrived.

When Tony returned, he scribbled a note to the Princess:

Darling, it was the most terrible thing I have ever seen. I managed to get to see everyone in both the hospitals and also visit a lot of homes. I gave your love and sympathy to everyone, especially the nurses, and it cheered them up a lot.

I'm sorry, darling, I couldn't come up last night. I asked Philip what he thought, and he thought that people would understand. I tried to ring you again this morning but you weren't awake yet. I somehow could not go to bed last night although I'd only had under two hours the night before. I just drove around thinking. It was all so awful seeing grown men, really tough miners, crying and crying. One turned to me and said: 'I've lost both mine – Tony, you'll understand, because you have two as well.' Then coming home and seeing David and Sarah and realising it was children just like them . . .

Two days later, Tony was still in such distress that at 7 a.m. on Sunday morning, with Margaret away, he rang up James Cousins to ask: 'Could we meet?' adding, with what must have been a subconscious memory of its therapeutic powers, 'Could we go over to Old House?' But the Cousinses were going out to lunch and, instead, took him with them.

Aberfan was a memory that would haunt him for years. 'It was awful, awful, awful. Partly what made it so terrible was the sheer numbers. I went on thinking about it for days, months, years. I think it was probably the worst day of my life.' Years later, at a party in Cardiff he had organised, Tony's half-brother Peregrine was approached by Lord Tonypandy, who as George Thomas had been a minister at the Welsh Office at the time of Aberfan and was later a famous Speaker of the House of Commons. 'I just must say to you', said Lord Tonypandy to the youthful Peregrine, 'that when Aberfan took place your brother changed everything for a lot of people.' It was a tribute as heartfelt as it was deserved.

9

Harsh Words

❊

Like jagged rocks revealed as the tide of passion ebbed, certain inescapable facts in the Snowdon marriage were becoming ever more obvious. Tony was never going to spend his time as a permanent number two, his prime job to be the perfect royal consort. He loved the perks and the prestige of being royal but he also wanted, to use an idiom that was just coming in, 'to do his own thing'. Chiefly this was because of his urge to work, but it also involved the streak of contrariness in his nature that manifested itself in various floutings of established custom or order. Equally Margaret, despite dipping her toes in Tony's world, would go on fulfilling the royal role to which she had been brought up – and behaving in the way she had always behaved. 'She was royal in an age when the old-fashioned Queen-Mary-type royalty was diminishing,' said her cousin Lord Lichfield. 'She was very much a schizophrenic in that sense – the moment people became too matey her reaction was "Don't forget who I am".'

Above all, both were used to being at the centre of the limelight – and both had grown up used to having their own way. Nor was either about to change. Confrontations were inevitable, yet the mutual attraction was still there and no matter what rows they had, sleeping together was still a regular and enjoyable part of their life.

Inside their marriage, each was feeling isolated. The words written by Francis Wyndham in his article on loneliness that appeared in the *Sunday Times Magazine* of 18 December 1966, with its evocative accompanying photographs by Tony, must have held a certain resonance for them: 'Loneliness may be defined as the condition of an individual who desires contact with others but is unable to achieve it. This inability may be inherent in his or her character, or it may be due to external circumstances. Thus, there are two types of lonely people: the temperamental and the temporary. For the first ("Hell is other people") salvation may lie only in the mysteries of psychiatry; but for the second ("no man is an island") something sometimes can be done.' For the Snowdons, this meant reaching out to other people.

For some time, 'other people', as Tony would later vaguely put it, had been part of his life. These minor infidelities were so discreetly conducted that no one outside his immediate circle realised that he had taken this or that girl home – nor could they have known at what time he returned to Kensington Palace. Some rumours spread across the Atlantic: newspapers reported that Tony's friendship with the beautiful American editor Pamela Colin had caused a secret discussion on divorce at Buckingham Palace, an allegation hotly denied by the Princess's Press Secretary, Major John Griffin.

Some affairs were more visible. Kenneth Tynan, never the most discreet of men, would retail hilarious stories of these short-term liaisons to close and trusted friends like the Gilliatts. But as far as the general public was concerned, Tony's persona was one of great talent, genuine hard work and a growing compassion for unfortunates – all of which was true.

Margaret had become aware of Tony's interest in other women and what seemed a growing antipathy towards herself. She was beautiful, she was wretched and she was still in love with her husband. She had not even begun to contemplate the possibility of her marriage breaking up but she hated finding herself more and more alone and she was used to male admiration and male company.

Towards the end of 1966, one of the men she had known since she was eighteen came back into her life as more than the friend he had formerly been. This was Robin Douglas-Home,* a charming, sensitive, lighthearted dilettante who had been commissioned into

---

* Nephew of the Prime Minister Sir Alec Douglas-Home (later the 14th Earl of Home) and his brother the playwright William Douglas-Home.

the Coldstream Guards but later joined an advertising agency. He was a talented pianist who played at smart hotels like the Ritz and the Berkeley and was well known for his love affairs. One of the first women he fell seriously in love with was Princess Margaretha of Sweden but he was seen off by the Swedish royal family, who did not consider a nightclub pianist a suitable match for the young princess. In 1959 he married the beautiful eighteen-year-old model Sandra Paul.* This, however, did not stop him pursuing other women and in 1965 Sandra was granted a divorce on account of his adultery.

But he was much more than just a charming lothario. He was popular with men and women alike: his photograph albums were full of off-duty photographs of the famous who had become his friends – Jackie Kennedy, Elizabeth Taylor and Richard Burton. He was also sensitive, well educated and cultivated – his red leather commonplace book with its gilt lock is full of Greek poems (written in Greek), phrases from Spinoza, verses from the romantic poets and Latin epigraphs. Perhaps there is a hint that the constant questing of his amatory life brought him no satisfaction in one of the couplets written in his clear, even hand, with the deep loops on letters like g and y that denote an emotional nature: 'The sweets we wish for turn to loathed sours/Even in the moment that we call them ours.'†

Robin had often been to Kensington Palace, where he would play the piano and the Princess sing during evenings when Margaret entertained groups of friends. After they ran into each other again at the Society Restaurant in Jermyn Street, where Douglas-Home was playing its horseshoe-shaped piano, Margaret once more began to invite him round to Kensington Palace. Intuitive, empathetic and a practised seducer, he quickly realised that the Princess, depressed, lonely and neglected, was ripe for an affair. Her feelings of unhappiness were exacerbated by Tony's absence on location in Tokyo. The two had argued violently about it, Margaret begging him to postpone his trip but he had refused. The last time they were seen out together before he left on the

---

* Now the wife of the politician Michael Howard.
† From *The Rape of Lucrece* by Shakespeare.

Tokyo assignment was on 29 January 1967. As usual, once there he failed either to write to or telephone his wife; and Douglas-Home's visits continued, usually with other people.

A man who made her feel a desirable woman again, who wanted to be near her rather than away from her, was a huge comfort – in the short term. For what she did not want to do was threaten her marriage. Though she no longer attended the prayer group of her earlier years her religious faith, which encompassed the sanctity of marriage, was profound: she went regularly to Communion, was interested in theology and never travelled without the small white leather Bible she had been given on her Confirmation. And despite their difficulties, Tony was still the man she loved.

One February evening she made a gesture of affection to Robin, telling him, it is alleged, what a comfort he was to her and adding: 'I don't know what I'd do without you.' It was the green light. A passionate but brief liaison followed, with Margaret visiting Douglas-Home at his house, Meadowbrook, in West Chiltington, Sussex. Here were all the felicitous attentions that turn a pleasant evening into a memorably romantic one: soft lights, candles, a delicious meal cooked by Douglas-Home, music and loving words.

On Monday, the day before Valentine's Day, he drove her back to Kensington Palace. The next day she wrote him a letter, which she called her bread-and-butter letter. 'Darling, thank you for a perfect weekend.... Thank you for making me live again. Thank you for being gentle when it was unexpected, which gave me back self-confidence. Thank you for everything nice, which everything was. With best love. M.' Significantly, the only person who called her M and to whom she signed herself in such a way was Tony.

Tony, in Tokyo, learned of the affair when alerted by a friend. He rang Margaret from New York (whither he had flown to see Alex Liberman, the Editorial Director of *Vogue*), slipping into the city unnoticed on 20 February 1967, a day earlier than planned and disguised by the beard he had grown to render him more anonymous when working in Japan. He was furious and jealous. Forcefully he told her that Douglas-Home was never to be allowed into Kensington Palace again. By now the rough edges in their marriage were the subject of such gossip that Tony took the unusual step of denying that there was a rift. Adept as always at handling the press, he told them: 'It's news to me and I would be the first to know. When I am away – and I'm away quite a lot on assignments for my paper – I write home and I telephone like other husbands in love with their wives.' The trouble was, of course, that he did not – but Margaret could hardly say so.

The strain she was suffering over the difficulties in her marriage and the loss of her lover affected her badly and her doctor, Sir Ronald Bodley Scott, advised a check-up in the King Edward VII Hospital in Beaumont Street. At her first public appearance since the reports of the rift – at the premiere of the Burton–Taylor film *The Taming of the Shrew* – she was visibly tense, although glamorous in a cream satin dress with fur-trimmed hem and, ironically, the turquoise and diamond Poltimore tiara she had worn for her wedding. Meanwhile, Tony's plausibility, apparent openness and natural charm won over the American press and temporarily scotched the rumours to such effect that the Queen, on a visit to the Bahamas, wrote to congratulate him on his 'masterly appearance on TV' and on having 'quietened things down considerably'.

The final expression of their togetherness was when Princess Margaret flew out to Nassau where, on 10 March, she and Tony staged a loving reunion, hugging and kissing for the benefit of the world's press, before taking a ten-day holiday in the Bahamas, where Jocelyn Stevens had offered them his villa La Carina at Lyford Cay (his wife Janie flew out with Margaret, acting as her lady-in-waiting). At home, their children were recuperating from measles.

When they got back to England, the Princess telephoned Douglas-Home and told him she would never be able to see him again. To Tony she said: 'He wasn't nearly as good a lover as you, darling' (a phrase that she would use again to her husband several times in the future). Such was the emotional upheaval through which Tony and Margaret had passed that the burglary that took place at their home that week passed almost unnoticed. Douglas-Home immediately wrote her a long and emotional letter, to which Margaret replied:

This is to be a bleak time for love. I am only encouraged by the knowledge that I am secure in yours and I would do anything, as you know, to make you happy and not hurt you.

I am hampered by thoughts and hearts being divided at this moment when a real effort must be made on my side to make the marriage work.

I feel I can do this, curiously enough, more convincingly with this happiness of security in you and feeling of being upheld by you, than without....

What I don't want us to do is to yearn, and long, and eat our hearts out wanting something that is forbidden.

We must make the most of this wonder that has happened to us to do particularly wonderful things ... so that people will marvel at them, and they won't know why we are doing such excellent things in such a special way.

... I shall try and speak to you as much as possible but I am in fear of him, and I don't know what lengths he won't go to, jealous as he is, to find out what I am up to, and your movements too.... Know always that I want you – that thread that holds us is quite strong – know too that it is only because I *cannot* – that I will not be able to see or speak to you so much; know that it will always make me happy when I can do so. Trust me as I trust you, and love me as I love you.

Promise that you will never give up, that you will go on encouraging me to make the marriage a success, and that given a good and safe chance, I will try and come back to you one day. I daren't at the moment.

You are good and loyal, think that I am too, whatever I may seem to do or say.

All my love, my darling, M.

It was tenderly and indeed lovingly written, but it was unmistakably goodbye.

This episode did not, of course, improve relations between the couple; invited to stay with Quentin Crewe and his wife Angela Huth, Tony told Margaret at the last minute on Friday afternoon that he was not going to come with her. She went by herself, putting as brave a face on it as possible. The only sign of her inner distress was her request to Angela (an Italian-speaker) to translate some Italian articles for her to see what they were saying about her marriage and the Douglas-Home affair.

After the Douglas-Home affair, Tony flung himself into yet more physical activities. With Jocelyn Stevens and Anthony Richardson, secretary of the British Water Ski Federation, in a boat driven by Tommy Sopwith, he set off with fifty-two other teams in a cross-Channel waterski race at the end of May 1967, in such dreadful conditions, with waves up to sixteen feet high, that only six teams finished the Greatstone–Cap Gris Nez and back course. Tony's team came in fourth, with a time of four hours three minutes. In July he made a ski-kite flight, rising to more than seventy feet at his first attempt and remaining airborne for ten minutes. His instructor at the Princes Water Ski Club, near Staines, Middlesex, was so impressed that he remarked, 'I have never seen anything like it at the first attempt.'

On the surface, especially with friends and especially abroad, the glittering façade seemed intact. Tony had even begun to wear a present Margaret had given him, a pre-Inca gold eagle necklet on a gold chain, that had once belonged to Tito Arias; after the assassination attempt on him in 1964 his wife, the ballerina Margot Fonteyn, had given it to the Princess who in turn had given it to her husband.

When they stayed in Sardinia with the Aga Khan at his Hotel Pitrizza, to be joined by Peter Sellers and Britt Ekland in Sellers' new yacht *Bobo*, this new toy, fitted with the latest in modern technology, fascinated Tony; while Sellers' jokes, wit and constant tumblings into the water off his expensive new waterskis caused much laughter. Interest in the Snowdons was greater than ever. In London Margaret had had a nearby restaurant – Maggie Jones – named after her; here in Sardinia they were followed everywhere by reporters and photographers. Ann Fleming, the widow of James Bond creator Ian Fleming, was also in Sardinia; staying with her were the politician Roy Jenkins (Home Secretary at the time) and his wife Jennifer, the Oxford don Maurice Bowra and Cyril Connolly, famous as critic and editor. On 26 August 1967 Ann wrote (to the Duchess of Devonshire) that 'a flotilla anchored below our windows, the Snowdons and the Aga, better than the Derby through field glasses but grisly for Roy, for reporters and police swarmed.' Nevertheless, the social prestige of contact with the Snowdons was such that she reported that Connolly was 'made fearfully restless by vicinity of Snowdons, saying not to meet them was like being in Garden of Eden without seeing God!'

On trips to Italy with Jocelyn and Janie Stevens, staying in Rome with the Princess's friend Judy Gendel and her husband Milton, there was plenty of fun and laughing. Princess Margaret was an avid sightseer, culturally knowledgeable and anxious to learn as much as she could about the works of art that they saw, and would remember from one year to the next exactly what she had learned or been told about them. Talking to intelligent people, learning about things that interested her, with people whom she liked and who, she knew, liked her, she was at her best. Tony loved the waterskiing, the driving in fast cars; both soaked up sunshine like lizards. For them holidays meant the delights of sun, sea, sand, sex and sightseeing – but holidays lasted all too short a time.

At home, the Snowdons' life was so hectic that their servants, always hardworking, were beginning to feel the strain. Neither Margaret nor Tony would hesitate, on their way out to a party, to say: 'By the way, there will be eight for dinner tonight after the theatre,' meaning that chef, kitchen man, butler and footman would be on duty at least until midnight – ensured by the washing-up alone, done by the footman as the butler felt it was not part of his duties. It was clear something had to be done. 'Whatever time off we are able to give these men [butler and footman],' wrote the Princess's Private Secretary, 'it is safe to say that each will work about 70/80 hours a week, and the only way to alleviate this would be to engage a third man.'

The kitchen staff were better off, as one of the two was generally able to go off duty in the afternoon. The head housemaid and under-housemaid worked hard at cleaning from 7 a.m. until 1 p.m., remaining on duty until 8.30 or 9.30, with two or three hours off on some unspecified days of the week. Only if the children, their nanny and a nursemaid were away for the weekend were Saturday afternoons and Sundays free. The Private Secretary wound up with the plea: 'Would it be possible for there to be one day in the week (say Wednesdays) when you did not entertain?'

Entertaining was one way of avoiding the difficulties of being alone together. Tony's irritation and uncaringness showed itself in various ways. Typically, he would roar out on his motorbike to the annoyance of other residents in the Palace complex. One elderly courtier was so maddened by the din that when Tony, unrecognisable in his cycle helmet, halted on his bike at the policeman's box he rushed out of his house and pushed him off the bike. He was horrified when he discovered it was not a noisy despatch rider but the husband of the Queen's sister. Tony, however, good humour restored and amused by the man's spirit, just laughed.

The royal family were unhappily aware that all was not well in the Snowdon marriage. Their view of Tony was, naturally, coloured by his behaviour toward them and they, in turn, appeared to bring out the best in him. He was always at his best and sunniest when in the presence of the Queen, for whom his admiration, respect and affection were enormous, and of the Queen Mother, to whom he was wholly devoted. His relationship with Philip was less warm but good – earlier that year, the Duke had offered him a small speedboat called the *Albatross*, which had been in the royal yacht *Britannia*, in case it would be of use to him waterskiing on the lake at Sunninghill. As all of her family knew how difficult the Princess could be, they laid the Snowdons' marital discord at Margaret's door.

This was understandable, as the Princess's own nature militated against her. Her family, and many of those outside it, knew that she could be imperious, arrogant and capricious, her temper flashing when asked to do something or meet someone she did not wish to. Even among those devoted to her, she was known for her lack of social consideration.

At dinner parties, where naturally she was served first, she would begin to eat straightaway and, a quick eater, finish quite a long time before others. As protocol forbade anyone continuing to eat after the Princess, those who could not bolt their food often got only half a dinner. It was the same with departure times: no one could leave before she did and if she wanted to stay until 4 a.m. – as she often did – everyone else also had to. Tony, like anyone who worked, wanted to go home at a more reasonable hour, and sometimes did so. Sometimes this was with the Princess's agreement, but increasingly it happened without a word to her.

On the night of Norman St John-Stevas's housewarming party in Hampstead Tony asked the Gilliatts at 2 a.m. if they would drive him home, as he had to leave early for Holland next morning. 'What about Princess Margaret?' they asked. 'Oh, she's fine – she wants to stay anyway,' he replied. Back at Kensington Palace, he invited the Gilliatts and John Betjeman in to listen quickly to a tape he had made before going home. As they were doing so, Princess Margaret came in weeping bitterly, having arrived by taxi. 'How would you like it', she sobbed to Mary Gilliatt, 'if Roger had left you at a party?' The Gilliatts left quickly.

Friends who had known them since the early days of their marriage began to find themselves witness to ever more painful scenes, from rows in front of the servants to outbursts of misery. Several told me: 'She would ring at one or two in the morning and one would dress and go round and there she'd be in floods and the whisky bottle would be empty and he'd be in the basement. Next day, as likely as not, the two of them would be constantly on the telephone to each other.'

Tony was, however, still adamant that the boundary between his work and private life should not be breached. When Francis Wyndham, who often accompanied Tony even when he was not writing the story, dined with the Snowdons one evening before Tony set off to photograph Joan Crawford, who was making the 1967 horror film *Berserk* in a circus on Blackheath, Margaret longed to come with them as Crawford was her favourite film star. It was extremely difficult for Wyndham to refuse her, as Tony insisted, but eventually they set off in the pouring rain with Margaret's words 'Do tell Miss Crawford I'm such a fan of all her films!' ringing in their ears. On the way, Wyndham warned Tony: 'Whatever you do, don't mention Coca-Cola, because she owns Pepsi-Cola.'

The resulting interview was made memorable by Crawford's veneration for Tony as near-royalty and her crispness with those around her. Ushered to Crawford's caravan, they were greeted by her in her circus tights, her plump make-up man hovering behind her. At the sight of Tony she sank into a deep curtsey and asked: 'What can I offer you?' 'I'd love a Coca-Cola,' responded the incorrigible Tony. She handed it to him and then turned to snarl 'Get your fat butt outta here!' at the make-up man as he tried to edge his way past her, swinging round to simper at Tony: 'I saw your darling little wife at a dinner the other night – what a fairytale Princess!' He and Wyndham watched her do a scene that had her galloping round the ring on a horse; every time she passed Tony she would smile and bow. The session was a great success.

Seven years into the marriage, the circles in which the Snowdons now moved were hedonistic, racy and largely friends whom Tony already knew or whom he had met through his work. The old barriers of class and money had been swept aside; now talent, looks, cleverness, ambition and a gift for the outrageous were the benchmarks of social success, with prudishness the ultimate sin.

At the parties given by Kenneth Tynan, the drama critic who saw it as a mission to push the boundaries of permissibility on stage or in the written word as far as possible, blue films were sometimes shown ('Do her good,' said Tony, when Ken expressed doubts about watching these in Princess Margaret's presence). At others, George Melly would do his well-known turn of going out of the room and then returning first as a man, then as a woman and finally as a bulldog. He would suddenly disappear, take off all his clothes outside, then come in with arms raised and chest puffed out, as a man; enter again with his hands over his groin as a woman, and finally reappear backwards on all fours with his testicles sticking out between his legs as a bulldog. He was so proud of this trick he would often sign his letters, 'Yours, man, woman and bulldog' and perform it as the whim took him. Once, according to a mutual friend, Princess Margaret was among the spectators; so embarrassed was Melly's wife Diana that all she could say was: 'Look at George's varicose veins!'

For Tony and his friends, the sixties were a time of excess and of sudden liberation from the old constraints. Marijuana, with its mantra 'Make Love Not War', was widely used, its distinctive aroma hanging over hippie communes and the post-prandial tables of avant-garde dinner parties alike. Tony often kept a lump of hash in his pocket.

As usual, Tony was at the forefront of all the new trends. Even in such minor matters as clothes he made waves. At restaurants like the Connaught, the Savoy and the Mirabelle, where ties were the rule – some restaurants even lent ties to customers who arrived without them – and at black tie dinners, he would wear a black, or more usually white, poloneck sweater under a midnight blue velvet smoking jacket. 'Tonight at the Italian plays in the Aldwych', wrote Cynthia Gladwyn on 14 May 1968, 'I sat immediately behind Tony Snowdon, dressed in his white polo-neck jersey, his now auburn-coloured hair dressed in two handsome waves, the perfection of which seemed to occupy him very much.'

Above all, there was a loosening of the strict corset of sexual morality hitherto worn by most of society. Premarital sex was increasingly accepted and the pill had begun to revolutionise women's lives. The sexually adventurous took advantage of the climate of permissiveness to experiment with drugs like amyl nitrate to heighten pleasurable sensations.* This, a sweet-smelling, clear pale liquid, often came in capsules that had to be snapped or popped open so that the liquid could be inhaled (hence their everyday name of 'poppers'). Tony's friend Peter Sellers, who found that they 'assisted his physical endurance' (to quote his wife Britt Ekland), was a regular user, a habit brought to an end when he suffered a near-fatal series of heart attacks one night.

Sellers, extremely close to Tony and determined to remain so, not only introduced him to these pleasure pills – so effective that Tony eventually kept a bottle of the liquid in the Kensington Palace fridge – but also showered him with presents – once, even, a Riva speedboat. 'If Tony just happened to remark that he liked a new camera, or a new set of lenses that Sellers had bought then my husband would give it to him,' wrote Britt of that period. Sellers's gift for fantasy and self-deception had led him to hope that Princess Margaret would be prepared to marry him, and with his own weird reasoning he saw these gifts as a form of part-exchange for the Princess.

---

* Originally produced in the nineteenth century, amyl nitrate was then used to ease the chest pains of angina and first became popular for recreational use in the early 1970s. Said to smell of old socks when stale.

For the Princess, although she was fascinated by the intelligence and wit of these new friends, such parties were not always comfortable. It was difficult to be both bohemian and royal and if discomfited she would retreat into hauteur – especially if any of the remarks of her new friends seemed to hint at disrespect to the Queen. Her former 'set' knew exactly how to behave – and how far to go – with royalty, but while in these bohemian circles there were a number who came from the same background, most found the presence of a princess somewhat disconcerting. Attempts at familiarity might be rebuffed by one of her glacial stares, while those who did not want to give offence sought desperately for a 'safe' subject of conversation, neither of which made for easy chatting. Tony, always quickly surrounded, did not help by often ignoring her.

Parties at Kensington Palace could also be difficult. In 1968, Tony made his first film for television, *Don't Count the Candles*, inviting a number of friends to a private showing there. What he did not tell them was that he had also hidden microphones at various spots round the room, feeding back into his study next door where he was working the projector. With their host out of sight, the gossip began immediately, largely about his affairs and relationships. On his return, he confronted his discomfited friends with what they had said.

The film itself, an hour-long documentary on the loneliness of old age, was broadcast on 4 April 1968 on ITV at the peak time of 9.05 p.m. It won Emmys for him and his collaborator, Derek Hart (Tony spray-painted his black because he thought it looked better that way) and a number of different prizes in foreign countries, where it sold so well that Sir Lew (later Lord) Grade made the pair an extra, ex gratia payment of £1,000.

In all it was shown in twenty-one countries, earned six awards and was acclaimed by the critics. It had come about because the American television company CBS had been impressed by his photographs on the same subject for the *Sunday Times Magazine* and asked him to do something similar with a television camera. 'It is very rare that you get any television as good as *Don't Count the Candles*,' wrote one reviewer, adding, 'It should become a classic and we should get a chance to see it often again.' Typical of the congratulations from friends was the note from John Julius Norwich. 'I can't resist writing to tell you how brilliantly good Anne and I both thought it. Your photography was, as always, a delight in its endless inventiveness without ever a gimmick. Please make lots more.'

The film that emerged from weeks of hard work was moving, poignant and funny, opening with a shot of a child blowing out a candle on a birthday cake while Derek Hart quoted Jonathan Swift: 'Every man would like to live long, but no one would be old.' There were gruesome descriptions of the use of cells, from the foetuses of specially selected Swiss sheep killed halfway through their pregnancy, to maintain a look of youth and a hilarious scene where Tony's friend Robert Belton tried on a wig. ('What happens if someone catches their umbrella in it?' asked Belton. 'They don't usually,' replied the baffled wigmaker. 'Well, it's the law of universal cussedness that they probably would,' replied Belton.)

The 86-year-old Compton Mackenzie said that the only grudge he had against old age ('I never think about it') was the rapidity with which time flew by; Noël Coward thought that the saddest thing was one's contemporaries dying. One elderly woman, who could hardly move ('If I could get out, I wouldn't feel so lonely'), talked of her parrot and her doll as company. Probably the sculptor Barbara Hepworth best summed up Tony's own views when she said: 'You have to live with work – live with it, make it and complete it. Everything is work.' Or as Lady Asquith remarked: 'I've made no terms with old age at all. I've been far too busy living.'

The introverted Cecil Beaton, persuaded by Tony to do an ad hoc interview for the film, was greatly upset by the result because so much emphasis was put on his age, sixty-four, although, as he wrote in his diary, 'I looked extremely young and attractive.' This did not stop him describing with a certain gruesome relish 'the ghastly things that happen, the turkey gobbet under the chin and the sagging muscles around the mouth, the false teeth that click'. *Time* magazine reported that he had trouble with his dentures and, he wrote, 'worse – it has made me feel venerable'. He telephoned Tony to tell him of his displeasure, but this gave him little satisfaction, 'for I know Tony was only too pleased to think he might have found himself in a lot of trouble, but had just managed to get away with it'.

At the same time, Tony was extraordinarily thoughtful to others in small things. When Princess Marina, Duchess of Kent, died her Secretary, Sir Philip Hay, was in a state of utter misery. Upon Margaret and Tony's return from her funeral (on 30 August 1968) Tony, who had noticed Sir Philip's wretchedness, told Richard Wood to make up a beautiful bunch of flowers from their garden and immediately took this round to Sir Philip.

Almost nothing was a greater cause of trouble in the increasingly tempestuous Snowdon marriage than the question of a house in the country. This had preoccupied them for some time. Tony in particular found Royal Lodge, their frequent weekend destination, constraining. He was someone who badly needed his own space in the form of workshop or studio where he could spend hours doing what he most enjoyed, designing or making anything from a small crystal clock to the facsimile of a Georgian architrave. Instead, at Royal Lodge, the main amusement was when he, Margaret and the Queen Mother would eat dinner at a card table set up in the large drawing room while watching television. Both he and Margaret wanted somewhere to which they could escape from the formality of life at Kensington Palace and where the children could have plenty of space and freedom, but none of the houses at which they had looked during the previous year had seemed suitable, either because of price, distance from London, size or lack of privacy.

After one of these house-hunting forays Tony, describing the one they had just seen to his old friend Bob Belton, remarked: 'Really, you've got the most beautiful house in England.' Belton grasped the subtext immediately. 'Would you like Old House back?' he asked. 'Would you miss it?' responded Tony. 'Well, yes,' replied Belton, 'but it will never be mine. So you must have it back.' At the same time, the Queen offered Princess Margaret a site near Sunninghill. She was delighted, believing that there, with Tony's flair for design, they could build exactly the house they wanted. They would be completely private, without the public access afforded by the right of way past Old House, it was near Windsor, close to the lake on which they waterskied and, above all, she would be near both her mother and her sister.

Tony, Old House within his grasp, argued vigorously in its favour; the Princess was equally adamant on the virtues of Sunninghill. Neither would give an inch, and disagreement escalated into constant, furious rows. Francis Legh, Margaret's Comptroller, would arrive home exhausted from the strain, at around 6 p.m. 'Give me a drink, quick!' he would demand, then describe what, to a courtier of the old school, was almost unbelievable behaviour. 'They were shouting and screaming at each other up the stairs, *in front of the butler.*'

What the Princess did not know was that Tony had already negotiated with the National Trust for the alterations he planned to make to Old House, and had been down there some time earlier with Oliver Messel and James Cousins, who did a report on its condition and drawings of the alterations Tony proposed. Through Cousins Tony had found a builder – who was ordered to start work straightaway.

With the arguments still raging, the two of them agreed to ask an independent adviser whether Old House or the Sunninghill site would be best and to abide by whatever decision he reached. Their arbiter came down in favour of Sunninghill, largely for security considerations. These, naturally, involved the proximity of the right of way that had originally so worried the Princess.

But her triumph was short-lived: she soon discovered that Tony was pressing on with his plans regardless and that, willy-nilly, she had to accept them. It was at this point that she telephoned Colin Tennant and asked if he had meant what he had said about giving her a piece of land on Mustique (by now cleared of mosquitoes, and with a landing strip, hotel and a few villas). 'Of course, Ma'am,' replied Tennant. When Tennant returned to London, he went to see her at Kensington Palace, taking a map of the island and, by deed of consideration in marriage (which meant it would be free of estate duty), formally gave her the land; and said he would build her a villa on it.

At first Tony attempted to cajole the Princess into accepting his decision, reassuring her with perfect truth that it would be his own money he spent on Old House and pleading with her for them to work out a way of life that was happy and relaxed. 'You have everything at your feet,' he told her in one letter. 'Great talent, appreciation of the arts, when you do a job, however boring and dull, you always make it exciting and wonderful for everyone and I love you very much.'

For Tony, Old House had everything. Not only was it at the core of his childhood, it had belonged to Oliver, whom he worshipped; and it had been in his family for even longer. It was *his* in a way no brand-new house could have been, while anywhere near Royal Lodge, with the likelihood of visits to and from the royal family, would have involved more formality – and he and Margaret already went regularly to Balmoral, Sandringham and Windsor Castle. In addition, it was the project to end all projects – a place he loved better than any other house he had known, and which demanded an immense amount of what he most enjoyed: designing and making things.

When he took it over, the interior was dark owing to high banks nearby. One of the first steps was to bulldoze these down roughly (a great motto of his was 'As long as it's eye-pretty, that's enough'). He created images or vistas by clever use of *trompe l'œil*, had several chimneys removed ('there were too many'), made 'instant Chippendale' corners for the dressers, painted the kitchen walls yellow with paint from Venice mixed with white spirit and a little white oil paint, and rubbed it on with a Brillo pad, hanging a painting of his grandmother by Oliver on one wall. The round basin in the downstairs cloakroom, fitted by Tony, was a pretty old patterned pudding bowl, its waste hole drilled out by his dentist.

He upholstered the mahogany gout stool, made the pelmets, the engraving round the bottom of the birdcage lamp and the façade of what looked like a Gothic folly in his workshop there. Behind this was a small room in which he seated two nude shop-window mannequins in deck chairs. Much of the china was made by friends of the family, in a kiln Tony had put in. Upstairs, the installation of a four-poster bed from Nymans in the guest bedroom had required much ingenuity and the removal of a balcony; as it was, ceiling clearance was only an inch.

The only heating in the house came from an eight-foot-high cast-iron stove which, although efficient, failed to heat bedrooms or bathrooms, and an open fire. There were objects that took him straight back to earlier happy days spent there: a nursery fender and the walking pig made of chamois leather that when wound up wagged its head from side to side and grunted, beloved by him and Susan as children.

The entrance hall was dominated by a huge white sixteenth-century bread oven, French windows were installed to lead onto a formal terraced garden. He found a kelim instead of a cloth for the big pine table he made, around which ten could eat in the large, brick-floored kitchen on cold days, and outside on hot ones – nearby, he made an iron gravity-powered spit for barbecues, turned by a bicycle chain.

The whole house, he said, was a tribute to Oliver who, because of his declining health, had gone to live in Barbados at the end of 1966. Oliver's masks and designs hung everywhere; there was even a small stage – the hall and the wide steps leading down to the kitchen were framed with carved swags of wooden cloth and curtains held back by ropes (bought for twenty-five shillings in the village), visual reminders more potent even than the long letters Oliver wrote regularly.

In the garden Tony concocted cascades and fountains and put in a 'stone' statue of the Madonna – in reality a fibreglass mock-up from a film set. The biggest task was digging out the swampy ground lower down from the house to make a lake, a process that he thought would take a weekend but, with the aid of an earth-mover and twelve willing hands, took a year. It was only a foot deep but appeared bottomless, thanks to its lining of black plastic. In all, the improvements would take twenty years, for Tony a constant source of joy and pleasure – as well as asking countless friends down, he could now spend hours in his favourite occupation, designing things and then making them.

Once plumbing and electricity had been installed and a certain amount of decoration completed, Tony brought down Princess Margaret for the weekend, accompanied by baby, nanny and detective. At the same time he invited Belton who had, as Tony had promised when he took the house back from his friend, continued to come and stay. Margaret's visit was not a success. With Tony, Belton had usually eaten out or they had had a scrap meal. Now there were five adult mouths to feed and though the Princess was anxious to help, she had never in her life cooked. Discussions in the kitchen were punctuated by remarks like: 'Should you put the lid on boiled potatoes?' from the Princess, with the response from the equally ignorant Belton, 'I don't suppose it matters.'

Eventually a meal was produced. Then where to eat it? The only place was the big sitting room, with its two small tables, at one of which sat Tony, Margaret and Belton, with the nanny and detective at the other. All were well within earshot of each other, which made for stilted conversation on both sides. Nor was the Princess used to being without her dresser; the newsagent's sister from the village, who would occasionally pop down during the day, was not quite the same thing. Worst of all was the right of way close to the house, with its potential for the curious to come and gawk.

From then on, it was clear that staying at Old House would not be popular with Margaret. It was not part of her childhood as it had been for Tony's, and she found it claustrophobic. 'It's so small and poky,' she would say much later. 'I was born at Glamis, where the rooms are huge – and here people can walk past just a few feet from the window. On my sister's estate I can relax, because there I know all the people and they know me and we're protected and taken for granted.'

Old House soon became a focal point for Tony's friends in the world of art and entertainment in which he moved so easily. The novelist Edna O'Brien would come down, perhaps with another visitor, Nicky Haslam, who would often collect the food for these lunches from Kensington Palace. Jackie Rufus-Isaacs and her brother Anthony (two of the children of Lord and Lady Reading, who lived nearby) would appear, and Peter and Britt Sellers were constant visitors, sometimes bringing Lorenzo and Mara Berni, whose guest presents might be a cold roast, some delicious Italian pudding from the kitchen at San Lorenzo and several bottles of wine.

Once the Bernis arrived to find a rabbit that Tony had shot. Lorenzo, pronouncing it insufficient, borrowed one of Tony's beautiful shotguns, potted another and then, fortifying himself first with a large Scotch, skinned and gutted both of them to produce a memorable rabbit stew.

Inevitably, Old House pressed home the wedge between the Snowdons. Margaret, who disliked it intensely, seldom came down; so that increasingly the Snowdons spent weekends apart, each with their respective friends. Margaret would visit friends like Lord and Lady Rupert Nevill, Lady Penn, the Douglas-Homes or her lady-in-waiting Lady Juliet Townsend, driven there by Larkin, who would return to pick her up on Sunday. Such visits were of course private, an informality marked by the Princess's habit of sitting in front beside her chauffeur rather than as, on official occasions, in the back.

By now Larkin was a great favourite, his discretion and loyalty absolutely trusted, to the extent that the Princess's usual insistence on protocol often disappeared. 'Take me to Lilibet's house,' she would say as she slid into the passenger seat. Sometimes on the way down to friends on a Friday evening, the Princess would suggest 'stopping for a drink' at some attractive-looking pub. Larkin would take off his chauffeur's coat and hat and put on an old tweed jacket kept in the boot for such occasions; the Princess, in headscarf and simple country clothes, would slip in and sit at a table in a dark corner while Larkin fetched the drinks.

The sheer unlikeliness of her presence in a local pub meant that she was seldom recognised but occasionally Larkin would be asked as he stood at the bar: 'Is that who I think it is?' 'Well, who do you think it is?' he would respond. 'Er – Princess Margaret?' the questioner would say, in tones already doubtful. Larkin would laugh and reply: 'Well if it was Princess Margaret, she wouldn't come in here, would she?' To which the questioner would back off saying, 'Oh no, of course not.'

On other occasions this discretion was tested to the limit. On hot summer weekends, when he was driving Margaret to Royal Lodge to stay with her mother for the weekend, she would sometimes say: 'Can we stop for a swim?' Larkin would park by the lake the Snowdons used for waterskiing – for which he would often drive the boat – but which was otherwise deserted, the Princess would withdraw to a discreet distance, take off her clothes and skinny-dip.

Since his love affair with Princess Margaret, Robin Douglas-Home had been drinking heavily. In a depression exacerbated by gambling debts and alcohol, he committed suicide on the evening of 15 October 1968, at his country cottage, Meadowbrook.

That night James Cousins was having supper alone with the Princess. As was her frequent habit when alone or with an old friend, she was watching television, when the news of Douglas-Home's death came through. There was not, Cousins recalled later, a single flicker of emotion from her. Yet although she did not, in his words, bat an eyelid, at the meeting she attended the following day she fell deeply asleep – something she had never been known to do before. Cousins wondered if she had spent the night weeping.

The popular press believed that Douglas-Home had killed himself in the wake of his affair with the Princess. Before taking the fatal overdose, he had left a last message on his tape recorder. 'There comes a time when one comes to the conclusion that continuing to live is pointless.' Or as he had earlier written in his commonplace book:

> The mind has a thousand eyes
> And the heart but one
> Yet the light of a whole life dies
> When love is done.

10

Old House and Les Jolies Eaux

❖

Getting on badly with her husband, loving the sun and conscious of her plot of land in Mustique, Margaret began to think in terms of a Caribbean villa. First, she wanted to refresh her memory. She asked her friends the Tennants if she could come and stay during the winter of 1968. Although their original house had burned down and they were living very primitively, with little furniture and no hot water or electric light and the only nod to civilisation a cold shower, under Colin Tennant's aegis the island was slowly becoming more sophisticated.

Most of the scrub that had originally covered it had been cleared, cotton planted and a new village for the workers created. Tennant also initiated the planting of coconut groves and limes, oranges, grapefruit and vegetables. The expansion in air travel was bringing more and more distant spots within reach; an airstrip and airfield were under construction (they were opened in 1969); and a charter negotiated between Colin Tennant's Mustique Company and the government of St Vincent (which included Mustique) provided for the building of a maximum of 120 private homes while maintaining the essential character of the island. Already, through the Tennants' wide circle of friends, word of this beautiful, unspoilt island had begun to spread and Colin, who had invested heavily in the place, was selling parcels of land at around £15,000 each.

Knowing that the Princess liked her comforts, Anne Tennant asked if she was sure she wanted to come, explaining that there was no electricity, the house was furnished with plastic garden furniture and that the rainwater they collected was coloured orange by the roof tiles. 'Yes,' said Margaret, 'I'd like to come.'

'You and Tony?' asked Anne Tennant 'No, just me,' replied Margaret. The visit was such a success that Margaret asked Colin Tennant if he had really meant his offer of a villa on his island. Tennant, knowing that the presence of the Princess on the island would secure its future as the tourist attraction he was hoping to make it, answered: 'Yes, of course.' Tennant and the Princess, dressed in a pair of his pyjamas to protect her from the scrub, marked out a plot with stakes. Tennant set aside £30,000 for the villa's construction.

He asked Oliver Messel to design it, hoping that his uncle's involvement would entice Tony out too. Oliver's own house on the Barbadian coast was enchanting, with its courtyard between two colonnaded cloisters, open loggia dining room where Oliver gave dinner parties at which hibiscus and frangipani were piled on the table between silver, crystal and porcelain, and a garden planted to create a Rousseau-esque jungle that gave glimpses of the sea below. So exquisite was it that Oliver was quickly asked to design a number of the other handsome villas on Mustique.

Earlier in their marriage Margaret had hoped that she and Tony would be able to plan their house on the island together. But Tony, who cordially detested both the idea of Mustique (always calling it 'mistake') and its owner, Colin Tennant, refused to have anything to do with it, Oliver or no Oliver. That spring, after an operation to remove her tonsils, Margaret flew first to Barbados to stay with Oliver, and then on to Mustique in a light plane. It was as primitive as Anne Tennant had warned her but she was enchanted with the view from 'her' peninsula, and the island's potential. Building began.

The villa that finally emerged, 'Les Jolies Eaux', was a simple, single-storey four-bedroom house (later, it was extended to seven bedrooms) built in a U shape round a paved courtyard. The large glass-panelled sitting room windows folded back to make the most of the spectacular view, a thatched gazebo stood beside the small swimming pool and the garden was brilliant with bougainvillea, oleanders and hibiscus. Paths led down through pines to the beaches of white sand.

Margaret did all its simple decoration, going off with Anne Tennant on countless shopping trips to the Sloane Square department store Peter Jones where she bought everything that it would need – construction took several years and it was not until late 1972 that it was finally habitable. From then on she would visit it twice a year, in February and the late autumn. It was one of only fifteen villas on the island, the occupants of which all knew each other, moving freely in and out of each other's houses.

It was a relaxed, informal, beach-bohemian lifestyle and the Princess soon became the uncrowned queen of this small, intimate society. But although a number of her friends came out to stay, she never brought her children. When Anne Tennant, arriving with her own children, suggested one day that David and Sarah come, the response was immediate and unequivocal. 'Oh, no, Anne,' replied the Princess. 'It's *my* holiday.' She even had her special 'holiday' jewellery, a suite of faux ruby and paste necklace and earrings and various coral pieces that she wore when her skin was tanned.

One of the contradictions in Tony's nature most difficult for those who loved him to come to terms with was the thoughtfulness and compassion he showed to others – particularly those from a less fortunate background than his own – and his genuine desire to see them treated on equal terms, while at the same time 'being beastly' as one victim put it, to those, particularly women, to whom he was close. Yet for those he thought had been treated unjustly or dealt a bad hand by fate he would campaign, write numerous time-consuming letters and lobby people who could help.

Unsurprisingly, after the severe bout of polio he had suffered in his early years, his sympathy was engaged by fellow sufferers. For some time, he had served on the committee of the charity that started as the Polio Research Fund (now Action Research), which funded medical research into disability. A fellow committee member was his friend Quentin Crewe whose illness, muscular dystrophy,* was now handicapping him physically more and more. Although Crewe refused to allow it to limit his life in any way –

---

* Muscular dystrophy is a group of genetic diseases characterised by progressive weakness and degeneration of the skeletal muscles that control movement.

in the mid-sixties, almost chair-bound, he had joined an expedition across the Saudi Arabian desert – he, like other disabled people, found the wheelchairs of those days cumbersome and difficult to handle. In the summer of 1968, Tony decided to help him by designing a powered chair that could integrate its user more fully into the life around him.

As always, Tony worked from the basis of what he wanted the chair to do, rather than building an improved version of what had been done before. This meant – as with the Snowdon Aviary – disregarding the conventional approach to wheelchairs and producing something where form literally followed function. What he came up with was, in essence, a motorised chair-base on which seating of different types and heights could be fitted, and which was small enough to pass through a standard door and fit into a small bathroom.

As many wheelchair users have found, unless someone squats down to talk to them there is a tendency to refer to them as to children, in the third instead of the second person ('Would he like another drink?'); alternatively, constant talking with people standing up leads to neck strain for the wheelchair user. With a high stool on the chair platform, Crewe could be at the same height as other people, making conversations both easier and socially more equitable. Other seats could be for sitting and reading, or for moving from one place to another. The prototype Chairmobile, with its adjustable steering column, was powered by a battery removed from one of his children's toys.

The chair was an immediate success. Crewe used his for fifteen years ('it was a wonderful little machine') and Tony persuaded Sir Alfred Owen, head of the engineering firm Rubery Owen, to manufacture it. There was no problem in garnering publicity and soon the Mirror Group bought 2,500 of the new chairs, to sell at the discounted price of £99.50 (about half the cost of other wheelchairs) to readers of the *Sunday Mirror*. It was to have a great success in the next few years: Scotland Yard gave one to a disabled policeman and Sir Joseph Kagan presented six to the Parliamentary All-Party Disablement Group. For Tony personally, this initial project was to fire an interest in the problems of disabled people that would become a lifelong campaign.

The disastrous 1968 famine in Biafra (in south-east Nigeria) appealed to the collective conscience of the West, with its terrible pictures of pot-bellied, stick-limbed children gazing at the camera. Tony, like many others, wanted to help in some way. He knew he could not nurse, but felt he could be useful driving food to where it was needed and he quickly organised a small group to leave almost at once: his friends Jocelyn Stevens and Tommy Sopwith and a physiotherapist called Jean Cooper. He had a motorbike and got hold of a Land Rover and, when she heard of his plan, the Queen also lent a Land Rover. Then, within twenty-four hours of take-off from Stansted Airport, the Prime Minister, Harold Wilson, telephoned to say they could not go. 'I never found out why,' recalled Tony later.

For Margaret, 1968 saw trips to the USA and France, naturally viewed by her as part of her 'job'. But for Tony, their glamour had worn off. Despite his fondness for Margaret's lady-in-waiting, Lady Elizabeth Cavendish, he found them exhausting ('Princess Margaret was naturally the star, so one went at her pace. It's much less tiring if you're setting it but if you're hanging on behind it's far more tiring') and worse still, boring. Often he would rebel in the only way he knew how: by being disagreeable.

When they holidayed in Sardinia as guests of the Aga Khan he would attempt to get hold of a separate boat; once he ignored Margaret's birthday completely, failing not only to get her a present but even to say 'Happy Birthday' – something especially significant to the Princess, for whom birthdays and anniversaries were of supreme importance. At a nightclub that evening, where they had gone to celebrate with their friends the Gendels, he remarked: 'Should one celebrate a birthday after eighteen?' After they left the nightclub Margaret, chagrined, walked ahead with Judy. Milton Gendel took the opportunity to say to Tony: 'Was that necessary?' The only answer was a furious silence. But Margaret's desire to make the marriage work was still – just – proof against such painful snubs.

At home, Tony still found many of the trappings of royalty highly enjoyable, notably the shooting parties in Windsor Great Park, at Sandringham and at Balmoral; at the last two one of the keepers was his loader. At Windsor Great Park it was the

Snowdons' chauffeur, Larkin, who had become a quick and proficient loader after Tony had taught him – he would first drive the Snowdons down, then load for Tony when the drives began. A typical shoot at Balmoral, with the Duke of Edinburgh, Prince Charles, the Marquis of Douro, Angus Ogilvy, Lord Plunket and Tony saw a bag of fifty-nine brace of grouse. On Boxing Day 1968, in cold but fine weather, the Dukes of Edinburgh and Kent, the Prince of Wales, Prince Michael, Lord Elphinstone, Lord Plunket and Tony had a bag between them of 336 pheasants. The following day, with the same weather and almost the same people – bar Michael Adeane in place of Lord Elphinstone – there was a similar bag, of 355 pheasants.

But the atmosphere within Kensington Palace was poisonous. To all intents and purposes, the relationship between the Snowdons was degenerating into open warfare, with Tony's quickness of wit and lack of scruple giving him the edge. He would make lists of 'things I hate about you' and leave them in the book she was reading, on her writing desk, under her pillow or lying around the house – the most famous was 'You look like a Jewish manicurist', found in her glove drawer.

If she was singing at the piano with friends gathered round he would stand behind her and mimic her, make faces indicating ridicule or perform a mock curtsey. He was invariably very funny when he did this but for mutual friends it was horribly embarrassing, as was his habit of asking everyone except Margaret what they would like to drink and when she asked for a glass of whisky simply ignoring her. Margaret, ashamed, would not know what to do. En route to official occasions Tony would open the window of the Rolls, Margaret's carefully done hair would blow all over the place and a violent scene would ensue as she shouted, 'Put that window up,' and he refused.

Dinner parties were another minefield. 'If I was invited to dinner there,' remembered Patrick Lichfield, 'I always hoped there would be other people rather than just me and my girl-friend or wife, because they were so prone to fight – over people, over lifestyles – and then each of them would try to draw one to their side. And I always felt obliged to be on Princess Margaret's because she was my cousin and it was through her I got to know Tony. Whom I thought in a class of his own as a photographer.'

Although their private life was floundering, Tony remained a hardworking member of 'the team' on official engagements. The tour of Japan, Cambodia, Thailand and Iran that autumn of 1969 was a great success, especially for its inclusion of the first royal walkabout. Like all royal tours, however painstaking and detailed the planning beforehand, the unexpected had a way of cropping up. On one occasion on this tour, it was Tony's natural ingenuity that saved the day.

As always, presents had to be taken for the hosts. The Princess took her youthful lady-in-waiting, Lady Juliet Smith (granddaughter of the famous F.E. Smith) to shop for the most important ones. For the Emperor of Japan there were Joseph Banks books from the Natural History Museum – the Emperor was a marine biologist and the Princess herself enthusiastic about shells – for Cambodia's Head of State, Prince Norodom Sihanouk, Margaret chose two beautiful but comparatively modest-looking modern silver goblets, against the reservations of Lady Juliet, who pointed out that silver was the one thing of which there was plenty in the Far East 'and wouldn't this look, well, a bit *small*, Ma'am?' 'Nonsense,' responded Margaret, 'British sterling silver is famous the world over.'

After British Week (26 September–5 October 1969) in Tokyo, they arrived in Cambodia, where the ceremonial for them was held in the Presidential Palace in Pnomh Penh under a large canopy, with stilted conversation to the sound of guns booming as North and South Vietnam fought each other in the Mekong Delta. ('The more Vietnamese that kill each other the better it is for us, tee hee hee,' said the Prince in his strange falsetto voice.) After dinner, enormous double doors were flung open to reveal the Prince's presents to the royal couple on a long table. It was covered from end to end with quantities of glittering silver objects.

Fortunately, the Snowdon gifts did not have to be presented until the following day. That night, there was an agonised conference: two smallish silver goblets could hardly compete with the extravagance of a tableful of silverware. Juliet, who had with difficulty bitten back the words 'I told you so,' had little to contribute and the Princess took a lofty line. 'This stuff is rubbish. Anyway, who is this man? – he won't be here in a few years.' (She was right: he was deposed a mere six months later, although no one anticipated this at the time.)

The situation was saved by Tony, with typical ingenuity. Using the cardboard boxes in which the various presents had been packed, he piled them up together so that they formed several small display platforms. Acquiring a length of silk, he draped this over the boxes, then set about putting on this improvised display with all the presents they had, from the silver goblets and a large silver-framed photograph of Tony and Margaret to an impressive silver cigarette box (brought for the Ambassador but loyally handed back by him in this hour of pressing need) and a huge crocodile handbag destined for Madame Monique, Prince Sihanouk's beautiful, and favourite, mistress. When he had completed setting all the objects out on the hidden boxes, framed in luscious folds of silk, the effect, to sighs of relief all round, was of a rich hoard of opulent gifts.

Constitutionally, this tour was of great importance, since Margaret and Tony were the forerunners for the later State Visit of Emperor Hirohito of Japan (when the Emperor and Empress arrived in England on 5 October 1971 it was the Snowdons who were sent to perform the first, ceremonial greeting). Tony's behaviour on the trip, as with all the royal tours on which he accompanied the Princess, was a typical mixture of the hardworking and exemplary in public with impish asides and tricks. During a conversation on dancing with Tony and the Ambassador to Japan, Sir John Pilcher, Prince Mikasa, the brother of the Emperor, remarked: 'I do like dances but I prefer my balls on ice.' Thereafter, at every smart line-up when important dignitaries were waiting to be presented, Tony would murmur to the Ambassador beside him: 'Do you like your balls on ice, Sir John?'

His natural gift for contrariness also came into play, as in the episode of the tailcoat. Protocol decreed that when being received by the Emperor, black tailcoats should be worn. Tony, who invariably liked to be different, declared that he would only wear a grey one. A special dispensation was sought, and granted, and the grey tailcoat travelled out in his luggage. Unfortunately, when on arrival at the British Embassy (where the Snowdons were staying) Tony's valet Richard pressed it, he was unaware that the iron was filled with charcoal – and the coat was scorched. Wood immediately told Prince William of Gloucester (he had worked for the Gloucesters before coming to the Snowdons), who was Counsellor at the Embassy. 'We'll get the black one sent out, Richard,' said Prince William, adding, 'so he'll be wearing black to meet the Emperor after all.'

Although Margaret was a person of mood swings and might well refuse to attend some 'boring' event, if she did go she would, usually, perform impeccably in public, although one observer described her as 'pretty, tough, disillusioned and spoilt'. As their relationship worsened Tony would often subtly ridicule her as she fulfilled these official duties, to the embarrassed discomfort of those in attendance, although he was careful never to do this in front of any other member of the royal family.

One of her chief complaints was that he would reduce her to bouts of weeping on the day of a grand ball or public engagement so that she appeared puffy-faced and red-eyed. Another trick was to wait until the last minute before joining her, so that the cavalcade had to roar down the wrong side of the road to reach the destination in time – seeming thoughtlessness for which Margaret got the blame. There would be occasions when both would be leaving a party and, after posing for photographers, Tony would dart back inside leaving the Princess standing forlornly on the steps. Late one night, after a gala to raise funds for a John Cranko studio at Sadler's Wells, followed by dinner at Osbert Lancaster's Eaton Square flat, when both had been talking to other people, the Princess called out: 'Oh darling, I'd like to go home.' 'I'm not your chauffeur!' shouted Tony, to the frozen embarrassment of the thirty-strong party who heard. The charitable view was that he needed to show others that he was not, as one of them put it, 'walking along behind her with his hands behind his back'.

Occasionally, Margaret managed a crushing riposte. On one Saturday afternoon when the Snowdons and a few friends were sitting around on the drawing room sofas, Tony produced a packet of cigarettes and offered them to everyone except his wife. 'Oh, darling, I'd like one too,' she said. Tony lit it – and then threw it at her. 'That's a terrible thing to do,' Margaret remarked angrily. 'You might have burned this dress.' 'I wouldn't care if I had,' he answered. 'I've never liked that material.' Margaret drew herself up and with all the royal hauteur of which she was capable replied: '*We* call it "stuff".' There was, too, the day when her children came back from their day school complaining that the other children would say, 'Here come the royals,' when they arrived. 'But darlings, you're not royal,'* the Princess told her children, adding pointedly, 'And Papa's *certainly* not royal.'

There was even a wall between Tony and his children, largely erected by Nanny Sumner, who would ignore him if he went into the nursery and simply continue talking to the children; and if he did manage to attract their attention, answer for them. If he wanted to take them out she would refuse and if he remonstrated, would flounce out of the room saying: 'I'm going to speak to the Queen.' As she kept the children immaculately clean and looked after them extremely well Margaret, who needed someone she could trust completely when she went away, relied on her heavily. Since, in front of the Princess, who in any case seldom went into the nursery, Nanny Sumner's behaviour was impeccable, Margaret found it easier to disregard Tony's complaints.

Occasionally, to Nanny Sumner's frustration, Tony was able to whisk his children down to his workshop, where she was not allowed, and where David's growing interest in making things could be encouraged. As she had always worked in the grandest of houses where a nanny had her own staff of under-nurse, nursery-maid and footman, she was fiercely status-conscious, often behaving as if she had taken on the identity of her employer. She would insist on taking her 'own' nursery equipment, from kettle to clothes dryer, with her, even to Windsor, so that a special van had to be sent to bring these belongings down and the idea of taking the children anywhere in a taxi was not even considered ('Oh no, I

---

* Princess Margaret was quite right. Her grandfather George V, worried by the plethora of descendants of Queen Victoria, had decreed that only the children of the sovereign and the children of the sons of the sovereign were entitled to be called royal, with the prefix HRH in front of their names.

can't have my Sarah in a taxi – you don't know who's been sitting on the seats').

'Just to think poor David will never travel on a red London bus,' she said one day. 'What do you mean?' asked Tony sharply. 'Well, in his position …' she simpered. 'Nanny, I've got news for you,' said Tony grimly. 'David will go on a red bus, and I will take him.' 'You can't, you can't!' she cried. But it was in vain; a few days later, Tony took David off for his first ride on a London bus.

Tony had begun to visit Old House regularly and Princess Margaret would occasionally, unwillingly, come with him, bringing the children. Psychologically, the visits were a dismal failure, in part because the basic attitude of each was the polar opposite of the other. For Tony it was a haven, a return to the happiest part of his childhood, a place that was his own, where he could introduce his preferred carefree, bohemian, impromptu way of life among like-minded friends and where he could spend happy hours remodelling and embellishing this or that or simply disappear into his workshop. One of the reasons he had come not to enjoy weekends at Royal Lodge so much was that he had no workshop there: for Tony, hours spent concentrating closely on making things were both soothing and exciting – more, they were essential to his happiness.

Margaret, who never in a thousand years would have thought of spending Sunday afternoon on a tractor digging out the foundations of a lake, gamely tried to play along for the first few years. If their friend Pamela Colin came down with them Pamela would cook and Margaret would don her rubber gloves to do the washing-up. But the Petit Trianon aspect of her stab at housekeeping was underlined by the fact that anyone helping her still had to remember to add 'Ma'am' to mundane requests like 'Pass the tea towel, please,' if they were not to incur frosty looks. As she later told Tony – and several friends – she had been born and bred in a castle and she wasn't going to live in a cottage.

More than any of this, however, Margaret still felt deeply hurt that Tony had presented Old House to her as a fait accompli, simply saying: 'I've done it up, and that's where we're going to be,' instead of accepting their arbiter's decision that the Sunninghill site was more suitable; subsequently, she was never consulted about any alterations or arrangements to it. She thought the drive to Old House was a dreadful way out of London – it took anything from one and a half to two hours to get there – compared with the ease with which they could have reached Windsor and her home ground. Once there, it was desperately uncomfortable: there was no central heating, the only bathroom was down a passage, so icy in winter that wise guests took all their clothes along for the chilly run back.

Besides, she detested the cottage itself. It was a place where everybody 'mucked in' as there was no living-in servant – nor any room for one – and Margaret did not know how to cook, clean, wash or iron. (The lack of servants did not affect Nanny Sumner, who would simply leave her shoes outside her door for Tony to clean.) In addition, the Princess believed the house to be haunted. Once, while sitting there, she saw a man whom she thought was dressed rather oddly in breeches and a cravat, but assumed it was someone who had been riding. On Tony's return to the room she said: 'I think a friend of yours must have arrived – some man has just passed me.' 'No,' said Tony, 'no one has come.' Later, one of her detectives saw the same man and had the same reaction.

Tony, whether subconsciously wishing to keep this special place for himself or not, used one of his characteristically oblique methods to underline the growing distance between them and to put Margaret off Old House even more. Instead of encouraging her to cook simple things like scrambled eggs (or as she, equally characteristically, retorted: 'We call them "buttered eggs"') he would buy food that required complicated cooking, and then watch her fail hopelessly. 'Of course she was difficult,' said one friend who watched the long, slow process of marital unravelling. 'But he would taunt her. He would go for the weaker points, and the weaker points were the things she couldn't, physically, do. It was awful to watch.'

As Margaret's visits became fewer, another cause arose for anger and tension. Tony, who loved entertaining, would often give impromptu lunch parties for eight or ten friends at Old House. To feed them, he would raid the Kensington Palace fridge and larder, packing lobsters, cheese, wine or fruit in a hamper to stow in the back of the Aston Martin. As most of these foodstuffs had been bought in on Friday ready to prepare for Monday, when the chef found the cupboard bare and told the Princess there was an inevitable explosion: 'Why should I be expected to feed all your friends? Why must you disrupt arrangements without a word to anybody?' on the one side, to 'Can I not take food from my own house?' on the other.

While Margaret was becoming increasingly lonely, Tony's life had never been busier. As well as accompanying Princess Margaret on some of her official duties and undertaking as many photographic assignments as possible, he was making his second film for television, *Love of a Kind*, a fifty-minute documentary about the devotion of the British to their pets; again, Derek Hart wrote the script. It was shown on 28 October 1969. 'That love makes the world go round is a laconic scientific observation,' wrote television critic Peter Black. 'People who can't get it from other people will find the emotional outlet they need in looking after animals. As we saw, the fact that the power and the love are one-sided sometimes makes the relationship neurotic. One old woman loved her dogs so much she's going to have them all done in when she dies.'

The film, which showed two men breakfasting with their pet monkey, a woman hatching an ostrich egg in her capacious bosom and another who earnestly hoped God would take her and her pet parrot on the same day, attracted plenty of comment. Not all of it was favourable. A zoologist complained because he felt the pet-human relationship was too private to exhibit on the small screen; others queried that anyone spoke to his or her pet as if they were a person – one woman was shown cooing to her parrot as if it were a lover. Derek Hart riposted that 'if you tape-recorded someone talking to their pets, they would hear themselves do it. Everyone thinks their relationship with their animal is "normal" – but what is normality? If you listen to a normal person talking to his pet, it is quite different from your point of view from what it means to them.'

The shots of the woman hatching an egg in her cleavage were more controversial than anything else. Finally she came forward to confess that this was a reconstruction of an episode eleven years earlier when a twenty-one-day incubation of an egg held in a container in her bra resulted in a successful hatching. 'I could never do that now,' she said. 'I suffer from arthritis and I'm in a corset all day with a special bra I could never get an egg into.'

What spare time Tony had was mopped up chiefly by his great friend Peter Sellers, more emotionally needy than ever after divorcing Britt Ekland ('he bit off more than he could screw,' said Tony when he heard the news). Sometimes Sellers would telephone him, talking for hours on end, oblivious of the time; once, when it was nearly dawn, Tony ended the conversation as gently as he could, only to receive a telegram immediately: 'WHY DID YOU HANG UP?' At other times Tony would rush to Sellers's side when he rang full of unhappiness, often to find that his friend had had a lightning change of mood by the time he arrived – or else was in a gloom so profound that nothing Tony said or did, no jokes, no mimicry, no funny stories, could lift it, and Tony found himself sinking into Peter's slough of despond.

Overriding all these varied demands on his time, however, was one supreme commission: the Queen had asked him to design the setting for the Investiture of her son Prince Charles as Prince of Wales in July 1969.

Planning for the Investiture had begun as early as 1967, and for the first time was to include television. To present this medieval ceremony as a worldwide spectacular without it appearing either ludicrous or completely irrelevant to the life of the country meant that as well as those authoritative in its traditions someone with the vision to create the right setting was also needed. As the royal family knew, in Tony they had within their ranks an expert in design who was creative to his fingertips, abreast of contemporary thought and who was, moreover, Welsh (his grandfather could speak the language, although he could not).

The ancient title Prince of Wales had been created in 1301 by Edward I for his son, hoping this would please the Welsh while he was fighting the Scots. Charles, who had become the twenty-first Prince of Wales in 1958, had an abundance of titles, which included those of Earl of Chester, Duke of Cornwall, Duke of Rothesay, Earl of Carrick, Baron Renfrew, Lord of the Isles and Great Steward of Scotland, Knight of the Most Noble Order of the Garter, Knight of the Most Ancient and Most Noble Order of the Thistle, and Great Master and Principal Knight Grand Cross of the Most Honourable Order of the Bath – but to be officially invested as Prince of Wales marked both his majority and his adult fulfilment of the role.

There was, however, considerable opposition to the idea of the Investiture, largely from those who held a Welsh separatist point of view and who would not hesitate to express their feelings in physical form. In view of this, four terms after Charles had begun as an undergraduate at Cambridge, the government wanted him to spend some time at a Welsh university, to study Welsh. Charles was duly enrolled at Aberystwyth University and learned enough of the language to be able to deliver his Investiture speech in fluent Welsh.

For security's sake Tony, whose walkie-talkie radio was in his Aston Martin, suggested to the Buckingham Palace switchboard that as people could listen in on that waveband, he should have a code name. 'Call me Daffodil,' he suggested. 'Don't forget.' 'Yes, me lord,' replied the girl on the telephone exchange. A few minutes later, Tony tried to ring his wife, only to hear the telephonist put him through with 'Oh, Your Royal Highness, it's his lordship on the phone, calling himself Daffodil.' It was the end of that particular attempt at discretion.

Tony was deeply conscious both of the historic significance of the occasion and the fact that it would be watched by a worldwide audience of millions. He had to propose something that maintained the dignity and solemnity of the ceremony, during which Charles would pledge his loyalty to his mother the Queen, and which would allow every nuance to be seen: nothing must obstruct the view of the watching millions and the television cameras therefore must be invisible – two, which occasionally had to take higher shots, were on hydraulic cranes so that they could be moved out of sight after each shot. As the first royal broadcast in colour, it also had to be a glamorous spectacle that would hold audiences through the six hours set aside for it by the BBC.

His solution, using a budget of £50,000, was dramatic, effective and boldly modern while drawing on the historic pageantry of the past. This meant a minimalist approach, so that the Castle could speak for itself. As always, Tony determined to use daylight rather than any artificial lighting, with the overall effect as of theatre in the round.

In the middle of the grass courtyard, against the grey walls of the Castle, he put a dais of slate with three raised thrones, also of Welsh slate, for the Queen, the Duke and the Prince. This came from the quarry owned by Tony's godfather, Michael Duff, who generously made a gift of it. To shield them from any rain that might fall there was a clear Perspex canopy, the model for which was made in Tony's workshop at Kensington Palace. Sometimes his son David was co-opted as assistant, perhaps holding one end of a piece of metal with Tony and a welding torch at the other. This canopy, at 25-foot-square the largest piece of Perspex used to that date, squeezed through the Castle entrance with a mere half-inch clearance. It was embossed with nine-foot-high Prince of Wales feathers, with the feather tips towards the forward edge of the canopy ('this made them look softer') and was supported on pikestaffs made of steel, rather as if it were a tent. As Tony later pointed out: 'It was a romantic dais – we were actually doing what they would have done for Henry V if they'd had Perspex then.'

Tony showed his designs to the Queen and to Prince Philip ('he was very helpful'). When Tony asked if the Duke would mind not having a back to his throne, he replied: 'Not at all – I never lean back, anyway.' The Queen's throne had a back to it; and Prince Charles's had a red cushion – three thrones were considered more pleasing design-wise than two. The correct height for the respective thrones was achieved at Clarence House, using chairs and tele-phone books (in the real ones, of slate, there were hidden micro-phones to relay the service).

The Castle was closed six months before the ceremony and Tony began to spend most weeks in Wales. He co-opted two designers to work with him: Carl Toms, whom he knew from his days with Oliver Messel and whose bias was towards the romantic, and John Pound, a brutalist.

No detail was too small to escape Tony's notice. The abundant notices that adorned the Castle walls were ruthlessly pruned, reduced in size and often re-sited where they were less obtrusive but still visible to the public. Stained glass was protected with Perspex instead of mesh, unsightly chicken wire removed from windows, the risers on the steps to the royal dais painted to resemble their slate surroundings, the sizes of the rope 'banisters' up various spiral staircases standardised. He pointed out that if lights were to be needed at the back of the orchestra these should not be tungsten ones because of the televising difficulties they would create, and made a note to himself to tell the Queen that she would be walking on grass so that she could choose appropriate shoes.

He was lent a small speedboat, and to keep himself in trim would go waterskiing with Toms and Pound in the early morning before work – as an excellent sailor, bouncing about on choppy waves never worried him, although once he was nearly sunk. Running up the coast one day with Pound in the speedy little boat they realised they were opposite Lord Newborough's property, where a large crowd was gathered round a cannon that had been installed there during an invasion scare in the Napoleonic wars. Almost at the same moment there was a loud explosion and only Tony's almost instantaneous opening-up of the throttle saved them – the next second another cannonball landed in their wake, covering them with spray. Coolly, Tony remembered that the Newboroughs were having a cocktail party to which he had been invited. The two landed, and had a restorative drink. On land, he got about in his Aston Martin or, more often, on his Triumph 500 motorbike.

The ceremony was under the overall charge of the Earl Marshal. This was the Duke of Norfolk, Britain's premier earl and a man of enormous experience in handling State ceremonies – he had been in charge of the State funeral of George VI in 1952, the Coronation in 1953, and Tony's own marriage in 1960. As Constable of the Castle, Tony worked closely with him.

'We hear that the Earl Marshal and the Constable of Caernarvon Castle hate each other,' wrote Cynthia Gladwyn (one feels a trifle gleefully) on 29 June 1969. 'The former is the most excellent and efficient organiser of ceremonial and the latter is only concerned with television publicity.' Later that day, at dinner, Field Marshal Templer told the Gladwyns 'that the Duke of Norfolk and Snowdon are now on such bad terms that it is no longer a question of them not speaking to each other, they cannot even bear to look at each other'. It was far from the truth. On the prospect of television, the Duke of Norfolk had already commented: 'If people invent these things you've got to live with them,' and was immediately prepared to be co-operative with Tony, who later described him as 'super'.

When Sir Anthony Wagner, Garter King-of-Arms, wanted a striped awning leading to the thrones to keep the Queen dry should rain pelt down, the Duke vetoed it as being out of keeping, a move which met with Tony's entire approbation.

Although he found working with the Duke, who told him, 'You know about art, you get on with it,' easy and enjoyable, Tony and Sir Anthony got across each other from the beginning. One argument involved whether the Welsh dragons emblazoned on the scarlet banners should have knots in their tails, the Snowdon team saying that they should, Garter disagreeing. 'All dragons have knots in their tails,' insisted Toms. Garter stood his ground until eventually Tony said: 'Oh come on, Garter darling, can't you be a bit more elastic?' In the face of the hoots this produced, Garter unwillingly succumbed.

Tony's main reverse was not being allowed to bring his children – the Queen had vetoed children – but it was left to the Earl Marshal to tell Princess Margaret. Instead, Tony took the children to the Constable's Room in the Tower, where they watched the ceremony on a rented colour television. Nor did Sir Anthony care for it when, during one rehearsal when the Heralds were solemnly processing to their appointed places, a Sandie Shaw song rang out through the loudspeakers, substituted by Tony for the more dignified music selected (this ranged from Schubert's *Marche Militaire*, *Tannhäuser* and *Lohengrin* from Wagner and Handel's *Hallelujah Chorus* to specially commissioned works based on old Welsh airs).

Not only were their ideas different, they were temperamental opposites, Sir Anthony thoughtful, considered and traditional in approach, Tony mercurial, fast-talking, anxious to include new ideas and against anything he considered smacked of old-fashioned snobbery. 'The Ministry of Works were such snobs,' he later recalled. 'They wanted the VIPs to have grand chairs and the riff-raff, as they called them, to sit on planks on the scaffolding. But we [Tony and his fellow designers] wouldn't have it.' Instead, there were 4,000 chairs made of scarlet wood, with scarlet Welsh tweed seats, backs and seats to which legs were attached by screws. After the Investiture those who had sat on them were asked if they would like to buy their seats for £12; if so, the chairs arrived packed flat in a box (somewhat of a novelty then). These sales helped to defray the cost of the ceremony, a subject of close parliamentary scrutiny. Tony bought six, used to this day.

The Prince wore his Commander-in-Chief's uniform, and over it a purple surcoat trimmed with ermine. Tony had envisaged a simple coronet of gold for Charles – rather like that in *Henry V* – which would have been perfect. But unfortunately Sir Anthony had a much larger and more ornate affair of velvet and gold, replete with jewels, crosses and fleurs-de-lys made up on his own initiative. The result, the Queen later told Noël Coward, was 'like a candle snuffer' on Charles's head. Tony had also wanted all the women to wear long dresses, as in the Garter procession, but again was overruled.

However, he was able to design his own uniform as Constable and in keeping with his minimal approach it lacked buttons, braid or any other superfluous trimming. Cynthia Gladwyn described it: 'The Constable of the Castle wore a self-designed uniform of bottle green which would have been very suitable for a com-missionaire. His complexion was bronzed (I fancy it was made up for television) and he was darting here, there and everywhere.' With its zip-fastened, roll-collared jacket and narrow trousers, it earned him several nicknames: 'Buttons', 'The Green Elf', 'Peter Pan' and 'Principal Boy' among them. Tony, however, liked it so much that with his hallmark streak of contrariness he would wear it instead of a dinner jacket for dinner at Balmoral.

The investiture took place at the medieval castle of Caernarvon on 1 July 1969, when the Prince was aged twenty. The ceremony, watched by television audiences worldwide, marked not only his presentation to his constituency, but also his integration into public life. He now had official duties and responsibilities to fulfil, the first of which was a tour of Wales, where to his apparent surprise he was met with great warmth and cheer.

What would have happened if it had rained? Tony's response was: 'As the Duke of Norfolk said at the Coronation, "Well, we'll all get bloody wet".' The only precaution that could be taken was to cover the scarlet chairs with polythene – when this was removed at the beginning of the ceremony there was a sudden burst of scarlet.

Although there had earlier been bombs from Welsh protesters (the BBC had even organised prerecorded obituary tributes in case the Prince should be assassinated), on the day nothing went wrong, although as Tony himself said: 'I was in agony, I was so nervous. That's why I minded Jeremy Thorpe wearing a mackintosh when it didn't even rain.'

The ceremony opened with the Queen's arrival, upon which Patrick Plunket, Master of the Household, knocked on the Castle's Water Gate. This was opened by Tony, who bore a fifteen-inch key. 'Madam, I surrender the key of this Castle into your hand,' he said, whereupon the Queen touched it, saying: 'Sir Constable, I return the key of the Castle into your keeping.' The Queen, with the Duke, then went to the slate thrones beneath the Perspex canopy and the Prince appeared with his procession, which included six Welsh peers carrying the insignia of the Princes of Wales. The Queen then invested him with the insignia and he knelt, placed his hands between hers, and swore: 'I, Charles, Prince of Wales, do become your liege man of life and limb and of earthly worship, and faith and truth I will bear unto you to live and die against all manner of folks.'

Both the Queen and the Prince are on record as saying they found the ceremony extremely moving and at the time their deep and obvious belief in the importance of the words they were saying was apparent not only to those watching in person but also to the wider television audience. George Thomas, the Secretary of State for Wales, thought that 'it was a far greater triumph than we had a right to expect. He really was the Prince Charming'. Later, a survey showed that this programme had heightened awareness of the royal family's apartness from everyday life but at the same time increased support for the monarchy.

Tony's *mise-en-scène* was considered such a triumph that he was cheered as he left the Castle; and he was awarded the GCVO in the Investiture Honours. The Queen wrote to him with thanks and congratulations, confessing that she had initially been sceptical and was delighted to have been proved wrong. When she described the view of the ceremony on television as 'spectacular and breathtaking' she was summing up the opinion of a global audience: nothing like it had ever been seen before. It was simple, elegant, modern yet at the same time it expressed the historic past.

Congratulations flooded in from all over the world, most amply vindicating Tony's decision to allow the simplicity and grandeur of the ceremony to speak for itself to the widest possible audience without irrelevant intervention. 'The authentic medieval atmosphere was a perfect complement to the grandeur of the ceremony but what impressed most of us was the complete lack of clutter,' wrote a twenty-year-old drama student from Sydney. 'I know I can speak for my family and all my friends who watched, when I say how appreciative we were that you gave such prime importance to the world audience, not just those fortunate enough to be present.' 'For once we TV viewers were able to see all of this historic event without the scene being blocked by unnecessary clutter,' wrote Mrs Judith Pritchard from Telford, Shropshire. Barbara Walters, the NBC network queen, wrote: 'The Investiture was received with such joy by Americans and it may interest you to know that our coverage on NBC had the largest rating of all the networks. We had sixty-seven per cent of the national audience and it was the highest rating for that time period that the network has ever had.'

There were letters from the royal family, best represented by a comment from that of Sir Angus Ogilvy: 'It is not often one can say with sincerity "It would have been hard to improve on" but Tuesday was certainly one of those occasions.' Lord Mountbatten wrote from Broadlands: 'Having taken part in more royal occasions than anybody in the family except Harry Gloucester and Alice Athlone (who were neither of them there) I would like to pay a tribute to the decorations at Caernarvon Castle. They were the most impressive because of their simplicity and good taste I have ever seen.'

George Thomas, writing to congratulate Tony on his recognition by the Queen ('no one more richly deserved it'), continued with: 'I have already told you how superbly you did your part.' Even his earlier opponent, Garter King-of-Arms, apologising for leaving behind a mackintosh, umbrella and KCVO star, gave a generous accolade: 'The Castle looked splendid. Keeping the skyline clear meant everything.'

John Betjeman summed up many of the points made by others when he wrote: 'It was really one of *the* great days of my life. I can't quite put into words its tremendous effect. It was local and intimate and yet international. It was a family event and yet for everyone; it was a beautiful clear ritual like the Book of Common Prayer; it kept Wales as a separate country; it was superbly staged. The decorations seemed to me perfect, they weren't fake medieval and they weren't aggressive contemporary.'

For Tony, the immense success of the setting he had designed was a personal triumph, an achievement that could have been matched by few others. In a life crowded with extraordinary events, it was a high point; along with the Snowdon Aviary, it was one of the two design projects in his life of which he would remain most proud.

11

Feeling Trapped

❊

Another marital disaster stemming from Tony's fixation with Old House was about to emerge publicly. The path to Old House led off Staplefield Green and passed Staplefield Grange, then the home of the Marquis and Marchioness of Reading. Tony had first met these neighbours, who lived only a quarter of a mile away, when he asked if he could put two concrete tracks up their path to reach Old House as there was virtually no access for vehicles other than tractors or Land Rovers. Naturally enough, Lord and Lady Reading agreed, although Lady Reading already had a presentiment that this might lead to difficulties.

The first was that once Tony and his friends increasingly began to use the previously semi-private lane that led towards the Reading house, so did many other people, from firemen to dog-walkers, and the privacy the Readings had so valued disappeared. The second problem was infinitely more serious but the Readings would not realise it for some time. As Princess Margaret came down several times during Tony's first occupancy of Old House, the Readings met her and the Armstrong-Jones children, whose small grey pony was kept in their field. All of them noticed the contrast in styles between Tony and his wife and, gradually, the increasing acrimony – Tony, determined to show who was boss in the marriage, would often say sharply when Margaret was speaking: 'Shut up and let someone intelligent talk.' But Margot Reading's disapproval of rudeness to a spouse in front of others was overwhelmed by the effect of Tony's charm.

As Margaret's visits decreased, Tony often came down by himself on his motorbike. One reason was that their son David was a boarder at Ashdown House, a £200-a-term preparatory school a few miles from Old House, and Tony was anxious to see as much as possible of him. Every free day his son was allowed Tony (if he was in England) would spend with him at Old House, where Tony taught him to fish in the lake (encouraging his interest by stocking it with fish which soon took the bait), teaching him to use a camera and nurturing his growing bent for making things.

Often, Tony dropped in on the Readings, joining them for most meals at Margot Reading's huge kitchen table (absent-mindedly, Lady Reading had ordered it in yards rather than feet) or inviting them up to Old House. Quickly he became an intimate, charming them all with his charismatic personality, his endless flow of jokes and his gift for making the simplest walk in the fields or family supper something vivid and exciting. 'He was like a firework bursting into our lives,' said one of the family later.

There were endless jokes, from Tony's oblique and funny remarks to practical ones that ranged from humiliating to childish – a favourite, when there were grand or pompous visitors, was to make an imitation dog-mess out of crumbled ginger biscuits moulded with water, pretend to spot it suddenly, then say: 'Oh, look what the dog's done,' scoop it up and eat it. There would be games with corks – 'Watch what I do and then do it', would be the command as he made passes in the air and over his face, the only difference being that Tony's was a clean cork and the unsuspecting victim's marked with cigarette ash. On other evenings they would sortie out to the houses of neighbours they knew to be out or away and rearrange all the furniture – pranks that seem silly and childish but, done with Tony's panache and high spirits, kept everyone laughing helplessly.

After a while, it was noticeable that he was seeing more of two of the Reading children than the rest of the family: their son Lord Anthony Rufus-Isaacs and their daughter Lady Jacqueline (always known as Jackie). All of them, however, witnessed at first hand the difficulties in the Snowdon marriage and, as time passed, became aware that it was close to collapse.

Jackie, born in November 1946, had been fourteen or fifteen when she first met Tony, then in the early, happy days of his marriage to the Princess, at her parents' home. As the two families' friendship grew, and Jackie became older, she would visit Old House more frequently; at the same time, the Princess was seen there less often. By 1968 Jackie, an acknowledged beauty, was a favourite of the gossip columns with an established London life, working as a model and in the Bond Street boutique of the designer Yves St Laurent. What no one, including her family, knew was that she and Tony were in love and having an affair. She was slim, blonde, sexy, well educated, sharp-witted and with a zest for life as appealing as it was attractive. It would have been a strange man indeed who, seeing her so constantly, did not succumb. The susceptible Tony was not that man.

As most of Jackie's friends knew, her family home was close to the Snowdons' weekend retreat, so to see her in a party with Tony at first aroused no suspicions, although there was an early 'near-miss' with the unsuspecting Princess Margaret when the Princess, on her way back from staying for the weekend with Lord and Lady Rupert Nevill in Sussex, said to her chauffeur Larkin, 'Let's call in at Old House.' Larkin, who knew much more about Tony's activities than did his employer, wondered frantically what he could do to avert what he felt might be a catastrophic confrontation that would cause the Princess pain. Knowing how quick Tony was to pick up signals, he flashed the headlights of the Vauxhall estate car (in which the Princess often travelled on private visits) off and on all the way up the track to Old House.

When they arrived, Tony was there to meet them. After greeting Margaret affectionately, he turned to Larkin and said, with a meaningful look unseen by the Princess: 'The Aston Martin wants some petrol in it – you'll get some in the village.' Larkin, whose responsibilities included filling the tanks of the royal cars, knew perfectly well that there was plenty of petrol in the Aston Martin's. Accordingly, he drove the car to nearby Staplefield Green where he opened the boot – to see Jackie curled up inside it. From the village she could walk back to her parents' house openly and innocently.

What was noted publicly was that although Princess Margaret and Tony had watched the 11 December 1969 premiere of Peter Sellers's film *The Magic Christian* together, they arrived separately at the gala party afterwards at the nightclub Les Ambassadeurs.

Margaret gazes lovingly at Tony on their San Francisco visit in November 1965.

Tony and Margaret with their children in front of No.1A
Kensington Palace in 1965.

The Snowdon Aviary at London Zoo in 1965.
It had been opened the year before.

Tony walking along the
internal bridge at the
Snowdon Aviary, 1965.

Bob Belton with Tony (*left*) and Princess Margaret (*below*) on the Princess's birthday in August 1960. Margaret and Tony had taken Belton with them to stay at Birr and Lady Rosse had chartered a boat for the day.

Richard Wood (*left*) and Malcolm Higgins in the Kensington Palace livery worn for special occasions in the mid-sixties. Princess Margaret's spaniel Rowley is between them.

Tony's sister Susan, married to Viscount de Vesci.

Robin Douglas-Home in the 1960s.

Tony and Prince Charles at Caernarvon Castle, before Charles's Investiture as Prince of Wales in July 1969.

Tony in wetsuit, ready for waterskiing, one of his favourite sports.

Tony and Judy Gendel (formerly Judy Montagu) reading magazines at the Caffè Gilli in Florence in 1968.

Jackie Rufus-Isaacs in
modelling pose,
July 1970.

Jackie Rufus-Isaacs and Tony at Les Ambassadeurs Club,
December 1969.

A view of Old House from across the lake created by Tony.

Once there, Princess Margaret sat at a table with friends like Jocelyn Stevens and her cousin Lord Lichfield and Tony went to the table occupied by Jackie and her brother Anthony. Britt Ekland, too, shortly before her divorce, noticed 'a closeness between the couple'. And once Jackie said to her: 'You are lucky to be able to go out with someone openly – I can't.'

Jackie often had dinner with Tony in London, but in a well-known restaurant it would be in a party, or with Anthony, who would tactfully slip away at the end of the evening. When he wanted to pick her up from work, Tony would resort to the subterfuge of a pseudonym. The shop's telephone would ring, and the voice at the other end would say: 'Can I speak to Lady Jacqueline? It's Dr Ricketts.' If the coast was clear, the black-leather-clad figure of Tony would roar up on the bike, Jackie would hop nimbly on the back and they would be away. For suppers *à deux* the favoured place was San Lorenzo, where he could rely on the discretion of his friends Lorenzo and Mara Berni. Few had noticed that sometimes his car was parked all night outside the block in Cundy Street where Jackie had a flat.

If the Reading parents had known what was going on they would have been desperately worried that their beautiful daughter, with her life ahead of her, was entangled not simply with a man who was married but with one who was married to the sister of the Queen of England. At the very least, a scandal of enormous proportions would have ensued. As it was, Lady Reading, in whom Tony had finally confided what was increasingly obvious, that his marriage was on the rocks, had become sufficiently disturbed by the closeness she had noticed between her daughter and Tony and his disruptive effect on their lives that one night, just before midnight, she walked up to Old House to see him. She spoke to him straightforwardly: 'Tony, I think you have got to step back out of our lives. You're getting too involved and it's not fair. And you don't really love any of us.' 'But I do,' he said. 'Well, it's a funny way of showing it,' replied Lady Reading.

The Snowdons now often went to parties by themselves or visited separate friends. Larkin would take the Princess to the Notting Hill Gate house of Derek Hart, where she and Hart would enjoy a romantic lunch, picking her up later at around three or three-thirty. Nor was Margaret at the grand party *Vogue* Editor Beatrix Miller gave for Lesley Blanch (author of *The Wilder Shores of Love*) at her house in Mulberry Walk, Chelsea, its large drawing room in different shades of russet acting as a backdrop for the sartorial vagaries of the fashionable guests – Susan Crewe* in black velvet knee breeches, the writer Marina Warner in Turkish clothes and Tony himself in a billowing white shirt, black velvet trousers, huge gold bracelet and oversize watch.

Gradually the circle round Margaret, and Margaret herself, became aware of Jackie's involvement in Tony's life. When Tony – in part to avoid Christmas at Sandringham with his wife – chose 17 December 1970 to enter the London Clinic for an operation for piles (he emerged on 19 December), it was Jackie who spent long hours by his bedside, on occasions narrowly missing a visit by Margaret. For Margaret this proof of Tony's closeness to the young beauty who was seemingly desperately in love with him was devastating. For someone so proud, the public humiliation was hard to bear and with her only perspective on relationships that of the constrained royal circles in which she had been brought up, it was difficult for her to know how to counter this threat. Reproaches had no effect, nor did sweet talk.

Once – perhaps to frighten Jackie off, perhaps to show that as the wife she was still pre-eminent – she went down to Old House with her lady-in-waiting. This did not stop Tony asking Jackie over to lunch. 'I'm so worried Princess Margaret won't be nice to her – will you be there and smooth it over?' he said to the lady-in-waiting, who felt outraged on Margaret's behalf at such a request. There were times when Margaret was so unhappy that she would sob on the shoulder of the devoted Larkin. Once or twice, although aware of the rule that no one must touch royalty, he gave the weeping Princess a hug. 'It'll be all right,' he would tell her comfortingly. 'He's just messing about.'

Yet although by now they appeared to be leading virtually separate lives, with never-ending rows, the reality was that both still felt themselves tied to the other and both, the intimate side of their relationship still intact, suffered the sexual jealousy that now

---

* Susan Cavendish married Quentin Crewe in 1970.

had Margaret in its grip. 'I drove Princess Margaret home from a dinner party one night at that time,' recalled the distinguished doctor Frank Tait (a close friend of Lady Elizabeth Cavendish), 'and she was terribly upset. She said to me: "I could nurse him well – you know, when I was a Girl Guide I got a badge for nursing."'

Unhappy as she was, Margaret was still doing her best to keep the marriage going. She could not quite believe in, or understand, Tony's unkindness to her, while at the same time failing to realise how difficult she herself could be. Sometimes she would ask one of her confidantes, usually a lady-in-waiting: 'Do you think Tony's got a point?' 'Should I have been able to be housekeeper and bottlewasher at Old House?' she would often say to Anne Tennant (who had become her lady-in-waiting in 1970), adding a moment later: 'But I just couldn't do it, and I hated being there. *He* chose it, he didn't ask me if I wanted to go there – then of course he would go down with the women.'

Jackie was another reason that Margaret ceased to come down to Old House – to watch her husband at his best and most tender with a woman she knew he was in love with was more than she could bear. The affair upset her deeply although she did her best not to let those closest to her see how upset she was. Occasionally a chance remark would give away her feelings. When the painter Bryan Organ lunched with her *à deux* she told him that his portrait of Tony 'captured his ruthlessness'. Roy Strong, who confided this to his diary on 21 January 1971, added: 'How long can this marriage go on?'

For those who entered it, or worked there, the toxic atmosphere in Kensington Palace now seemed all-pervasive. Most of the rows were about trivia, a constant battling to show who was 'top dog'. Margaret's upbringing and background had convinced her that she was always the most important person in the room; Tony was determined to show he was master in his own house and that he would not be bossed around. Thus if his wife asked: 'Tony, will you sit in the front of the car,' he would climb into the back. His sense of alienation and misery made him flail out, like the child he so often resembled, at those around him. Because the salaries of the staff in Margaret's office were paid by her, he viewed them as being in his wife's 'camp'. When one new member of her staff arrived he told her: 'You may think you're in the middle but you're really on their side – you can't be on my side.'

The small office and security staff – private secretary, policeman, lady-in-waiting, accountant and secretary – worked in a different building. If sent for, they would cross the cobbled courtyard, usually with a slight panic feeling as to why they were being summoned. Sometimes it would be the Princess saying stiffly: 'Would you please find out if my husband is coming to lunch?' Down to the workshop basement the hapless emissary would go, to receive the answer 'Perhaps', or 'I don't know yet', then up again to an icy Princess. 'It was worse when he did come,' recalled one lady-in-waiting, then in her early twenties. 'Sitting between them at lunch was terrible, a bit like one's worst moments at school – you never knew what was coming next.'

It was the same for the servants: driving with Margaret beside him in the car, Tony would ask the butler, Malcolm Higgins, sitting behind, to light a cigarette for him. Higgins would do this and hand it to him, then to his acute discomfort hear Margaret say plaintively, 'Darling, can't I do that for you?'

Margaret's Private Secretary, Lt-Col. Frederick Burnaby-Atkins, caught in the middle, came off even worse. As he was responsible for the smooth running of her life, he had to ensure that everything needed for this was in place and functioning properly. If Tony took her official Rolls-Royce, used for her public engagements, down to Old House to see Jackie, bringing it back covered with mud on a Sunday evening so that it could not be used for an early engagement on Monday morning, the Private Secretary had to remonstrate – and Tony would be furious to receive a note to this effect.

Food would now often disappear on a daily basis, taken by Tony for a meal cooked in his quarters at the other end of the house; as overseeing supplies was also the responsibility of Burnaby-Atkins, this too provoked remonstrances and an angry response, usually on the lines of: 'Is this my house, or isn't it?' The Private Secretary also had to deal with complaints from Nanny

Sumner: 'I won't have that man coming up my stairs smoking a cigarette,' with Tony's justifiable response: 'I won't be told in my own house that I can't see my own children.'

There were further difficulties if the Snowdons were asked as a couple to perform an engagement. Asked by Burnaby-Atkins if he was to accept on behalf of them both, the Princess would say: 'Oh, you'd better go and ask Tony.' As his reply was usually: 'I'm damned if I'm going,' Burnaby-Atkins would have to return and say: 'I'm afraid Tony isn't available.' If the Princess did not want to accept this, it was backwards and forwards down the corridor again, sometimes half a dozen times.

Sometimes there would be an angry call over the intercom from Tony: 'What is all this about – this note?' 'I'm sorry, which note?' would respond the lady-in-waiting at the other end, who might have sent numerous notes during the previous week. 'Well, did you or did you not send it?' 'I'm sure I did, but I can't remember – perhaps I'd better come over and see you.' 'I don't think I want to see you' – and down would slam the telephone. 'Nobody could be more charming or interesting when he wanted to be,' said one lady-in-waiting. 'He could be nicer than anyone. You'd go over and he'd *pour* charm over you. At other times he'd have you over and virtually pull your wings out, for the fun of it – in front of other people.' One warning sign that he had taken against someone or was cross with a friend was the sudden tacking-on of a surname where a Christian name only had been the norm.

So tense and difficult had the Snowdons' life together become that sometimes they even fought in front of the Queen Mother, shouting at each other across the drawing room at Clarence House. One argument, over a gala at the Royal Ballet, was so ferocious that the Queen Mother said to her page, William Tallon, 'Come on, William, we're going – into the pantry. We're not being privy to this.'

Tony was wretched in this desperate situation but at least he could fling himself into work. An account of one of his Design Council tours, to various Welsh factories, written in 1971 (by Douglas Keay) shows not only his commitment but also his phenomenal energy and impeccable eye for detail.

The group arrived in Caernarvon after 11 p.m.; Tony dragged

them out on a midnight walk round the Castle, where he pointed out that the floodlighting was all wrong ('too yellow'). For the next three days, tours started at eight-thirty as factory after factory was visited and the artefacts each made closely inspected. 'The design of the tooling that makes the engine that goes inside the washing machine is every bit as important as – maybe more important than – the outside casing,' said Tony. 'Equally, if a coffee pot does not pour properly, it's a badly designed coffee pot, no matter how beautiful it looks.'

Away from work – and life without work was meaningless to Tony – there were the constraints and difficulties involved in the whole business of being royal, from the forcing of his whole personality into an accepted mould to what he saw as traditions so outmoded as no longer to have any meaning. While on the one hand he was fiercely monarchist and enjoyed the perks that came with his status as the Queen's brother-in-law and – as for anyone of 'celebrity' status – the insidious pleasure of being recognised, on the other he was insistently democratic. He could not stand the stuffy attitudes of many in the Household and he rebelled against them in small ways.

These polarised attitudes were reflected in his sometimes contradictory approach. He would, for instance, be thoughtful over his assistants' comfort, insist that they ate with him and if anything went wrong be extremely understanding. Yet while travelling economy on an ordinary passenger flight he would demand a Bellini while still on the ground 'because I always have one on take-off' (as he did on royal flights with the Princess) or attempt to use a walkie-talkie on descending to alert his driver and make a fuss when the air steward told him it was against the rules. At home, this dichotomy was reflected in the battles with someone as determined as himself to get her own way, culminating in rows or icy silences.

Above all he felt trapped. He had always 'moved on' – to use one of his favourite phrases – when the spirit took him; indeed, the spontaneity that was part of his charm was also an essential part of his character. With Jackie, apart from the flattery implicit in the adoration of a beautiful young woman, there was a return to the happy, hedonistic, carefree days before he had become enmeshed in the demands of Palace life. With Jackie, for instance, he had torn round the Isle of Wight one sunny day in the speedboat he had been lent for the Investiture, both of them smoking joints; with Jackie he laughed constantly, with Jackie there was youth, love, fun, hours spent in the place he loved the best – and no hint ever of being expected to walk two steps behind with folded hands.

He began seriously to consider the idea of divorce; and to speak of marriage to Jackie. At the beginning of his marriage the whole idea had been anathema to him, not simply because of his feelings for Princess Margaret but because the thought of the presence at his wedding of his father's three wives had filled him with ashamed distaste.

Then, in January 1971, their hands were forced. Nigel Dempster (of the *Daily Express*, later famous for his column in the *Daily Mail*) was such a friend of Jackie's brother Anthony that he came to stay constantly at the Grange for weekends and had become rather like another son of the house. He had learned that a New York paper was about to run a story saying that the Snowdons' marriage was falling apart and linking Tony with Jackie.

When Dempster told the Readings this they decided that Jackie, who had said that the story was untrue, should accept the invitation of a Sussex friend and neighbour, Anita Fuglesang, to stay with her in Gsteig, near the ski resort of Gstaad in Switzerland, to keep out of the way of the inevitable publicity. Jackie's eldest brother, Simon (Lord Erleigh) and two other friends had also been invited on this skiing holiday.

A night or two before Jackie left, she ran into two brothers who were friends of hers, one of whom was destined to deliver the final death blow to the Snowdon marriage. These were David and Roderic Llewellyn, always known as Dai and Roddy, the sons of the famous showjumper Harry Llewellyn.* 'Why don't you come out to Switzerland too?' she asked them. A few days later, her mother also came to stay and shortly afterwards, the Llewellyn brothers arrived, by car, with Dai driving and Roddy perched on the bonnet.

---

* Harry Llewellyn, who went on to have a distinguished and philanthropic career, was knighted in 1977 and became a baronet on the death of his brother the following year.

When the story broke (on 7 January 1971, in the *New York Daily News*) it was immediately picked up by the British papers and reported on radio and television news broadcasts. Lord Reading angrily denied that there was anything in it, which is what he believed at the time. 'I have no doubt that my daughter sees Lord Snowdon in London. My son and my wife also see him in London,' he said. In Switzerland, Jackie found herself besieged, with newspapermen and CBS News camped outside the door of the chalet. In a telephone call, Tony told her to deny everything. 'I really cannot understand why my name should be linked with Lord Snowdon's – he sees much more of my brother Anthony,' was Jackie's dismissive comment, duly reported by Dempster from Gstaad the following day and picked up by papers as far afield as Perth, Western Australia. There were more denials at home, from Lord Reading and Lady Reading, from Buckingham Palace and from Kensington Palace.

Once back at home, however, and pressed by her father, Jackie broke down and eventually admitted that she and Tony were having an affair. The Readings were furious. Quite apart from the fact that Tony was married – and to the second best-known woman in Britain – they felt that their trust and hospitality had been abused. There were threats of horsewhipping and he was banned from the Grange. To scotch the rumours, Tony and his sister Susan flew to Barbados, to stay with their uncle Oliver; eight days later, Margaret flew out to join him – Oliver had built a small pavilion for them in his luxuriant garden to give them a degree of privacy whenever they came to stay. On her arrival at the airport they were photographed embracing and looking happily and affectionately at each other before climbing into Oliver's air-conditioned Rolls-Royce. The affair was effectively over.

The constraints of Tony's life seemed to be closing in on him. His world was changing: as well as losing Jackie, and with her, the friendship of her family – if he bumped into the Readings on their shared path they turned away – another great friend was in trouble. In August 1970 Peter Sellers had married Miranda Quarry, the daughter of Lord Mancroft, whom he had met at the start of the

London to Melbourne car rally at Crystal Palace in 1969. For the first year they lived in Cheyne Gardens and then left to live a few miles outside Dublin in the palatial Carton House, with its thousand acres of parkland, in the village of Maynooth in County Kildare. Their farewell party was in San Lorenzo, hung for the occasion with emerald green balloons and streamers. Sellers would, he announced, be opening a branch of San Lorenzo in Dublin. But already the Sellerses' marriage was beginning to unravel. Miranda had been brought up in an ambience altogether different from the world with which Sellers was familiar. As Tony told the story, one evening when Sellers was handing round port after dinner, Miranda said to him 'Don't you know that port goes round the other way?' This criticism and implied reproof pressed all the wrong buttons in the volatile Sellers psyche. As Tony recorded: 'He went berserk, screaming: "Nah, I fuckin' don't. I'm a fuckin' Jewish actor." Miranda had lots of birds in cages and he let them all out and hit them round the room with a tennis racket. We then left and I took him to my sister's.'

They drove through the night, arriving at Abbey Leix at about 6 a.m. and threw gravel at Susan's window. She leaned out and, unflappable and welcoming as usual, simply said: 'Oh, good morning, darling, have you had breakfast?' They went in and ate and stayed there for the day until Sellers, whose boredom threshold was even lower than Tony's, suggested they moved on. To the pleasure of Sellers, always impressed by titles, they drove to Birr. A day or two later Tony took Sellers back to his house, where he knew Sellers's manservant Bert (Mortimer), 'the great Bert', who did everything for him, would look after him.

Once back in England, and still worried about his friend, so subject to deep depressions, he telephoned to find out if all was well. The telephone was answered by Spike Milligan, pretending to be a Chinese manservant. All that could be heard above the noise of an uproarious party was Milligan declaring that Mr Sellers had gone out dancing. It was a moment's light relief in a gloomy overall picture.

An added irritant was the attention of the press to everything the Princess, and Tony, did. One in particular, the photographer Ray Bellisario, continued to drive them mad: bobbing out from behind a bush in the most unlikely settings, he would walk backwards a few feet in front of the Princess, snapping away almost in her face. One day Tony, driven beyond endurance at the village fête at Staplefield Green, reversed his car into Bellisario's, who promptly issued three summonses against him: driving a motor car in a manner dangerous to the public, driving without due care and attention and, thirdly, reversing for an unreasonable distance. The case was heard in the Haywards Heath Magistrates Court on 9 September 1971. The first and third charges were dismissed out of hand and the second, of careless driving, proved. Tony was fined £20 with £20 costs and his licence was endorsed. From his point of view, it was money well spent: Bellisario was far less troublesome after that.

Only work seemed to be going well. That June Tony joined the royal family for the traditional carriage drive up the course for Royal Ascot, sitting beside Princess Alexandra, but did not attend for the rest of Ascot Week, nor did he make one of the Queen's Windsor Castle house party. Although his work commitments would in any case have prevented this – he was photographing for *Vogue* almost constantly – he disliked racing, finding it boring; nor did he much care for those involved in it. To him, the racing circle round the royal family represented the stuffier side of Palace life that he so much disliked.

This dislike took open form at a party for 400 given by the canned-food millionaire Jack Heinz and his wife Drue at their Mayfair home on 10 June 1971, where Tony spotted the beautiful Countess of Westmorland dancing with the Queen Mother's trainer, Peter Cazalet. Like many another man, Tony was a great admirer of Lady Westmorland, and tried to cut in on Peter Cazalet. Cazalet, however, was not prepared to relinquish his dance with the Countess and responded by saying: 'We don't do that here – that's an American habit.' Next time the couple came round, Tony threw a glass of white wine over Cazalet's shirt front. Not content with that, when they revolved round again, he grasped the top of Cazalet's trousers, pulling them outward, and poured another glass of wine down inside them. 'I thought it should be red wine this time,' he said. Cazalet, determined not to embarrass his hosts, did not make a scene, but the incident found its way into the following day's papers.

Tony's work commitments alone would have given him plenty of excuses to be absent from home. With Derek Hart, who had become a close friend of both the Snowdons since first interviewing him about the Snowdon Aviary, he was making what became another highly successful film for the BBC. This was *Born to be Small*, an hour-long documentary, screened on 6 December 1971, on what the world called dwarfs, or midgets, but whom Tony invariably referred to as 'people of restricted growth'; in Britain alone there were an estimated 3,000.

Such was Tony and Margaret's relationship now that she believed the film was a dig at her – she had always minded greatly that she was so small since her childhood, when her grandmother Queen Mary would look down at her and remark: 'Oh, I see Margaret hasn't grown.' Her complex about this was not helped by *Private Eye*'s frequent references to 'the Royal Dwarfs'. Even four years later, when congratulated by the actor Gordon Jackson on her husband's film, she responded: 'Not my cup of tea at all. Bit too near home, I'm afraid.'

Restricted growth was a brave and unusual subject to tackle. As well as the major issues, it focused on many less obvious problems that anyone of this height (around that of the average six-year-old child) might face, from not being able to see over shop counters, having to jump to take the receiver off the hook in a public telephone booth, being pushed around unseen in the rush hour to putting up with continual staring and comments from children and the never-ceasing difficulty of finding employment – one reason why so many said they ended up in circuses or on the stage. What came across most strongly was the cheerfulness, courage and good nature of the small subjects interviewed, although some of their stories were heart-rending. It was seen by fourteen million in Britain and came eighth in the ratings for that week – an extraordinarily high placing for a documentary. The reviews were uniformly excellent. 'The film, directed by Lord Snowdon and produced by Derek Hart, was consistently fascinating and contained images to be remembered when all the other television documentaries of the year have been forgotten,' wrote Sean Day-Lewis in *The Daily Telegraph*. 'The justification of this documentary is that it is a microcosm of the enormous problem of abnormality and public prejudice, patronage, ignorance, cruelty and jeering fear,' wrote Nancy Banks-Smith in *The Guardian*; in the London *Evening Standard* Penelope Mortimer told readers: 'What will really haunt me for a long time were the twins, minuscule Katharine Hepburns, who sat identically dressed on a small sofa, and looking at each other with gigantic love, tenderness and a sense of irony, said: "We're an act of God, aren't we?"' Peter Black of the *Daily Mail* summed up the approach that would become Tony's credo in his future work with those in some way handicapped by a physical condition: 'The moral Snowdon and Hart were pointing to was that people who are "different" ought to be accepted naturally in areas where their difference makes no difference.'

Letters flowed in. The noted film critic Alex Walker wrote the following morning: '"Compassion" is an easy word to write, but a rare thing to be able to feel these days. ... I can't recall seeing or reading anything so affectionately revealing as TV showed me last night.' Quentin Crewe sent a telegram in the small hours: 'We were still talking about it at 1 a.m.,' and his former wife Angie Huth sent a telegram saying: 'Well done well done I don't know how you avoided every pitfall and left one with tears but quite without words. It was brilliant.' Margaret, despite her earlier hurt feelings, sent him a note on a piece of memo paper: 'All here enjoyed the film enormously. Well done. Lots of Love M.' In the 'To' section at the top of the sheet it was addressed simply 'Darling'.

His committed attitude was emphasised when, in 1972, he became a trustee of the National Fund for Research into Crippling Diseases and a member of its Council – another member, who would play a great part in his future work for disabled people, was Andrew Farquhar, an extraordinarily effective worker for charity.

As with the Cazalet episode, Tony had become less concerned at keeping in with friends he saw as belonging entirely to Margaret's side. When asked to Badminton in spring 1972 for the horse trials held there annually, he at first refused because, he said, they bored him; then, two days before they began, said he would come after all. The diarist James Lees-Milne, whose house was on the Badminton estate, recorded (on 30 May 1972) that Tony 'infuriated the Duke [of Beaufort] by saying that hunting was cruel, which the Duke resolutely denied. Then he said: "The competitors in the horse trials must be *terrified*." "Equestrians are never terrified," the Duke said. "Only cissies are terrified." He began belabouring the fire with a poker. Princess Margaret, wanting to calm his rage, said: "Tony doesn't mean terrified really. He means nervous." "No, I don't. I mean terrified," Tony insisted. Whereupon the Duke, completely out of temper, shouted as he banged away at the fireplace, bending the poker, "Damn this fire, I tell you. Damn it, damn it!" Tony thereupon left that afternoon while the party were at the trials without saying goodbye.'

Lees-Milne observed another event a month later, on 28 June. This time it was Princess Margaret in a difficult mood and Tony all charm, at a private dinner in the restaurant Rules in Maiden Lane after the premiere of John Betjeman's film on Australia. First comes the vignette of Tony: 'While having drinks at the bar of the cinema Tony Snowdon arrived, ran up to us and talked about Bath,* full of vitality and cheer. Then Princess Margaret came up to Tony and, small though he is, she almost tiptoed to kiss his ear and whisper. Tony said: "You know Jim?" "Yes," she said, and moved away.' After watching her for the rest of the evening Lees-Milne came to the conclusion that 'PM is far from charming, is cross, exacting, too sophisticated, and sharp. She is physically attractive in a bun-like way, with trussed-up bosom, and hair like two cottage loaves, one balancing on the other.' He also noted that although it was Betjeman's film and he was guest of honour 'she did not talk to John once.'

Yet although by now the couple were leading virtually separate lives, both upheld the forms, still – in letters – addressing each other as 'Darling'. When, after an official tour of the Virgin Islands in March 1972 Margaret spent her first holiday at her Mustique villa, she wrote to him ('My darling') ecstatically, describing a dinner party at the Cotton House (the island's only hotel) with the Tennants and her old beau Dominic Elliot, where they were joined

---

* James Lees-Milne was a trustee of the Bath Preservation Trust.

by her cousin Patrick, Lord Lichfield, and the models he was photographing, when up the steps came an impromptu band 'so we all danced and sang like anything'.

Nor did the bitter rows prevent them from sleeping together, one confidante remarking astutely that the fights 'were almost a form of foreplay'. Possibly for this reason, Tony was still the only person who could persuade Margaret to do something against her will. When he accompanied her on a visit to the Seychelles and Western Australia in late 1972 one of the events the couple attended was the socially important floodlit trotting race meeting, at the end of which she was supposed to say a few words. She refused flatly to do this. Burnaby-Atkins, aware of the insult this would be to her hosts and also that she was to be presented with a gift, wrote out a few suitable sentences on a piece of paper to make her task easier. Margaret simply crumpled it up and tossed it away.

Desperately, Burnaby-Atkins, seated in the row behind, crept along until he reached Tony, sitting in front, and begged him to persuade the Princess to speak briefly on the lines he had suggested. After the races, she was presented with a silver horse statuette, and in response expressed her gratitude gracefully – in exactly the words Burnaby-Atkins had suggested. When she turned and faced him before climbing up the stairs she made an almost imperceptible gesture of complicity, as if to say: 'There! You see?'

Relations on the trip, as so often when the pair were abroad together, were perfectly pleasant, although several of the royal party noticed that on the flight back Margaret, seated in the first-class compartment out of sight of Tony, was making a play for the Air Commodore in charge of the flight. 'She really cuddled up to him,' said one of her retinue.

On their return, the uneasy truce continued for a while. Though gossip about the marriage was rife, the Snowdons were still asked out together and the mystique of royalty still held. Marlon Brando, asked to dine with the Princess in a small party, was so overawed that he could not speak to her directly but had to do it through his host: 'Would you ask Princess Margaret what she thinks of ... etc.' This effect was so marked that when a fellow member of the House of Lords told Lord Donaldson of Kingsbridge that he had been at a party with Princess Margaret and how sorry he felt for her, and Jack Donaldson asked why, the man replied: 'She hasn't the faintest idea of what anyone is like. When she came into the room we all changed.'

Tony plunged back into work, his portraits as in demand as ever, as this letter from the former Goon Spike Milligan shows: 'Thank you for the really super photographs. I really do not know what to say. I think I will say three Our Fathers and one Hail Mary – people are not saying them like they used to. Super, super, super photographs (there is no such person as David Frost, it's a baptised weather report). Phone me – we can dine and drink wine and talk and talk and sometimes laugh. If you can't laugh, smile, and apply for an extension. Love, light and peace, Spike.'

The end of 1972 brought several changes. Both Snowdons lost friends: Judy Gendel died in November of a heart attack and a month later Oliver Messel lost his lifelong companion Vagn, who had been part of Tony's life ever since he could remember. More positively Tony, who had always empathised with those handicapped either physically or by the circumstances of their lives, was asked by Lord Goodman to join a Committee on Integration of the Disabled, to recommend, as Lord Goodman's letter of invitation stated, 'ways in which the disabled can have more usefully effective and fuller lives'. It was a project close to Tony's heart – as Lord Goodman's letter had continued, 'I know of the most practical concern you have manifested for people under disability or disadvantage.'

In December Lt-Col. Burnaby-Atkins, endlessly caught between his employer and his employer's husband ('I carried out your instructions re a driver for your dinner party at Apsley House and was then told by Princess Margaret I should not have done so'), found himself swamped by the difficulties of his position combined with Tony's enmity, and left. It was not until six months later that his replacement, Lord Napier and Ettrick, an old friend of the royal family and former Tory whip in the House of Lords, was appointed as the Princess's Private Secretary, Comptroller and

Equerry.* The year 1972 also saw the departure of John Larkin, much against the Princess's will; although he refused to tell her the reason for his departure it was the simple and straightforward one that he, too, could no longer cope with being in the middle of the battlefield.

By now the marriage had deteriorated to a point of no return. For the first six weeks that Lord Napier worked for her, Princess Margaret deliberately kept him away from Tony and when they did meet, it was by accident. When the Princess sent for him one day just before lunch, Nigel Napier let himself into the house with the key he had been given and saw that the Princess, standing in the hall, was talking to Tony. As Napier walked in, the Princess said to Tony in her most regal tones: 'I don't think you've met my new Private Secretary?' Without batting an eyelid Tony responded: 'Only twenty-five years ago.' What the Princess did not know was that they had been at Eton together, although not in the same house. That link, and the fact that Napier, like Tony, had had polio when young, meant that Napier was always able to communicate with his employer's husband – an ability that rapidly became indispensable to Princess Margaret.

Margaret's increasing unhappiness was having deleterious physical effects: she was drinking heavily, she was putting on weight and there were sudden forays into flirtation. 'Sometimes she almost threw herself at men,' said one of her closest friends. 'Partly it was to make Tony jealous, partly to prove to herself that she was still attractive.' Her misery was largely because, despite everything, she wanted her marriage to continue: a divorce was against all the tenets of her upbringing, her religious faith and her own inclinations. She knew how unhappy it would make her sister the Queen; and she herself was proud. Divorce, to her, spelt failure.

---

* Lord Napier and Ettrick held this position from 1973 to 1998, after which he became the Princess's Treasurer until her death in 2002.

12

Lucy

⋇

Towards the end of 1972, Tony met the woman who would become his second wife. This was Lucy Lindsay-Hogg, née Davies, the daughter of one of Ireland's most successful clothing manufacturers, Donald Brook Davies. In the sixties, Donald Davies shirt dresses, made of the softest Irish tweed in delicious colours, were as popular and versatile as the wrap dress was later to become. Lucy, born in 1941, grew up in Ireland in the picturesque village of Enniskerry, set in the foothills of the Wicklow mountains. In 1966 she married the talented film director Michael Lindsay-Hogg;* in 1971, the year before Tony met her, they were divorced.

Lucy and Tony had first been introduced when she and the Snowdons were invited to a dinner party at the large Chelsea house of Colin Clark.† For both of them, it was a purely social encounter. Lucy was also a friend of Tony's great friend, Derek Hart – *Venice*, the book written by Hart, with Tony's photographs (for which he was paid £4,000 plus expenses by Olivetti, the sponsors of the book), was published in October 1972. She was asked to work on a film with them, subsequently cancelled before it began, but the team idea stuck.

As Tony and Hart were also working together on another television film, *Happy being Happy*, she became Tony's assistant. She was tall – she overtopped Tony by several inches – slim and elegant with, as Tony once described her, the dark good looks of a Spanish marquesa. She was shy, gentle, loyal and kind, less

---

* Now Sir Michael Lindsay-Hogg, 5th Baronet.
† Younger brother of the diarist and MP Alan Clark.

physical in her approach than Margaret and far more prepared to dedicate herself to the happiness of those she loved. It was easy for them to meet, as Tony was spending more and more time away from home, largely on work assignments: his diary is filled with sittings for *Vogue*, assignments for the *Sunday Times* and, increasingly, more television work, largely for the BBC. In between there were visits to Old House or lunches at San Lorenzo, in the knowledge that the discretion of his friends Mara and Lorenzo Berni was total.

Links with other old friends were maintained, in particular Peter Sellers, whose shower of gifts continued. 'I am sure that this nifty little camera will be just what you are looking for to capture those elusive moments of vérité that you strive so hard to achieve,' wrote Sellers on 2 January 1973 in the jokey vein of his happier days. 'PLEASE REMEMBER to read *carefully* the weeny booklet in which you will find the relevant instructions because without this vital information this minuscule can easily be abused and cause you to go blind.'

As for Margaret, her early spring visits to the Caribbean were now routine. On 14 February she left London for Mustique, there to stay with the Tennants while the final touches were made to Les Jolies Eaux. A week later she moved in. Interestingly, it was still referred to in the press as 'the Snowdons'' rather than 'Princess Margaret's' island home. From it she wrote ecstatically to Tony: 'It all looks frightfully nice, I do wish you were here to see it all. The lamps are lovely and the loo works and we've had a bath and we're just about to go to bed for the first time. With masses of love from Your loving M.' She concluded her letter with the familiar admonition: 'Please write', underlined.

While she was away Tony invited the Queen and the Queen Mother to lunch at Old House, on 4 March, recorded in several happy, smiling photographs. The Queen Mother performed the opening ceremony for the lake Tony had made, snipping a ribbon with a pair of shears and taking the first steps across the stepping stones laid across the narrow end of the lake. Afterwards she congratulated 'Dearest Tony' warmly on the layout of the house and the effect of the lake and saying how she had enjoyed herself, in her letter of thanks (written on 6 March): 'To eat marvellous food, in the company of dear friends, in a very pretty house, is my idea of bliss! It was all such fun and having dropped David back at school I went home to Royal Lodge in a daze of martinis, red wine, that excellent yellow stuff and CHAMPAGNE. It took me a few hours to surface!'

The summer of 1973 was the last family holiday the Snowdons took with their children, now aged eleven and nine. But the semblance of normality, even affection, that they had always managed to maintain between them in the more relaxed atmosphere of a holiday, had evaporated for good. There were rows in front of the children. 'Papa, Mummy is talking to you,' one of them would say, to which Tony would respond with a blank air of indifference, 'Yes, I know,' and continue to ignore Margaret.

They went first to Sardinia, again to stay with the Aga Khan, and from Sardinia to Italy. This time they did not stay with Judy and Milton Gendel: Judy, Margaret's great friend, had died (of a heart attack) the previous November. Gendel had arranged for them to be put up instead in the palazzo of a friend of his, Princess Caracciolo. It was about thirty minutes' drive from Porto Ercole, the resort for smart Romans and their yachts. Everyone knew that the Snowdon marriage was, to say the least, bumpy, but it was quickly obvious to Princess Caracciolo that the mutual attraction was still as strong as ever. Not certain of their sleeping arrangements, she had tactfully arranged for them to stay in a separate wing of the palazzo, where each of them had been allotted one of the two double bedrooms there. When she took the Princess to her room Margaret's first action was to jump on the bed to test the mattress. 'Oh, it's far too hard!' she exclaimed. 'There may be a softer one in the other room, Ma'am,' said Judy Caracciolo, to which the Princess responded: 'Oh, but I want to be sleeping with Tony.'

Great trouble was taken to provide as many diversions as possible to keep both of them in a good humour. They loved the sun and sea; for Tony this largely meant waterskiing, for the Princess, sunbathing or swimming from a yacht and Judy Caracciolo managed to fix up outings on a different boat each day. The routine was simple. The Princess would have her breakfast in bed and the others – Judy Caracciolo's daughter was the same age as Sarah, and Milton Gendel's little daughter Anna was also with them – would breakfast downstairs at around ten. By the time they were all ready to set off it was eleven-thirty, when they would drive to Porto Ercole, board whatever boat had been lent for the day, head for an unspoilt bay along the coast and anchor there.

What everyone noticed was how much the Snowdons were drinking: Tony drank vodka – a new bottle was sent down to the chosen yacht every day – while the Princess stuck to gin. Both followed this with wine at lunch. In addition, Tony had a supply of 'uppers', doling them out on request. After lunch Tony would waterski and the Princess sunbathe in her sedate skirted one-piece swimsuit. On the return drive to the palazzo there was always a stop at the small town of Orbitello for the children to have ice creams. Back at the house, there would be baths or showers and a change of clothes, before drinks started again from six-thirty onwards and, usually, dinner out – Princess Caracciolo had persuaded her friends to give dinner parties to help her in keeping the Snowdons amused.

Before one of these, such a blistering row erupted between the couple that Margaret refused to go, demanding scrambled eggs on the lawn instead. Although Princess Caracciolo could not order Margaret about she could, and did, tell Tony that after all the trouble her friends had gone to she could not turn up without either of them. Tony, who agreed, behaving perfectly at the party, nevertheless cut short his holiday and departed almost immediately for London, leaving Margaret and the children to complete their holiday in a palazzo belonging to the d'Orso family, near Positano. Here Margaret had another flirtation, this time with Luigi, one of the younger d'Orso brothers. It was clear to onlookers that what she craved was attention – in the sense of reassurance that she had not lost her power to allure – and uncomplicated affection. Soon she would meet a man who supplied these wants lavishly.

At home, the Snowdons had reached the stage of communicating largely through the Princess's Private Secretary, Lord Napier. To a certain degree this was natural: as private secretaries know all about their employer's movements or engagements, much communication is through them. In this case, though, it was not simply a question of checking diaries but of Lord Napier being used as messenger boy, as neither could bear to speak to the other.

For the first two or three years of Napier's incumbency Tony attempted to make life so difficult for him that he would leave, thus demonstrating that Margaret could not keep anyone who worked for her. There would be telephone calls when he knew people had come to see Napier. 'I don't want cars parking in the forecourt. Tell them all to move at once. Security.' 'It's not your house, it's Princess Margaret's house,' Napier would reply, 'but I will discuss it with Her Royal Highness.' When he did so, she would exclaim: 'How dare he! Tell him to forget it.' And back Napier would go again.

There was the same trouble over the household accounts as under the aegis of Lt-Col. Burnaby-Atkins. The Princess paid all the food bills (Tony contributed towards the rates and paid half the children's school fees). With a couple in harmony, everything might have worked out smoothly; as it was, with the Private Secretary's job to safeguard his employer's interests, there were bound to be difficulties, especially over Tony's ongoing habit of removing food from the kitchen to feed guests at Old House – none of whom were anything to do with the Princess. From Tony's perspective his actions seemed entirely fair. 'You and I agreed the other day it seems to be quite reasonable to take food down to the country at the expense of the housekeeping account,' ran one note. 'If this seriously is to be paid then one must take into account the fact that the staff are not employed when I am away and also food bills etc. Also if one is going to do the thing one must include the price of food returned.'

For Napier, life was easier when the two were apart. Like the rest of the staff, he found almost unendurable the lunches at which he had to sit with the warring couple, sometimes in icy silence, sometimes with a shouting match bubbling beneath the surface only to burst out at some unforeseen trigger word. Their heavy drinking lessened their inhibitions about quarrelling in front of others; the Princess had given up gin in favour of whisky and Tony would often remain in the dining room drinking wine until three-thirty or four in the afternoon.

The atmosphere between them was so glacial that it was impossible to disguise. On official occasions when both were invited they would arrive separately and leave separately. Not only did they not speak to each other, the organisers had to be extremely careful to see that their paths did not cross. 'Just keep them away from each other,' whispered a lady-in-waiting to the chairman at an exhibition arranged by Barnardo's, a charity of which Princess Margaret was president.

To add to Margaret's problems, her Civil List allowance was being disputed. Inflation throughout the sixties had meant that the entitlements for the various members of the royal family considered eligible, which had been fixed in 1952, had become inadequate and some of the costs incurred in carrying out public duties or meeting their official expenses were coming out of their private funds. The Queen accordingly requested an increase in the Civil List and the Prime Minister, Harold Wilson, had set up a Select Committee in 1966 to investigate this but it had not yet reached its conclusions when the Labour government fell in June 1970. The new Conservative Prime Minister, Edward Heath, formed another Committee; and in 1972 the whole matter was the subject of heated controversy in Parliament.

What troubled MPs was not so much the question of raising the Queen's allowance – as the fact that it was more than doubled (to £980,000 a year) demonstrated – but those of other members of the family. And it was the proposed increase of Princess Margaret's from the £15,000 a year granted on her marriage to £35,000 that aroused the greatest controversy. Most of the members of the Committee believed that she was, to put it bluntly, not worth it. Her lifestyle was more exotic than that of any other royal personage, her holidays abroad with what would today be known as the jet set, and the fact that her husband worked, were all held against her. She had, said the Committee, only spent thirty-one days outside London (on official duties) during the whole of 1970. 'Your Committee do not feel it right to ask the taxpayer to continue the annuity; free housing should be adequate recompense for services rendered,' concluded the official 1971–2 Report from the Select Committee on the Civil List.

In short, what they were recommending was the complete

withdrawal of her Civil List allowance, with that regular scourge of the royal family, the Labour MP Willie Hamilton, calling her 'an expensive kept woman'. But after fierce debate the increases were put through, MPs no doubt recollecting that Margaret had paid official visits to Yugoslavia, France, Canada, the British Virgin Islands, Italy, West Germany, the Seychelles, Western Australia and Singapore in the preceding two years; and that, although her official staff numbered twelve, only three – private secretary, personal secretary and lady-in-waiting – were salaried.

Happy being Happy was transmitted on Monday 10 December 1973 at the peak time of 8 p.m. It attracted the usual flood of fan letters. Lady Antonia Fraser wrote to say that she found it both excellently made and moving – 'it was rather like listening to good music'. Jonathan Aitken sent a note: 'This is just a fan letter, to tell you I thought your programme on happiness was marvellous.' Lady Elizabeth Cavendish, who also loved it, condoled with him about poor reviews in *The Times* and *Telegraph*, fiercely castigating the critics for their lack of empathy and adding, 'I don't know why you and John [Betjeman] get so upset by these [despicable] creatures.'

Even with his great success and well-established reputation the urge to be different, to kick against convention, had not left Tony. At a group photograph of the royal family at Christmas 1973 by the Queen's photographer cousin Patrick (the Earl of Lichfield), in which the men wore smart, well-tailored suits in the usual dark colours and fine worsted cloth, Tony stood out in a corduroy suit. The togetherness evinced in the photograph was only for Lichfield's lens. The breach between the Snowdons was now an unbridgeable gulf.

Where most couples would have looked, individually, into their own hearts and minds to see if there was any way they could have spoken or acted differently, neither Margaret nor Tony possessed the necessary amount of introspection for self-analysis. Tony spent as much time as possible away, usually with Lucy, who lived in a flat in nearby Kensington Church Street and was still ostensibly his assistant. In the evening, he would slip out of the house; no one knew when he returned but sometimes his wet footmarks would be seen in the hall early in the morning by the housekeeper. Lucy's invisible presence was a constant hurt to Margaret, who minded very much indeed that Tony was in love with someone else. She would refer to Lucy as 'the thing', and would say with heavy meaning, 'Ugh – he's *working* again.'

When together, it was no longer a question of 'If?' but 'When?' One day, in a moment of confidence Napier, who had always got on with Tony, boldly said to him what everyone close to the Snowdons was thinking: 'You cannot go on like this – you are destroying each other.' It was clear that Tony realised this, and agreed. A photograph taken around this time shows a forlorn Margaret, clad in a mackintosh, at a desolate site near Sunninghill, where once there had been plans for a house to be built for them. On the photograph, written in Margaret's hand, are the words: 'This is where we might have built a house but Tony went off without a word to me to Old House and did it up, thus ending our marriage.'

On 20 August 1973, the day before Margaret's forty-third birthday, Tony left for more BBC filming, from which he would not return until 28 September (after which there would be a further six weeks spent editing). This was to direct a film on Mary Kingsley in *The Explorers* series, for which he would be paid £2,400. Flowers from Tony arrived at Kensington Palace to mark the day but it was not until almost three weeks later that Margaret discovered where he was and could send a telegram to thank him – it turned out to be Libreville, the capital of Gabon, on the west coast of Africa. Depressed, ignorant of the whereabouts of her husband and – despite being accompanied by her children – lonely, and unable to envisage the future, she left for Balmoral.

Her friends the Tennants, knowing her low and unhappy state, had asked her to stay with them at Glen, the Tennant family place near Innerleithen, Peeblesshire. So wretched that she could hardly make up her mind about anything, she only accepted at the last minute. She was driven there in early September, in one of the Queen's cars with her detective; her children and their nanny and her dresser were to follow later.

At Glen there had been a mild panic: the Princess's late acceptance had meant that the house party was one short of the necessary men to balance the numbers – the one invited for her had dropped out, also at the last minute. Unable to think of anyone at this late date, Anne Tennant telephoned an aunt of Colin's, Violet Wyndham, who had a wide circle of friends, including plenty of young men. 'I know a very nice young man who works in the College of Heralds,' she replied. 'You could try him.' It was Roddy Llewellyn. When telephoned by Anne Tennant, he expressed himself delighted. The Tennants offered to pay his fare as the journey was expensive for a young man with little money (his job at the College of Heralds brought him in £70 a month).

Margaret and the eldest Tennant son, Charlie, drove into Edinburgh with Colin to meet Roddy's train and then to link up with her children, nanny and dresser, Elizabeth Greenfield, outside the Café Royal, where the whole party was to have lunch. As all ate at the same table, Mrs Greenfield noticed immediately that, in her words, the Princess had eyes for no one but Roddy. After lunch, before driving back to Glen, Margaret took Roddy off to buy him some swimming trunks so that he could take advantage of his hosts' heated swimming pool. They chose a pair emblazoned with a Union Jack.

During the drive into Edinburgh the Princess, naturally, was seated beside Colin, who was chauffeuring them. When they returned to Glen, Anne Tennant was staggered to see that Margaret was sitting in the back with Roddy. It was instantly apparent that they had established a rapport and the moment Roddy got out of the car Anne Tennant realised that something – she could not quite tell what – had begun. 'Heavens, what have I done?' she thought.

Roderic Llewellyn, born on 9 October 1947, was almost eighteen years younger than Margaret and, as almost everyone who met him noticed immediately, extraordinarily like Tony in appearance. He too was Welsh. In character, they could not have been more different: Roddy was gentle, thoughtful, kind and quite often depressed, though when on form he was extremely funny. He got on particularly well with older women, many of whom, like Violet Wyndham, became great friends.

When he came to London from the parental home, Llanvair Grange, an estate near Abergavenny in South Wales, he had done a series of odd jobs while living in a small flat in the Old Brompton Road, then had moved in with the interior designer Nicky Haslam (whom he had met through Jackie Rufus-Isaacs).

Along with gardening, one of Roddy's interests was genealogy, so the College of Heralds was a natural destination. At his school, Shrewsbury, *Burke's Peerage* was a favourite read as a refuge from what he regarded as its philistine atmosphere; as he grew up, the appeal of ancient aristocratic families and grand houses became ever stronger. Thus when he was invited to Glen, although he did not know his hosts or any of the rest of the party, despite a natural shyness he never hesitated for a moment. Haslam, an Old Etonian and great social figure, had 'launched' Roddy by introducing him to many of his own social circle. Ironically, Haslam also knew Tony, whom he had met in 1955, and had often been at one of the luncheon or weekend parties held by Tony at Old House. Sooner or later, Roddy too would inevitably have met Tony; as it was, he was destined to meet Tony's wife first – and become the second major 'hate' figure in Tony's life.

Roddy, young, often rather uncertain and inoffensive, did not seem at first glance the sort of rival to inspire virulent dislike in even the most jealous husband. He was quite different from Margaret's previous admirers: he had neither the tall, striking good looks of Anthony Barton nor the expertise in love of Robin Douglas-Home. Amusing and pleasant as he was, he was an unlikely lothario, especially for an experienced, much older princess.

At Glen they talked endlessly, swam in the pool, held hands, went for long walks in the lovely autumn weather and sang songs round the piano. Roddy was also good at having fun: at a fancy dress party at Glen shortly after they met – for which Princess Margaret dressed as a Southern belle in scarlet crinoline and a huge red hat – Roddy had overcome his initial shyness sufficiently to sport a mini-kilt. He was fascinated by this sophisticated, voluptuous woman, so amusing and so easy to talk to, who made it plain how attracted she was to him. For Margaret, it was a case of falling in love again. She not only had a new man, she had a new interest in her life, someone whom she believed she could help, both socially and in his career. Her 'comfort eating' stopped and she lost weight; her staff noticed that whenever Roddy came round to Kensington Palace she was in a happy mood; away from him, she often wept.

Her life was now so separate from Tony's that when he underwent a hernia operation on 17 November 1973 Princess Margaret was staying with friends in the country. She returned to London to see him – and found Lucy at his bedside. For Margaret, proud, still possessive about her husband and, like him, still sexually jealous, it was a humiliating encounter.

Roddy by now was living in a basement flat in Walham Grove, Fulham. After a quarrel with Nicky Haslam he had moved out and gone to stay with his older brother Dai but clearly, if he were to entertain the Princess, he needed a place of his own. His new dwelling consisted of a good-sized sitting room, its size increased by a large mirror, in one corner of which was tucked an attractive photograph of Margaret (not by her husband) and which also held an upright piano. Off this were a small kitchenette and a large bedroom. The entrance hall passage was striped and tented – an idea that came from the Princess. Margaret, in the first flush of love, helped Roddy furnish it by buying household necessities from Peter Jones – and to Tony's chagrin, putting them on their household account.

What neither the Princess nor Roddy realised was that his Walham Grove basement was only two doors from the house belonging to Tony's friend Bob Belton. On visits to Belton, Tony would relieve his wounded *amour propre* by remarks designed to be heard by the nearby occupant. Standing on Belton's top-floor balcony that overlooked the garden two doors away in which Roddy was often to be seen, he would comment in the effortlessly carrying voice that had been part of his equipment in his rowing days: 'What a peculiar garden down there. Who on earth could have bought such vulgar plant pots?' On evenings when Margaret's Rolls was to be seen parked outside (often to remain all night), his comments were particularly acerbic, and he would sometimes neatly block her car in by double-parking his own Aston Martin.

That Christmas of 1973, James Lees-Milne, staying with Lord and Lady Drogheda at their house in Englefield Green, was asked with them to a drink in the Dean's house after the service in St George's Chapel, Windsor,* which they attended on Christmas Day. He gave a vivid résumé of Margaret and Tony's misery. Princess Margaret, he thought, 'looked sorry and slight ...'

> Then Tony Snowdon caught my hand. He looks grey, his hand shakes, and he chain-smokes one cigarette after another. I asked him how he was. He said laughing that he felt worse since his operation. I don't know what his trouble is beyond general unhappiness. This stands out a mile.
>
> The same old business ensued. Princess Margaret wanted to go. It was time, and she approached Tony, who said: 'No, I want to go on with my drink.' So I said to him: 'No, you must toss it down, and hurry along.' 'I won't be hurried,' he said. Princess M then said rather crossly, 'Then I shall have to walk home by myself,' and began to leave the room.

Yet amid the wreckage there were still signs of the depth and closeness of the bond that had originally drawn them together. Right until the last gasp of the dying marriage, they continued to use their usual endearments to each other in letters – Margaret would end hers 'with masses of love from your loving M' – and they continued to sleep together. For both, the sexual attraction between them was too strong to be denied. Tony would cross the bathroom that lay between their bedrooms then, in Margaret's words (to three of the ladies-in-waiting to whom she was closest): 'He would fling open my bedroom door, stand there with no clothes on and then – well, what could I do?' He was, she said later, so masterful that she could only acquiesce.

Perhaps it was this sexual domination by her husband that made Margaret submit to him in another aspect of her life. Her unhappiness, combined with her natural wilfulness (not to speak, perhaps, of reaction to the amount she had drunk the night before), often caused her to flout that absolute of royal obligation: always to fulfil an engagement unless accident, illness or calamity prevented. Sometimes she would say to her lady-in-waiting about something that had been arranged months beforehand: 'I don't want to go.' 'But, Ma'am, you said you would – you've got to.' 'I

---

* Lord Drogheda had been created a Knight of the Garter in 1972.

don't feel well. I won't do it – I won't.' Everyone knew that the only person who could change Margaret's mind on these occasions was Tony; and if he were in the house there would be an emergency dash to his office.

On other occasions there would be no need for this. If Tony had discovered earlier that she wanted to renege on something, he would take steps to prevent her. When her dresser, Elizabeth Greenfield, called her at nine with a trolley holding tea and a glass of freshly squeezed orange juice, the Princess might say that she would not be going to a planned engagement because she had a cold. As on every day, Mrs Greenfield would then go upstairs to Margaret's wardrobe room, which was directly above Tony's dressing room. While she was pressing or mending a dress or washing the Princess's underwear she would hear the dressing room door slam below and a few minutes later the Princess's bell would ring in the wardrobe room. Down the dresser would go. 'I think I will go, after all,' the Princess would say. Recalled Mrs Greenfield: 'It was because Lord Snowdon had been in and said to her: "Come on, rouse yourself – you've *got* to go."'

Tony's success in overcoming his wife's reluctance to do anything she thought would be boring or that she had tried to cancel at the last minute further endeared him to the Queen Mother, who had frequently felt that her daughter did not always show enough sense of duty. At this point neither the Queen nor the Queen Mother realised – or wanted to realise – in any comprehensive way what was going on. Margaret's relationship with her mother, whom she saw more frequently than her sister, was prickly and often bossily unpleasant. 'God, it's hot in here – why can't we have some air,' she would announce as she walked into the Royal Lodge drawing room, or 'Why do you spoil your servants so – it's so stupid.'

Tony was uncomplicatedly admiring and fond of both Elizabeths and always at his best with them. In their presence he was charming, pleasant, funny and amiable to his wife. Nor did they see him often, so any other aspect of his nature was hidden from them. Whereas Margaret, as both well knew, could be extremely difficult, spoilt and generally maddening. The result was that their sympathies lay almost entirely with Tony. And it was Tony who would emerge from the forthcoming maelstrom as the injured party.

13

'Tell Your Friend to Keep Out of My House'

Margaret's relationship with Roddy soon became so important to her that she invited him to stay with her on Mustique when she took her annual spring holiday there, with the Tennants as fellow guests. Margaret flew out on 2 March 1974; Roddy, who had been discreetly told that the holiday would cost him nothing apart from tips for the staff, travelled quite separately from the Princess.

The holiday went well and, for Roddy, was a step towards his eventual successful career as a landscape gardener – while there, he remodelled the garden of Les Jolies Eaux and, with the aid of the local gardener, planted it up. For Tony, it consolidated his antipathy to the Tennants. He felt that not only had they encouraged Margaret to have a life separate from him, they had also introduced her to someone with whom she would form a long and important relationship.

There were several reasons for his intense dislike of Roddy, probably the only man by whom he felt threatened during the course of his marriage. First and most obviously, here was someone who was almost a blueprint of himself but young, kind and attentive – although Roddy had no money to speak of, he would take immense trouble to search out objects that might please Margaret or plan what he hoped she would enjoy. Also, and another profound cause of dislike, it was clear Margaret really did love her young admirer – her previous infidelities had usually lasted weeks rather than months, let alone years – while Roddy, for his part, was thrilled with her and intensely grateful for all she did for him.

In May 1974 Margaret and Tony made an official visit to the US, timed so that they could attend the hundredth anniversary of the Kentucky Derby, run annually on the first Saturday in May. Here there appeared to be the harmony between them so important to convey to the thousands of eyes that would be watching them. In New York, where they were due to attend a performance of the Royal Ballet, they stayed at the Waldorf Towers.

On their arrival, on 7 May, reporters in the lobby asked them unexpectedly if they knew the Duchess of Windsor was there; Wallis Simpson was also staying at the Waldorf Towers, in a suite on the fortieth floor. Margaret was prepared to ignore this news. Wallis was, after all, the woman whose marriage to Margaret's uncle David had forced her beloved father onto the throne and, in her mother's eyes if not her own, caused his early death. If Margaret ever referred to her, it was as 'that ghastly woman' or, more pointedly, 'the woman who ruined my uncle'.

Tony's reaction was kinder and more pragmatic. 'Oh, come on, M,' he said. 'It's all gone on too long – we're going to go up and see her.' Up they went, with Margaret, about to set off for a ballet gala, in full evening dress, to visit the Duchess, now an ageing and pathetic figure. Although they spent only fifteen minutes with her, they had the presence of mind to suggest that Margaret and the Duchess be photographed together; the subsequent pictures appeared all over the world. 'I will remember, with the greatest pleasure, the honour of meeting the Duchess of Windsor,' said Tony afterwards to the waiting press in the hotel lobby. 'We discovered she was in the hotel and just rang up to see how she was, and asked if she would like us to come and see her.'

The show of unity between the Snowdons was deceptive. Later in the trip, there was a squabble when Tony refused to walk in behind the Princess to the convention hall where 300 women were waiting to be addressed at ten-thirty one morning. He delayed for a minute and then entered, to peahen-like screeches of 'Oh, Tony!' from the assembled women. Those accompanying Margaret believed it was done deliberately, to minimise her impact, but it could equally well have been the ingrained perversity of spirit that made him want always to do something different from others – and which expressed itself in his creative life as brilliant originality.

In June 1974, soon after they got home, Margaret asked Tony to move out of Kensington Palace. He refused – it was, after all, his home as well as hers and, in part, his place of business, holding his study, office, darkroom and workroom, all considerations important to someone with a living to earn. If Tony had agreed to go, it would have made one aspect of Margaret's romantic life much easier. Although the Tennants allowed her and Roddy to use their large and beautiful white house in Tite Street, and although they were invited together to stay with friends in the country at weekends, she naturally wanted to entertain her own friends in her own house. Equally naturally, Tony bitterly resented Margaret's new young lover entering the place he still saw as home, and said so. 'Tell your friend to keep out of my house,' he once shouted at Margaret.

To Roddy, the knowledge of the unseen but looming presence of the husband of the woman he loved, with all a husband's moral rights over both her house and her body, added to the pressures that now seemed to be enveloping him on all sides. He had never had a long relationship with a woman before; now he was involved with one who was not only far richer and older but who had a demanding, intense and possessive personality. Also, according to his brother Dai, the physical side of the relationship was proving difficult to sustain. In every sense, everything was becoming 'too much'.

There were warning signs of the strain he was suffering from: inexplicable, and unexplained, disappearances, from which he had to be tracked down by Margaret's personal secretary Muriel Murray Brown, failures to turn up for dinner à deux with the Princess at Kensington Palace. One day, soon after taking Margaret to visit his parents in the family home of Llanvair, he cracked. Leaping up from the restaurant table where he was having lunch, he rushed home, threw a few things in a suitcase, drew some money from the bank, telephoned his mother and Princess Margaret to say that he was going away, and left for Heathrow airport.

Here he got on the first available plane, which happened to be going to Guernsey, but was back at Heathrow in two days. This time, he caught a plane to Istanbul and then spent several weeks travelling round Turkey by bus. He is said to have told someone he met on his travels that he 'had been having an affair with a married woman and that it had all got too much for him and the sex had become a problem'.

Margaret was shattered by his sudden disappearance. She knew that her marriage was in every real sense over, and now she had seemingly lost the love that had so suddenly and wonderfully come into her life. Exhausted by nervous strain, miserable and distraught, she took several of the Mogadon sleeping tablets she kept in her room. 'I was so exhausted by everything, I just wanted to sleep,' she later told her authorised biographer Christopher Warwick. Nevertheless, rumours that she was having a nervous breakdown or had tried to commit suicide flew around. When she came to, she sat motionless in bed for hours, the letter Roddy had sent her when he fled clasped in her hand, her head bent over it. What was certain was that she needed rest and quiet to recover, both physically and psychologically.

She remained alone in her bedroom, as prescribed by the doctor, who stationed two of her ladies-in-waiting outside her door to prevent anyone unauthorised entering – specifically mentioning Tony, as he thought he might upset her. 'She has to sleep,' said the doctor. At first, the only person Margaret asked to see was Lady Anne Tennant, her own great friend and a friend of Roddy's, as she thought Anne might know where he had gone.

As Anne emerged from Margaret's room, she was spotted by Tony, his jealousy of the effect Roddy's absence was having on Margaret at full throttle, and angrily accused of 'finding someone for my wife to go off with'. His furious tirade was only cut short by Anne fleeing to the safety of the office where the ladies-in-waiting worked. Tony, baulked of entering his wife's room, got into his car in a rage and drove round and round the cobbled courtyard in front of the house, blaring the horn. No one who heard this could doubt that the marriage was over (later, he told one of Margaret's friends how difficult he had found 'seeing one's wife have a nervous breakdown because her lover had left her').

Margaret, miserable and despairing, refused to leave her room, wanting only her closest friends to look after her – which meant night-time duty as well as day. Finally one of them, exhausted, rang the Queen, who took her away for a weekend at Windsor, remarking as she arrived at Kensington Palace at four in the afternoon, 'I feel exactly like the night nurse taking over from the day nurse.' With Margaret, head bowed, supported out to the car by her maid, the analogy was all too realistic. The Queen, however, was able to take a more robust stance towards her sister than anyone non-royal.

On 5 December 1974 Tony left for Australia, first for a fortnight in Sydney to research a film on Burke and Wills for the BBC series *The Explorers*, returning to Australia again on 3 February 1975 and coming home on 5 April. For most of this time Lucy, as assistant on the film, was with him.

Tony and Margaret did their best to maintain a normal relationship in front of their children. To Tony's everlasting credit, he managed to persuade Margaret away from her view that their son should follow a traditional royal path: Eton, followed by the Navy (chosen rather than the Army because her father had served in the Royal Navy).

Tony was determined that David should go to a school better suited to his particular talents than Eton where, self-confessedly not being particularly academic, he might have struggled to keep up. He was accepted for Bedales, the forward-looking co-educational establishment, on 1 April. Here, a boarder at £1,344 a term, he flourished, his father noting with pleasure his skill in carpentry and design. Later that month, on 10 April, Tony made his maiden speech in the House of Lords, rising nervously at 3.53 p.m. to talk on the handicaps in everyday life suffered by disabled people.

When Roddy eventually returned to England – he spent a further few months in South America – his relationship with Margaret was resumed, although on less intense terms, as well as a career change for him. His other great interest, gardening, now came to the fore when he was invited in June to become one of a loose-knit group who lived at Surrendell, a beautiful 1628 Jacobean manor house with forty-seven acres near Hullavington in Wiltshire.

Its nine bedrooms were home to a miscellaneous group, best

described at that stage of their lives as upper-class hippies: Prince George Galitzine, Lady Sarah Ponsonby, daughter of the 11th Earl of Bessborough, Sarah's boyfriend John Rendall, Tessa Codrington, and the architect Mike Tickner. Others, like the actress Helen Mirren, came down frequently. There were eight bedrooms in the main house, and an annexe in which Rendall's sister lived. Rendall, Tickner and Lady Sarah were the main investors in the house.

It was semi-derelict when they bought it; those who could afford it made contributions towards its renovation and everyone mucked in with housework, looking after the cows, geese, pigs, chickens and horses they kept and working in the garden. To generate an income they opened a restaurant in nearby Bath, called Parsenn Sally (named after a prize cow at the farm where they had previously lived). Its interior was designed by Mike Tickner, with the addition of ferns hung from the ceiling by Roddy, who had become one of the floating group who lived there semi-permanently. He designed the garden, in which they grew produce to be eaten in the restaurant, becoming ex officio head gardener.

It was a restful ambience, a place far from the complications that had been making his life so unhappy, with congenial people all working towards the same goal. The atmosphere was relaxed, the inmates sporting ponchos, kaftans or, in Roddy's case, long suede boots with jeans. Sometimes there was bare-skinned work in the summer sunshine or Sarah Ponsonby, when not working on one of her colourful paintings, would dig the cabbage patch topless. What the country people living in the little nearby village of Hullavington thought of Surrendell life caused one inhabitant to sum it up as 'frolicsome'.

At first keeping in regular touch with Margaret was difficult for Roddy as both were anxious not to attract any attention and the ensuing publicity. Again the Tennants came to the rescue, inviting Margaret and Roddy round for the evening to their house in Tite Street, Chelsea. Every Thursday, Roddy would come up from Surrendell and Margaret would arrive with a big picnic hamper from Kensington Palace.

Roddy's descriptions of life at Surrendell made Margaret want to see the place where her lover was so happy. Her first visit was for lunch, with John and Michelle Phillips of the well-known

Californian band the Mamas and the Papas. After this, Margaret said she would like to come and stay. There was no room for her driver – she had arrived in her Rolls-Royce – so he was put up in the village. All the group from Surrendell went to dinner at Parsenn Sally, where Roddy played the piano for a general sing-song, in which Margaret joined.

Her visits were easy and relaxed. It was known that she was Roddy's special friend but the relationship was never mentioned, let alone discussed. 'Everything was very proper,' recalled John Rendall later. Nor did Tony's name ever come up, except when Margaret once remarked apropos of some snapshots: 'My husband is the most wonderful, talented photographer.' She was given the largest and best room in the house, normally slept in by Mike Tickner (there was no question of sharing a room with Roddy), which had a comfortable mattress on the floor and Indian blankets hung round the walls. Lady Edith Foxwell, the recently divorced wife of the film-maker Ivan Foxwell, who lived nearby, would come over as a nominal lady-in-waiting. Roddy would take her up a cup of tea in the morning and later she would appear for breakfast. After meals she would help to clear the table and after dinner, where the drink was often scrumpy made by the Surrendell group, there would be hours of chat or sing-songs, all seated in and around the huge ingle-nook fireplace.

There was only one mildly tricky moment. The cooking in the large kitchen was done on an old solid-fuel Aga, which had been nicknamed Argret by the inhabitants of Surrendell. One morning when the Princess came down after Roddy had brought her her tea she overheard someone saying: 'Has someone stoked Argret today?' The famous blue eyes flashed and a frosty look spread over her face. Then she caught the eye of John Rendall and burst out laughing.

Inevitably, and especially with her driver staying in the village, word that Surrendell had a royal visitor leaked out and the little community was besieged by the press. (Later, police interest was aroused when a thriving cannabis plantation was discovered in the garden.) It was trying for all of them – none had had any experience of the press before.

For the Queen, Margaret's indiscreet behaviour was a cause of distress. She was well aware of the difficulties within the Snow-dons' marriage but had hoped that, as Tony was to write later, both could have led their own lives while remaining reasonably harmoniously under the same roof. She believed that Margaret's conduct in becoming involved with an indigent young man of no settled profession who was roughly half her age was, to say the least, undignified. Tony, it still appeared to both her and the Queen Mother, was more sinned against than sinning. A letter from the Queen Mother to 'Dearest Tony', written on 16 October 1975, looks forward to the Snowdon children coming to Royal Lodge for the weekend and invites him to stay also, with the ending 'Much love and I do hope to see you.'

By the time the Snowdons' 1975 visit to Australia was due, their relationship was that of two people living in hostility in the same house. Sometimes they could barely bring themselves to speak to each other. By now, Margaret's own view of Tony's affair could have been expressed as: 'If that's what he wants after me – well, really!' Finally she sent for her Private Secretary, Lord Napier, and said: 'I don't think I want Tony to come. In fact, if he goes, I won't.' Napier was put in the unenviable position of telling his employer's husband that, although he had been invited to visit Australia by its Prime Minister, the Princess did not want him to go there with her. 'I don't know how you're going to get out of that one,' said Tony. 'You can't say I'm otherwise engaged because I ain't.' It appeared to be stalemate. But in the end, by dint of Napier simply saying that the royal party was setting off without him, Tony accepted the situation, with Lord Napier feeling that he might in fact have been quite relieved. A notice was put in the paper to the effect that Lord Snowdon was unable to accompany Princess Margaret owing to his other engagements.

If Roy Strong's diary of 25 November 1975 is anything to go by, Napier's reaction was correct. 'Princess Margaret [described by Strong as 'tiresome, spoilt, idle and irritating'] had just come back from Australia which she had hated and, worse, it had rained. Traffic lights were not cancelled any more, no escort and no crowds. She smokes non-stop.' The following day they met at a grand dinner at Versailles, where Margaret 'slugged through the whisky and sodas', then 'suddenly raved on about Tony. She had returned from Australia to find that he'd nearly driven away the chauffeur, he'd upset the nanny, he went away for weekends she didn't know where and she didn't know his friends or anything. It was bitter and sad. She looked lonely and soured by it all.'

Tony had finally lost all patience with Nanny Sumner. Summoning Napier as a witness, he sent for Miss Sumner and proceeded to berate her so bitterly that Napier, who knew Nanny Sumner's good points and how much the Princess relied on her, especially when she went on extended royal visits abroad, was distressed to the point of saying: 'Tony, you really shouldn't have done that. What's it achieved?' By contrast, he was as usual loving and generous to his own old nanny, who wrote to him and Susan from her retirement in Oxted, Surrey, in the same month: 'It is so very, very kind of you all to send me more money. I do not know how to thank you enough, it is so generous of you. I don't deserve your wonderful kindness as I only tried to do my duty when I was with you all and a very happy time it was. You have all been such darlings to me and I love you as though you were my own.'

The end was rapidly approaching. On 26 November Margaret, who had already removed her wedding ring, sent Nigel Napier to inform Tony that in future he was not to accompany her to any public engagement, nor was he to be informed of any private invitations or activities – irrespective of whether or not they had both been asked. The drawbridge had finally been pulled up.

For his part, Tony wrote to the Queen at the end of November 1975 a letter that set out his point of view about their marital discord and pointing out that he now had little hand in their children's upbringing. He felt, he said, that their life together had reached a stage which, finally, he could no longer tolerate and that he could not contemplate wasting the rest of his life in the conditions prevailing in their house. 'The atmosphere is appalling for all concerned – the children, the staff, the few remaining loyal friends and she and I both,' he said, in a sentence with which all who lived, worked in or visited Kensington Palace would have agreed.

Three weeks later, the Queen responded. His letter, she said, had been devastating, the reason for her delay in replying. She intimated that she was aware of how bad their relationship had become before saying that she realised the situation was now intolerable for both of them. However, she begged that nothing precipitate be done before Christmas, adding that of course she would like to talk to him as soon as possible.

It was a nightmare situation for the royal family. Although a separation was all that had been mentioned, the overwhelming likelihood was that it would lead to a divorce, the first in the royal family since Henry VIII had divorced Anne of Cleves in 1540. With the Queen head of the Church of England, divorce was in any case a word not to be mentioned in the Palace without a shudder of horror. Everyone knew that the Queen's own uncle had given up the throne for love of a twice-divorced woman and the seismic upheaval this had caused. Only the impeccable behaviour of the new King and Queen and Elizabeth herself had restored the monarchy to the popularity it now enjoyed. Was this carefully restored image now to be shattered?

At first it seemed not. Tony, invariably mindful of the Queen's wishes, said no more, although his resentment of Roddy and his place in the affections of the Princess continued to rankle – irrespective of his own deepening love affair with Lucy. Like the child that in so many ways inhabited his inner landscape, his view of the world around him was self-centred. Soon, he would have the opportunity of what he really wanted: a break for freedom.

Behind the scenes, frantic discussions were going on about the Snowdon marriage (later publicly admitted by the Palace). It was already known that the Queen would not wish any marriage troubles within her family to come to a head in 1977 – the year of her Silver Jubilee – so the problem, already known to the Cabinet, took on a new urgency. From the Palace point of view, the best time to announce any separation was Easter 1976, when the Snowdon children would have arrived home from school and the news could be broken to them quietly at home.

His private problems did not stop Tony hitting out in a struggle that was becoming increasingly important to him: the fight to improve conditions for disabled people.

With Marjorie Wallace (later campaigning journalist and Chief Executive of SANE, the charity she founded)* there were stories that would take them 'on the road' together for anything up to a fortnight. One reason why these assignments fell to Marjorie, young and heavily dependent on her *Sunday Times* salary, was because many of her colleagues found that working with Tony, as Marjorie tactfully put it, was 'not always the easiest task'.

For a start, there was the question of recognition. 'Wherever we went, he would insist on being incognito,' said Marjorie. 'So I would ring up the hotel and tell them to expect Miss Wallace and Mr Smith. We would arrive and his face if they didn't recognise him was a study. If the red carpet wasn't then unrolled or a great welcome given he would angrily ask for the visitors' book, then with a huge flourish and scratching of his black pen he would write "Snowdon". I would be standing there shaking, as would the receptionist. I was so in awe of him – I thought this must be how you behaved if you were royal or semi-royal.'

Together they worked out a techique for ensuring Tony got the compelling pictures that were his trademark. One series, on what were then known as asylums, serves as example. Tony would give an unobtrusive signal, upon which Marjorie created a diversion with conversation or a request for tea. Tony would then slip unnoticed out of the room where the pair were being entertained by a welcoming party and go into the wards, quietly snapping away with his small Leica. He would return just in time to be taken round on the official tour with Marjorie.

Once, in Birmingham, to achieve the pictures they wanted, they staged what Tony called a 'Dawn Raid', arriving outside the lock-ed hospital gates at 5 a.m. on an early spring day in 1975. All was quiet and they were in any case not expected until 11 a.m. Undaunted, Tony muffled the lower part of his face with an old scarf, filled a camera bag with stuff lying around and told Marjorie to say to whoever answered the bell: 'I'm delivering the laundry.' They took the car in, parked and went straight to the women's ward, where the nurses were dressing the inmates. Tony used his

---

* SANE was founded in 1986 as *Schizophrenia – A National Emergency* but has widened its concern to all serious mental illness. Its patron is the Prince of Wales.

charm and Marjorie explained they were campaigning to change conditions. Unfortunately, although the pictures were some of Tony's best, the story was considered a failure and not used: what the *Sunday Times* had wanted was an exposé of abuse, neglect and the cruelty of nurses. Instead, what Tony and Marjorie had found, in the twelve dank and gloomy institutions they visited, was an extraordinary level of compassion and care. 'One beautiful nurse, for instance, spent a good hour trying gently to feed a small hydrocephalic child,' she remembered.

She found Tony, as so many had, fascinating, endearing and maddening. 'Boring' was a word she learned to dread. Sometimes it meant total silence in the car, sometimes that the potential photograph was not exciting enough, with a consequent effect on Tony's mood. Once, on a visit to a training centre in Lincoln for young people damaged by rubella (German measles) he decided that 'straightforward photographs would be too predictable. Hands – I'm only going to take pictures of hands,' he told the startled Marjorie, who knew this was not what the *Sunday Times* was expecting. But the pictures proved him right – a blind boy's hands on an electric saw guided by the teacher, a deaf girl gripping a pencil as she sketched a church window – and the story was used under the title 'A World in Their Hands.'

Although his behaviour to the subjects of these photographs was always impeccably courteous and gentle, working with him had its ups and downs. In the car, for instance, he would always insist on having the window open, even when rain was coming in. 'Could we have the window up, Tony?' Marjorie asked once, with water pouring down her shoulder. 'But if I close it, how on earth will they recognise me?' answered a surprised Tony. Marjorie remained wet. At other times, there were 'great moments' when he was funny, charming, appreciative – and very kind.

When, as a former sufferer from polio, Tony had been asked (in 1975) by Duncan Guthrie, Director of the National Fund for Research into Crippling Diseases, to chair a working party formed to produce a survey on the needs of disabled people and what was required both to help them lead as normal a life as possible and to minimise their isolation from the rest of society, he was glad to accept. Many of his friends – Quentin Crewe, Lady Elizabeth

Cavendish, Janie Stevens, Simon Sainsbury and Mary Gilliatt among them – were co-opted. One of the most influential of the group would be John Hannam, MP.

As Tony's foreword to the survey, published in 1976, put it: the report's dominant theme 'is a demand, in the name of humanity, for the better and wider understanding at all levels in our society, of the emotional and material needs of disabled people.... Need disabled people still be put in herds – in schools, buses, homes – and labelled as such? Can they not instead have the equal opportunity, so commonly enjoyed, to go where they want, how they want, and when they want. ... Must they be treated as a category "to be put up with"? They are not second-class citizens and must never be made to feel so.'

They were words elaborated on by Duncan Guthrie. As he pointed out, disabled people were institutionalised where they pleaded to be individuals, thus complicating their social problems and making harder the breaking-down of social barriers, while through their consequent unfamiliarity with disablement – at school, during leisure, at work – able-bodied children or adults were often at a loss as to how to respond, whether in conversation or in offers of help – would it seem patronising, or was it needed?

Much of the evidence for the Snowdon working party came in the form of letters, many heartbreaking in their descriptions of how minimal help then was. 'I do all shopping, cooking, cleaning, ironing, when able,' wrote a 41-year-old mother of four who had had to give up work three years earlier when disabled by multiple sclerosis. 'I have a home help for two hours a week which my husband pays for. I was offered a bus pass but wasn't able to get as far as the Town Hall to fetch it – I can only go out leaning on a pushchair.'

Another disabled mother wrote that children's playgrounds (there were plenty more then) were usually in the middle of open spaces where parking was forbidden so that she was unable to take her children there. A disabled woman was barred from promotion because she was only allowed to work on the ground floor of her organisation – in an emergency, the lifts would be switched off – and all the better jobs were on higher floors. 'The needs of the disabled are too numerous to mention,' wrote a woman with a chronically ill husband, a daughter of sixteen on a year's college course and a son of eleven at Grammar school, 'but with a liveable weekly income many of these needs could be fulfilled without having to beg. No-one asks to be born disabled, surely that is punishment enough without having to scratch and worry over every penny. As it is, sub-standard citizens are all the disabled can be called.'

The survey proved a valuable first step towards the aim declared in its title: *Integrating the Disabled* (if Tony had known of this title in advance, he would have insisted on the word 'People' being added). By the time it was published, Guthrie had retired and Andrew Farquhar, who felt he was too young to take on the post of Director, became Deputy Director.

Then, hearing on the radio that guide dogs were excluded from the Chelsea Flower Show, Tony took on its President, Lord Aberconway. The action began with a long letter from Tony in *The Times* of 14 January 1976 in which he quoted from the letter sent by the Royal Horticultural Society's official spokesman to the National Federation of the Blind. 'There are no aural or tactile pleasures available and so the only pleasure which could be enjoyed by them is that of scent ... only another person can say what the flowers are, what they look like and so on. A guide dog cannot perform these functions and that is why guide dogs are excluded.'

Tony's two-column letter was not all criticism: he continued by suggesting that the RHS arranged for 'a few keen horticultural volunteer guides' to stand by for the four days of the Show 'to accompany those at present treated like social outcasts'. He concluded by pointing out that in the US and Australia there were gardens in which all the exhibits were labelled in Braille. His letter, and Lord Aberconway's reply, attracted a large correspondence – not all on Tony's side; some of it pointed out that no guide dogs could be expected to operate satisfactorily in the surging throngs that often congested the Flower Show – and gave rise to a Parliamentary question (on 2 February).

The last letter, on 14 February from Alfred Morris, Joint Parliamentary Under-Secretary of State at the Department of Health and Social Security, effectively brokered a deal between Tony's claims and those of the RHS. Guide dogs were to be left and cared for at the entrance to the Show until departure; if the blind person wished, a volunteer, probably a Fellow of the RHS, would act as guide to the Show. 'I am naturally very pleased with the Society's offer of an important new facility for blind people at the Chelsea Flower Show,' wrote Morris. 'I am sure that these arrangements will be welcomed as much by Members of Parliament as they have been by the major organisations representing blind people.' From Tony's point of view, it was another small step forward in his efforts to promote greater equality of treatment for disabled people.

In February 1976 the Princess set off for her annual three-week holiday in Mustique, as usual flying first to Barbados and then by island-hopper on to Mustique. It was the third time she and Roddy had been to the island together, sometimes travelling as Mr and Mrs Brown, and by now the rumours, hints and minor stories about them were building up. Soon they would explode into front-page headlines, with their relationship treated as a national scandal. All the ingredients, already in place and waiting for the touch-paper, were there: royalty, the age gulf – regarded as disgraceful by many of those who would not have blinked at a similar one with the sexes reversed – and, above all, the perception of the Princess as someone who led a gilded lifestyle but did little for the money put up by the taxpayer except take holidays in the sun (the fact that several other members of the royal family took two holidays a year was conveniently ignored).

The spark that lit the bonfire of scandal was a photograph taken by a journalist who had slipped through Colin Tennant's security net via an upmarket package holiday to the island. Also in the original photograph were Anne Tennant's brother Lord Coke and his wife, who were sitting opposite each other on either side of the table (the Princess's Private Secretary, Lord Napier, had also been staying in the villa but had just left, in order to be back at Kensington Palace when she returned).

Napier arrived home on Saturday 21 February. The next day, the photograph was printed in the *News of the World*. Fuzzy though it was, it clearly showed the Princess, wearing one of her usual one-piece, corseted and skirted bathing costumes, sitting at a wooden table, with Roddy, in the Union Jack trunks she had bought him on their first meeting, beside her. The two figures were silhouetted against a background of ocean. The Cokes, and others nearby, had been cut out, so that what appeared was apparently a photograph of Margaret sitting alone and intimately with her young lover in one of the world's most romantic settings.

On Monday Napier went as usual into his office. Tony, in his own basement office, pressed the buzzer and said to Napier: 'Will you come across and see me?' 'Of course,' said Napier, who crossed the courtyard, entered Tony's little office and sat down. 'Well, come on,' said Tony. 'What's going on?' 'Don't be so stupid – you know perfectly well what's going on,' responded Napier. 'You've seen the newspapers, and you know what's been happening.'

Tony sent for his secretary, Dorothy Everard. When she entered he announced: 'Dotty [as he always called her], we're moving out.' Saying this in front of Napier was a clear statement of intent – and meant to be passed on to Napier's employer.

Napier's first duty was of course to inform the Princess who, in Mustique, without newspapers and with no particular reason to ring Kensington Palace, would have no idea of developments. As Napier had to talk to her on an ordinary telephone line he had to be extraordinarily careful in the way he phrased the information that her husband was moving out in case some unauthorised person overheard and leaked it to the press.

Suddenly he remembered that Tony's Christian names were Antony Charles Robert. Charles might have been confusing but no one in the royal family was called Robert so that if anyone had been listening in they would probably have thought he was referring to a footman. He telephoned Margaret with the words: 'Ma'am, I have to tell you that Robert has given notice and he's leaving at the weekend.' 'Say that again,' said the Princess, momentarily puzzled. Napier repeated the same sentence and Margaret immediately grasped his meaning. 'Nigel, that is the best news you have ever given me!' she cried.

By the time Margaret returned alone (save for her detective; Roddy, who returned later, fled at once to Surrendell) on 3 March 1976, her head wrapped in a turquoise scarf and her eyes hidden by dark glasses, Tony had left Kensington Palace for good. He went straight to a tiny basement flat in West Halkin Street, belonging to his friend Jeremy Fry.

On 16 March, five days after he had turned sixty, the Prime Minister, Harold Wilson, resigned, to the shock and surprise of almost the entire nation. He had then held the supreme post in government for longer than any other premier in the twentieth century and had been Labour leader for thirteen years. He told his stunned Cabinet in the morning and went to see the Queen in the afternoon (although it was understood that he had informed her of what he intended to do the previous December). The precise timing of his resignation was a chivalrous gesture intended to divert attention from what he knew would be another 'headliner': the official announcement that the Snowdons were separating. Unfortunately, Tony had left on assignment for Hong Kong on the same day, and before he departed had told a friend in Beaverbrook Newspapers that he and Margaret would soon be legally separated, that the subject had been discussed by the royal family and that the Queen had given her consent to it. As soon as this story appeared in the *Daily Express* (on 17 March) it completely drowned the Wilson resignation story instead of the other way round.

In England, the massed ranks of the media closed in on Surrendell. The next day, Roddy managed to drive his blue transit van out of a back gate and across fields already sown with corn to the farm of his friend Diane Cilento five miles away.

Tony, who flew on to Australia where an exhibition of his photographs was being held, found the press was waiting in force at the airport when he arrived on 17 March. He had little option but to call an immediate, impromptu press conference. Hands trembling, face drawn, and with a halting voice he read out, from a sheet of paper which he held near his knee, the words: 'I am naturally desperately sad in every way that this had to happen. And I would just like to say three things. First to pray for the understanding of our two children. Secondly, to wish Princess Margaret every happiness for her future. Thirdly, to express, with the utmost humility, the love, admiration and respect I will always have for her sister, her mother and indeed her entire family.'

It was all perfectly true: his feelings for the Queen, the Queen

Mother and the royal family remained all his life exactly as he had said; his future comments about Margaret were invariably admiring and affectionate, and he certainly wanted the understanding of his children. At the same time, his statement was a public relations coup. His very sincerity made it an emotional tour de force that put the public firmly on his side. Princess Margaret, to the fury and distress of her friends, all of whom had seen Tony's treatment of her and knew of his affair with Lucy, was firmly cast as the villain of the piece: an abandoned 45-year-old woman who had – horrors! – taken a lover nearer her son's age than her own and who was luxuriating with him on a holiday island behind her hard-working husband's back. Margaret, who watched Tony's performance on the BBC television news, is alleged to have commented: 'I have never seen such good acting.'

From Clarence House, Major John Griffin, Press Secretary to the Queen Mother and the Princess, issued a statement. 'A separation has been a possibility for some time,' he said, 'and once the final decision had been reached it was obviously best to implement it straight away. It was the best course to take in all the circumstances bearing in mind in particular the interests of the two children.'

Behind the scenes the Palace machinery was working frenziedly. Two days after Tony's emotional words from the other side of the world, the parting of the Snowdons was made official with a bleak, uncompromising announcement on Friday 19 March 1976: 'Her Royal Highness, the Princess Margaret, Countess of Snowdon, and the Earl of Snowdon have mutually agreed to live apart. The Princess will carry out her public duties and functions unaccompanied by Lord Snowdon. There are no plans for divorce proceedings.'

14

Separation

※

As the Snowdon separation was the most serious marital drama in the royal family since the Abdication, all parties recognised the need to avoid the dread word 'divorce'. In 1976, the advantage of a legal separation was that arrangements could be made over both children and money without going to court. Also, after two years, it was relatively easy for one of the parties to obtain a divorce – provided he or she had the consent of the other. If there was no such consent, a divorce could take place after five years with no consent required.

Buckingham Palace stated officially that the Queen was 'terribly sad' about the break-up. The Queen Mother, as ever unwilling to face unpleasant facts, put it down to media interference. As she emerged from her lady-in-waiting's sitting room after the announcement, her page William Tallon was unable to refrain from saying: 'Your Majesty, I feel so sad.' 'It should never have happened,' she replied. 'It was all that wretched *Daily Express*.'

Margaret herself was, at first, miserable. Depressed, dreading the future, she felt unable to be alone. Her 'first eleven' of friends was on constant duty at Kensington Palace, offering support, what cheering words they could and seeing that she did nothing rash – twice there were attempts at an overdose. Others, like her cousin Lady Elizabeth Anson, were equally on call: Margaret might want to come to dinner several nights running. If there were obstacles, real or pretended ('Listen, Ma'am, there's a domestic crisis', or 'I haven't bought any food'), when the strain of attempting to alleviate her wretchedness became too much, she would simply say 'That's all right, I'm not hungry – I'll just come round and talk.'

Princess Margaret enjoying two of her favourite occupations: sunbathing and smoking, on the *Fior di Mare*, the boat belonging to Prince and Princess Caracciolo, summer 1973.

Tony, Margaret and their children among a group during the 1973 holiday they spent with the Caracciolos at their country villa near Porto Ercole. It was the last family holiday they took together.

Tony and Peter Sellers fooling around at Sellers's Beverley Hills home in the mid-1970s.

Tony in Australia in 1975, making a BBC documentary (on the ill-fated 1860 expedition of Burke and Wills).

Colin Tennant on Mustique, 1973.

Roddy Llewellyn in the 1970s.

The *News of the World* photograph of 22 February 1976 that blew the Snowdons' marriage apart. Others seated at the table were cut out of the picture.

A lunch party at Old House – guests include the novelist Edna O'Brien and, opposite her, the satirist John Wells and the interior designer Nicky Haslam.

The maestro relaxes after an arduous photo shoot, a moment captured by his assistant Richard Dudley-Smith.

Carl Toms in 1981, taken by Tony.

Family christening group for Lady Frances Armstrong-Jones in October 1979. *From left*: David Linley, Lady Rosse, Lucy holding Frances, Tony and Sarah.

Polly Fry aged twenty-three.

Lucy and Frances in 1983.

Lucy Snowdon, by her husband.

Tony and André Leon Talley of *Vogue* at the Palazzo Ruspoli in Rome in 1987, spoofing the Fendi fur fashion show they were covering.

At weekends, she would go to Royal Lodge, where she took out her unhappiness on her mother in countless small, irritating ways. If the Queen Mother closed a door because of a draught Margaret, sitting on the sofa doing her daily *Times* crossword puzzle, would pointedly get up and open it again.

For the Queen Mother, accepting that divorce could be of benefit even to people as wretched together as the Snowdons was almost impossible. When one friend commented that in their circumstances – shut away from each other, unable to communicate and fighting if they did speak – it was the only solution, her reply was that as all marriages had ups and downs, surely they could come to some arrangement. Divorce, so contrary to all she had been brought up to believe in and the code by which she had lived her life, filled her with a kind of horror.

The couple's solicitors, with Lord Goodman acting for Tony, had already negotiated a Separation Agreement that provided for the Princess remaining at Kensington Palace with the children and Tony having free access to them. The financial arrangements had still to be worked out.

The whole affair was a gift to the world's media. They could not beseige Kensington Palace – in any case, Princess Margaret had driven straight to Royal Lodge – but they could and did descend first on Surrendell and thence to Diane Cilento's farm where Roddy was staying. Badgered for interviews or comments, Roddy finally decided, with Diane Cilento's agreement, that the only way to stop this harassment would be to issue a statement, first telephoning Princess Margaret's office to clear it. Here Lord Napier briskly rejected it as being full of the sort of sentiments that would, he said, be a gift to the tabloid press.

Instead, Roddy composed a more suitable one that was, after being passed by Napier, issued to the Press Association on 24 March 1976:

> I am not prepared to comment on any of the events of last week. I much regret any embarrassment caused to Her Majesty the Queen and the royal family, for whom I wish to express the greatest respect, admiration and loyalty.
>
> I thank my own family for their confidence and support, and I am very grateful for the help of my friends at the farm who, with

myself, share a common interest in restoring a house to its original order and beauty, and in farming land which it is hoped will provide food for our Parsenn Sally restaurant in Bath.

Could we please be permitted by the media, who have besieged us, to carry on with our work and private lives without further interference.

But soon afterwards, the Surrendell venture came to an end. Parsenn Sally was so much in debt that it had to close and thereafter, as various members of the group drifted away, Surrendell was gradually abandoned. Roddy went back to his parents' home in Wales and later began a year's course at the Merrist Wood Agricultural College, near Guildford, Surrey (from which he graduated the following August with a national Certificate of Horticulture). Already, within weeks of the separation announcement, Princess Margaret and Roddy were seeing each other again.

Tony, who left Australia on 3 April 1976, arrived home on the 4th and went straight to the flat in West Halkin Street. It was, of course, staked out by the press. Due to photograph a cover for the American edition of *GQ Magazine* the next day, he made arrangements with the editor supervising the shoot, Meredith Etherington-Smith, to leave the flat at 5.30 a.m. 'There were about five photographers camped out around the front door,' she recalled, 'so we made a bolt for it. Fortunately they were not expecting us to leave at that hour.'

The shoot was taken against a barn door in the country to give a plain background. It was to feature the Russian ballet star Rudolf Nureyev, by now an old friend of Tony's, dressed in some beautifully cut clothes by the Savile Row tailors Anderson and Shepherd. Nureyev, all flaring nostrils, high cheekbones and fiercely focused gaze, looked immaculate if almost too virile. Tony, well versed in the tricks by which male ballet dancers enhanced their physiques, said to his assistant: 'Go and tell Rudy to take out whatever he's got stuffed down the front of his trousers – it spoils the hang of the clothes.' Tentatively, the assistant approached the great star to suggest that perhaps one of his socks had been somehow caught up as he dressed? 'That is not sock,' said Nureyev crossly. 'It is *me*.' It became a story destined to be many times repeated.

Although both Meredith and Tony roared with laughter at the episode, she was aware that beneath Tony's gaiety there was a deep unhappiness and considerable stress – his cigarette consumption had gone up to sixty a day. He felt bereft, and sad, emotions heightened by the gloom of the basement flat in which he was living, perpetually dark unless the light was switched on, with windows through which no daylight ever came, an especial deprivation as natural light was at the core of his work. For someone with his powerful and demanding visual sense, who took endless trouble to make anywhere he lived or worked as pleasing as possible, depressing surroundings or objects – such as the bare lightbulbs in the kitchenette – carried an added emotional charge. How much he missed the life he had lost was evident to Meredith when, after finishing a telephone call, he said sadly: 'They're so lovely, the switchboard at the Palace – they're so adorable.'

There was, however, still a connection with his former royal life, which he would always take care to maintain. The Nureyev pictures were developed, as usual, in the darkroom at Kensington Palace. He continued to use these facilities, entering as before through the separate basement door that led to his office and darkroom so that there was no danger of running into Princess Margaret. She, in any case, would have given him a wide berth. 'By the time of the separation she had come to really loathe him,' confirmed all those close to her. 'She hated him. They put on a front for the sake of the children but whenever he rang up she found it a frightful bore. It's no good pretending otherwise.' When she was told by a friend at a party that he had seen on a newspaper billboard that Tony's pictures in his Australian exhibition had been slashed, her response was: 'Good!'

Tony, on the other hand, spoke to no one of his feelings about his estranged wife. Neither then, nor at any time later in his life, did he ever utter a word against the Princess – or allow anything derogatory of her to be said in his presence, a gentlemanly discretion that enabled later meetings to be first civilised and then even affectionate. In any case, both had always taken great care not to inflict the stresses of their marriage on David and Sarah; when Tony had returned from Australia they went together to Bedales to tell them jointly of their parting. In an echo of Tony's own childhood, they planned that the children would spend half the holidays with each parent.

Tony, in addition, went further than simply remaining silent about the Princess. For the rest of his life, he would spring to her defence both privately and, when he felt something unjust had been written about her, publicly. When they separated he said to Angela Huth, who stuck by Margaret, 'If you ever do anything against Princess Margaret I'd kill you'; and he was always anxious to point out her contribution to public life. Of one proposed biography of the Princess he wrote to the publisher: 'I wish the project well if it is to be a serious book concentrating on Princess Margaret's many achievements, her work, her duties, her great contribution to the arts in general and to the ballet in particular, which has seldom been acclaimed in the way it should have been.'

It was not only a loyalty that endured for the rest of the Princess's life but an approach that further endeared him to those members of the royal family about whom he cared deeply.

House-hunting was an immediate priority, varied only by meetings with Lord Goodman, senior partner in the noted law firm Goodman Derrick and Co., and adviser and confidant to public figures who needed negotiations conducted delicately. Aware of every current, at the centre of a wide and influential network, he was exactly the right person to handle the fine details of a parting between two such well-known figures. Another business meeting to prove of great importance in his life was with Peter Lyster Todd.

They had first met in the early seventies when Lyster Todd was a partner in David Puttnam Associates, an agency that represented the new breed of photographers such as David Bailey, Norman Parkinson and Tony himself, whose names were even better known than their pictures. When Puttnam decided to become a film producer, Lyster Todd set up his own firm with a friend called Roger Barker, and was followed there by Tony. Over lunch in May 1976, they agreed that Lyster Todd would now represent Tony, a happy arrangement that continued for about twenty years until Lyster Todd finally shifted towards the music business.

Tony's first thought for temporary accommodation was that as there was plenty of room in his mother's house in Stafford Terrace, Kensington, he could stay there until he found a place of his own. So at Easter (Easter Sunday, that year, was on 18 April), he asked Anne if he could come to Stafford Terrace. Grudgingly, she agreed, but added, 'You can't stay longer than ten days.' Where most mothers would have unhesitatingly offered a son in that position a home for as long as he needed it – and Tony had made it quite plain that he only wanted to stay until he found somewhere of his own – she remained true to her guiding principle of climbing to the peak of the social mountain and staying there, no matter what the view around her. She was frightened, it transpired, of appearing to be on her son's side in the Snowdons' marital split, and thus prejudice her position vis-à-vis the royal family. She particularly wanted to keep in with Princess Margaret and the longer Tony stayed with her the more she would appear to be taking his part.

For Tony, there was support as always from his sister Susan – the one constant star in his life, with whom he had never had a cross word, on whom he could always depend. 'My darling,' she had written on 15 February 1976, after she had been to stay with him, 'You gave me such a happy time – for all those lovely evenings, thank you so much. The weekend at Old House was marvellous and I just loved being there with you – a million more thanks for that, and for driving me to Oxford, and on and on and on. . . .'

Two days after his arrival in his mother's house, there was a large, black-tie dinner party at Windsor to which Anne Rosse had been invited. 'Of course, you won't be going now,' she said to Tony. To her dismayed surprise, he replied: 'Well, actually I am.' It made no difference to her attitude to his visit; and twelve days later he returned to the Fry basement, renting it in the first instance until mid-June – Jeremy, then at Le Grand Banc, the Provençal hamlet he had restored, had moved to Royal Crescent, Bath.

The emotional bruising from the break-up of his marriage and his love affair with Lucy made little difference to Tony's attitude to any woman who seemed available. One of the first was a beautiful young woman (later to marry a peer), a good head taller than himself, with whom he quickly began a liaison. Athough she paid tribute both to his physical attributes and his virility, she found the West Halkin Street flat depressing. 'I remember it as bare and soulless, an atmosphere of gloom and order, with the telephone ringing incessantly with calls from Princess Margaret,' she told the author.

Even after Tony's departure from Stafford Terrace, there was an occasional pertinent reminder of him. Shortly afterwards, Anne Rosse, who had managed to achieve her aim of remaining on good terms with Princess Margaret, went to lunch with her and at one point visited the lavatory, using the one nearest to the dining room, by the front door. She had been gone some time when Margaret heard a plaintive cry of 'Ma'am! Ma'am!' coming from inside. It turned out that the integral lock (chosen by Tony) had got stuck and Anne Rosse could not make it turn. In the end the hapless Countess was rescued from ignominious captivity by Margaret's butler, who climbed through the window and managed to turn the lock. 'That's your son for you,' said Margaret crisply. Soon afterwards, the lock was replaced by an old-fashioned sliding bolt.

When Margaret left for a trip to Monaco (on 28 April 1976) Tony was able to see plenty of the children. They lunched at his flat and he then took them back to school. Sometimes they came down to Old House for weekends, at other times they went to Royal Lodge with their mother.

By the beginning of July 1976 the Separation Agreement had been quietly concluded and the couple's financial affairs settled, with Tony receiving £100,000 from the Princess and the understanding that a house would be purchased for him, to be held in trust for the children. As he had always done, he continued to pay half the children's school fees (with extras such as special tuition, art materials, examination fees and postage, these amounted to well over £1,000 a term each). The question of their furniture, some of which came from one side, some from the other and some of which was jointly owned, was to be left until Tony had found a house.

A friend, Bobby Cooper-Coles, who worked for the estate agents Druce, had already been house-hunting for a year. Then a house about which Tony already knew as its tenant, Lady Waleran, had been a friend of his father, came on the market. After her husband had died she was unable to afford to buy it outright and the owners wanted her out. That August, thinking that it might suit the son of her old friend, she telephoned Tony.

The house he went to see was in Launceston Place, a white stucco villa built in the 1840s that stood at the end of a quiet, short Kensington street. Launceston Place – then known as Sussex Place – was the last to be built of a group of streets round about with similar semi-detached houses. The house had one additional feature: a lead-capped turret, probably added by its second owner, Spiridone Gambardella, a self-styled astronomer and painter, to aid his view of the stars (Sr Gambardella, born in Corfu, appears in the census of 1851). Although not particularly large, it had a feeling of space and serenity. Stone steps led up to the front door, which opened into a wide hall. Off this led, to the right, a drawing room and dining room; above were two further floors of bedrooms and bathrooms; around and at the back was a quiet garden.

The moment Tony saw it he knew it was the one. 'I came in through the door and fell in love with it straightaway,' he said. Tony was represented by Savills and on 31 August 1976 the agent for the Trustees wrote to Savills to confirm his offer 'to purchase the freehold of the above-mentioned property subject to contract and survey for £75,000'. Although Tony's name was given as the buyer, the money for its purchase came from the Queen, coupled with the proviso that while Tony had it for his lifetime, it was in trust for the Snowdon children, David and Sarah Armstrong-Jones.

Work, always a raison d'être, was now also a consolation. There were portrait photographs – of Elizabeth Harrison,* of Jacqueline du Pré, of Elisabeth Frink, meetings with lawyers, agents, editors, several commissions from Beatrix Miller, the Editor of *Vogue*. Almost the whole of that autumn was spent abroad on assignments. He flew to Tokyo, he went to Hong Kong and thence to Australia – while there, there was almost a hiccup over the purchase of the Launceston Place house when another would-be purchaser offered £80,000, but a furious letter from Tony's solicitor John Humphries on 25 October ('I would, with respect, point out that the fact that your firm are acting for Trustees does not

---

* Recently divorced from the actor Rex Harrison.

SNOWDON

justify them in either gazumping or running a Dutch Auction')
soon brought them to heel. They might have reacted even quicker
had they known who was really buying the house.

His seven-week tour of Australia, Japan, Canada, parts of Africa
and the Middle East (involving 102 landings and take-offs) continued at an ever more frenzied pace, photographing car factories in
Singapore, flying to Brunei to photograph a floating village, taking
a helicopter to photograph logging operations. Fatigue was taking
its toll: his diary is spattered with references to 'ghastly dinner',
'longed to swim but no time'. Not until 6 November did he receive
a cable telling him that the Launceston Place house was now his.

It was his first Christmas for a long time when he had neither
visited Windsor Castle nor Sandringham. But there was no question of his severing contact with his former in-laws – nor forfeiting
their affection – as attested by a charming letter from Prince
Charles thanking him for a present. 'Needless to say, your jollity
and effervescent wit has been greatly missed over Xmas, certainly
by me if by no one else!' wrote the Prince on 27 December 1976,
adding that perhaps one day they might see him back again.
Margaret, meanwhile, made her usual visit to Mustique, where she
attended her friend Colin Tennant's gold-themed fiftieth birthday
party, for which the beach was sprayed gold and the gold-clad
guests entered under a golden arch of palm leaves to dance to a
steel band.

Early in 1977, at a conference for the disabled, Tony met a
journalist who found him electrically attractive from the start. A
few days later, according to one of her friends, she turned up at
the West Halkin Street basement where he was still living
(completion on the new house had not yet taken place). When he
opened the door she said: 'I am a journalist and I want to do a
story on you. But I also want to have an affair with you.' He did
not think twice about either proposition ('if ladies who are quite
attractive throw themselves at one it is very difficult to resist').
The affair began immediately and her interview with him was
published in March 1977, in *Social Services*, a small, little-known
magazine.

252

The name of his new lover was Ann Hills. Born on 7 January 1941, she was thirty-six when they met, and married to an architect, Nicholas Hills. She was pretty, with dark hair, blue-green eyes and a slim figure, effervescent, untidy, often scruffy in her person, cultured – she was totally familiar with and extremely knowledgeable about the Wallace Collection, for example – energetic, dynamic and a loyal friend. Like Tony, she was small, four feet ten inches; like him, she had a difficult mother and, like him, a voracious appetite for sex. As one close friend put it: 'Where sex was concerned, Ann was impulsive and compulsive. She always said she could get a man into bed within five minutes of meeting him.' In many cases it was true.

She was also given to depression. Her father, Elliot Philipp, a distinguished gynaecologist whom she adored, once had to drive through the night to her (non-collegiate) college at Oxford, St Clare's, after she had telephoned him to ask: 'What pills should I take – I want to commit suicide.' Another friend remembered having several conversations with her about different ways of ending one's life.

To the outside world, she was a hard-working journalist who specialised in pursuing interesting stories in different countries – sleeping with anyone who took her fancy en route – writing extremely quickly and selling different versions of the same basic story to different small publications. She was deeply interested in and worked hard for the rights of the disadvantaged – hence her interest in disabled people – and had won the Nancy Astor Award for her campaigning work for the 300 Group, which lobbied for women in politics. Through her energy and enterprise, she not only paid the rent of her flat but also educated her two sons at Westminster School.

Her architect husband had designed their large top-floor flat in York House, on the corner of Upper Montagu Street and York Street, Marylebone. On the rooftop terrace, which the Hills also owned, there was a turret, where her circular bedroom was; this held a large nine-foot-diameter round bed. Inside the flat, glass walls could be moved and repositioned to change the shape of the main living area. To a visitor, this could be disconcerting, as half the bathroom walls were glass, as were the walls of Ann's dressing room. 'So if you were having a shower and she was changing in her dressing room – well, you didn't always know where to look,' said one (platonic) male guest. Nor did she have any qualms of conscience about her way of life. She had persuaded herself that if she was discreet her promiscuous behaviour was doing no one any harm – and indeed, many of her affairs were fleeting – and she had no hesitation in indulging it. Any of her friends staying with her were liable to be told: 'Can you guys not come back until 5 p.m. – I have a tryst.'

She was fascinated by Tony from the moment they met. She knew, of course, that he was separated from Princess Margaret; she also knew that he was seeing Lucy. 'That wouldn't have worried her at all,' said her father later. 'She would have said to herself, "We enjoy one another's company and I'm not doing anybody any harm." She would have fooled herself, although in other ways she was very perceptive.'

Certainly, the article she wrote after their first meeting was well researched, thoughtful and sensitive. It began by telling readers that as a result of Tony's attack on the Royal Horticultural Society blind people could that year, for the first time, visit the Chelsea Flower Show, where they would be taken round by volunteers while their guide dogs were looked after away from the flower beds. She went on to list other victories:

> Snowdon recently supported the *Daily Mirror* in its campaign on behalf of a group of spina bifida children from Consett, County Durham, who were barred from a holiday camp near Scarborough on the grounds that 'customers might find it upsetting to have a large group of severely disabled people on holiday with them'. Snowdon, 'appalled at the ban', intervened by asking the owners of the Primrose Valley Holiday Park for more information and the end result is that the holiday camp have now accepted the booking. Publicity drew offers from Butlins, the Irish Caravan Council and other holiday firms who may now invite holiday-less handicapped children to their own resorts.

Tony's ongoing crusade for a better life for the handicapped was an aspect of his personality that had a powerful appeal for Ann, herself deeply interested in social problems. Soon aware that this affair would mean more to her than any other, she told her husband about it – an uncomfortable honesty was another of her personality traits. As the mother of young children, she was determined not to do anything to break up her family so, from the start, it was to be a liaison conducted entirely behind closed doors.

Ironically, at the time she was writing a book (with Tony Lake) entitled *Affairs – How to Deal with Extra-Marital Relationships,* published in 1979. It is a book that makes clear her belief that affairs are just as much a part of normal life as marriage; and the extramarital affair is 'an honest attempt to achieve more growth'. One of its sentiments, in the chapter headed 'Ready for an Affair,' could have applied to either Ann or Tony:

> The extra-marital affair is an attempt by someone who is married to meet through individual, extra-marital behaviour some personal objective, some private aim, that the marriage itself either has not met or has not radically altered. In this sense it is selfish behaviour. It may often appear to make no sense when seen in relation to the marriage, yet it may make a great deal of sense in terms of the individual's personal and emotional development. This development, of course, begins long before marriage. It is rooted in childhood, grows through adolescence and pre-marital adulthood and, despite the tradition that young men and women who marry should 'settle down', it continues through marriage.

The beginning of a later chapter set out the parameters for their liaison: 'Affairs are usually surrounded by a protective web of lies and deceit.'

Ann would visit Tony in West Halkin Street or he would ring her, each time with a different name and using one of the voices his gift for mimicry allowed him to put on at will. Sometimes he would go round to her flat in the morning, between nine and nine-thirty – easy if the boys were out of the flat during term time, more difficult if they were at home when they were sent out into the (safe) square garden to play. The number of their meetings varied: it could be two or three times a week or sometimes, to Ann's distress, not for two or three weeks, alleviated only by the occasional telephone call; nor would there be any rendezvous in public. Although determined to be discreet, she told a number of her closest friends under oath of secrecy, so that none of them ever spoke to each other about it. Neither Ann nor Tony could have guessed how long such a liaison, started so light-heartedly, would go on.

Tony's new house in Launceston Place needed much doing to it. Work on it began in February 1977, with a number of men specialised in their different trades of carpentry, roofing, plumbing, brickwork and painting up from Bath, where they had worked for Jeremy Fry, 'and all of them a pleasure to work with,' wrote Tony in his record of the house's makeover. They camped first in Dorothy's room, then the future kitchen and then moved up to the attic. It was a long job, as Tony naturally wanted to be involved at all stages.

The house progressed steadily. Picture rails were removed, embossed paper peeled off ceilings, doors blocked up and the internal stairs, from basement to bedroom floor, stripped of six coats of paint back to the original stone. 'One had the luxury of being able to discuss things each day, try things out, experiment and if necessary change one's mind,' wrote Tony. It was a project after his own heart: never happier than when designing, making things alongside sympathetic fellow craftsmen, using his eclectic eye to gain the effect he wanted – often by some ingenious and far cheaper method than anyone else could have managed – he was then also at his sunniest. At the end of June 1977 he was able to move in.

All the time, he had been working as hard as ever. One of his most powerful and moving essays in photojournalism was a feature on the mentally afflicted in the *Sunday Times Magazine* of 13 March 1977. It had a profound effect on those who saw these photographs, portraying their subjects both with dignity and pathos. (All had, of course, been printed with the agreement of those concerned: no one had been photographed unless they were willing, each photograph, taken to the relevant home or hospital, had to have a stamp of approval on the back and any considered not suitable for publication were abandoned.) It was, for Tony, one step nearer the campaigning work for disabled people with which he would soon be associated.

In private life, busy and sought-after as he was, he could easily have confined his acquaintanceship to the rich, powerful or those who would be a help in his career, but letter after letter shows that this was not so. 'Darling Tony,' wrote his old nanny in September 1977, 'I came home from hospital on Sunday. It was sweet of you to come with David and Sarah to see me, Sarah is so pretty. Thank you too for the delicious fruit you brought me, I very much enjoyed it. . . . with much love to you and take care of yourself, lots of love from Nanny.'

Later that month, wondering if he was spending too much, Tony asked Savills to do a valuation. They sent their assessment of its new freehold value to Tony's solicitor on 31 October. Commenting that 'this house is arguably the best house in Launceston Place', they continued: 'We are of the opinion that the freehold interest if placed on the open market at today's date would be fairly represented in a figure of £125,000.' This was already a sum far in excess of the combined purchase price and the £30,000 the alterations would eventually cost.

Soon after the work to make it habitable was completed, Tony invited Margaret there, saying he had something he wanted to talk to her about. She arrived, there were pleasantries, they had a drink. Margaret waited for Tony to broach whatever it was he wanted to talk about but nothing particular was mentioned. When she was leaving, she turned to him at the door and said: 'Didn't you have something you wanted to talk to me about?' 'No,' said Tony, sounding slightly surprised. 'Oh,' said Margaret, 'I thought you were going to ask me for a divorce'. 'I don't want one,' he replied.

As Princess Margaret's life slowly returned to what it had been earlier, the bitterness she felt towards her husband slowly leached away. Both were in any case determined that their children should suffer as little as possible, so that any such feelings would never have been displayed in front of David or Sarah. They would always greet each other affectionately, with a kiss on meeting or parting, and there was no bickering over the length of time the children spent with either parent – often, Margaret's chauffeur David Griffin (who joined her after Larkin's departure in early 1977) would take them down to Old House on a Friday evening to stay the weekend with their father. 'He would always ask me in for coffee – he would never leave me outside,' remembered Griffin. 'He was very considerate.'

Both would go to sports days at Bedales, in Margaret's case and to Tony's disapproval accompanied by Nanny Sumner, who had triumphantly outlasted Tony (she remained at Kensington Palace until David was seventeen). Occasionally, at Bedales, when Princess Margaret sent Griffin to fetch David, Nanny Sumner would insist on accompanying him, to the embarrassment of the fifteen-year-old David, who could not bear the thought of his friends seeing him with a nanny.

Another teenage boy, only a fortnight younger than David, who came back into Tony's life was his half-brother, Peregrine Armstrong-Jones. There had been a long gap during Peregrine's early years, after their father Ronnie had died and left Plas Dinas away from Tony, the eldest son, to his widow Jenifer and her son Peregrine. But when Peregrine's stepfather died, Tony telephoned at once. After asking the sixteen-year-old Peregrine down for the weekend to Old House, he said to him: 'If you ever want to use Old House I'll give you the keys and you can use it if you feel you and your mother are getting on top of each other, or if you want to live in the studio here you can, or if you feel you can't cope, just call me.' It was practical sympathy and kindness of the most welcome sort.

Margaret's love affair with Roddy Llewellyn was still going strong. Now that it was public knowledge, she did not seem to mind it being obvious. At dinner parties, Roddy would sit opposite her in the role of host ('rather unnerving', reported Roy Strong). At the beginning of September she and Roddy stayed at Glen with the Tennants; on 23 September Margaret, in a pink and gold evening dress, went with Roddy and another couple to an Alec Guinness play.

Roy Strong, in his diary entry of 28 November, gives a vivid picture of an evening at Kensington Palace (and also illustrates Anne Rosse's success in keeping in with the Princess while milking the situation for all it was worth):

The drawing room at Kensington Palace presented its usual scene. HRH in plumny red with a gold belt, smoking and drinking whisky, in good form surrounded by a motley crowd, some of whose identity we never established but included the Harlechs, the Rosses, the Tennants, a young Bacon boy, a Ramsay and Roddy [Llewellyn]. We'd never met him before. He was like Tony round again, thirty-ish, rather dapper, but very polite and assigned to a kind of 'host' role, getting drinks and ferrying them to people. HRH showed no overt interest in him, although he would spring up and actively join in anything that she wanted.

Anne Rosse, in her usual low-cut dress with a slit hemline and manacled in diamond stars, was very unhappy. It did seem rather tactless to ask Anne and Michael with Roddy there. She was in fact shocked and confided her embarrassment at being present at a party where her own son was replaced before her eyes by Roddy. ... I asked the million dollar question, 'Does Roddy stay here?' 'Yes,' was the reply. He's agreeable, not nearly as bright as Tony, rather silly and giggly but kind and she hasn't had much of that.

Others saw it differently. Strong's wife Julia, to whom Roddy had had a long chat the same evening, believed his motives were selfish 'and he should get as much out of it as possible'.

This may have been because Roddy was about to attempt another line of work. For in spite of his now well-known association with the Princess, his new career as a landscape gardener did not at first go well, and he decided it was time for another change of direction. This time, he would fling himself into the music business. He had a pleasant voice, he had plenty of connections, both social and – through his brother Dai – business. Claude Wolff, the husband of the singer Petula Clark, signed him up and he was launched with a duet sung with Petula ('Pet' as she was known) on French television. There was plenty of publicity in newspapers and television but singing, too, proved a dead end. One of the final blows was his almost immediate collapse on arrival in Mustique in March 1978 with a gastro-intestinal haemorrhage. He was flown for emergency treatment to Barbados, followed there two days later by a distraught Margaret.

Within days, pictures of the lovers began to appear in British papers, the signal for another outburst against the Princess. By now the image of a hedonistic Margaret enjoying herself with her toyboy lover was firmly fixed in the public mind. Within the royal family, matters were complicated by the fact that the Queen, for whom dignity and reticence were a given, although she wished for her sister's happiness neither liked Roddy nor approved of her sister's liaison with him. Lord Charteris* is on record as saying, 'she thought the Princess was behaving badly' and that she once referred to her sister's 'guttersnipe life'. As one for whom duty was everything, she must have felt further dismay at the articles about her sister on the theme of 'What does she do for the money we pay her?' that were now appearing with depressing regularity.

For Margaret, this was particularly unfortunate timing, as the Barbados episode coincided with another Parliamentary Review of the payments made to members of the royal family on the Civil List. It had been proposed that the annual payment to Princess Margaret be raised to £59,000 (from £55,000), a motion that to Willie Hamilton – and several other MPs – seemed a direct challenge.

Hamilton, in the most virulent attack he had yet made, suggested that, as the Elizabeth Garrett Anderson Hospital for Women in Euston Road was facing closure because repairs would cost up to £30,000, the money be taken from Margaret's allowance. 'If she thumbs her nose at taxpayers by flying off to Mustique to see this pop-singer chap, she shouldn't expect the workers of this country to pay for it.' Denis Canavan, the Labour MP for Falkirk West, called her 'a royal parasite'. Gallantly Roddy sprang to her defence ('I would like to see Willie Hamilton or any of the others do all her jobs in the marvellous way she does'), only to have Hamilton point out that the Princess had fulfilled a mere eight engagements in the previous three months – during which time she had drawn £14,000. After this, Roddy was advised to lie low for a bit. Soon, he slipped out of the country to visit Tangier. It was a move both wise and discreet, given what was to follow.

On 10 May 1978, a statement was issued from Kensington Palace: 'Her Royal Highness The Princess Margaret, Countess of Snowdon, and the Earl of Snowdon, after two years of separation, have agreed that their marriage should formally be ended. Accordingly Her Royal Highness will start the necessary legal proceedings.'

---

* The Queen's Private Secretary until the previous year.

The day after the announcement, the Princess left the King Edward VII Hospital, in which she had been for eight days, suffering from gastro-intestinal trouble. Tony, on the other side of the Atlantic in Brazil, had completed an assignment to photograph the train robber Ronnie Biggs at home and was busy with photographs to illustrate an article on the plight of the indigenous Brazilian Indians.

Public sympathy was with Tony. 'Seeing your sad face on television I write to express the sadness I feel about the situation you and your family find yourselves in,' began one letter. 'You came to my traffic-control box in T2, LHR, on the 13 April on arriving from France because you were upset about an announcement in Paris about your delayed flight, remember? I will *never* forget your manner of approach – your warm handshake and your charming self. Never have I met such a gentleman quite like you.' The writer ended with a PS: 'I've never heard a bad word against you. Everyone is saying "It's a damn shame." What more can I say?'

Past thoughtfulness was remembered. Lord George-Brown, better known as George Brown, the former Foreign Secretary, wrote a note: 'I do not wish to poke my nose in where it is none of my business but you were once very kind to me when I felt rather miserably depressed by the media, so now I would like you to know both Sophie and I are thinking of *you* during recent events.'

The divorce petition that followed, on 24 May 1978, was no. 3628b, last in a twelve-page list of couples seeking 'quickie' postal divorces. These could be applied for with the consent of both parties on the grounds that the marriage had 'irretrievably broken down'. The Snowdons' petition did not mention adultery but merely cited 'irreconcilable differences'. As well as simplicity, it had the merit of economy: it cost merely a £16 court fee plus postage, and a £1 swearing fee to a Commissioner of Oaths.

The day afterwards Princess Margaret, who had been given custody of the children, was taken to hospital with hepatitis, where she had to forfeit her favourite drink of two parts water, one part Famous Grouse whisky and ice, in favour of barley water. Or as Roy Strong put it in his diary entry for 31 May, 'Poor Princess Margaret was carted off to hospital with hepatitis. And now the divorce with Snowdon is announced. How little people will understand the agonies she has gone through as a practising Anglican to let the divorce happen. How silly but understandable to fall for Roddy and what an inevitable end. The loneliness of it all for her must be terrible.'

The royal divorce was heard in Court No. 44 of the London Divorce Court. The Princess was represented by her solicitor, Matthew Farrer, and Tony by John Humphries, the solicitor who looked after him all his life without a fee. Within minutes, the decree nisi was pronounced, to be followed six weeks later, on 11 July, by the decree absolute. When it was announced on the 1 p.m. news, with a comment by Tony, Princess Margaret was sitting in the back of her Rolls with Sarah; in front were her detective and chauffeur David Griffin. Griffin switched the car radio off at once, to be told by the Princess: 'There's no need to be diplomatic – we're all grown-up people here.' 'I'm sorry, Your Royal Highness,' said Griffin, 'but I didn't think you'd want Lady Sarah to hear this.' 'Yes, let's hear what he's got to say,' said Margaret. Soon, to the embarrassment of both chauffeur and detective, they were laughing and talking about it.

The feelings of other members of the royal family towards Tony were little changed – in particular those of the Queen Mother, to whom he had always been particularly close. Soon after the divorce, Princess Margaret had said to her: 'Mummy, who shall we have for Christmas?' 'Oh,' replied the Queen Mother, 'it would be so lovely if Tony came.' To which Princess Margaret replied, in understandably forceful tones: 'Don't you understand – I'm divorced now. How could you suggest we have him for Christmas?'

Tony's feelings were ambivalent. Like everyone who marries for love, he had hoped and believed his marriage would endure. Towards the end, both had found it intolerable. Never given to introspection, questioning or self-doubt, he had asked himself little about the reasons why; and soon his gift for airbrushing unpleasant episodes or emotions from the past came into play.

In that moment of the final sundering of his own marriage, one of the sentences in a letter received four days earlier showed what might have been. Always remarkably thoughtful himself at sending off letters even in the midst of demanding work – he had been photographing Jack Nicholson, Elaine Stritch and Noël Coward among others – he had written to Lord Hailsham expressing his sympathy over the death of his beloved wife Mary. Lord Hailsham, who had known his father Ronnie well, sent a touching reply. After saying how much Tony's letter had helped him, he continued: 'I never knew until the blow fell how much I loved Mary, and even amid all the tears and tribulations of the last week I have never ceased to wonder at my good fortune at having had thirty-four years of her serene, humorous and loyal companionship.' It was a sentence that must have cut to the quick.

Tony was soon to suffer a bitter blow of his own. On 13 July 1978 Oliver Messel, whose health had been deteriorating for some time, died at Maddox, his house in Barbados. He had designed it himself, and there he had spent the last twelve years of his life. Although in the Caribbean he had reinvented himself as an architect, designing and decorating houses for private clients and for Colin Tennant on Mustique, he had become beset with financial problems so severe that he died in debt. His affairs had become chaotic since Vagn, his lifelong lover and business manager, had died two years earlier.

Oliver's ashes were brought back to England and buried in the magnolia garden at Nymans, the house where he was brought up, and a memorial service held for him on 9 November at St Martin-in-the-Fields. It was attended not only by Anne Rosse – drawn-looking in black fur hat and veils – but also by Margaret, accompanied by Anne Tennant. Tony and Thomas Messel (the son of Oliver and Anne's brother Linley), his two nephews and joint heirs, read the lessons. Afterwards Tony told James Lees-Milne that he had been terrified at the thought of reading it; when Lees-Milne reported this later to Anne Rosse, she said crossly that 'it was high time he snapped out of this rot and made a speech somewhere'.

Both Tony and Thomas were in agreement that Maddox should be sold and the sale was quietly organised through Nick Paravicini, the leading Barbadian estate agent. One of Paravicini's friends, Anthony Johnson, who often visited Barbados, had already made known his interest in finding a handsome property. Maddox, theatrical and beautiful, with its own beach and one and a quarter acres of land, appeared to be the answer.

After some hard negotiating, Johnson secured it for $400,000 (then about £250,000). As Johnson was not a resident in Barbados, he would have been subject to a non-resident's purchase tax on the house, so the plan was that he should first buy the contents, which allowed him to move in and, after several months, complete the contract as a resident. This was agreed by Thomas Messel and Tony, and Johnson duly bought the contents, from Oliver's gilt mirrors, antique furniture, pineapple table and the seventeenth-century Sicilian gold and coral devotional carving above it, to the dining chairs that were replicas of a Chinese Chippendale chair once owned by the actor David Garrick, with the (agreed) exception of around half a dozen pieces withheld by Tony. 'When you're settled in,' he said to Johnson, 'can I come and stay and we'll make arrangements for shipping them back.'

Most of Oliver's other possessions, including his drawings and stage designs, were left to Tony, whom he had regarded almost as a son. Other items were sold piecemeal but not all of the family were aware of this. The present Lord Rosse managed to buy one of his pictures, of lilies, that had been painted at Birr, when he heard that it was being sold; its restoration added another £5,000 to the bill.

Princess Margaret, who had been on a royal tour of islands in the South Pacific and then Japan, followed by a private visit to Los Angeles and thence to Mustique, returned to Britain in November to be greeted by the news that Tony was marrying Lucy Lindsay-Hogg. Their wedding at Kensington Register Office, then in Marloes Road, took place on 15 December 1978, just over five months after his divorce from the Princess. It was a simple ceremony: Lucy, dressed in a blue and white coat and skirt and blue printed blouse, arrived from her flat at 15 Kensington Square in a small brown Volvo; Tony turned up in his 1972 blue estate car. Instead of the Buckingham Palace balcony and the cheering crowds of thousands, the newly-weds jumped into Tony's car and drove back to Launceston Place.

That morning Ann Hills opened her paper to read that her famous lover was going to marry someone else. Devastated, she realised she would have to accept the situation or give Tony up – and that, she knew, she could not do.

15

Remarriage

⊰│⊱

Margaret, like Tony, relished her new-found freedom (although even after her divorce she continued to wear her engagement ring). One of the busiest people on her staff was her chauffeur, David Griffin. His day began around 8 a.m., when he would arrive at Kensington Palace, have a cup of coffee and piece of toast with the chef, then go to the garage to see that all the cars were clean, their engines checked and the tanks full of petrol, a job that would take until around 10 a.m. He would then visit the office and collect any letters that needed delivery from the Princess's private secretary or lady-in-waiting or sometimes the Princess herself – all letters of any importance were hand-delivered. 'I want you to put this in the hand of Michael Caine – or Zandra Rhodes or my doctor,' the Princess would say as she handed over the envelope with her distinctive looped handwriting on it.

Occasionally a letter would be sent to Tony – remembered by Griffin as 'very pleasant and nice, with impeccable manners' – who would sometimes ask the chauffeur to wait while he scribbled a reply. If this was impossible, and Tony rang the Kensington Palace office to ask if Griffin could return and collect his reply, Margaret would always refuse. 'No, he's got other things to do.'

The 'other things' were usually to do with enjoyment. Shortly after eleven the Princess would appear, ready to be taken by Griffin to her hairdressers, by now David and Joseph in South Audley Street, and when she emerged at around 1 p.m. perhaps to lunch at the Ritz. Lunch would last for two or three hours and then it was back to Kensington Palace for a rest. About 4.30 Griffin would take her to Buckingham Palace to swim in the pool there, then back to the hairdressers for a comb-out before drinks at Kensington Palace, followed by the theatre or ballet with friends, after which came dinner, often at the Savoy, with an evening that ended around 2 a.m.*

Unless Margaret was staying with friends, weekends were spent at Royal Lodge, regardless of whether or not the Queen Mother might be entertaining a house party. Margaret's relationship with her mother, never easy, sometimes verged on the disruptive – showing that she was bored or staying in bed all morning was commonplace. Only occasionally did the Queen Mother allow herself to be ruffled out of her usual serenity by this baiting. Once, after Margaret's only visit to stay with her in her beloved Castle of Mey,† Margaret commented: 'I can't understand why you want to go and live in a dump like that.' 'Well, darling,' responded the Queen Mother sweetly, 'you needn't come next time.'

Margaret's evening entertaining at Kensington Palace almost always included Roddy. The Princess's affair with him was still going strong, although it was frowned on by her family. This was made plain during the organisation of her fiftieth birthday party, celebrated on 4 November 1980 at the Ritz in London (her actual birthday, on 21 August, took place as usual at Balmoral). Margaret naturally wanted Roddy there, among the forty guests invited to the dinner itself, but the Queen refused to allow it as she felt that if she attended a party at which Roddy was present it would appear that she was countenancing their relationship. Once more the loyal Tennants came to the rescue: instead of attending the dinner for Margaret they took Roddy off elsewhere. A number of guests had been asked to join the party after 10.30, when dinner was over and, as a compromise, Roddy was allowed to come with these.

---

* Griffin's usefulness was the indirect cause of the end of Nanny Sumner's long reign. When David reached the age of seventeen, Griffin was asked to teach him to drive, upon which Nanny Sumner kicked up such a fuss that even Princess Margaret realised it was finally time for her to leave. The driving lessons, of course, continued.

† The most northerly castle on the British mainland, the Castle of Mey, looking out to sea over the Pentland Firth, was in a state of disrepair when bought by the Queen Mother in 1952 after the death of her husband. She would stay there in August and October.

*

Work on Launceston Place, where Tony and Lucy were now well established and expecting their first (and as it turned out, only) child, was well under way. All the decoration was done by Tony and his friend Carl Toms, with some of the furniture from Kensington Palace that had originally been brought there by Tony or given him by members of his family on his marriage to Princess Margaret. Lucy, who had sold her flat, bought other pieces. Believing that her husband was badly off, she also often paid restaurant and other bills.

There was no problem over the arrival of what had been in Kensington Palace. When the Princess first decided that it was time Tony took away his things, she informed him through her private secretary, but by the time it came to clearing out his possessions wholesale from Kensington Palace the first wave of fury and resentment on the Princess's part had disappeared. As she had come to accept the situation and the marriage to Lucy, the removal of his possessions was managed amicably, with certain pieces of Tony's furniture – such as the piano and a gold and white clock in the drawing room, a John Piper painting in the dining room and a Perspex chandelier by Buckminster Fuller on the stairs – left there because Tony felt that to remove them would leave too much of a gap. Some objects of value, such as Tony's collection of cufflinks, remained in her safe, which was not cleared until her death.

Unlike Tony, whose feelings towards Roddy Llewellyn did not mellow, Princess Margaret's attitude towards her successor was civilised in the extreme. Spotting Lucy across the room at a wedding reception at St James's Palace, she told the friend she was talking to that she had never met her but would like to. Lucy was brought over with the words: 'Princess Margaret would like to have a word with you.' Lucy curtsied; and the pair spent several minutes in easy chat.

Life with Lucy was quite different in every way from Tony's previous existence as royal consort. His working life was less affected by the change. Although he had always been insistently democratic in the studio, he was now so much more famous than many of his clients that they often treated him as if he really were royal, letting him do exactly what he wanted in terms of photography, terrified to argue with him. At home there would be suppers with old friends, often in the kitchen, with its eau-de-Nil painted dresser and cupboards, large and beautiful chandelier hanging over the table and porcelain sink – Tony, who eschewed most modern technology, would not hear of a dishwasher.

To Tony Lucy's presence was deeply reassuring. She knew of his unhappy childhood, of his rejection by his mother and, of course, of his unhappiness as his marriage to Margaret began to disintegrate; she knew that he would, as she put it, 'push people to the brink' and she thought that perhaps it was because he so feared rejection that he would do this, to see if it happened. She loved him, and she had always vowed that he would know she loved him because she would always stay with him through thick and thin – *she* would not be pushed 'over the edge'. She would never let him down in any way, she would always be there.

Tony's 'new beginning' with Lucy continued to bring him closer to other members of his family. His kindness to Peregrine continued. When Peregrine needed help over proposed changes to Plas Dinas, he took the architectural plans round to Tony, who could easily have refused to have anything to do with what he might have seen as his lost inheritance. Instead, he jotted down some well-thought-out ideas for changes that would help Peregrine develop it in the way he wanted.

He also advised the boy on, or rather against, the career he thought he wanted. Peregrine, at the Royal Agricultural College near Cirencester, aspired to be an interior decorator. When Tony told him he was unsuited to this, Peregrine questioned why. Tony's response was to ask: 'Who are your top ten favourite interior decorators in this country?' Peregrine could not name a single one.* Gently Tony said: 'If you don't even know who they are – how can you be one?'

It was at this time, too, that he began to establish a truly close relationship with his cousin Thomas Messel – again, helped largely by Lucy, warm and welcoming to all her husband's relations and

---

* Peregrine Armstrong-Jones later struck out with great success as a party planner, organising and arranging events as diverse as a State Banquet for the Queen, Princess Anne's fortieth birthday party at her home Gatcombe Park and the wedding of David and Victoria Beckham.

friends. Thomas and Lucy first met at Old House, where Lucy put in central heating (many visitors had complained of how cold it was before), filled it with chintz and made a kitchen. She would drive down on a Friday afternoon with her car full of food, unpack and prepare the house for Tony and whatever friends he wanted to bring down, then do all the packing-up on a Sunday. A little later there was another Lucy addition, a swimming pool in the old walled garden. Tony, meanwhile, would be blissfully working at whichever of the Old House projects – the lake, a new pavilion – was demanding his attention.

He threw the same work and vision into creating exactly the home he wanted at 22 Launceston Place. What he did is worth recounting as it shows the tireless enthusiasm, energy and ingenuity with which he approached all projects close to his heart.

When the house was bought, its garage was separate, reached by a concrete slope downwards – like many London houses, the bottom floor was a semi-basement in front but at garden level at the back. The garden could be reached by a path on either side of the garage. The space between the garage and the house was now roofed over, floored and made into a room that doubled as utility room and sitters' changing room – beneath a wide flat counter were washing-machine and tumble-dryer, with the wall above the counter mirrored. Access to this was through the original tradesmen's entrance, a side door now fitted with a loud, clanging bell impossible not to hear (as opposed to the more discreet one at the front door entrance).

On the right of the 'tradesmen's entrance' was an office where his secretary could work; next to it, a darkroom, its walls fitted with shelves and cupboards for storage. The ground floor (first floor seen from the back) held a spacious hall, double drawing room and dining room and kitchen, with the Snowdons' bedroom and bathroom on the first floor. The top floor, with its large nursery, bedroom and bathroom, was devoted to their baby daughter Frances, born on 17 July 1979. Tony also added a balcony and a small domed 'pepperpot' containing a single room that could be used as a study.

Much care was devoted to building a studio, the room on which his work depended. This, in the basement at the rear of the house, was floored with reject quarry tiles from Wales, with French windows opening into the garden. It was not as high as he had wished: because of building regulations, the final dimensions were ten foot wide by fourteen foot long but only seven foot high although, as Tony said, there was something to be said for the studio being smallish. 'Sitters are not too intimidated.'

It was roofed with ordinary greenhouse glass to allow plenty of natural daylight. Under this were pinned two layers of frosted plastic to diffuse the light, and every surface that was not glass was painted black ('I find it easier to add light than to subtract it,' he said). The room's adjustable shelving, the shelves fitted onto a threaded rod so that one half-turn of the supporting nut raised or lowered them, came from Kensington Palace: it was what he had made for his workroom there.

The bedroom, painted a deep soft blue, of Tony and his new Countess held the four-poster bed that had belonged to his Messel grandmother (it had been in the spare room at Kensington Palace), hung with white draperies and covered by a white bedspread with a pale blue motif. The wall to a second bedroom next door had been knocked through to provide a large and luxurious bathroom. Here the louvred cupboards made by Tony at Kensington Palace were installed along the whole of one wall.

There was more furniture from Nymans in the rest of the house: his grandmother's huge gilded mirror on the wall of the staircase and an elegant eighteenth-century bed with a pale blue wall canopy in the spare room. The ugly wooden banisters were replaced – luckily some elegant iron ones were found in the garage, and the unattractive stain stripped from their wooden handrail. The drawing room with its magenta and gold carpet was given large comfortable sofas in burgundy and gold; the other half of the room, through double doors, became the dining room. Here ten chairs with vivid flower prints stood around the round table, framed by the white-shuttered window hung with dark red velvet curtains.

With most of the house finished, the 'extras' began. The back of the house, a plain white slab of wall, was, thought Tony, 'very bleak'. It needed a porch, he decided. This was made of soft wood, with a zinc roof and supported by some tracery ironwork originally from Ascot racecourse that Tony remembered had been lying in a field at Royal Lodge for the past fifteen years.

The safety of his children when they visited him at Launceston Place was paramount to Tony. He had a panic button connected direct to Kensington police station; the Deputy Assistant Commissioner in charge of Protection in the borough wrote to him with other recommendations, too – even then, kidnapping or some kind of harm was considered a possible threat. To modern eyes most of the precautions appear fairly normal compared with the high-tech security that would probably be in place today: a spyhole and chain on the side basement door and a lockable grille fitted inside one of the rear windows were two suggestions. The Commissioner also thought that a door with a lock should be installed so that the basement offices could if necessary be sealed off from the rest of the house 'and so physically exclude further intrusion by callers'; as well as one room designated as a 'safe retreat' for the children within the house.

His two older children visited often. Lucy was kind and loving to them and a warm relationship between the three of them quickly built up. Sarah in particular was to become extremely close to her stepmother.

Perhaps because of the warmth engendered by this happy family life, Tony's involvement with those less fortunate deepened and he continued to raise his voice in support of people afflicted by a disability. On 16 February 1977 he spoke in the House of Lords, putting his finger on the problem when he said that 'a long process of imaginative education was needed before there would be real integration'; and criticising the Department of Health for continuing to refuse to replace unacceptable invalid tricycles with safe vehicles that would ensure that disabled people could at least get to work on equal terms with everyone else.

On 1 July 1979, Michael Rosse died. For Tony it was almost as sad as for Michael's own sons; as Tony said, 'He always treated me like a beloved son.' To keep his property in the family it was naturally left to his own sons; his affection for Tony was shown in his bequest of £1,000.

Anne Rosse was devastated ('I suppose no woman ever loved her husband more,' wrote James Lees-Milne); ' . . . now I must put on another suit of armour, without that total understanding that Michael gave me,' she wrote to Tony. 'You yourself will become something I can lean on against the evil winds that have suddenly blown up.' It was only a momentary softening. Shorn of Michael's temperate, restraining influence, certain aspects of her behaviour gradually deteriorated. She began to drink more and became yet more intolerant of her son after his divorce from the Princess – when Lees-Milne lunched with her on 19 July 1979, he noted in his diary that she 'quite clearly does not like Tony and says she always lamented that he was made an earl "for stud purposes". Earlier she said he was the least chivalrous of her sons.'

It was a problem that got worse with time. Anne Rosse's relentless drive towards social success had hit the equivalent of an invisible buffer when her son's marriage to Princess Margaret had crumbled. Lucy, kind and gentle, did everything she could to make friends with her new husband's mother, running endless errands for her. But to Anne this seemed to count for little, and she largely ignored Lucy. Although she managed to remain on good terms with the Princess, she could not pretend to be on the same level of intimacy as when Margaret was her daughter-in-law. Gone were the days when she could say: 'I'm just dropping into Kensington Palace for tea.' The blame for this, naturally, was laid at Tony's door. However lovingly her letters to him were addressed ('My darling boy') and however flowery the sentiments that flowed across the page in her spidery handwriting, an underlying resentment was building up.

When Lucy's great friend, the noted writer Anita Leslie, wanted to write Anne's biography Anne was at first pleased but then said: 'Of course, you're not to mention my marriage to Ronnie – that's not to come into the book at all!' As 'blanking' this marriage would mean denying Tony's existence – perhaps his mother's idea – Anita Leslie dropped the whole idea.

When James Lees-Milne stayed with the Garnetts at their house, Bradley Court, the following summer, he found Tony there too. 'He greeted me with warm hugs. Very sweet and charming as usual. How small he is, almost a dwarf, but large hands I noticed, which suggest potency,' he wrote in his diary for 25 June 1980. 'After dinner he sat at my feet by the sofa and talked about Anne and the family. Complains that she doesn't "play straight" and is alienating the children who are ready to be as kind to her as they can. She has already driven off young Tom Messel who was her slave. She refuses to meet or speak to Tony's new wife Lucy. He invites his mother to luncheon, asks others to meet her, cooks delicious meal (has no servant) and Anne chucks at last moment on spurious grounds that she does not feel well, though he later finds she entertained sixty to drinks that evening . . . .'

That summer Anne Rosse sold the Linley Sambourne house in Stafford Terrace,* where she had been living, to the Greater London Council for £250,000, and moved to Nymans ('the potting shed' as she used to call it). Leaving 18 Stafford Terrace was hard for her. She had grown up with its dark rooms and diamond-paned windows, heavy chintz curtains and late-Victorian furniture and although her own taste was ebullient and theatrical her sense of family piety meant that she lovingly cherished this shrine to the grandfather from whom she and Oliver had inherited so much artistic talent.

At Nymans, she furnished the rooms in which she lived mainly with oak furniture of the period, but brought down some other pieces from her different homes – a pair of 1735 walnut and gilt pier mirrors from Womersley, a George III mahogany and satinwood bookcase, a William and Mary walnut and marquetry chest. Among these pieces and the Old Masters on the walls were a pair of white plaster swans by her brother Oliver from his legendary production *Helen!*† and some of his signature masks.

Living here, she found an outlet for her great talent as a gardener. At Nymans she directed the maintenance of the exquisite gardens with the aid of six gardeners (paid for by the National Trust,

---

* In 1874 Edward Linley Sambourne married Marion Herapath, the daughter of a wealthy stockbroker. Helped by Marion's father, the couple paid £2,000 for an 89-year lease on 18 Stafford Terrace, built in the 1870s in classical Italianate style. Through Maud Messel and then her daughter Anne Rosse, the house, with original furnishings, has been preserved as a unique example of a late Victorian townhouse.

† The all-white sets of *Helen!* for C.B. Cochran, in 1932, launched the vogue for the white-on-white décor popular in the thirties.

which had owned the gardens since 1954). She was highly know-ledgeable, conversant with the name of every plant and gifted with great natural taste, romantically making the most of the ruined house with flowers pouring out of the empty windows. There were plenty of visitors, mostly luncheon guests greeted with Lord Rosse's special Bacardi cocktail – a lethal brew of two parts Bacardi, one of Dubonnet, one of orange, with added sugar.

Tony, in London, was completing the makeover of his Launceston Place house. By June 1980 he was casting replacement cornices for the ceilings, bookshelves had been built in the drawing room and it was time to think of the garden. Two of the men working on the house, Bob and Ernie, made a pond and Tony designed the fountain set in the wall. It was based on the one Oliver Messel had at his Barbadian house Maddox – Oliver had taught the local craftsmen to make not only furniture and metal-work but also a fake terracotta out of the local coral stone. The fountain's mouldings were cut in Bath and brought up by Ernie. Tony created the 'antique' head from whose mouth gushes water by buying a modern head in the King's Road for £13, drilling out the eyes and ageing it with Bath-stone dust. The effect was impressively ancient. Nerving himself, Tony asked the great garden designer Lanning Roper to help with the planting. 'I felt it was like asking Capability Brown to design a window box,' he recalled. But Roper agreed.

One of the final touches was a fanlight over the front door – again, not what it seemed at first sight. Having unblocked the half-moon area above the door, Tony dipped plastic strips into boiling water so that they became bendable, shaped them into the desired pattern, painted them to resemble lead and glazed them.

His mother's drinking was not the only distress Tony suffered that summer. On 24 July 1980 Peter Sellers died of a heart attack. Sellers had been married to his third wife, Lynne Frederick, who inherited his £4.5 million estate, for the past three years and Tony had naturally got to know her well, so that despite his horror of speaking in public he agreed to read the 23rd Psalm at Sellers's memorial service at St Martin-in-the-Fields (on 8 September, the date that would have been Sellers's fifty-fifth birthday). He also spoke about his friend. 'My thanks come with much love and gratitude,' Lynne wrote to him afterwards.

Tony was as busy as ever. In 1980 alone, among those he photographed were the Duchess of Kent at her most dazzling, the actress Catherine Oxenberg, Ninette de Valois, the founder and inspiration of the Royal Ballet, Simon Callow, Lady Romsey and several of the Mitford sisters. He was a guest (on 9 July) on 'Desert Island Discs', the long-running radio show in which the well-known are asked to choose their favourite music, a book and a luxury, and give a rundown of their life.

Tone-deaf and completely unmusical, Tony rang his former wife for help – 'the name of that song I like – you know ....' With her assistance, he selected 'The Green Cockatoo', 'London Pride', 'Night and Day', 'The Boys in the Back Room', sung by his old friend Marlene Dietrich, the waltz from Act One of *Swan Lake* – the ballet he and Margaret had first seen together – Beethoven's Ninth and 'Land of Our Fathers', from the music played at the Investiture. The musical Margaret's indignant comment to a friend was: 'They should be asking *me* to come on it.' Sure enough, six months later, Margaret was the Desert castaway; her choices included 'Guide Me O Thou Great Redeemer' and the Band of the Highland Light Infantry playing 'Scotland the Brave'. Unsurprisingly, her luxury item was a piano.

The Princess's romantic life was to suffer a further blow. At a birthday party in 1980, given for him by the nightclub owner Peter Stringfellow, Roddy again met Tania Soskin, the daughter of a Russian film producer whom he had first seen when she visited Surrendell in his early Margaret days, and of whom he later said: 'I was very struck by her. You always know, don't you. I didn't actually have to talk to her. I knew she was the one.'

This time, he fell in love with her and soon realised that his relationship with Margaret would have to change. Again, there were signs of his growing lack of interest and disengagement. When Margaret had visited the Klondike in northern Canada the previous year, she had worn a frothy pink dress that showed her curvy figure to advantage at a party featuring the early days of the

Gold Rush. When she put it on to show Roddy one evening, instead of the rapturous compliments of former days all she got was: 'You look like a strawberry ice cream.' He had also become more casual about their meetings, often turning up late for dinner. Finally, in February 1981, during their now regular visit to Mustique together, Margaret tackled Roddy about his altered behaviour towards her. The reason, he confessed to her, was that he was in love with Tania and wanted to marry her.

Margaret's behaviour was both exemplary and intelligent. Determined not to lose the affection of someone to whom she had been so close, she turned herself from lover into an older-sister figure, welcoming Tania as a new friend and, when they announced their engagement on 4 April 1981, giving a luncheon party for them. The result was an ongoing friendship: the Princess often went to stay with the Llewellyns and became godmother to their first child. (Many years later, Roddy described the affectionate relationship that ensued. 'She was an extremely easy guest. She helped with the washing-up – you couldn't stop her. Our daughters adored her. She liked quiet weekends with us, just seeing a few friends. She was the greatest company. She'd whizz effortlessly through the *Times* crossword puzzle and could contribute to a conversation on any subject, which was extraordinary considering she'd had so little formal education.')

On Barbados, it had taken Anthony Johnson about eighteen months to make Oliver Messel's house suitable for him and his wife; one of his discoveries while redecorating was that the mirror on one bedroom wall was two-way. Finally, on 1 October 1980, they moved in, arriving in Barbados on a banana boat with two huge containers of furniture and a car. On 25 October Tony and his daughter Sarah arrived to stay.

Thanks to prior notification by Tony's secretary to the High Commission in Barbados, their arrival was treated as if he was still a royal consort, with no question of formalities such as Passport Control. For Tony it was an emotional visit. 'It's so heart-rending for me to be here without my darling Oliver,' he would tell Johnson, as he looked round the house he knew so well. The staff were greeted – and bade farewell when he and Sarah left a week later – with kisses and a liberal spatter of 'darlings'.

Sometimes he would take Sarah to see someone on the island whom he and Princess Margaret had once visited, invariably – and typically – walking straight into the house even if they were not there. Equally typically, the six items he had wanted to keep turned out to be considerably more, but Johnson, thrilled with the house, was not prepared to quibble and amicable arrangements were made to ship them back in due course. Neither of them could guess how tricky this would prove.

In 1981 Ann Hills divorced her husband. Consequently freer, she had hoped to see Tony more. She had been miserable when she read of his marriage to Lucy; although she had known he was pursuing Lucy, what she – married herself and promiscuous – thought of as just another affair on Tony's side had not worried her. What she had not realised was how much he would come to mean to her. 'I cannot break off this relationship. It is absolutely vital to my being – to my life,' she said to one of her few platonic male friends, to whom she had often poured out details of her many brief liaisons.

She also had to face a dilemma central to her whole being: she detested anything false or dishonest – yet here she was proposing to continue her affair with a man who had recently married someone else by whom he had fathered a child. Somehow she justified this by telling herself that she was there first, so that when her father remonstrated with her, saying 'He's got a wife and child, you know,' she would reply: 'Well, he can break it off but I'm not going to.'

Once, Tony gave her a piece of jewellery, an ornate German-made Victorian gold and diamond brooch that had belonged to his mother. When she left it temporarily with her father for safe-keeping, he was told by a jeweller friend that it was worth several thousand pounds. To Ann it became her greatest treasure: the equivalent of an eternity ring, a token of commitment and, as a possession of his mother, an endorsement of their relationship. She always wore it for her meetings with Tony but never at other times – again, for fear it might give rise to speculation.

Their affair had taken on a regular pattern. Mostly their meetings were at her flat; sometimes, after them, Tony would turn up at the offices of his agent Peter Lyster Todd, handily nearby in Marylebone Street, who, not knowing of Ann's existence, was often surprised to see him arrive so unexpectedly. Sometimes Tony took her down to Old House and, occasionally, back to Launceston Place. Having alerted her, he would park his car round the corner, she would casually wander round and, when no one was looking, slip into the car. For Ann, one of the strangest aspects of the whole affair was that, as she put it, 'nobody ever cottoned on'.

Their meetings were not nearly as frequent as she wished. Sometimes there would be a month between trysts and she wanted many more. 'She told me that if she had been able to see him at least once, possibly twice a week she would have been delirious,' said one friend, 'and if she did not see "the man I really want in my life" she would be on edge. What she really wished was that he would come and live with her.' She was also unhappy that they could not be together openly. Once, after he had been to America for a fortnight, she said sadly to a friend: 'He's just driven past me – and I couldn't even wave.'

Nor, despite the secrecy of their liaison, did she feel she was compromising the honesty that was central to her. She had told her husband and when, occasionally, she visited Launceston Place openly, it was on the pretext of helping Tony with one of the speeches he was increasingly called upon to make on the welfare of disabled people, an excuse that was all the more convincing because it happened to be true. As such, her fleeting presence was accepted without either suspicion or qualm by Lucy, who in any case seldom came down to Tony's basement studio and office during his working day and who knew how much of his time was taken up with his work for disabled people.

One of the most important steps forward in this was achieved when the second edition of *Integrating the Disabled* was published in 1977. Much of the material showed how simple thoughtfulness rather than elaborate schemes could alleviate the handicaps of many. Those who were severely scarred, for example, often balked at communal changing rooms, relying instead on shops or mail order catalogues that offered a no-questions full refund policy. Why could these people not be given a special card by their doctors, asked the report, on production of which any shop would allow them to take clothes 'on approval' to try on in the privacy of their homes?

One young disabled woman, who had built up a career for herself as a telephone salesgirl and canvasser, pointed out that the housebound were not catered for at all with regard to employment but that many could do anything from telephone selling or market research to taking messages for tradesmen like plumbers or electricians who were out a lot (this was, of course, before the days of mobiles) and suggested that Social Services could help. One man on a respirator with a petrol-driven generator, in case of electricity cuts, complained that when the price of fuel went up, operating his respirator cost more. 'For me the cost of living literally means the cost of staying alive.' Other suggestions ranged from remote control appliances to a slot for a walking stick on a wheelchair for those who could walk a little after reaching their destination.

What rose off all the letters and reports like steam was the desperate desire of the handicapped to live at home and lead as normal a life as possible rather than be sent – as were many disabled sons or daughters – to a care home when their able-bodied parents died.

Suggestions for improvements to life ranged from putting electric sockets at waist level rather than on skirting boards, lavatory door locks that locked from the inside but could be opened from the outside in case of a fall, taps like levers that were easy for arthritic hands to grip and dining tables with swivel ends to pull over disabled laps. Worst of all, the motorised tricycles on which many depended to get about were withdrawn in favour of a £5 mobility allowance (except to men over sixty-five and women over sixty). 'Apparently you don't need to get about for companionship,' wrote one woman bitterly. 'You're far too old to want to get out and enjoy yourself at sixty and sixty-five. So just sit back and rot!'

Tony was determined to maintain his relationships with the royal family and they, for their part, were not about to lose someone for whom they not only felt affection but who was also their favourite photographer. In February 1981 he took Charles and Diana's engagement pictures. When the Duke and Duchess of Kent came to a 'kitchen supper' with Tony and Lucy at Launceston Place in September 1981 – an invitation accepted by the Duchess with the words that they would much rather relax round a kitchen table and enjoy themselves than make an effort at a more formal dinner party – the Kents asked Tony if he would consider taking some photographs of their daughter Lady Helen Windsor the following summer, when she would be eighteen.

There were other royal photographs, notably of Princess Anne (for the Save the Children Fund, of which she was President); in her affectionate letter of thanks she commented that it was a help 'to see what doesn't work in terms of hair, clothes, etc.' as well as what did. Above all his special relationship with the Queen Mother remained untouched. In many ways he felt closer to her than to his own mother; Queen Elizabeth's affection was unwavering rather than, as with Anne Rosse, fluctuating according to his social achievements. Although he admired his mother's skills – she had much of Oliver's flair for colour and design and was an expert needlewoman – he felt relaxed and easy with the Queen Mother. He amused her, she admired his work greatly, and she felt that her daughter, rather than Tony, must have been responsible for the final marriage break-up. His discretion, the fact that he did not seek to raise difficult issues, his obvious devotion to herself and, above all, his hands-on love for his children, the two grandchildren who spent most time at Royal Lodge, made him very much *persona grata* at Clarence House. When he invited her to perform 'an opening ceremony' on the small bridge he had recently completed at Old House, she accepted (on 20 October 1981), in terms of jokey affection that illustrate the continuing depth of their relationship:

> Dearest Tony, I was thrilled to receive an invitation to open (or perform the opening ceremony) of the recently completed Great Bridge at Old House and I would like to congratulate you most heartily on bringing this great project to a happy conclusion. I have read many articles in the press about the difficulties of the terrain, the depth of water, the strong current and, of course, the great

length of the many spans. It will be a great pleasure for me to take part on this momentous occasion and I suggest that we have a meeting with your agents at some further date to discuss ways and means and dates. But, bar chaff, it looks *so* pretty and very much at home with the various shrubs and weeping tree. With my love ever your affectionate ER.

Tony, too, would end his letters in a way that blended affection with the respectful formula due: 'with deepest admiration, respect and love'.

16

Campaigning

※

1981 was inaugurated as the International Year of Disabled Persons, for which Tony had been asked (in late 1980) to become President for England. It was something towards which he had been working for a long time – not consciously but in a series of steps that showed his increasing concern for anyone suffering some kind of physical handicap. He had always spoken out on their behalf, most notably in the Snowdon Working Party that he had chaired in 1975–6; now he had a greater role, and therefore a more recognisable platform, from which to conduct his campaigning on their behalf.

To launch it, he gave a number of passionately felt interviews. 'In the name of humanity, we demand a better, wider understanding at all levels of our society for the emotional and material needs of disabled people,' he told the *News of the World* on 23 November 1980. 'Anyone, in a split second, on the motorway, in the street or at home or at work, can find themselves in the minority of people who are physically handicapped.'

Government figures showed that in England there were 350,000 physically handicapped adults under sixty-five and 50,000 handicapped children living at home. In words that are as true today as they were then, he continued: 'I am not saying that people intentionally set out to do something to the detriment of a disabled person. An architect who is designing a public building doesn't say to himself: "I'll put in revolving doors so that a disabled person can't get in." He just never considers the difficulties the doors will cause.' In those days, although wheelchair users were permitted to cruise the Festival Hall alone, to go into the auditorium they had to be accompanied by what one of them bitterly referred to as their 'symbol of mobility' (who could if necessary be a deaf great-aunt of ninety-three with failing sight and a pronounced limp). Nor were the blind allowed in EMI cinemas unaccompanied.

Tony's greatest venom was reserved for British Rail. Railway carriages then had narrow doors with a handle on the outside, so that alighting passengers had to open the window, lean out and open the door. When the train was about to depart, the guard would walk along the platform, slamming any doors left open – hence the trains' nickname of 'slam-door' trains. These doors, of course, were not wide enough to admit a wheelchair. The only door on the train big enough to do this was that of the guard's van, which had an internal metal cage to secure goods or prevent any animals in the van that happened to break free, from escaping. Wheelchair users had to travel in this van, without a companion, surrounded by whatever else was there, from crates of fish to bicycles, homing pigeons or dogs. As there was no heating, it was icy cold in the winter. Nor, of course, was there a lavatory. This was absolutely unacceptable to Tony. The injustice of slam-door trains became an ongoing obsession for him and he mentioned it in virtually every speech he gave at the annual presentations of the Snowdon Award Scheme (slam-door trains were phased out so gradually that even in 2005 some were still running).

As well as his own illness while growing up there might, perhaps, have been an inherited reason for Tony's sympathy with the handicapped. His grandfather, Sir Robert Armstrong-Jones, had used all his influence and knowledge to alter the character of what were then called lunatic asylums (it was for his services to mental health that he was knighted). His attitude, highly unusual in his day, was that just as anyone who breaks an arm receives therapy in the form of a plaster cast, similarly anyone who is mentally ill also needs therapy.

Added to his usual work Tony now had the serious business of campaigning. With his presidency of the International Year of Disabled Persons about to begin, this seemed the moment to launch a plan he had been considering for some time. He had always wanted to help disabled youngsters with the money he had put aside from his royal photographs twenty years earlier; and in November 1980 he decided to set up a special fund for this purpose, helped by Andrew Farquhar, called the Snowdon Award Scheme. Its aim was to encourage the government of the day to take note of the needs of disabled students and the lack of financial support available to cover the disability-related costs – such as special travel arrangements for carers and interpreters – of taking up places in further education; and to help them where it could.

But £14,000 – the original £10,000 plus £4,000 interest that had accrued through the years – was not enough to set up a national charity, said Farquhar. Straightaway, Tony wrote to various of his wealthier friends and to organisations, asking them to contribute. A few weeks later, he returned to Farquhar with the words: 'Will £100,000 do?' It would indeed, said Farquhar; now all they had to do was to wait for sufficient of the money promised to arrive before the scheme could be officially launched as a charity.

When Tony spoke at the press launch for the Year of Disabled Persons in early January 1981 he said he desperately hoped the year would be more than that – rather, the first twelve months of a new era of understanding and action to start breaking down the social barriers of fear, prejudice and ignorance as well as exposing the many architectural and economic excuses that had existed for so long. 'It is very important that all decisions about disabled people should be [made] with them, not for them.'

He was determined, as in all the honorary posts he took on, to act as much more than a mere figurehead, and if he discovered unfairness or an inequity he would not hesitate to castigate. Finding out in December 1980 that wheelchair users were not allowed into the Chelsea Flower Show, although this featured a garden for wheelchair users designed by a husband for his disabled wife, the winning entry in a competition for 'wheelchair gardens', he sprang into action.

A tactful letter was sent from Buckingham Palace by the Prince of Wales's Private Secretary, Edward Adeane (the Prince was Patron of the Year of Disabled Persons) expressing the hope that the organisers, the Royal Horticultural Society, could 'stretch a point' this year, as it *was* the Year of Disabled Persons, and let disabled RHS members in on Monday (the least crowded, because royal, day). It only met with the response, on 5 January 1981, from the head of the RHS, Lord Aberconway (with whom Tony had duelled in 1976), that 'it is quite impractical, for many reasons, to let disabled people into the grounds on the Monday. I am sorry about this.'

The Sunday Times, which had organised the competition, asked Tony if he could use his influence to persuade the organisers of the Show to open it to wheelchair users for two hours after the royal party had gone round. Tony's support was immediate. He launched an attack on Lord Aberconway through the columns of *The Times*, well aware that other papers would pick up the story. 'Flowers but no hearts' was the *Daily Mirror*'s headline. At first Lord Aberconway refused to give way. He then modified his stance to say that if wheelchair users could be there by 8 a.m., they could see it before the crowds poured in. Tony's indignant response was that few wheelchair users could manage to be there by eight in the morning. He went on to make two appeals to allow a special time to be set aside for disabled people before the official opening, but with no success.

He then rallied parliamentary support through Alf Morris, former Minister for the Disabled and, as Chairman of the Year of the Disabled, in close contact with Tony. On 9 February, thirty-five MPs backed the motion 'That this House urges the Royal Horticultural Society to facilitate the visit of disabled people to the 1981 Chelsea Flower Show as a contribution to the International Year of the Disabled; and particularly requests that the disabled be admitted on the royal opening day.' The motion was passed overwhelmingly, and was followed by a letter from Hugh Rossi, the Minister for the Disabled, to Lord Aberconway.

Climbdown came on 17 February with a press release from the RHS issued to all newspapers, stating that twenty disabled RHS members, who would be chosen by ballot, would be allowed entry at 6 p.m. The release also contained the sentence: 'The Society wishes to make it clear that the disabled have always been and are welcome to the Chelsea Show when it is open.' It was not a clear-cut victory but it was a major step, as a letter of congratulation on 19 February from the Secretary of State for Social Services to Tony makes clear: 'Just a line to offer a word of congratulation ... I have no doubt at all that this progress would not have been made without the authority of your own voice and influence.' In

March there was a further step forward when British Rail Chairman Sir Peter Parker announced that cheap rail travel was on the way for severely disabled people.

Tony put the maximum effort into his year as President, speaking and writing as much as possible. On 22 April he wrote a guest column for the *Sheffield Evening Telegraph* urging various practical alleviations as well as a change in attitude: 'After the encouraging decision to remove VAT from cars bought under the mobility scheme, could not the Government also remove it from the cost of car adaptations? And could the Treasury examine how all disabled people might be allowed to buy a set amount of petrol – perhaps related to their work needs – every month free of duty?' Above all, he called for a different approach, 'not so much for charity as for understanding and action, not just for money but for determination to make social integration real for everyone. Disabled people are not rejects. They are not manufacturers' seconds, to be treated cheaply. Their rights and opportunities must be the same as the rest, for they are as much part of humanity as the rest.'

He managed to get the name of the Hospital for Incurables in Putney changed to the Royal Putney Hospital. As a listed building, to have its name changed needed the permission of English Heritage, who at first refused. When Tony wrote to them, their answer stated that: 'In any case, because of the trees you can hardly see it from the road.' 'Try going past it in winter,' wrote Tony.*

Even the Design Council seemed unaware that disabled people had to be specially designed for. On 13 May its Chairman wrote to Miss Marion Janner of the Muscular Dystrophy Group of Great Britain apologising for the Centre's shortcomings 'from the point of view of wheelchair users'. Although they were trying to improve the situation, he said (a ramp was recently installed at the front entrance), their financial position meant that major changes would only be made gradually. There were stairlifts, but these could only be used for those who had enough muscular control and mobility to get in and out of the seat unaided.

---

* It is now the Royal Hospital for Neuro-Disability, Putney. The frieze which carried the words 'Hospital for Incurables' was covered over in the 1990s, with the permission of English Heritage, although the words are still there under the rendering.

Finally, on 22 May 1981, came the day when the Snowdon Award Scheme was created as a charity. Apart from Tony, its ten other Trustees were the wheelchair-bound Baroness Masham, the deaf MP Jack Ashley, the Editor of the *Sunday Mirror*, Bob Edwards, Moss Evans, head of the TGWU, John Hannam, the MP for Exeter (and Chairman of the All-Party Disablement Group), Sir Frederick Catherwood, the Hon. John Astor, Alan McLintock of the well-known accountants Thomson McLintock, Alfred Morris, MP and Simon Sainsbury. At that first meeting, by which time £40,000 was already on the table, the main declared aim of the charity was laid down. 'To award a bursary or bursaries annually to one or more needy physically disabled student(s) for the purpose of assisting the Benificiary(s) to pursue some academic, scientific or practical achievement which would otherwise be beyond his/her financial means on account of disability, such bursary to be for periods of either one year or two years each and awarded on the recommendation of the Administering Charity, provided that preference shall be given to Beneficiaries between the ages of seventeen and twenty-five years.'

From the start, there was an annual meeting, when students who had benefited were invited to come and meet Tony. At first this meeting was held in the NatWest Tower – the Bank was a great supporter in the early years – and later in the Glaziers' Hall. That first year, the Scheme gave away £6,000, which rose to £9,000 the next. In 2007 £1.7 million was given to 1,400 students.

Money – or rather, the lack of it – was always the main problem for disabled students. Sometimes extra cash was needed for obvious purposes, at other times for something only imaginable by talking to someone disabled – and few in the average government department had done that. Many disabled students needed wheelchairs, but few universities had ramps up which these could be propelled. Deaf students – before the age of computers these, along with wheelchair users, were the largest category needing help – needed someone to assist them by translating the spoken word into sign language, which usually meant someone who needed paying. There was no specially equipped accommodation, nor was there any recognition that quite often the university nearest the disabled student's home was not necessarily the most suitable for them ... which meant extra expense in the form of transport.

When, on 8 June, Tony visited the headquarters of Action Research for the Crippled Child, he was able to tell them not only that the money in the Award Scheme had now reached £75,000 but also that he was bestowing his Raspberry of the Year on Westminster Council for putting a lavatory for the disabled at the bottom of nineteen steps. The Council's response was that disabled people had only to call out and someone would come up and carry them down.

Tony, as a public figure who clearly knew what he was talking about, was able to focus attention on all these anomalies. As his secretary, the invaluable Dorothy Everard, wrote to him on 27 August, 'Darling Tony, the International Year of the Disabled certainly has been a success, so much more so than the Year of the Child. One feels that people are now aware of the disabled in our society – more notices in public places, holiday firms offering help and advice, etc. Well done, Tony. You were a lucky one when you recovered from your childhood illness but your efforts on behalf of those not so lucky have been magnificent.'

The same year a further, damning report was published. It was written by the Committee on Restrictions Against Disabled People. This report stated that discrimination was caused by the failure of society to recognise that it excluded disabled people in many areas of life. Buses were inaccessible. So were most buildings. Insurance companies added extra premiums onto their policies even though there was no evidence of extra risk. The solution, it said, was to change society – not disabled people.

Progress in removing these difficulties was slow. Throughout the 1980s a Bill proposing changes that would alleviate the lot of disabled people went to Parliament every year and every year it was defeated. Gradually, however, successive governments began to realise that more had to be done and a number of victories were won. One was the design of an accessible taxi (today, all of London's black cabs can carry people in wheelchairs and they have provision for people with other impairments); another that in the mid-1980s the access requirements of disabled people were incorporated into building regulations and hence in all new public buildings.

Tony was often approached to speak or write on such issues and, if it seemed he could be effective, would usually do it. Becoming Patron or President was a different matter: as he invariably threw himself into anything to which he had lent his name, the time involved became a pressing factor. So when the International Polio Campaign run by the Rotarians, Polio Plus for Rotarians, approached him by telephone to ask if he would be President (in this country) of their appeal, he asked Andrew Farquhar, himself a Rotarian, if this was one to accept. Farquhar went to the Rotary headquarters in Warwickshire to find out what would be involved; when he returned he told Tony: 'This is something to which I think you could make a real difference.' Tony agreed to accept, provided the National Fund for Research into Crippling Diseases would give Farquhar, their Company Secretary, the time to help him.

What followed was a year of visits and speeches at meetings, the largest the RIBI (Rotary International British Isles) annual conference in Blackpool where there was an audience of 4,000. For Tony (and his secretaries) these speeches were a supreme ordeal. Each had to be typed, after which he would alter it innumerable times – each involving a full retyping – finally underlining points of emphasis.

Then came the actual speech, before which he would shake with nerves. Once, at a meeting in Southampton, he trembled and shook so badly that he nearly toppled off the stage and had to be saved by Farquhar, who was by now running the Award Scheme. This stage fright had one unexpected bonus: he would usually lose his place in the speech and have to continue off the cuff – as an ad-lib speaker with a gift for anecdote his words came across far more effectively than in the speeches he had worked on so painstakingly.

Although Tony would never have dreamed of drawing attention to it, his life in these years was in sharp contrast to that of his former wife. Since Roddy Llewellyn's marriage in 1981, friends noted that she needed male companionship 'almost as if she were collecting scalps' as one put it. Other escorts came forward, most of them touted as the 'new man' in her life. One was a wealthy

Italian merchant banker named Mario d'Urso, with whom she had holidayed alone apart from her detective; another was the tall, attractive Norman Lonsdale whom she had known for a number of years, who became a regular escort although, eventually, her night-owl hours were too much for Lonsdale, a hardworking businessman.

More seriously for Margaret's health, her drinking had become legendary – though she never showed a sign of it in public – and she smoked constantly, so much so that when she went into hospital on 5 January 1985 with a shadow on her lung it was feared she might have lung cancer, although with removal of a small section of the lung it proved to be non-malignant; but she took the precaution of switching to filter-tip cigarettes, smoked through an even longer holder, and gave up her favourite Famous Grouse whisky in favour of barley water.

She was, of course, still undertaking official engagements – and certain visits almost unheard of then, made privately and never yet mentioned, though later made famous by Diana, Princess of Wales. In the early eighties, Aids was a new and dreadful disease, with most people frightened to have any contact with a sufferer. Without fuss, without warning the press, and taking everything entirely naturally Margaret, accompanied by Anne Tennant, would visit the Lighthouse, in Notting Hill, west London, the establishment that took in young men with Aids who had lost a partner or been abandoned by their families. When she went to see Anne's son Henry, dying of Aids, she would always hug him.

As well as the time and trouble involved in his campaigning, Tony was also working as hard as ever. The portraits he took during those years read like a roll-call of the famous and the brilliant: Anthony Burgess, Ava Gardner, Graham Greene, Princess Anne and Carmen Callil.

In 1982, Sarah, too, went to Bedales, its fees then just under £1,200 a term. 'I still don't believe I've got in!' she wrote to Tony in a letter thanking him for being such a 'wonderful, thoughtful father'. It was a time of great happiness with his children. Many of their letters are to thank him for some thoughtful present.

'Darling Papa, I *love* my [there follows a drawing of a jacket]. Thank you so much. All best and fondest love. Ya Ya [Sarah's childhood nickname].'

Tony was determined not to let Oliver Messel's reputation and memory disappear. An exhibition was arranged at the Victoria and Albert Museum, under the aegis of Roy Strong, to run from 22 June to 30 October 1983. Anxious to show as many aspects of Oliver's spectacular talent as possible, he wrote to Anthony Johnson to ask for pieces that Oliver had left him as well as the loan of certain others Johnson had bought with the purchase of Maddox, to display in the V&A. Unfortunately, during the intervening eighteen months Johnson and his wife had parted, an acrimonious split that involved the removal of a number of these items from Maddox. Most had been put into a local furniture store called Forbes, which was legally bound not to hand them over to Johnson. Johnson explained the position to Tony, and suggested he wrote to the store direct.

As the deadline approached Tony's letters became more plaintive. 'I would rather have them delivered to someone in Barbados, so that they can bring them over next time they come but it would be best to send them to the British High Commission. I will write to them as soon as you get Forbes's okay. As regards the other things of mine, I think it best if you and I discuss it as obviously I cannot make arrangements without the two of you making arrangements. It surely cannot be hard for you to get a quote and send them to arrive in time for the V and A. As you both know, it is only because you said you admired Oliver's work that you got Maddox in the first place. I beg of you to act fast.'

Johnson did his best but to no avail. Tony, waiting to hear whether or not the promised pieces would arrive, asked his former wife to open the exhibition; Margaret had been extremely fond of Oliver, and the house he had designed for her was the scene of some of her happiest moments. She did not hesitate to accept and, as Tony wrote on 17 June to the Queen Mother ('Dearest Ma'am') when thanking her for the loan of some sketches and two Messel wall candelabra, 'Margaret is very sweetly opening it – with a speech written by me!'

Dramatic tension was provided by Anne Rosse, who had worked

herself into a fever of nerves – as Roy Strong's diary entry for 20 June 1983 makes clear:

> The whole day has been blighted by the run-up to the Oliver Messel exhibition. Tony Snowdon on the phone: had I seen the *Daily Mail*? No. I saw it later and it said that Tony was miffed that Princess Margaret was opening the show. Not true. No, I insisted, the speech had to be in the tent room. Then a letter by hand from Anne Rosse. She had wept all over the catalogue yesterday. Would she come? Wouldn't she come? Princess Margaret mercifully laid down the law: 'You must go to the Messel opening.'
>
> The heat was stifling, with no air-conditioning, leaving the ageing actresses and aristocrats melting, Dorothy Dickson, Elisabeth Welch, Anna Neagle and Ninette de Valois among them. The HRH gang were there in force – Carl Toms, Derek Hart, Milton Gendel, Jane Stevens, etc. Diana Cooper turned up on Patrick Proktor's arm, complaining that I now cut her (not true!). There was a vast battery of photographers to get the photograph they all longed for. Tony, having said that he'd not mingle with the crowd, did precisely what I thought he would. Immediately on HRH's entry, he embraced her. Blaze of flashlights. In fact he's fascinated by her. Anne Rosse in trailing black taffeta acted as Queen Mother manqué.

After the Messel opening at the V&A there was a dinner at Kensington Palace that, as Strong later learned, 'almost never happened because Anne Rosse (now eighty-three) sat transfixed with emotion and refused to eat for hours'.

A week later, Tony wrote again to Johnson. 'As yet I have not heard a word from Forbes. It is extremely sad for me as I really would have liked them at the exhibition, which has already opened. I really would like the other things that are mine as soon as possible. Yours Tony.' The postscript was sad: while negotiations were going on, the Forbes store burned down, and with it most of the items that had been Oliver's that Tony had wanted to borrow. In all he received two plaques back from Maddox; the two urns and lamps he had been left were in the Forbes store. Unhappy though this ending was, Tony remained on good terms with Johnson, writing to him later: 'Thank you for letter and the photographs of Maddox. I was so pleased to see you have kept so much as it was in Oliver's lifetime. I hope that one day I can come over to visit although it would sadden my heart without Oliver, and Vagn. How were the staff. If they've left can you please convey to them my warmest wishes.'

Soon afterwards, in October, Tony's brother-in-law Lord de Vesci died. Susan, no longer châtelaine of Abbey Leix, the famous Irish estate where she had spent her married life, moved first to Womersley (which she had always loved) and then to the small Leicestershire village of Smeeton. Soon afterwards, it was discovered that she had cancer. Lucy, who had been to stay with her there, visited her often in the Princess Grace Hospital in Nottingham Place, London, to which she came for chemotherapy and where she spent the last six weeks of her life – she died two years later, in 1986. Tony was photographing when the news reached him: a shoot for Italian *Men's Vogue*, using the Linley Sambourne house as a background and several friends as male models. One of them was Michael Dover, his tall and handsome editor at Weidenfeld & Nicolson, who had known him for around three years. As Tony snapped away, the telephone rang. When he returned from the call, he was, in Dover's words, 'completely destroyed', sobbing uncontrollably into his friend's shoulder for a long time. It was a rare glimpse of the deep well of emotion usually kept so carefully hidden.

The rest of his family remained devoted, sending him letters that breathed love, a longing to see him, and thanks for generosity. After spending a month with him in India – as she noted, the longest time they had ever been together in their lives – Sarah wrote on 26 April 1984: 'Darling Papa, I am unable to tell you how much I loved going to India with you.... I can only thank you, darling Pa, for being such an ace father and taking me to work with you as it certainly is an experience I will never forget. I loved it all. It is so hard to show how grateful I am. With all my best love, Ya Ya.' David wrote to thank him for some elegant cufflinks, Frances sent him home-made birthday cards. 'I love you, dear Papa, with love from Frances and loads of kisses and hugs.'

At eighteen, David had begun a two-year course in cabinet-making at the John Makepeace School for Craftsmen in Wood at Parnham, in Dorset. On leaving, aged twenty, in 1982, he and a partner set up their own cabinet-making business in Dorking.

Three years later, he opened his own shop in New King's Road (later he moved to Pimlico). His pieces, beautifully made and expensive, were known particularly for his skill in marquetry. Now independent, he bought his own flat and moved out of Kensington Palace.

Sarah's path to an independent life was less high-profile. Her interest had always been in painting – her only A-level at Bedales was in art – and on leaving school she went to Camberwell School of Art, to which she pedalled every morning on her bicycle from Kensington Palace. Once arrived, she was just another student. This and the course she later attended at the Royal Academy art school resulted in a successful career as a painter. She too moved out of Kensington Palace, in 1985 (soon after she had turned twenty-one), into a small, pretty terrace house in South Kensington, bought for her by Princess Margaret.

Although they were now independent, both children saw a lot of their mother. When a visit by Margaret to China was proposed for 1987 the Chinese government invited her to bring David and Sarah as well. The relationship between Margaret and Tony was now so amicable that she was able to consult him on this.

Always deft at dealing with the public relations side of any official engagement or tour, as he had been in the days when he was married to Margaret, his advice was shrewd and succinct. 'It seems fine to me to accept the kind and generous hospitality from the Chinese government but I do think questions might be asked if the taxpayer had to foot the bill for two first-class return tickets. Could they not go on the same aeroplane, tourist, and pay privately? As they will be going Pacific Airways rather than British it's up to the airline if they want to upgrade them. It's just the thing the press would get hold of and it would damage the goodwill of the tour. Hope you are well. Will you mention this to the Foreign Office?' His advice was followed.

17

Working Ever Harder

⊁⊰

During this decade and the next Tony's Launceston Place studio had never been busier nor his work more varied. He photographed political heavyweights like the Prime Ministers John Major and Tony Blair and the Lord Chancellor, as well as stars like Joan Collins and Lenny Henry and Britain's most prolific novelist, Barbara Cartland. In 1981 his photographs of two nineteen-year-olds, Lady Diana Spencer and the Hon. Louisa Napier, appeared in the February issue of *Vogue*; that August, the magazine carried his official portraits of the Prince of Wales in full-dress naval uniform wearing his Garter sash and his fiancée Diana in a deep blue-green full-skirted, puff-sleeved taffeta ballgown. He was in such demand that in June the *Sunday Times* wrote suggesting that his annual retainer alone be raised 'immediately' from £10,000 to £12,500.

In 1982 another royal commission came his way when he was asked to undertake the photography for a special definitive version of the stamps to commemorate the Queen's coronation. For this he was offered a fee of £10,000. It was one of the few occasions in his career that he did not retain copyright, which in this case went to the Post Office.

In December there was 'Leafy London', two glamorous pictures of his London garden and that at Old House; in 1984 the official portrait of Princess Margaret just before her visit to Bermuda and Dallas. Although the lustrous softness that characterised his early portraits of her had disappeared with the vanishing of their love, his skill at making the most of his subject's looks remained, with the pure line of the Princess's profile balanced by her upswept dark chestnut hair, tiara and long diamond earrings gleaming, smooth shoulders rising creamily from the deep sapphire blue silk taffeta of her dress. The visits of the Princess to his studio were managed so discreetly that no one was aware of them. Her car would glide down the slight incline into the garage, after which the door would close behind it and the Princess would step out, go through the little door at the back of the garage into the garden, and enter the studio through its French doors.

The most profitable work came from advertising, where fees were much higher. Here two of his most salient characteristics were in evidence: his great creativity and his firm control, sometimes amounting to bullying, of agency art directors for whom his fame, his reputation and his former close links with royalty could be overwhelming. Some would fly over from France just for a meeting, to be greeted with innocent-sounding phrases like: 'Tell me – what does an art director actually *do*?' with any mumbling or stumbling mercilessly pounced on. But the lucrative commissions kept on coming (some of the proceeds of this torrent of gold were put into a settlement of £104,000 in August 1988 to be held in trust for Frances until she reached the age of twenty-five; later, he gifted another £150,000-odd).

One of the commissions he received was from the impresario Victoria Charlton and her then husband Peter Brightman. Their company, Entertainment Corporation, had arranged with the Russian authorities to bring the Moscow State Circus and the important Russian ballet companies to perform in the UK. Victoria had written to Tony's agent, Peter Lyster Todd, to ask if Tony would be prepared to come to Russia and, in the first instance, take photographs of the Circus performers and dancers of the Bolshoi Ballet. Other assignments soon followed.

The trips were a great success. For the first one, the group left London on 4 December 1985 and travelled round a number of USSR republics from which the various acts in the State Circus came. In most of them they went to official dinners, made noteworthy by the endless speeches and toasts and the huge amount of drink – each person was allotted a large bottle of water, a large bottle of Coke, a bottle of wine and a bottle of vodka. On other of their sorties there were exactly the kind of improvisations that

Tony loved. They had to iron the backdrops for the pictures and produce their own food – Victoria always took plenty, and a microwave to cook it, often backstage, where the dancers sniffed hungrily at the aroma of beef or chicken casserole, or sometimes in the hotel room as the cooks in their KGB hotel left at 10 p.m. sharp.

For those who were not frightened, working with him could be a revelation. For a jewellery advertisement that focused on rings, he showed them on a collection of hands – those of a newborn baby, a 95-year-old man, the gnarled hands of a gardener, dark hands of African men and the supple hands of a Thai dancer that bent back gracefully. For one magazine there was Damien Hirst in a glass tank; for an American one, Germaine Greer on a red motorbike with Placido Domingo – they had asked her what would be her two greatest pleasures in life, to which she replied: 'Singing with Placido Domingo on a red motorbike.' He also took a photograph of the Prince and Princess of Wales with their two children, posing like models in a Fortnum's catalogue with a picnic hamper, that was one of the few misjudgements of his career. It was roundly castigated by the critics; engagingly, Tony agreed with them.

Assistants came and went. Working with someone so brilliant and famous in his own field was a magnetic draw to any would-be young photographer; against this, the appeal of the job was offset by the long hours, the poor pay and the mercurial temperament of the employer, which on occasions shaded into downright bullying. When Julian Broad, then aged twenty-one, driving back from a shoot, accidentally bumped into the kerb and damaged the suspension of Tony's van, it was Julian who had to pay for its repair – nor was he ever allowed to forget his 'crime'. Work was hard: his hours were 7.30 a.m. until 7 p.m., the pay £70 a month, with £15 or £7.50 a day respectively extra for every full or half-day's editorial work on Vogue (billed to Condé Nast). And just as the Pimlico Road assistants had found, the concept of work stretched to include non-photographic tasks. 'I painted Frances's room and washed the outside walls of the house,' said Broad (now a well-known photographer in his own right and on excellent terms with Tony).

One anecdote illustrates both Tony's charm and the relentless insistence on getting what he wanted, no matter what travails the other person was undergoing. The set designer Sue Odell, who worked enjoyably with him for a number of years, continuing to do so through a pregnancy, left one evening having acquired all the props necessary for the shoot at his studio the following day. In the middle of the night her baby arrived. Conscientious even in the hours after childbirth, she rang her courier service at 8 a.m. to tell them to collect the props in a van and take them to the studio. Almost at once a fax arrived from Tony: 'My darling, what a wonderful excuse for not turning up at the most boring shoot in the world.' She smiled – and settled back to enjoy her new baby. Her peace was short-lived: four times that morning Tony's assistant rang to ask her to order in a new and different prop and have it delivered to his studio.

In February 1987 Tony resigned from the Council of Industrial Design, which he had first joined in 1961. He had been dissatisfied for some time with its increasingly stuffy, bureaucratic approach and after a confrontational interview with the Council chairman, Simon Hornby, he left – he himself said he had been sacked. Terence Conran, founder of the Habitat chain that virtually introduced good, cheap design to Britain, weighed in on Tony's side, saying that the Council had become a victim of bureaucracy and turned a deaf ear to criticism. Most of Britain's top designers, much of whose work was showcased in the Design Centre, supported Tony's views. In the same month, under the headline 'Dead as a Dodo? Why do the words Design Council make one yawn with ennui?' in a *Vogue* interview with Hornby, he called the Council's magazine, *Design*, 'unreadable, unfashionable and out-of-touch'. It is only fair to point out that Hornby agreed with him, adding for good measure that he found the magazine 'impossible to read; it lacks continuity and excitement'.

He continued speaking and writing to help disabled people throughout the eighties. One of these initiatives caused a considerable stir. In their February issue of 1988, *Vogue* published a heavy-hitting interview between Tony and Sir Robert Reid, the Chairman of British Rail since 1983. Sir Robert, who had been expecting a reasonably congratulatory exchange based on the introduction of BR's new colour schemes, instead got an earful on BR's treatment of disabled people. Tony's attack was based on a journey he had made with a young disabled student, Karen Jenkins, who had achieved a place to read French at Sussex University, gone on to work for the Brighton and Hove Federation for the Disabled, and who travelled up to London once a month, partly by local train and then on the Brighton–London train.

Her journey was invariably in the luggage van or, as BR called it, the 'security cage', locked in throughout the journey, so that going to the lavatory was impossible, and she had to wear extra clothing as the cage was not heated. She carried a strap in her handbag to tie herself to the grille bars of the security cage to prevent her wheelchair slipping or falling over – she was almost invariably alone – as there was no bell or means of calling for help. When she reached her destination she was dependent on a guard bringing a ramp to take her in and out of the van – once, she was left in the van at Victoria until the guard came to take the train back to Brighton. If she wanted to travel by InterCity she had to make a reservation several days in advance to allow for time to remove two seats to fit her wheelchair in. Impromptu journeys were out of the question. As always, Tony sprinkled various practical solutions throughout the interview.

His opening broadside was to ask Reid if he commuted himself and what he did if annoyed that his train from Purley was grubby. 'I speak to the guy who's responsible for carriage cleaning,' said Reid, upon which Tony asked him if the Purley train was now cleaner as a result. When Reid replied: 'No, I shouldn't think so,' Tony said silkily: 'So your complaints haven't had any effect at all?' He then extracted from Reid that British Rail was an equal opportunities employer, eliciting the following exchange: 'So how many blacks have you got on the board?' Reid: 'I have none at the moment but I have two ladies.' Tony: 'White?' Reid: 'They happen to be white but that's not important, surely?'

Tony then moved on to the journey he had taken with Karen Jenkins, pointing out that while there was a small notice that asked 'Please Give Up Your Seat If A Disabled Person Needs It', the doors to the carriages were twenty-two inches wide and the minimum width of a wheelchair was twenty-five inches. 'So there is no way', he concluded, 'that a person in a wheelchair can get to such a seat.' He went on to say that it was intolerable that anyone in a wheelchair should have to travel among bicycles, trunks, dogs and chickens. 'Not chickens,' said the unhappy Reid. 'They'd have been pullets.'

The last major 'foray' with Marjorie Wallace, now a close friend, took place the following month, as part of the Care in the Community campaign* that was to release many of the mentally ill from the grim institutions in which they had been confined into the community where, supposedly, there would be sufficient supervision and support to allow them to live as normal a life as possible.

As Marjorie pointed out in her articles, 'The trouble is that independence may simply mean loneliness,' and the habitations into which these former patients were released were barely suitable, since few landladies had been informed about mental conditions. At one of these addresses that Marjorie had been given, in a back street in Southampton, there came the sound of ferocious barking from behind the door – the landlady kept a dozen rottweilers. 'You go in,' said Tony hastily, burying his head in the car boot. 'I have a little problem with my camera.' Marjorie found herself inside, with the rottweilers and an alcoholic landlady, eventually to be joined by an apprehensive Tony. There also was an inmate with a huge bandage around his thigh, the result of a savaging by one of the dogs. Fortunately Marjorie and Tony escaped untouched.

In Liverpool, where they went to photograph those who had ended up homeless on the streets, there was a different challenge. They arrived late at their hotel, the Adelphi, and after dinner, announcing that he was tired and wanted to go to bed, Tony told Marjorie, who had a bad cold, to go out and set up potential subjects for the next day's shooting. 'So alone, at 11 p.m., in a strange city to which I had never been, I had to go and look for down-and-outs who would be prepared to be photographed. I asked the police where they congregated, sat down among them,

---

* This eventually resulted in the Community Care Act of 1990.

and asked if they would be willing to be photographed the next day. Of course by the next day they weren't there – they were only in their cardboard boxes at night. Tony got more and more ratty and I thought my career was on the line. Luckily we found a genial drunk Irishman with a bottle of meths and that saved the day.' Their feature, with Tony's extraordinarily moving photographs, was published in the *Sunday Times Colour Magazine* of 3 May 1987. Later Tony was to comment: 'The hardest thing to photograph is dirt – and loneliness is harder still.'

In November 1989, Peter Lyster Todd negotiated a contract with the *Telegraph Sunday Magazine*, under its editor Nigel Horne, that lured Tony away from the *Sunday Times*. It was for a minimum of five years, thereafter to run from year to year with six months' notice on either side. Tony was to have an annual retainer of £35,000, with another £35,000 to cover the twelve assignments a year they hoped for. Extra work would be paid at the rate of £2,916 per shoot and he was free to accept any other freelance offers, with the exception of rival newspaper colour supplements circulating in the UK. He would also be given forty per cent of all syndication fees. It was an extremely generous contract – at just under £6,000 per assignment, plus expenses – but Peter Lyster Todd even managed to include a clause to the effect that the retainer be revised upwards by an annual five per cent for the fourth and any subsequent year(s) plus extra money if assignments took more than two days. Horne hoped that he would work mostly on portraits and fashion, with at least one reportage piece a year.

Lucy, whose admiration of her husband's work was immense, could often be his sternest critic. She was so convinced of his brilliance that if, in her view, something fell short of what she felt he was capable of, she did not hesitate to say so. But criticism, even loving, constructive criticism, is often hard to take and Tony, the small child in him to the fore on such occasions, could be resentful.

Speech-writing, over which he was meticulous, was often based on help given him by either Andrew Farquhar or Ann Hills; the pair met several times at Launceston Place and also at the annual meetings – by the early nineties, when these took place at Glaziers' Hall, Ann attended whenever possible. Only later did Lucy Snowdon, who often wondered why she was never invited to these meetings, realise the reason. Like all those who knew Tony well, she was aware of his habit of 'compartmentalising' his life; at the time this seemed just another manifestation of this trait. She did, however, have her suspicions that his old habit of extramarital flings had not died out, so much so that she once asked the opinion of one of his photographic assistants to whom he was close; the boy, torn between truthfulness and loyalty to his employer, gave a non-committal answer.

Lucy was, in any case, extremely busy with her own life. Not only did she have to account for every penny of the housekeeping money allowed her by Tony's accountant, she was also giving a great deal of attention to Tony's ageing mother. Despite Lady Rosse's rudeness and unpleasantness to her at the beginning of her marriage to Tony, Lucy was generously determined not to hold this against her. Sensitive to others, she realised that her mother-in-law was in fact lonely. She fetched and carried for Anne, ran errands for her, went down to Nymans to see her and checked that Anne was taking the pills and potions prescribed by her doctors and often asked her to lunch. 'Lucy fags for her ceaselessly which Anne takes for granted,' wrote James Lees-Milne on 6 November 1988. One reason for Anne's declining health was her increasing dependence on alcohol. There are accounts of her – as at one luncheon at Old House – appearing in her customary bejewelled elegance and then, to the embarrassment of the other guests, toppling forward at the lunch table in an alcoholic stupor.

Tony's ceaseless campaigning for the disabled or physically handicapped continued. In early February 1989 he opened a symposium on the technological aspects of hearing aids, organised by the Royal National Institute for the Deaf. Instead of the expected bland introductory remarks, he made a speech bitterly critical of the design and price of hearing aids. Why, for instance, he asked, should a hearing aid supplied to the Department of Health and

Social Security at a cost of only £25 cost more than £200 when sold privately?

He followed this with an attack on the sales methods used by some manufacturers. He himself had been working for seven years on what he called a 'hearing device' (rather than a hearing aid); its purpose was to cut out the background noise, as at meetings, parties or restaurants, that adds enormously to the difficulties of those with impaired hearing. His invention was based on a tiny pocket receiver, to be used in conjunction with a small microphone and, possibly, headphones connected to a hearing aid. When objections were raised as to its visibility, he pointed out that one of the reasons a premium was placed on a hearing aid's invisibility was that deafness was so often treated as a source of ridicule. 'Personal stereos are obvious and yet perfectly acceptable – and *they* don't have to be tiny and flesh-coloured.'

He was also approached by Lord McColl,* the distinguished professor who in 1986 had produced the McColl Report on aids for disabled people (this had recommended sweeping changes to the Artificial Limb and Appliance Service management, and the services provided for disabled people). When Lord McColl heard that Tony had designed a wooden wheelchair that was small-wheeled and flexible and could thus go more or less anywhere, he asked Tony if he could borrow one. This he took to the wheelchair-bound Baroness Darcy de Knayth, crossbench campaigner in the House of Lords for the rights of disabled people. Because of its manoeuvrability, she found that she was able to visit hitherto unseen parts of her north London garden. McColl recommended its manufacture to various companies but few were interested in it as a commercial proposition.

Early in 1992, the Snowdon Award Scheme received a major boost when the London Marathon approached Tony to ask if he would be prepared to start it that April. At once, Tony realised this could be of benefit to his Scheme and got in touch with Andrew Farquhar. Farquhar, very conscious that the Scheme did not have enough money to help as many students as they wanted to, had already applied to the National Lottery but had been told they

---

* Ian McColl was created Baron McColl of Dulwich in 1989.

were the 'wrong category'. Now he went to see the Marathon's sponsors (then NutraSweet).

The London Marathon, which came into existence on 29 March 1981 with just under 7,500 runners, had become so popular that the number of starters had quadrupled. Entry was and is by ballot, but because four times the number apply as there are places for, many are disappointed. Both then and at the time of writing the only other way to participate is through charities, which are allowed to buy 10,000 places from the organisers. Charities will then allocate these to those who wish to race on condition they can vouch for a certain sum in sponsorship. Farquhar arranged that NutraSweet would give the Snowdon Award Scheme 200 places for three years, in return for which Tony would start the Marathon for those three years. This arrangement set the Award Scheme firmly on its financial feet, raising around £500,000, which was then invested. With the increased income, many more students could be helped – and with more students the Scheme was enabled to gather the large body of evidence that would eventually contribute greatly in getting the law changed in ways helpful to disabled people.

On a more personal note, Tony suggested to the Palace that in future guide dogs might be allowed at Investitures (early the following year, the Queen's private secretary wrote to say that a guide dog would be admitted with the next recipient of an honour who wished to bring one).

Later that year, at midday on 3 July 1992, Anne Rosse died of a heart attack. Lucy was with her when she died. Anne had spent her last years peacefully at Nymans, cushioned by alcohol. The copious letter-writing of her earlier life was a thing of the past and communicating with her by telephone was no longer possible, although her housekeeper gave news of her to those who rang up. When she died she was, as one obituarist tactfully put it, 'dwelling serenely in a world of her own'.

Her funeral at Womersley was spectacular. The description of it by James Lees-Milne in his diary entry of 9 July cannot be bettered, so it is here quoted in full:

By train to Doncaster with the Thomas Messels, from where we taxied to Womersley; where mourners assembled for stand-up luncheon. Martin [Parsons] looking like Mervyn the Badminton gamekeeper, florid-faced, thickset and boisterous in charming puppylike way; William Rosse by contrast frail and slight, and very Irish. Having not seen them for so long I had little to say to them, though they were very sweet to me. Lucy Snowdon a darling, and William's [Lord Rosse] wife nice and unassuming.

Service done in great theatrical style of which I approved. Tony [Snowdon] had arranged a marvellous display of white flowers in front of the Bodley roodscreen. Two priests, one Irish swinging a censer. Anne's coffin invisible under a golden pall smothered with wreaths and raised on a catafalque. Three lessons by the three sons, all beautifully [read]. John Cornforth gave a long address of which I heard little, being on the other side of the aisle. People said it was good but it sounded rather conventional to me. He is a stiff pudding. Six young men, one a grandson wearing pony tail, carried the coffin slowly down the nave through the west door, across the graveyard into the grounds of the house, where they put it into the hearse, a handsome, streamlined modern motor. From her own front door Anne was driven away for the last time with great dignity and in total silence. Moving moment.

This sympathetic, unknown, beautiful simple old house within its white limestone park walls has no land left to speak of, and is too large one would suppose for the impoverished Martin and his family.* I shall never go there again. I had a last look at Anne's little boudoir wherein she lived during the war, with Oliver's dazzling portrait of her.

One aspect of the funeral which would have appealed to Anne herself was also pointed out by Lees-Milne. 'Anne had the distinction of having two sons who were earls and three grandsons who were viscounts or barons at her funeral, along with ladies and hons galore.' As one of her obituaries pointed out: 'Socially she occupied a rare position. She was grand and very pretty [but] Society was occasionally disparaging about her.' Others spoke of her 'impeccable and inimitable dinner parties' and 'the remarkable resilience she showed in old age when the storm of 1987 struck

---

* They sold the house and forty-five acres of park in 2004.

Nymans and inflicted some of the worst damage suffered by any National Trust garden'.

The family jewellery – the Rosse emeralds and the Womersley diamond stars – were left to her sons William Rosse and Martin Parsons respectively (the stars were sold by Martin at Pontefract within a year). She had already given Princess Margaret a fair amount of her jewellery. Lucy, the person who had done so much for her, received practically none.

There was a final parting of a different kind for Princess Margaret. That summer of 1992, her former love Peter Townsend came over from his home in Paris to attend a reunion of those who had travelled with King George VI, Queen Elizabeth and the two princesses to South Africa on HMS *Vanguard* in 1947 – the trip that confirmed Margaret's love for him. He and his wife, the former Marie-Luce Jamagne, were staying at Searcy's in Knightsbridge.

'Do you think it would be all right if I gave a lunch party for Peter?' Margaret asked her Private Secretary Lord Napier, who agreed that it would be a nice idea. It was thirty-four years since Margaret and Townsend, respectively twenty-seven and forty-three, had seen each other; she was now sixty-one and he seventy-seven. The guests included Sir Eric and Lady Penn (Prue Penn was the half-sister of Tony's old friend Jocelyn Stevens), who had said they would pick up Townsend and his wife from Searcy's and take them back there after the lunch. When the Penns arrived, Marie-Luce emerged to say that she thought it better that she should not come, offering as her excuse that 'she had a cold coming on'. Although there would be a number of people at the luncheon, her presence would have subtly altered the dynamics of this meeting between the Princess and her former love, innocent though it was. This tactful gesture by Marie-Luce was much appreciated.

At lunch, Townsend was seated beside Margaret at her place at the centre of the table. After the meal was over, the Princess suggested that the party went out into the sunny garden for a stroll. Here she and Townsend were able to have a few brief semi-private words together. Then, calling Prue Penn, she handed Lady Penn her camera and asked if she would take a photograph of herself and Townsend together.

At the end of the party, the Princess came out onto the steps to say goodbye. As the Penns' car, with her former lover sitting inside it, drew away, she pulled a handkerchief out of her bag and waved it. Then, turning to Napier standing behind her, she said with one of her sweetest smiles: 'You know, Nigel, he hasn't changed a bit. But it's all a very long time ago.' She never saw him again.* At Searcy's, Marie-Luce was waiting and when Prue Penn said: 'We missed you,' she replied, 'But I'm sure I was right not to come.'

Although his attendance at church was not as regular as in the days when he had been to prayer meetings in Westminster Abbey, in September 1993 religions matters local to Old House claimed Tony's attention. The Vicar of Stapleford, Anthony Freeman, had caused countrywide outrage by the radical beliefs published that year in his book *God In Us*, roughly speaking a promulgation of humanism based on Christian ethics. God, he declared, was not an invisible spirit but existed in the human heart and mind as 'the sum of all our values and ideals', guiding and inspiring our lives. Tony, in support of the daughter of one of the previous vicars – and expressing his own view – wrote to the Bishop of Chichester to condemn Freeman's stance:

> Of course, Mr Freeman, as an individual, has every right to be an author, to publish his views, along with his strenuous efforts to obtain as much personal publicity in the media as possible to gain more sales of the tome. All I have to say is that with all the problems the Church of England is experiencing at the moment, I would have thought it extremely disadvantageous to employ someone with these beliefs within the Church. Did he make his views about God clear when he was appointed? If so, it surely was a strange appointment, if not, he should relinquish the post forthwith. It really is too feeble to say the situation will be reviewed in twelve months – if this is an accurate report in the papers.

The Bishop's reply, ten days later (on 13 September 1993) showed that the Church too had been taken by surprise: ' ... we had no idea that his views were as they appear in the book and

---

* Peter Townsend died on 19 June 1995.

indeed my impression is that they have developed only in the earlier part of this year. It has been a very difficult decision to think what to do with him.' He went on to say that after discussion with his two suffragan bishops and two retired professors of theology, the conclusion was that there was a chance of him moving back from his extreme position if given time for reflection. 'That is why he is being allowed to remain at Stapleford for the next twelve months. I have told him that I shall review the situation with him next May.' Freeman (who read first Chemistry and then Theology at Oxford) was dismissed from his parish for contravening Church teaching, but remained a priest in the Church of England, becoming a writer, editor and lecturer on theology and consciousness.

Other family events were the marriages of the Snowdons' children. On 8 October 1993 David Linley married Lord Petersham's only daughter Serena Stanhope, at St Margaret's, Westminster. It was a grand, high-society wedding, with the path from Parliament Square to the west door of the church covered in blue carpet (just as the nave of the nearby Abbey had been in 1960 for the wedding of David's parents). Serena wore Princess Margaret's 'second-best tiara'. The reception was held at St James's Palace.

The following year, on 14 July, Sarah Armstrong-Jones was married to the actor Daniel Chatto in a simple half-hour ceremony at the beautiful Wren church of St Stephen Walbrook, in the City of London, by Prebendary Chad Varah, founder of the Samaritans,* followed by a reception at Clarence House. Almost all the royal family as well as friends from film, theatre and television were among the 200 guests but compared to her brother's wedding Sarah's was a low-key affair – except for her dress. This, by Jasper Conran, was a simple, exquisite confection given her by Tony, to whom she wrote an ecstatic letter of thanks ('I've never worn a dress so utterly beautiful nor one that was so exactly what I dreamed it to be') from her honeymoon in Mumbai.

*

---

* The twenty-four-hour volunteer organisation offering confidential support to anyone in emotional distress or so despairing that they are contemplating suicide.

Tony and Prince Charles at Caernarvon Castle for the 25th anniversary
of the Investiture, July 1994.

Tony working the crowd at the Investiture anniversary.

Tony at the Snowdon Award ceremony of 1989 with Lady Boardman (wife of the chairman of NatWest Bank, who sponsored the ceremony) and Hugh McLeod, 20, from Gravesend, Kent, who was studying for a degree at University College, London, with the help of a Snowdon Award.

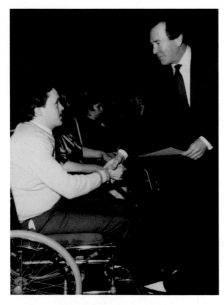

Tony talking to Huw Griffith-Jones, in a wheelchair owing to spinal injuries.

Ann Hills, who died on 31 December 1996.

Old House in 1991, after its extensive remodelling by Tony.

Anne Rosse when she was living at Nymans in the early 1980s.

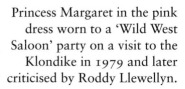

Princess Margaret in the pink dress worn to a 'Wild West Saloon' party on a visit to the Klondike in 1979 and later criticised by Roddy Llewellyn.

Melanie Cable-Alexander with her son Jasper.

Tony and his son Jasper (born in 1998).

Polly Higson with her five daughters.

Tony, in his robes as Provost of the Royal College of Art, greets the Queen at the Albert Memorial ceremony in October 1998. On the left is Sir Joceyln Stevens and on Tony's right is Sir Christopher Frayling, Rector of the RCA.

Tony with his daughters Sarah (left) and Frances at the opening party for the Retrospective of his work at the National Portrait Gallery in February 2000.

Tony, accompanied by Emmy Hirst, attending the funeral service for William Tallon, held at the Queen's Chapel, St James's Palace, in December 2007.

Tony and Marjorie Wallace lunching at the Caprice in 2005.

Tony, wearing his Cambridge Blue rowing cap from 1950, talking to fellow Cambridge Blue, Ewan Pearson, at Henley in July 2006.

Tony spends much of his day in his Launceton Place studio at the desk he used in Kensington Palace, made by him and designer James Cousins in his workshop there. On it and on the wall (to his left) are family photographs.

In 1994 Andrew Farquhar, who had decided to branch out on his own, left the National Fund for Research into Crippling Diseases. Tony, determined not to part company with anyone so hard-working and effective, asked him if he would take the Snowdon Award Scheme with him. Farquhar accepted; and at this point, although already a registered charity, it was hived off to become separate from the National Fund.

Slowly the attitude to disabled people was changing, from viewing them as people with a medical problem to seeing that they were men and women who should have equal rights with the able-bodied, and various piecemeal measures were achieved, though often against resistance. It was clear that what was needed was a comprehensive Act of Parliament. With this gradual sea-change in attitude came, eventually, legislation to give them equal rights. After a fifteen-year struggle by disabled people and their organ-isations, the Disability Discrimination Act was passed in 1995.

Its first clause defined what was meant by 'disability'. The intention of this was to create a common-sense definition which fitted the generally accepted perception of what is a disability and who is a disabled person and which provided certainty and avoided vagueness. The government of the day believed that the description they settled on – 'a physical or mental impairment which has a substantial and long-term adverse effect on the ability to carry out normal day-to-day activities' – would encompass the vast majority of the 8.6 million disabled persons in Britain (later, it was estimated that approximately 11.7 million adults or twenty per cent of the population are covered by the Act).

The Act's many clauses made it unlawful to discriminate in almost any way against a disabled person because of their dis-ability. It covered such commonplace (to others) activities as using public transport or hiring a taxi, entering libraries or other public places, travelling by train (Tony's particular bugbear), and aspects involving education – the focus of the Snowdon Award Scheme. In this important area – on it often depended the disabled person's later ability to earn a living – help depended mainly on local education authorities. Such help often took a considerable time to materialise, so much so that the Award Scheme Trustees believed that a comprehensive survey of what was needed was necessary.

This was commissioned from and compiled by the University of Leeds Disability Department, the cost of £30,000 being underwritten by one of the Scheme's Trustees, Evelyn de Rothschild.

Tony's own fund-raising continued: in March he collected £30,000 on behalf of his Award Scheme at the St George's Day Club annual luncheon, held at Grosvenor House, where roast beef and patriotic songs were the order of the day.

In June 1995 Tony's public career took a new and exciting turn. Already on the Appointments Board of the Royal College of Art, Britain's most prestigious establishment of further education for all branches of the creative arts, he was asked to become its Provost. It was an honorary post he was delighted to accept. In addition to his enormous interest in the visual arts, and in those studying them, this highly visible position brought another, special bonus. He was no longer royal or semi-royal, he had resigned from the Design Council; now he had a recognisable platform from which to relaunch himself into the world of designing for disablement.

Almost simultaneously, the new Rector, Professor Christopher Frayling, arrived. After a slightly edgy start – Tony said that he wished to ask Frayling some 'searching questions' and tape the answers; Frayling refused to be taped – the two established an excellent relationship. 'We must be on first name terms,' said Tony. 'I will call you "Rector" and you will call me "Provost".' (Once, a man standing in the doorway of a bank where the two met impromptu heard the brisk exchange: 'Morning Rector!', 'Morning Provost!' and called out 'Oh, I did enjoy that!')

One rite of passage for any new Rector was a Snowdon photograph (outside the Rector's office there is a 'Snowdon corridor', of framed portraits by Tony of former Rectors and notable graduates, including one of David Hockney in the famous gold lamé jacket he wore to the Convocation where he obtained his degree). Duly, Frayling arrived at Launceston Place that February 1995, smartly dressed in a suit with crisp white shirt. Tony gave him a critical look. 'A white shirt's not a good idea,' he said. 'It detracts from the face – too much light goes on to it. You need one that's slightly coloured.' As Frayling did not have another shirt with him Tony sent him up to the bedroom, saying that on the bed he would find a blue one, which would be much more appropriate. There on the bed lay a blue shirt with button-down collar – something Frayling had never worn in his life. He put it on, noticing that it was still slightly warm, and went downstairs again for the photograph.

Two months later he learned that only a few minutes earlier it had been taken off by Tony Blair, who had been photographed in it that morning (and whom Tony had told not to smile for the camera). It transpired that Blair had turned up in his best suit and a co-ordinated shirt and tie. Tony took one look at him, said 'Tut, tut,' and sent Blair to change into one of his own open-necked denim shirts. Throughout the years, blue shirts had become something of a Snowdon trademark: he had put subjects from Prince Charles (for his and Diana's engagement photograph) and the Duke of Edinburgh to Alan Bennett, Richard Branson and Terence Conran into one of his drawerful of blue shirts.

Although he loved the glamour and the theatricality of it, for Tony the most daunting aspect of being Provost was presiding at his first Convocation, the ceremony at which around 400 students get their degrees. At the time of writing, these annual gatherings take place in the Albert Hall, with the various College officials, in splendid robes, sitting at a long table on the stage. Proceedings begin with trumpeters from the Brigade of Guards giving the College fanfare, after which the Provost rises to his feet to say; 'I declare this Convocation open,' then calls upon the Rector to give his annual address. Later, he has to say: 'I call upon the Registrar to introduce us to the students.'

Tony, shaking with nerves, found the task almost impossible. The first year, instead of waiting for the trumpets to finish, he spoke over them so that no one could hear him; the following year he was so nervous that for a ghastly few moments nothing came out of his mouth at all until at last he was able to blurt the words out. The Latin phrase in another sentence was always mispronounced, so after a couple of stumbles Frayling wrote out cues for him that spelt these words phonetically – 'cowsa' instead of 'causa', for example. Fortunately, these difficulties only endeared him to the students. Despite Tony's stage fright, he loved the drama of it, and the formal, splendid robes. To do these justice the male officials, he decreed, should wear wing collars and white ties (many found these insufferably hot under their heavy robes) and he himself was not above a touch of make-up.

Where some Provosts treated the role as purely honorific, arriving twice a year for the Convocation and the College Court (the annual general meeting) Tony, as always, flung himself into what he saw as the demands of the job. He went to all the students' shows, from the range of interim shows put on individually by each department to the big, final summer show in May or June, talking to the students, finding out their views, discussing their plans and how they saw their work, and commenting on it.

Naturally, he had strong opinions on the work of the Photographic Department that did not always chime with the gallery-oriented ethos that was emerging – one student, who professed herself interested only in art shows, was referred to in a letter to the Head of the Department as 'rude, chippy and pathetic', in contrast to the eagerness and enthusiasm of the majority. Invariably self-deprecating, he would say: 'Just try and get it in focus,' or 'I take snaps, not works of art.' The students loved him.

By now, Tony was finding it increasingly difficult to get about even with a stick and he was limping badly. Post-polio syndrome was making itself felt. This weakness affects those who, like Tony, have had polio badly in their youth, and can strike anything from ten to forty years after recovery. It is caused by the death of individual nerve terminals in the motor units (nerve and muscle combinations) that remain after the original polio attack. As the leg, and in particular the knee joint, is protected by muscles, when these cease to work because the nerves die, the increasing muscular atrophy and joint pain cause loss of function. In Tony's case, he was gradually losing the use of his withered left leg.

What was most notable to everyone who knew him was his courage in facing this coupled with his extraordinary lack of self-pity. It would have been easy to complain of the narrowing of his physical horizons to the walls of whatever room he had to sit in for most of the day, but no one ever heard him do it.

Where the Royal College was concerned, to counter his increasing lameness he evolved a technique that did away with the need for him to process up the centre aisle with the College dignitaries. He would arrive at Door 1 of the Albert Hall, slip into a dressing room as the procession formed at the College, moving to his place on a specially raised chair at the centre of the table a few moments before it entered the Hall. As it did, he would rise to his feet, mortar-board firmly in place on his head, and remain standing during the fanfare. After he had opened the Convocation with the words, 'On behalf of the students, their tutors and the Honorands, I would like to give you all the warmest possible welcome this morning. I now declare the Convocation open and call upon the Rector, Professor Christopher Frayling, to give his address,' he would remove his mortar-board and sit on his high chair again.

At intervals throughout the ceremony he would be called upon to speak briefly – when conferring honorary doctorates, when presenting Fellows or honorary Fellows with scrolls and then shaking hands with the several hundred graduates, each of whom received a smile of genuine warmth. Finally, after the President of the Students' Union had made a speech, he would put on his mortar-board, stand and close the Convocation. After the ceremony was over, the procession would file out again, leaving Tony on the stage until someone came to help him down to his dressing room.

Soon the Rector noticed that as the procession left the Albert Hall there would be, behind him, immensely loud cheering from 800-odd people. Much of it came from the students sitting behind Tony at the table in admiration of his bravery in getting through what for him was clearly torture; the rest from the audience of parents and first-year students in the body of the Hall. Difficult as the whole procedure was for Tony, the result was highly effective, as Frayling evinced when he wrote: 'Thank you so much for chairing Convocation so effectively and well: a classic performance which has been praised by staff and students. Indeed "why wasn't it video-ed" was a constant refrain on Monday ... staff and students all felt that it was a joyous occasion: there's *never* been such a Collegiate atmosphere in the Albert Hall before.'

With a loving wife and devoted children, whose letters at this time breathe affection, admiration, love, a longing to see him and profound thanks for his generosity ('thank you also for the lovely boots, bracelet, egg, John Betjeman book and necklace. I love you very much and shall miss you,' wrote Frances), his home life could hardly have been happier. He had become a grandfather – Sarah and Daniel's children, Samuel David Benedict Chatto and Arthur Robert Nathaniel Chatto, were born in 1994 and 1999 respectively; David's children, the Hon. Charles Patrick Inigo Armstrong-Jones and the Hon. Margarita Elizabeth Rose Alleyn Armstrong-Jones, were born in 1999 and 2002.

Outside home, he had an honorary position that he adored, recognition – in 1995 he was guest of honour at the 141st Oxford and Cambridge Boat Race dinner – a campaign into which he could throw his heart and more work than he could cope with. Although his contract with the *Telegraph Sunday Magazine*, to which he had contributed nineteen covers and 223 pages in four years, was terminated by its new editor, Emma Soames, saying that they could no longer afford the 'reasonable fees' he commanded as a prestige photographer, he also received the biggest commission of his life. That November of 1995 he did a fifty-six-page all-star portfolio of notable Britons for *Vanity Fair* magazine, commissioned by its anglophile editor Graydon Carter, which took three months of solid work and eighty-five separate sittings. He called it 'Dad's Renaissance'. One of these photographs, of Tony Blair, adorned the New Labour leader's manifesto as he went into the seminal General Election of May 1997. At the same time, his portrait of the incumbent Prime Minister, John Major, whom he had photographed for *Vogue*, was used for Major's election posters.

At last Tony seemed to have arrived at life's sunny uplands. Nobody could have guessed how soon the view therefrom would change.

18

'I Need to Speak Urgently to Lord Snowdon'

❖

For Ann Hills, life was spiralling downwards. She had had a long-standing column in *The Guardian* but on the arrival of a new Woman's Editor it had been abruptly terminated, a mortifying blow that was followed by one or two rejections from other regular press outlets. As her friends knew, she was badly affected by these sudden withdrawals of regular work. Most people who have worked freelance know how easy it is to feel isolated or rejected, to think that if an article is refused one has 'lost one's touch', with consequent plummeting self-confidence. It is highly likely that Ann Hills, who in any case was prone to depressive tendencies and whose self-esteem and sense of identity were closely bound up in her work, suffered these feelings more forcibly than most.

Her personal life, too, was causing her distress. Since her divorce, her relationship with one live-in lover had broken up because she could not give him children and that with his successor was disintegrating – open and honest as always, she had told both of them about Tony, adding that they must 'disappear' when he visited her. She confided to those close to her that she feared she no longer had the emotional energy left to embark on another serious relationship.

Although still highly active sexually – when researching in Korea she had had her usual affair with a local – at fifty-five, despite looking much younger, she might have feared that even prom-iscuity might become more difficult. Her two sons, Guy and Adam, respectively twenty-nine and twenty-eight, were grown-up and independent, leaving her no real maternal role. Her health had become suspect: a year earlier she had been diagnosed with cervical cancer and although treatment appeared to have been successful, there were signs that it might be reappearing.

Then there was Tony. Although the sexual side of their relationship was no longer so paramount or so pressing, replaced by feelings – on Tony's side at least – more akin to friendship, her need for him had not diminished. She well knew that secrecy was the only option if she wished the affair to continue. Even her next-door neighbour, a young architect, was unaware of the relationship, while the men with whom she had a more casual sexual relationship, who might have suspected, simply knew that a tryst was never possible before 3 p.m. because her mystery lover 'T' might be there.

Unsurprisingly, after so many years, she longed for more openness and a greater commitment. When one male confidant, who knew virtually everything about the affair, took her out to dinner in December 1996, he asked: 'How's Tony?' knowing that she loved to talk about him. The question brought an instant explosion. 'How dare you say his name so loudly! People might hear.' Soon the reason for this outburst emerged. 'I'm feeling really pissed off about this affair,' she told her friend. 'At the best of times I don't see him nearly enough. And at Christmas, naturally, he's got to be with his family.'

She was a woman for whom the idea of suicide had throughout her adult life often been present. 'I would be frightened to live without the thought of suicide,' she said once.* 'It is an open door. Admittedly it opens into nowhere, but at the same time you can turn away from the dark room you are in.' With her personal life seemingly disintegrating, a stinging rejection from the newspaper for which she had worked for so long, the closing of several other doors and the prospect of a dwindling succession of lovers as she aged, it must have been a thought that emerged ever more frequently.

One of the sentences in the book she co-wrote, *Affairs*, was extraordinarily prescient. 'The person at the centre of multiple affairs is often very lonely, and the affairs can put off the day of

---

* To the writer Drusilla Beyfus, who interviewed her for her book *The English*.

reckoning when he or she comes to terms with the inner core of loneliness that lies at the centre of true maturity. If this is you, then only you can face the loneliness inside you, and render it powerless to hurt you.'

Ann Hills was unable to. She spent Christmas with her ex-husband Nicholas Hills, their two sons and Nicholas's second wife Susan (with whom Ann got on well) and then returned to her flat. On 29 December 1996 she took her elderly father to the theatre, to see Tennessee Williams's play, *A Streetcar Named Desire*. The two shared a special closeness and Elliot Philipp was well aware that his daughter's self-esteem was at rock bottom. 'She could not face not being a success at journalism,' he said. 'She also worried about the prospect of not having a man in her home.'

Desperately lonely, worried about her future, she rang Tony and left a message for him to call her. He responded, but no one knows whether or not she actually picked up his message. Announcing himself as usual by his coded name, he explained that he could not see her over Christmas and the New Year because 'we' would be under a spotlight. 'I'm really concerned. I would love to see you,' ran the message. 'Chin up!' he ended.

On 31 December, one of Ann's two closest friends, the writer Lesley Abdela, said to her partner Tim Symonds: 'Ann may be all by herself this New Year's Eve. Why don't we ask her over – she could easily hop on her bike and come.' A little later, around 8 p.m., after both had agreed on this, Lesley rang Ann's number only to get the answerphone. 'There's something odd about its message,' she said, alarmed. Symonds tried to reassure her that there was probably nothing to be anxious about but, worried, she sent her daughter over, who obtained a key to Ann's flat from a downstairs neighbour in the same block.

When the girl entered, the place seemed deserted. Apprehensive, she telephoned Ann's father, reporting that while she could see into Ann's room, where piles of papers lay about, there was no sign of Ann. 'Shall I call the police?' 'Yes, please do, and I'll come straightaway,' said Mr Philipp, instantly apprehensive that his daughter, of whose earlier suicidal tendencies he was well aware, might have 'done something'. He and Lesley Abdela hurried over.

Both saw the diaries that Ann wrote copiously every night lying around but there was otherwise no trace of her.

On her kitchen table lay the suicide note she had written hours earlier, telling of her problems, paying tribute to her father, requesting that her body be used for medical research – this proved impossible because of the pills she had taken – and asking for the brooch Tony had given her to be taken back to him, along with a note saying that she had always loved him and always would.

It was a freezing night. At minus 2–3°C (27–28°F) the temperature was well below zero and a biting wind from the northeast added to the chill. A light sprinkling of snow lay on the ground. For a while no one thought of looking outside on Ann's terrace roof garden, dark under the cloudy sky. This garden was something that had given her much pleasure over the years. In 1993 it had won for her the Westminster Roof Garden prize and had been featured in magazine articles.

When the police first went up there, they saw nothing untoward – chiefly because they could not believe that Ann owned the entire rooftop terrace. It was her father who found her, in the far corner by a chimney-stack. Her small body was clad in a black dress and the stiletto heels she invariably wore to add height to her doll-size frame. Beside her lay an empty bottle of Moët et Chandon champagne, given to her by Lesley and Tim a few days earlier and which she had intended to drink with the boyfriend who had left. Beside it was a china mug lined with a white, crystallised sediment, the remnants of the massive dose of tranquillisers and paracetamol that had killed her.

The police took away her diaries and the answerphone tape. It was easy enough to relate the diaries, comprehensively detailing the dead woman's turbulent love life and her emotional dependence on Tony, to the message on the answerphone. It became clear that her suicide was no spur of the moment decision. She had made a will six months before her death, so that all her affairs were in order and at the same time had mentioned to Tim Symonds that she thought she would commit suicide – something that at the time he found difficult to take seriously. Both Symonds and her father emphasised that nothing in her relationship with Tony, who had always been supportive, could have triggered the final, tragic conclusion.

At Launceston Place, Lucy was just off to India to stay with Jeremy Fry's cousin, the painter Anthony Fry, and his wife, who had bought a palace in Fort Cochin, Kerala, in southern India. She had ordered a taxi to take her to the airport and when the doorbell rang, thinking it was the taxi, she opened the door. There stood a man in an overcoat who stepped forward and said: 'I need to speak rather urgently with Lord Snowdon.'

Tony was downstairs in his studio as usual, so Lucy went down and said: 'There's somebody upstairs who urgently wants to see you – it sounds quite important.' At that moment her taxi arrived and she went off. The man to whom she had answered the door was a *Daily Mirror* reporter, who had learned of the message on the answerphone.

When Tony came down to speak to him after Lucy's departure to be faced with the news that his long-time friend and lover had committed suicide, he was deeply shocked and distressed. Tears sprang to his eyes as he said how sad he was. 'It's a horrid, horrid thing. Ann was terribly nice and great fun. I never thought she would take her own life. I don't know the details and I don't want to know them. I think a lot was wrong with her. I've seen her on and off over the years and never talked about her private life at all.' When the *Mirror* reporter told him that the paper was aware of his long sexual relationship with Ann, he put his hand up to his face and said only, 'Uh-huh. I'm not going to elaborate on this at all. I certainly wouldn't dream of talking about her in any way except that she was a friend and it's a very, very sad incident that has happened.'

Ann was cremated at Golders Green Cemetery on Friday 10 January 1997. There were twenty-three mourners and two of her Oxford women friends read tributes. After her death, her friends discovered that she had told many of them about her affair with Tony, swearing each one to secrecy, so that all believed they were one of only a handful to know about it; in one case, she told someone newly introduced to her that for a number of years she had had a relationship with an individual far too important to name and that often a chauffeur would drop him at her mansion block and return later to pick him up. As the lift she used went directly to her flat there was little danger of meeting other tenants in it. The copious notes in her diaries, many read at the inquest, revealed not only her tangled love life but also her deep feelings for Tony. The result was a blizzard of articles and headlines as the story was revealed to the world.

Lucy, in India, learned that her husband had had a mistress for the past twenty years from a copy of *The Times*. At home, Tony rang the headmaster of his daughter Frances's school, told him that he had been involved in a scandal that would break the next day, and asked him to tell Frances. To hear this kind of news not from one of her parents but from a comparative stranger must have been hard.

For Lucy it was a bombshell. The discovery that the woman introduced always as a journalist or 'someone who is helping me with my speeches' had been having an affair with her husband not only during their courtship but right through their marriage was deeply wounding, and to realise that her daughter had learned of it without her mother's comforting presence at her side must have been extraordinarily painful. Nor did Tony, who hated discussions of this kind, give Lucy any kind of full explanation on her return.

If she had known what was to come, she would have been even unhappier. A week or so earlier, Tony had been asked to a party at the Wallace Collection to mark the centenary of the magazine *Country Life*. Its Features Editor was a young woman by the name of Melanie Cable-Alexander. Tony had spotted her across the room and asked the man to whom he was talking if he knew her. By coincidence this was John Rendall, former part-owner of the Surrendell commune visited by Margaret. 'Yes,' said Rendall, 'cracking girl, isn't she?' and introduced them. The meeting made little impact on Melanie – but during the course of the evening Rendall could not help noticing Tony's obvious interest in her.

The following year, the annual meeting of the Snowdon Award Scheme and the presentation of its awards took place in the House of Commons for the first time, on 5 March 1998.* In his

---

* And for every year subsequently.

introductory address Tony, after welcoming Alan Howarth, a minister in the Department for Education and Employment with particular responsibility for the needs of anyone disabled (Labour had succeeded the Major government in the General Election of 1 May 1997), remarked that both Major and William Hague had formerly been Ministers with responsibility for disabled people ('I say this not to suggest that this appointment is always a stepping stone for better things') and that he hoped that the new government would continue to give the needs of disabled people the highest priority. He then presented the first Snowdon Special Award to Lord Morris of Manchester, as the designer and promoter of the first major Act for disabled people* and the first ever Minister for Disabled People (1974–9).

The new young Prime Minister, Tony Blair, responded, promising that in the coming review of the welfare state 'we will ensure that all disabled people get support and help tailored to their needs'. He concluded by saying: 'The Snowdon Awards are a valuable and important way of extending these opportunities.'

On 22 July 1998, the Survey commissioned by the Trustees of the Snowdon Award Scheme was published, launched with a ceremony in the Senior Common Room of the Royal College of Art. Again, it was inaugurated with a speech by Tony, first explaining what they had already done, what they were currently able to do – maximum grants of £2,500 for two years, 'a meagre sum but often the difference between giving up and carrying on' – and what they hoped to do. 'We want to know whether the experience we have gained in seventeen years could help the Government in bringing to reality its New Deal for underprivileged people – the concept of which we all applaud but which I sincerely hope will not be just a flippant label.' The words 'as "Cool Britannia" seems to have become' were tactfully crossed out.

The Survey was based on the evidence given to the Snowdon Working Party of 1997 by more than 200 disabled people (all sixteen or over) engaged academically in anything from GCSEs to doctoral research. Its main proposals were the extension of Disabled Students' Allowances to part-time, postgraduate and second-

---

* The Chronically Sick and Disabled Persons Act of 1970.

degree students; a fair system to replace discretionary awards; the creation of a single student support agency for England and Wales (as in Scotland), to reduce regional variations in financial support; and government spending reviews on Social Security benefits for disabled people.

Finance, as always, loomed large. As one paragraph pointed out, not only did disabled students usually require more money for accommodation and transport than the able-bodied, but also they did not have the cash-generating options open to others, such as student jobs in restaurants or bars, and because they could not do this it was more difficult both to acquire a student loan and to pay it back later. Only ten per cent of all the students interviewed felt that they received sufficient financial help from their Local Education Authority. A large majority – around three-quarters – of part-time students believed they had hardly been supported at all. One of the commonest complaints was that many LEAs expected students to pay for (non-medical) help first and reclaim later – but few had the funds to do this. Sometimes an LEA had not heard of certain responsibilities it was supposed to bear.

One undergraduate, unable to take notes during lectures, was told by the student counsellor that she was entitled to a tape recorder. Only when she showed a copy of the relevant regulations, where this was clearly stated, to her LEA did they pay up … a year later. Another put the same point in more overarching fashion. 'The main thing in my experience with the LEA and the DSS (Department of Social Security) is that you must approach them already knowing your rights and then you have a starting point – information is not forthcoming.' Even those who believed they had had good support spoke of the time and willpower needed to overcome the hurdles of red tape, production of the necessary evidence and delays caused by the slowness of official reaction.

Extending support to part-time (mainly postgraduate) students was another important point raised. The experience of one, who wrote seventy-five letters to charities – speaking to many more on the telephone – before receiving help summed it up. 'I could not claim Disabled Student Allowance, granted to me as an undergraduate but withheld from a postgrad course even though I must pass this course to practise [law]. Postgraduate study is in any case more vital for disabled people – we have to over-qualify in order to compete with "normal" people. I pointed out to the Local Authority that an MSc would increase my job prospects – but it made no difference at all.'

Sometimes students worried that attempting to educate themselves would mean they lost benefits – as would any kind of part-time work that they might be able to find. 'I was worried because I was assessed as eighty per cent disabled and incapable of ever working. I was afraid I would lose my benefits if I proved I could study a course,' said one.

Tony's work for disabled people meshed well with his position in the Royal College of Art. His suggestions to help disabled students resulted in a number of improvements to the College's facilities. Among the small but effective changes that he suggested were realigning the handrails at the front steps to make them more user-friendly, installing handrails on both sides of the wide steps in the link gallery, painting handrails in galleries a different colour from the walls to improve visibility, indicating changes in floor levels by a coloured strip and putting up prominent signs directing wheelchair users to the College's large lift. A little later he inaugurated a department called Designing for Disabilities, going with the students to the Disability Road Show. 'I wanted to get the students out of the College to meet disabled people so that they would understand the problems real people face and what's needed.'

He was becoming ever more attached to the College. He found himself energised by the young people there, he loved their creativity, which sparked his own, and he enjoyed talking to them. Even arguments in the photographic department were fun. Most of the students there regarded themselves as artists rather than reporters: their attitude was 'I want to get into the best art galleries,' rather than 'I want to take a good portrait,' or 'I want to be the best photojournalist.' Tony, who loathed pretentiousness of any sort, and refused to regard photography as an art, found the 'Tate Modern, here I come.' approach antipathetic. 'Just make sure you get the f-stop right, you use the right kind of film and you take the lens cap off,' he would say. Although photography had moved on, his track record was such that all listened to him with respect.

His relationship with the man he always meticulously called 'Rector' was fruitful and enjoyable. Sometimes he would visit Frayling at the latter's house in Bath, where Frayling spent weekends; and about once in every two months Frayling would come to Launceston Place for what became known as a Provostial breakfast – basically, a grand fry-up. Frayling would arrive around 7.30 and Tony, with help, would make the breakfast: bacon, sausage, fried egg and tomato, followed by toast and Marmite, dished out of a silver container. Frayling ate everything; Tony ate sparingly of the toast and Marmite. Over this feast, they would discuss College affairs, gossip would be exchanged, Tony would reminisce, perhaps about his childhood and nanny, perhaps about a photographic assignment that had meant much to him.

There were letters of congratulation in Tony's small, rapid handwriting. 'My dear Rector … could you please pass on my congratulations and best wishes to the students whose work I admired in Industrial Design, engineering, print-making, furniture and fashion.' 'My dear Rector, I was truly impressed by all the work in progress that I saw today – would you please convey my warmest thanks to Kate and Eleanor for arranging it all so splendidly.' 'I was *really* impressed by all the work I saw. Many congratulations.'

As well as visits to the shows and the students, he attended all the meetings, of which there were about half a dozen a year. He went to the lunches, where the College kitchen produced the traditional English dishes he liked, such as roast beef and bread and butter pudding of which, even though favourites, he would only eat sparingly.

As always, no detail was too small to escape him. 'My dear Provost,' runs one letter from Sir Christopher, 'Thank you so much for your letter about the back entrance and, in particular, the skip. The big problem is where to hide the skip while retaining as many parking spaces as possible. Watch this space ….'

The College, his own thriving studio work, the constant letters, the campaigning, left little time for anything else. Or so one would have thought – wrongly.

19

Melanie

❊

'Most people in Tony's life don't know what's going on in other areas,' one of his assistants once told the author. 'He is brilliant at keeping a lot of balls in the air at once – but sometimes, they all crash. And then there's massive fallout.' One of those times was about to follow.

Melanie Cable-Alexander, the young woman who was, in many senses, to prove Tony's nemesis, was a stylish, intelligent and attractive creature of thirty-three – the same age as Tony's daughter Sarah – when they first met briefly in February 1997. She had previously worked as a secretary on the *Financial Times*, which she had left seven years earlier to be a trainee journalist with *Country Life*, becoming its Features Editor a year later.

Born on 14 September 1963, she was the elder daughter of Lt-Col. Sir Patrick Cable-Alexander, 8th Baronet and Bursar of Lancing College since leaving the Scots Guards. Her parents divorced in 1976, Melanie and her younger sister remaining close to their mother, who married Brigadier David Edelsten (*Country Life's* polo correspondent) as her second husband, living with him in the village of Glanville Wootton, near Sherborne in Dorset. Tall and slim, with glossy brown hair, an excellent figure – often displayed in such un-*Country Life* attire as hot pants or leopard-skin tights – Melanie had a warm, open, sexy manner. Many men found her irresistibly attractive.

To celebrate its centenary, *Country Life* asked various people eminent in the field of the arts or design to guest-edit one of its fortnightly issues. Tony was asked if he would be the guest editor for the issue of 6 November 1997. With his knowledge of photography and layouts, his strong views on the presentation of a subject, he was a natural choice. It was a project that greatly appealed to him. As anyone who knew him could have foretold, his approach was hands-on (in this case, it would be all too literally). His enthusiasm and determination to be involved in every aspect of that November issue took everyone in the *Country Life* office by surprise – many of the guest editors had limited themselves to occasional visits to the office and a general approval of features they had suggested or, more likely, had had suggested to them.

Tony, on the other hand, as the magazine's staff were soon to find, took over completely. He was determined to oversee the whole issue from start to finish, his eye on every detail, with professional thoroughness. He would often stay until late in the evening, sitting in front of a computer screen working on layouts – his particular interest – surrounded by the increasingly weary staff of the magazine's art department. When the issue eventually appeared, it was stuffed with famous names, many of them Tony's friends, from Simon Callow and David Puttnam to Rabbi Lionel Blue and the novelist Mary Wesley.

The first real contact between Tony and Melanie was when Clive Aslett, the Editor of *Country Life*, took them both out to lunch to discuss Tony's issue and the shape it would take – as Features Editor, Melanie would be working closely with Tony. Melanie felt an immediate sense of rapport with this good-looking older man sparkling with ideas and fun. She found him, as so many had before, compelling; he had, she thought, great presence – not necessarily a comfortable presence but one of which it was impossible to be unaware.

As she lived in a flat in Gloucester Road, only a few minutes' walk from Launceston Place, she developed the habit of going there in the morning on the way to the office if there was anything that needed discussion or that Tony wanted doing. Her role, she quickly found, was that of an amanuensis: she had to prepare notes or layouts for him to look at, write to all the people he wanted to contribute to his issue or ring them up and cajole them if they were reluctant. Most difficult of all, and equally characteristic of Tony to hand on to someone else to do, was telling them if something they had done was not to his liking.

Faxes would arrive for her at the office addressed to 'Darling Melanie' – but then, he called everyone 'Darling' – and signed 'Snowdrop', but the idea that the two of them would ever embark on an affair never entered Melanie's head, although she enjoyed their lunches, often with the *Country Life* Art Editor. Attractive though she found Tony, he was twice her age and married. Moreover, she had just parted from a boyfriend with whom she had been living for some years.

One day he told her he would like her to see Old House. Although she did not immediately realise what a mark of favour this was, she gladly accepted his invitation to lunch there. After a contretemps over directions – he had said turn left at a telephone box but that morning the box had been removed – she finally arrived and, after a pleasant lunch with Tony, Lucy and Frances, left again for London.

Next time she went down, no one else was there. This time, Tony made it clear how attracted he was by her. After that, one thing led to another and by late May they had started an affair. From then on Melanie, deeply in love with him, visited Old House constantly. It became the place where they conducted their romance; at first Tony would drive Melanie down there for weekends, later she would drive Tony. Although they often met midweek in London, the visits to Launceston Place were largely for work.

At Old House local friends, who treated them as a couple, came over for coffee or a meal. Sometimes Tony's half-brother Peregrine and his wife Caroline came to stay, both of whom developed a great affection for Melanie. She was, they thought, extraordinarily kind to Tony. After dinner, cooked by the two women, Caroline and Melanie would wash up together – Tony's face was still resolutely set against any modern extravagances like dishwashers or microwaves. In their turn, the Armstrong-Joneses asked Melanie to come and stay in Wales with Tony.

To Melanie, Lucy seemed unhappy, both in herself and with Tony (as any wife might be who had only weeks earlier suffered the revelation of a long-term mistress). At Launceston Place the pair hardly met during the day: Lucy had always remained upstairs while Tony carried on his working life in and around the basement studio, secretary, assistants and assorted visitors coming and going constantly through the side door with its loud, echoing bell.

By September Melanie realised she was pregnant. Far from being a planned pregnancy, it was a complete shock – 'a mistake', she said later. Neither she nor Tony had wanted a child although it had been left to Melanie to ensure that they did not have one. Nervously she broke the news to Tony, uncertain of what his reaction would be. It was all that she could have hoped. It was entirely her decision as to whether or not she had the baby, he told her; if she decided to, he would stand by her.

At first Melanie was undecided. Pregnant by someone extremely well known but who wished to preserve his marriage and therefore wanted secrecy, she wondered what would be the effect on a child growing up with a father who could not be acknowledged. She was thirty-four – was this going to be her only chance of having a child by someone she loved? She had no real home (except with her mother in Dorset, which was far from Tony) and not much money. Could she look after a child *and* keep her job? With all these thoughts churning round in her head, coupled with the hormonal upset of pregnancy, she soon found herself plunged in a maelstrom of confusion and misery, exacerbated by the fact that she could not discuss them with Tony – despite his protectiveness of her, he simply would not take part in such conversations.

Although Melanie had always wanted children, she had intended that this would be in the context of a settled, firm, open relationship. The difficulties attendant on bringing up a child on her own, with a 'secret' but well-known father were daunting. Eventually she decided that the opportunity to have a child by someone she loved overrode all other considerations and she would go ahead and accept the consequences – later, when her son was in her arms, she was to wonder why she had ever hesitated.

As Melanie's pregnancy became more obvious, one of her visits to Launceston Place prompted Lucy to ask Tony who the father was. 'Oh, some man . . .' he replied vaguely. 'I think she had a one-night stand.' Lucy, who after the Ann Hills affair had perforce realised that her husband was practised at dissimulation, was not convinced. She felt confused and suspicious: if Tony turned out to be dissembling over this, what else was he concealing? He had always drunk a lot but now he was drinking more – and drink put a sharper edge to his tongue. She found it difficult to believe Tony's assurances of love – to Lucy, love was something based on truth and trust – but the alternative was almost unbearable. Melanie, on her side, had been telling her lover that she thought he should tell Lucy the truth; if he wanted the marriage to work, he should face square-on what was happening.

At the time, they were conducting what Melanie later described as 'a very strong relationship'. Then, in the New Year, when she was around six months pregnant, a different dialogue began. 'Lucy is asking me whose your baby is,' he would begin. 'What are you saying?' Melanie would respond. To which his response would be, 'Well, I don't know – whose is it?'

As any woman would be, Melanie was devastated at the implication. 'I probably lived most of my pregnancy in tears, and the months afterwards. It was the most awful time.' Tony, either unconvinced, hoping against hope, prompted by Lucy or desperately trying to save his marriage, said he thought Melanie had better have a DNA test. Melanie was happy to agree and the tests were organised by Melanie's gynaecologist from the Chelsea and Westminster Hospital, at a cost of £650, with Tony's name put forward as 'Mr Jones'. They proved without a shred of doubt that Tony was the father.

At last, in late January 1998, Lucy learned the truth unequivocally. One evening Tony telephoned Melanie, and said he was putting Lucy onto the telephone. She asked Melanie if the child she was carrying was Tony's. 'I'm really sorry but I'm afraid it is,' replied Melanie. 'Thank you very much,' said Lucy politely, 'I just wanted to know the truth.' For Lucy this confirmation of what she had suspected and feared was too much. Her love for Tony had been wholehearted and totally committed, she had vowed that she would never leave him and never cause him to feel rejected, as he had been by that early and fateful distancing by his mother; she believed that he would see that she, Lucy, would never repudiate him in any way.

Now she felt utterly betrayed. As someone to whom honesty was essential, what made this feeling like a dagger in her heart was that he had not, as she put it, 'been straight with her'. Originally she had never believed that the failure of his marriage to Princess Margaret was Tony's fault, an opinion that inevitably was changing. In mid-April she moved out of Launceston Place, telling reporters that she and Tony were having a trial separation. At the time this was put down as a reaction to the Ann Hills affair; Lucy, while neither confirming nor denying this theory, merely told the press: 'I feel I need some time alone. People have been very kind to me.'

Two weeks later, on 30 April 1998, Melanie's son Jasper William Oliver was born, after a seventeen-hour labour, on the NHS in the Chelsea and Westminster, weighing nine and a half pounds. Tony's name was not on the birth certificate. On her return from hospital Melanie had nowhere to live – before Jasper was born, she had stayed for a month in Hammersmith with a friend of her mother's but it was not a house to which she could bring a child. At first she moved from friend to friend, on a purely temporary basis. Since the identity of the baby's father was not known – except to a handful of her family and friends – nor yet suspected, Tony was not invited to Jasper's christening (as a christening present, he sent Jasper a small silver Peruvian horse). But, conscious of the need for her son to have as much support as possible in the future if he was to grow up without a publicly acknowledged father, he was given eight godparents.

Gradually rumours began to spread in the wider world that Melanie's child had been fathered by Tony. One day, returning home, Melanie saw two men walking backwards and forwards outside her door, as though waiting for someone. She took Jasper for a walk to the nearby Post Office and noticed they were following her. Suddenly she realised they might be journalists.

Nothing happened for a week, during which she did not see Tony: the physical difficulties of looking after a small baby, extreme fatigue – Jasper, like many newborns, woke up throughout the night – and hunting for somewhere to live consumed most of her time. One day he telephoned to ask her for a drink and to help him photograph a lodge he was including in a book about London that he was preparing. When he arrived to pick her up two photographers were waiting outside the door. That night, proofs of the story which was to appear in the following day's paper were pushed through their respective doors. After the story broke, on 28 July, press interest was intense – Christopher Frayling would often see paparazzi lurking outside Launceston Place when he arrived for one of his Provostial breakfasts.

The most pressing question was money to keep going. When she spoke to his lawyer, John Humphries, about this, he said that Tony was prepared to offer support. So that it could be put on a proper footing, Melanie too acquired a lawyer, feeling that it was best that the two lawyers thrashed things out between them (it was only now, with the need for clarity over financial affairs, that Lucy learned of her husband's divorce settlement from the royal family, with the Launceston Place house in trust for the children). Despite the difficulties inherent in this, amounting at times to confrontation over Melanie's needs and the amount Tony was prepared to offer, the affair continued.

After Lucy had left, they saw each other more and more, spending weekends at Old House together. For Tony sex, as always, was a motivating force, retaining its impetus even with the high intake of alcohol that had been a constant of his adult life. Melanie, for her part, as well as being in love with him, was trying to maintain their bond for Jasper's sake, so that he would have a relationship with his father. As small children, like animals – and Melanie had just acquired a Jack Russell terrier – had never appealed to Tony, this was not an easy process. The dog was not allowed into his house.

At the same time, Tony was desperately trying to patch up his marriage to Lucy. He wrote to her and persuaded friends to talk to her and plead his cause or try and arrange 'accidental' meetings. Frayling would receive telephone calls asking him to invite Lucy to such and such an exhibition at the Royal College where Tony could meet her 'by chance', or at dinners, against all protocol, they would be seated next to each other so that Tony might have a chance to regain some ground. But none of these efforts worked: Tony could not bring himself to do the one thing Lucy wanted – have a long and completely frank discussion between the two of them in which he would answer all her questions truthfully. One friend remembered walking down Bond Street with him after an art gallery private view, with Lucy and Sarah following behind. 'Do you think Lucy would ever come back to me?' asked Tony. 'Why are you asking me?' responded his friend. 'Why don't you ask *her*? But you'll have to talk to her – I mean, really *talk* to her.'

From Lucy's point of view, how could a marriage work without communication? For without communication, how could trust be rebuilt? She had been betrayed twice (to her knowledge); how did she know it was not going to happen a third time? She felt that if Tony wanted a divorce or to marry Melanie, he would have to ask her for it, and tell her the reason why. Her feelings could be summed up as: 'For once he was going to have to tell the truth'; that is, the truth of what happened – and why. But talking, in that sense, was something he could not do. Accordingly, she withdrew further from his life; on the practical side, she requested no further involvement in the Launceston Place housekeeping arrangements (formerly her province) and the monthly payments of £2,800 to the housekeeping account were stopped that October. Tony's secretary was put in charge of handling day-to-day payments and paying their wages, respectively £190 and £50, to the daily and the housekeeper Nettie.

The birth of Jasper polarised opinions among their friends. The majority took Lucy's part. She had, they felt, been an admirable wife, all those who had met her liked her greatly and, though most of the more long-standing ones knew that Tony was given to dalliances, these had been reasonably discreet. A baby was something else – something that could not be 'swept under the carpet'. David and Sarah, who loved Lucy, were deeply upset on her behalf. Several of those who knew Tony felt that Melanie had tried to trap him into marriage by starting a baby – something that hurt her bitterly when she discovered it – others that she had been hard done by. 'After all, it *does* take two to tango,' said one. 'And he has had a lot more experience in these things than her.' Or as his lawyer put it to Tony: 'If I were you, I should stick to women over fifty in future.'

His life at this point was dismal. For the first time for many years, much of his time was spent completely alone. To his friends –

those who remained close – he seemed low and depressed. One of them was the Vice-President of the Council of the Royal College of Art, Helen Robinson, whom he had first met during Pimlico Road days in the fifties, then again when he was working in New York for *Vogue*. After meetings, she would give him a lift back to Launceston Place in her car and check that a light was on indoors in case he fell – the house was invariably in darkness.

Asked to stay for a drink and then supper, she would go with him to the kitchen – he had stopped using the drawing room and dining room after Lucy's departure. Never a big eater, his needs were now simpler than ever. A rout round the fridge might produce some bread, butter and a couple of cold sausages; the elderly Nettie from down the road who looked after him would have laid one end of the scrubbed kitchen table for supper and the other for breakfast. Although Melanie came round when she could, most of her life was occupied by her job, her child and her flat and he, who hated being alone, was often on his own. It was a bleak scene, with another cause for depression the knowledge that one of his oldest friends, the designer Carl Toms, was dying.

He did his best to help, inviting Toms to come and stay, but this had become impossible. 'Dearest Tony,' replied Toms, 'Thank you for your loving and caring letter. It means a lot to me. I know you want what is best for me. So kind of you to ask me to stay with you but I am like a wounded animal and want to crawl under a stone. My love for you is boundless, my oldest friend. You have done so much to support me and I treasure your love but I must be left alone in my misery to cope as best as I can. I am so grateful that you care so much. I can't travel for any reason so I am here housebound. I don't mind that much as long as I am left alone. I am seventy-one you see and have severe emphysema. Love you a lot, ever Carl.'*

Tony's lifeline was work, although even here there were disappointments. The royal connection was still there, but the most glamorous member of the royal family had deserted him for another photographer. When Diana, Princess of Wales decided to sell seventy-nine of her dresses for charity at auction in New York

---

* Carl Toms died on 4 August 1999.

Tony had originally been chosen to take the fifteen-odd catalogue pictures. They were evening gowns and Diana was pictured made-up and in formal poses.

But both Diana and Meredith Etherington-Smith, who was handling the sale, realised that Diana had stepped aside from formality in more than her clothes. Fresh pictures were commissioned from the new star Mario Testino, who depicted a relaxed, laughing Diana, without shoes or jewellery. The catalogues alone, with these fifteen iconic images, accounted for a high proportion of the final £5.7 million raised. Tony was deeply upset at this snub to his work and from then on Testino's name raised his hackles. Paradoxically, Tony's own pictures of Princess Margaret during the early years of their marriage had the same quality of carefree glamour that Testino evoked.

Working with his hands, though, was still a pleasure – early in the year he received a note from his former wife enclosing the parts of a watch. ('Darling T, Just after you sent me the coaster you had mended, for which Mum was most grateful, I was tidying up at Royal Lodge and believe it or not there these [the watch parts] were at the back of a drawer ... love from M'.)

In May 1998 he received a morale-boosting mark of distinction when the Snowdon Aviary at the London Zoo was listed Grade II starred. In the autumn College affairs became a preoccupation: the Albert Memorial, newly refurbished by English Heritage, was due to be unveiled on 21 October by the Queen, who was also to visit the Royal College. Tony, as Provost, was much involved.

Preparations had begun early in the summer, when Sir Jocelyn Stevens, writing to Tony, told him that as well as opening the Memorial the Queen would present a new Charter to the nearby Imperial College after which she would meet senior dignitaries from the various institutions in the area founded by Prince Albert. Letters and faxes flew between Tony and Stevens (now head of English Heritage). He told Stevens that he was delighted his suggestions for the platform on which the Queen and the rest of the party would be seated were accepted. These echoed the philosophy of the Investiture in 1969 ('as simple as possible'), with Perspex canopies, plastic chairs and a Perspex lectern.

'It looks splendid,' he wrote on the very morning of the great day, 'but the two scaffolding stands are far too close. I beg of you to authorise them to be moved twenty foot further out – they will ruin every photograph as well as surely being too close to the Queen ... it only took $\frac{1}{2}$ an hour to put them up. It just would look much better and wiser for security reasons,' adding rather unconvincingly at the end, 'of course it's none of my business'. He was, naturally, right in his suggestions, which were immediately accepted.

The Queen's half-hour visit to the College began with her arrival at the front door at precisely 7.05, where she was met by Tony, who presented to her the Rector and Chairman with their wives and the Curator. At 7.30 she left for the Memorial and a twenty-minute son et lumière presentation, after which she declared the Memorial open. The following day Tony received a letter from her Private Secretary saying how much she had enjoyed the exhibition. 'She talked about it for some time after her return to Buckingham Palace.'

Tony was equally ready to concern himself with smaller matters to do with his beloved College. He wrote numerous times to Westminster Council to ask if their (licensed) ice cream traders could be allocated a different site, rather than the one they occupied outside the College front door. He pointed out that the vans permitted to park there, north of a disabled parking bay, blocked up the east–west pedestrian pavement, 'thereby forcing ped-estrians, children and wheelchair users into the busy mainstream traffic of Kensington Gore'. They also hid the posters and banners put up by the College to announce their exhibitions. But the main objection was their unsightliness in front of the newly refurbished Albert Memorial. 'It may be helpful for you to know that under the London Local Authorities Act 1990, visual amenity is not a ground for refusal of a licence,' the Council's Environment and Planning Department wrote back primly.

Finally, as a last hope, Tony wrote to Sir Paul Condon, the Metropolitan Police Commissioner, saying that the vans had been given all-day permission to park illegally on a double yellow line and had been supplied with pavement electricity 'presumably by the Council. Without doubt sooner or later someone will be knocked down. All it needs is for the approved site to be relocated south by twenty-five yards or so.' But it was no good. This was one battle Tony (and the Royal Albert Hall, which also complained) lost. Condon's reply stated that the licence, granted by Westminster City Council, effectively overrode parking restrictions and double yellow lines and that there was no evidence that the vans had ever contributed to any accident. In other words, nothing could be done.

In the New Year of 1999 Tony received a new honour that must have, even if obliquely, recognised the value of the work he was doing for disabled people. The reform of the House of Lords, with its concurrent ejection of most of the hereditary peers, was under way. Life peers, of whom the presumption was that they had 'earned' their ennoblement by meritorious actions or outstanding achievements, were to remain. Tony, however, was an hereditary peer of the first creation (i.e. the 1st Earl of Snowdon) and like all of those currently in the House of Lords for whom a hereditary peerage had been specifically created – as opposed to those who inherited it from an ancestor – he was offered a life peerage so that he might remain in the Upper House. In his letter of 19 January 1999 asking Tony if he would wish the Prime Minister to recommend to the Queen that she award him a life peerage, Tony Blair wrote: 'The Government recognises that in many important respects the first holders of hereditary peerages are akin to life peers and that the more controversial features of peerages by succession certainly do not apply to them.' On 21 January Tony replied: 'I would be delighted and honoured for you to go ahead with this recommendation.' On 16 November that year he became Baron Armstrong-Jones of Nymans in the County of West Sussex.

While critics could say that Tony had 'earned' his peerage merely by virtue of marrying the Queen's sister, one by-product of his hard and unremitting work for disabled people, for whom he was interested in improving conditions rather than following any kind of party line, was that he was considered a valuable addition to the House of Lords. The cheers of his fellow peers when he took the Oath of Allegiance to the Monarch at the despatch box on 2 December 1999 seem to prove this.

Soon after this, there was another example of his ongoing concern for the less fortunate. One night in 2000 Tony and his half-brother Peregrine visited the Millennium Dome but when they arrived Tony was not allowed entry because he was disabled. This was exactly the sort of injustice against which he had been campaigning for so long and he was so furious that he took action at once. He telephoned the Manager of the Dome and, speaking fiercely and authoritatively, told him that unless things were changed he would organise reporters there from newspapers the following day to expose this inequity. Cowed, the Manager gave way. Tony fired a final broadside. 'The only reason you're changing it', he said, 'is because I'm Lord Snowdon and you're scared of being exposed. But the reason I'm angry is that if I were a lady from Sheffield on a walking frame I wouldn't be able to get in. *That* is why you should be ashamed of yourself.'

In contrast to his articulacy and complete lack of embarrassment in speaking out against what he perceived as injustice, Tony still found even the simplest announcement in public a nerve-racking ordeal. When he was asked to open the new Dean Gallery in Edinburgh – a former orphanage refurbished to house the National Galleries of Scotland's collection of Surrealist art – it reduced him almost to a pulp. 'But Tony, you only have to say four sentences,' said the Countess of Airlie, Chairman of the Trustees, amazed that someone who had been so much in the public eye should be in such a state. Privately she wondered if he would be able to do it; in the event, he handled it perfectly. Surprisingly for such a veteran of royal tours, accustomed to being stared at by large crowds and adept at 'working' a roomful of strangers, this terror of public speaking never left him.

Melanie had been offered a great deal of money by various newspapers to tell her story but had refused them all – tempting though the million or so she could have made was to someone with not much money of her own and a child to care for. One of those that had approached her was *Hello!* magazine, which she turned down several times. Then, one day while she was still homeless and living with Jasper in one room in a friend's house, Tony asked her to accept *Hello!*'s lucrative offer in order to finance or part-finance a house. Hating the idea but longing for somewhere settled to live, she finally consented, thinking of it later as one of the most unhappy times of her life.

The interview, published on 13 February 1999, did, however, make two things absolutely clear: that she, and she alone, would be bringing Jasper up ('he's a Cable-Alexander and not an Armstrong-Jones and that's final') and that Tony was an absentee father. When asked how often he came to visit his son, she replied: 'He has never visited Jasper. He has seen him on a few occasions, though, when I've been out pushing the pram.' The feature, which brought in £250,000, financed half the house that was finally bought. The other half, bought by Tony, was to be owned by Melanie until Jasper's eighteenth birthday, when it would revert to Tony or to his estate. A month later, in March, Lucy moved into a flat nearby in Kensington.

As their affair continued, Melanie found that its drawbacks were beginning to outweigh the positive aspects. She was still in love with him, she found him fascinating and absorbing, and she was anxious that the relationship should continue for Jasper's sake. This, however, was proving more difficult to manage. Jasper was no longer a baby, asleep for most of the time and easily portable. With Tony's low boredom threshold, need to be constantly entertained, and preference for being the main focus of attention, he not only lacked the patience necessary to establish any kind of bond with a two-year-old but also disliked the idea of that two-year-old claiming most of its mother's attention.

Weekends at Old House were the times that the three of them spent together. Here Tony, who liked everything around him to be neatly ordered and arranged in its special place, would, even in the freedom of the country, try and discipline Jasper – attempts that were foiled by Melanie's more indulgent, gentle firmness. Although Jasper was not allowed to call him Papa like his other children, but Daddy, Tony did, however, acknowledge his son publicly, with an entry in the 106th edition of *Burke's Peerage and Baronetage* (published in 1999).

Melanie found her lover controlling and over-possessive of her time – something difficult to incorporate into life with a small child – and (as several other women have remarked unprompted to the author), too demanding sexually, with a libido higher than most men half his age. There would be half a dozen phone calls a day – partly because as his mobility declined, the telephone was becoming ever more of a lifeline, a way of reaching out to those he wanted or needed to see and reeling them in. Once, when she lost her mobile phone, she made no effort to find it or get another for a week in order to have some freedom.

At the same time, Tony was determined not to admit that his marriage had 'irretrievably broken down'; he and Lucy exchanged letters, telephoned and met each other. In both their minds was the possibility that one day they might be together again but their views of how this might happen were very different and, ultimately irreconcilable: Tony wished that the past could be forgiven and forgotten, Lucy believed that only by talking everything out fully and truthfully could they contemplate life together again. In the interim she wanted a temporary break of contact so that they could both consider how to proceed. She also needed financial support as, unaware of Tony's post-divorce settlement from Margaret, she had spent almost all her own money on Launceston Place and Old House.

Although Lucy had left there was no question of Melanie and Jasper moving into Launceston Place. Quite apart from Tony's hope that Lucy might perhaps return, to have a tiny child roaming free – as opposed to safely tethered on the top floor with a nanny – was for Tony the equivalent of inviting a tiger into his home. He would have been on edge all the time and as a consequence so would everyone else in the house. Nor would he have contemplated making Launceston Place into a childproof house. The result was that Melanie would call at the house on her way back from her work at *Country Life* before going home to release Jasper's childminder and cope with the rest of her life, from catching up with her friends to cooking or clothes-washing. It was an exhausting routine.

Gradually the affair began to crumble. With no help, Melanie found it difficult to go to Launceston Place as often as her lover wished. And as he had made clear, if she did not, he might stray. Nor did she feel able to take Jasper there: many of the surfaces in the house were covered with exquisite small objects that an ordinarily inquisitive child could pick up, drop, break or mislay. From

Tony's point of view a child was in the way. Children, in fact, only interested him as they got older, became able to ask questions and share in the sort of activities he enjoyed. Otherwise they should, as in his own early life, be seen and not heard: in a sense, his lack of interest in them replicated his own childhood.

His older children were a different matter. He was immensely proud of David's success, he greatly admired Sarah's painting and he could not do enough for Frances, who had gone over to Paris to work for French *Vogue*. He would go over by train to see her, taking his toolbox, with which he converted the bathroom of her flat and made shutters for it. It was, however, Frances's godmother Pamela Lady Harlech who gave Frances her twenty-first birthday party on 6 July 2000, dinner in the garden of her large house in Ladbroke Road, with dancing afterwards. The adults – a few friends like Simon Sainsbury and the Frys – sat at two tables pushed together but Tony, in one of his fits of contrariness, sat elsewhere, although his attempt at an early departure was firmly stopped by Pamela Harlech.

In 2000 Lucy filed for divorce. The decree nisi was granted on 18 September. In court she was asked exactly when she felt her marriage was over. 'In the light of the respondent's adultery, I came to the conclusion that the marriage was at an end,' she replied. Yet neither pushed for the decree nisi to be made absolute, so that in the eyes of the law they were still married. Lucy made it clear that if her husband came to her and said that he wished to marry someone else, she would agree to an absolute. From Tony's point of view the lack of an absolute not only nourished his hope, admittedly growing fainter, that Lucy might return to him but also was the perfect defence if anyone else should try and push him into marriage. From then on, if a newspaper referred to him as being divorced, he would write immediately to point out that, actually, he was still married.

Whatever the vicissitudes of his private life, they were not allowed to interfere with his work. His archive was huge; and when the National Portrait Gallery offered him a retrospective in February 2000, he was delighted. As his half-brother William, Lord Rosse, wrote to him, in a letter mingling congratulation with condolence: 'Never forget that however much of a pickle you might have got your personal life into just now, you have professionally just received a major record-breaking triumph with your retrospective exhibition.' This featured not only photographs but also a collection of souvenirs that bore images from the exhibition – the first time the Gallery had done so. These posters, calendars, mouse mats (with a Snowdon picture of a real mouse), diaries, a dragonfly brooch he designed out of safety pins and T-shirts proved to be money-spinners, with the merit that they continued selling after the exhibition was over. Tony and the NPG split all proceeds fifty-fifty.

The Royal College of Art continued to occupy much of Tony's time. Quite apart from his immense interest in the creative life humming under its roof, it was a welcome distraction from the increasing difficulties of his private life. His rapport with the Rector, and awareness of how much the latter was doing for the institution, meant that he was delighted when Frayling was awarded a knighthood in the New Year Honours of 2001. 'It was terrific of you to write and phone,' Frayling responded to Tony's congratulations. 'Yes, let's have a celebration fry-up at breakfast. I'll get into training for it!'

The College was also in the news for a Guildhall celebration banquet on 14 February 2001, with a Buckingham Palace prize-giving ceremony the following day. Tony, as Provost, was naturally expected to play his part. There were the usual immaculate Palace arrangements. 'I have learned that your Provost's robe is being taken to the reception in the Guildhall the night before by the RCA,' wrote the Deputy Master of the Household. 'At the end of the Guildhall function the robe will be taken from you and brought to Buckingham Palace on the Thursday morning.' There would be a lift up to the Picture Gallery where the assembly took place and a chair would be there ready, before the procession into the Ballroom where the twenty-three pairs of prize-winners would be given their medals by the Queen. For the presentation Tony, with the Duke and Duchess of Kent, would be seated in the front row near the Queen and the Duke of Edinburgh. It was a glittering occasion and a fitting acknowledgement of the part the College and its students played in the artistic and cultural life of the nation.

The day of the prize-giving was the first time Tony appeared publicly in a wheelchair. His mobility, already severely limited, had been deteriorating for some time so that when he, Melanie and Jasper visited the British Museum's Cleopatra exhibition, he had needed a wheelchair to transfer him to a special lift after Melanie had parked her car in the disabled bay. Once inside, she pushed him round the exhibits, with three-year-old Jasper scampering beside them.

Shortly afterwards, and after several attempts at gaining herself more space, she left him. Apart from the time and psychic energy needed to earn a living, the difficulties of bringing up a child on her own at the same time as handling a turbulent, complex relationship were too great. Nor, as she had come to realise, was there any future in the affair – and she wanted a life with a future. Dining together in a restaurant on her birthday, she told him that it was over – though of course they would continue to see each other for Jasper's sake. Tony, however, would not be alone for long.

20

Battling On

※

All his life, Tony was irresistible to women. From his earliest days they had buzzed about him like bees round a honeypot and, though several grew disillusioned – a disillusionment often proportionate to the intimacy of the relationship – most of them remained in contact. Gina Ward, his lover before he married Princess Margaret, wrote from Mexico, where she had settled, recalling the past and begging him to come and stay. Melanie (though refusing his frequent propositions) saw him reasonably often; old girlfriends came to lunch, and a new one soon appeared; once or twice strange girls were spotted under the duvet by the current housekeeper (Tony himself was an early riser) when she went up to make the bed.

Lucy, who had taken every step but the final one towards divorce, was in and out of the house. If she had severed all connection with her husband save that necessary over their daughter and financial matters everyone, from close friends and family to the casual readers of newspapers, would have understood. Instead, she made a conscious decision to stay in his life. A determination to do her best for their daughter was obviously one strand; another was less obvious but almost as important. Negative emotions, she felt, were corrosive; bitterness could warp personality and attitudes – and she did not want to become angry or twisted. There was, she believed, a fine line between love and hate – and she wanted to stay on the right side of the line.

Tony, for his part, hoped for some time that the lunches or dinners they enjoyed, and her sporadic but continuing presence in his house, often to pick up or leave some of her clothes, meant more. Every time they were photographed together there was renewed speculation by the press that a reconciliation was imminent; Tony himself still cherished the hope that the wife he loved dearly, despite the contradiction of his flagrant misbehaviour, would return to him. Meanwhile, with Melanie gone, there was the ever more pressing question of female companionship, with its subsidiary but important benefits.

For some time, partly owing to his increasing lameness, he had come to rely heavily on the telephone as social conduit. With Lucy gone, and many of their mutual friends less inclined to see him, he had become what no one would have predicted: lonely. He had always been good at keeping in touch; now people who had not seen him for a number of years suddenly found themselves at the receiving end of a call inviting them to lunch. A few were the servants who had worked in Kensington Palace or Clarence House. These lunches were simple affairs at the kitchen table: the housekeeper who came every morning until 12.30 would leave out smoked salmon and bread and butter or slip out to buy tuna baguettes; Tony would offer as much white or red wine as the guest could drink.

He enjoyed even more going out or being taken out to lunch at favourite restaurants, invariably choosing seats that faced into the room, partly to see but also to be seen, taking pleasure in the hum of recognition that ran round the room. Nor had his old habit of asking for something not on the menu deserted him ('I'll just have half an avocado', 'No, I want a baked potato, not mashed'). Failure to pander to these quirks, the unavailability of his usual table, the disappearance of a favourite waiter or waitress, slowness of service, could all result in the disappearance of his custom. ('Take the service charge off my bill! The food was bad and the service appalling.')

Lunch (out) had, in fact, become a ritual, with the Caprice in the lead as restaurant of choice. Marjorie Wallace, a frequent lunchtime companion, describes it. 'He carries a £50 note to pay the taxi. "You've seen one of these before? You've got change?" He comes in on my arm and I hand him over to a waiter, we make our way to "his" table – a corner one by the window, opposite the photograph of him by Bailey. If that table is ever taken I know there's going to be trouble but I've learned over the years to distract him. The waiters come over, there are kisses for favourites and he has the first of his three bullshots. He always eats the same thing – eggs Benedict followed by steak tartare, and insists on a bowl of allumettes which he never touches – though he makes a pretence of choosing. And glasses of port afterwards. So it's like a little dance – a child's nursery game.'

Old friends were still loyal but found that he could be difficult. Sometimes there was moodiness, sometimes a disregard of their commitments, a childlike mode of concentrating only on his own wants that had, earlier, been masked by the charm and spontaneity of youth.

Much of his early life had been spent subconsciously evolving a strategy for coping with feeling unloved, ranging from protecting his inner feelings by a carapace of frivolity to developing a hard-edged, hard-earned independence that included leading his life on his own terms, so that both alluring and manipulating those around him became second nature. Life under the mantle of royalty, with the superbly organised arrangements that facilitated everything from an official visit to a trip to a theatre, and the awareness that a thoughtful gesture or kindly word would probably be remembered by recipients to the ends of their lives, had also left its mark.

For anyone accustomed for years to being famous, famous is what, at some level, that person goes on expecting to be, with recognition of their celebrity, past or present, enhancing a sense of self and identity. Tony, for so long a performer on the public stage, was no different. Although consciously democratic, he still expected his housekeeper to call him 'Milord'. William Tallon, the Queen Mother's Steward until her death in 2002, an intimate for years and now his regular Sunday lunch guest, invariably called him 'My Lord' or 'Sir' – although always kissed hello and goodbye by Tony, as with Oliver's staff in the old Pelham Crescent days.

The psychiatrist Robert. B. Millman, of Cornell University Medical School, uses the phrase 'acquired situational narcissism'* to describe someone who becomes self-regarding as a result of

---

* In his book *Substance Abuse: A Comprehensive Textbook* (2005).

having fame, power and wealth thrust upon them, usually because they have quickly reached the top of their profession. He concludes: 'The result is behaviour that in many ways is similar to that of a child.' Or as one of Tony's oldest friends put it: 'the emotional map is that of a ten-year-old, coupled with a vast appetite for work and a huge sex drive'. The soft toys of his childhood – two dolls and a battered penguin – still rest on a chair in his bedroom and once, asked by a friend what his favourite book was, he answered, instantly and without hesitation, '*Peter Pan*'.

With Melanie gone, and with her the sexual aspect of their relationship – still, in his mid-seventies, as important to him as ever – more of his reeling-in calls were made to old girlfriends, or women who might be potential ones.

In the early autumn of 2001 Lucy, who had noticed the same car parked on the small slope between the front gate of 22 Launceston Place and the garage, eventually asked Tony whose it was. 'Oh, a friend down from Yorkshire who had asked if they could park their car there,' he said airily. Only when Lucy turned up unexpectedly early one morning, let herself in – she had kept her key – and, hearing voices, walked into the kitchen, did she see who the 'friend from Yorkshire' was. There she found Tony and a woman as yet unknown to her having breakfast.

Emily Hirst (always known as Emmy), the woman at the kitchen table, had a somewhat similar background to Melanie in that both their fathers were soldiers. Emmy's father, Brigadier John Hirst, was an extraordinarily handsome man, good at all sports from cricket to polo, who had served with distinction in Burma during World War II and, immediately afterwards, in French Indo-China (later to become Vietnam). Emmy herself was slim, blonde, elegant and beautiful. She had been a long-time friend and confidante of Tony's for much of her life – they had first met at Andy Garnett's twenty-first birthday party – so that when, at the beginning of September 2001, he moved the relationship up a gear, it seemed perfectly natural to both of them. Tony was, after all, as good as divorced and Emmy was completely free.

Deeply fond of him, she was anxious to help in any way she could: seeing someone whom she had known as so active, lively, sparkling and energetic now confined for most of the day to the swivel chair in front of his desk, roused pity among her other emotions. Like everyone who knew him, she admired his courage. No one had ever heard the mildest word of complaint from Tony, even when hauling himself laboriously upstairs by means of the thick rope banister he had installed up the circular stone staircase between basement and ground floor, or inching hand over hand from table to chest along a passage. 'I'm fine,' was always his response to any question about his health and nothing was more calculated to infuriate him than the adjective 'frail' attached to his name by a newspaper.

Kind, gentle, thoughtful and considerate, Emmy was balm to Tony's spirit after the loss of Lucy and the departure of Melanie. Their life together soon fell into a pattern, best described as a kind of reverse commuting. She would leave her flat in Chelsea in early evening, after the day's work could be presumed to have been finished, arrive at Launceston Place, and park her small car on the forecourt. Letting herself into the house, she and Tony would share a drink before she cooked supper on the ancient gas stove, its ignition system now requiring near-black-magic skills to induce a flame. They would eat, after which Tony would usually continue drinking and watch television – which, because of encroaching deafness, he liked on too loud for Emmy's taste – before mounting the two flights of stairs to the blue and white bedroom. Next morning, after breakfast (made by Emmy) she would leave. Sometimes they met for lunch; at weekends she might drive him to Old House or to stay with friends; more usually, she would cook his favourite roast chicken and bread sauce for Sunday lunch. It was a peaceful, almost domestic life, if quite hard work for Emmy.

By now Tony's alcohol consumption had risen to the point where those close to him had become worried. There would be two or three glasses of white wine before lunch, at which he drank red wine – and, if at a restaurant, he followed it up with port or brandy – and a regular intake of the good 'ordinary' claret from Berry Bros in the evening. But apart from a penchant for an afternoon nap, there was little sign during the day that he had drunk anything stronger than water.

*

On 9 February 2002 came a shock Tony had been dreading: the death of Princess Margaret. She had been ill for some time. In early 1998, at the end of her usual three-week visit to Mustique, she had attended a dinner party on 23 February, the day before she was scheduled to leave with her friends the Glenconners for Grand Cayman.* In the middle of dinner she had a stroke, slumping to one side of her seat. The Queen, Margaret's children and Tony were immediately telephoned and Margaret was taken via Miami to the Bayview Hospital in Barbados. On the 26th she was flown back to England, to the King Edward VII's Hospital, where she stayed for two weeks. She made a good recovery, with the stroke's only apparent legacy a tendency to tire more easily. Tony telephoned constantly to enquire about her health – attention that touched her deeply.

The following year she again went to Mustique in mid-February, joined there after a few days by her friend Janie Stevens. Stepping into the bath to wash her hair, she inadvertently turned on the bath taps instead of the shower head, and scalding water – caused by a faulty thermostat – poured over her feet. She was dazed, badly burned and in great pain. Worse still, she had to leave Les Jolies Eaux: her son David Linley, to whom it had belonged since she had transferred it to him on his twenty-seventh birthday on 3 November 1988, had let it and the new tenants were due to arrive.

For Anne Glenconner (who arrived to look after the Princess when Janie Stevens had to leave) the next fortnight was a nightmare. She had to find somewhere the seriously ill Princess could stay until she was fit to fly to hospital. After trying various people she telephoned a kindly American neighbour with a beach cottage, to which Margaret was taken by the island's ancient boneshaker ambulance. Once at the cottage, the only person Margaret would allow in her room was Anne, who had to take in her meals, clean her room and get up at night to attend to her when Margaret summoned her through the buzzer worn by Anne all the time.

Eventually, exhausted and with no sign from England, Anne telephoned the Queen and explained that she would either have to have nurses to help her or else the Princess must fly home, by

---

* Colin Tennant had succeded his father as 3rd Baron Glenconner in 1983.

Concorde, as she was just about fit enough to manage its much shorter flight time, though not that of an ordinary transatlantic flight. Concorde it was and the devoted Anne then took the Princess to the King Edward VII's Hospital. The only person who telephoned Anne after this epic feat of endurance and organisation was Tony, who said: 'I want to thank you for looking after Margaret so well,' following this up with a note of thanks.

Unable to walk, Margaret spent much of her time in her bedroom, at first in bed and then sitting in a wheelchair. It was a depressing time, as her feet took so long to heal, not helped by the knowledge that David Linley was going to sell Les Jolies Eaux, the only place that had ever been her own and where she had been so happy (it was sold in 1999 for £1.5 million).

Transporting the Princess to the different hospitals thought necessary for her treatment without publicity required ingenuity. Her chauffeur, David Griffin, found a Ford Galaxy from which the middle section was removed so that the Princess's wheelchair could be pushed in – without this, someone would have had to lift her bodily, something strictly against royal protocol.

Gradually she recovered, although she still often relied on a wheelchair – unlike her mother, who hated this vehicle and was determined to walk to the last. When the two of them went to Buckingham Palace, they would take the lift to the top-floor apartments, where the Queen had thoughtfully ordered a footman to have a wheelchair ready for the Queen Mother to traverse the lengthy passages. But when they emerged from the lift Princess Margaret would make for the chair and sit in it, to the annoyance of the Queen, who would exclaim crossly: 'For God's sake, Margaret – get out. That's meant for Mummy!' The Queen always maintained that her sister was well able to walk and, anyway, there was no excuse for taking their mother's wheelchair.

There was a similar scene at the Queen Mother's centenary (and Margaret's seventieth birthday), celebrated with a reception and dance in the State Apartments at Windsor Castle on 21 June 2000, where Margaret, elegant in cream silk, was able to enjoy herself. The Queen came back from greeting guests to say to her mother, who had been chatting to another group: 'Mummy, for goodness sake, come on – all your friends are arriving!' The Queen Mother's wheelchair was brought out but she brushed it aside and walked down the passage into the mass of people ahead, while Margaret nipped into the chair and was followed in by the 'fuming' (in the words of one onlooker) Queen.

After another, smaller, birthday party on 25 October arranged by David and Sarah, Margaret's health gradually began to deteriorate and on 4 January 2001 she suffered a second stroke. This time, her attitude to her former husband was quite different. She would refuse to take his calls and expressed herself as believing that his treatment of her had somehow precipitated her illness. Tony, naturally, found these misconceptions and her changed attitude deeply distressing – perhaps the reason for his outburst against their former mutual friend Angela Huth, who had remained steadfastly in the Princess's camp.

Angela, annoyed at the way many commentators were moralising about the effect of the Princess's earlier, hedonistic lifestyle on her health, had decided to write a supportive article pointing out Margaret's virtues as a friend – of which there were many. She first telephoned the Princess at her nursing home to find out if this would be acceptable and then, when the piece was written, sent it to her for approval or comment. Margaret told her that she was happy with it and it was published on 19 January 2001 in the *Daily Telegraph*. The immediate result was a furious telephone call from Tony, who told her that she should never have done such a thing. 'But she liked it!' said Angela. This made no difference: their relationship was ruptured until, with one of Tony's sudden voltes-face, it resumed again the following year with an invitation to lunch as if nothing had happened.

On 27 March 2001 Margaret had a third stroke. At the Queen Mother's 101st birthday celebrations on 4 August, the Princess presented a pathetic sight as she was pushed forward in a wheelchair. Her face was puffy and yet drawn, her left arm was in a sling and her eyes hidden behind large dark glasses. It was a sad and pitiable moment, made all the more poignant by the memory of her former beauty and glamour. Nine days later, Tony was also snapped being pushed along a platform in a wheelchair as he, Melanie (shortly before the end of their affair) and Jasper caught a train for Wales to stay with Peregrine. Newspapers did not hesitate to compare the plight of these two sixties icons.

Towards the end, Margaret's state was wretched. Tony was immensely concerned and rang up frequently; through the Buckingham Palace switchboard he would first be connected to one of Margaret's dressers and then, sometimes, to her. Often the Princess did not want to speak to anybody and at one stage even the Queen Mother could not get through (her solution was to arrive without warning one afternoon and walk into her daughter's bedroom). Even when Margaret agreed to see people it was only close friends like Janie Stevens or Anne Glenconner. Earlier, Roddy Llewellyn, still deeply fond of her, had been to see her but towards the end, conscious of how her once-beautiful face had altered, she refused to allow any male visitors. 'I look so awful now – I don't want them to remember me like this,' she told Anne.

On the night of 7 February she had yet another stroke. Two days later, at 6.30 a.m. on 9 February 2002, she died at the King Edward VII's Hospital, with Sarah and David by her side. Her funeral, attended by the whole royal family, took place on Friday 15 February at St George's Chapel, Windsor. Tony, who of course also came, sat with them in the choir. Against royal tradition but according to Margaret's own wishes, her body was cremated. Three days later, Tony wrote his son a heartfelt, loving letter, saying how well he had read the lesson. 'I know what agony it was for you but you did everything so perfectly. Reading the lesson must have been terrifying but you did it with such dignity and strength and at exactly the right pace.... You know how desperately proud I am of you with everything you do but this outshone them all. I hope that now you can get some time to think of all the very happy times we all had together.'

Tony remained deeply upset for months, a depression exacerbated by the death seven weeks later of the Queen Mother (on 30 March). He had kept all Margaret's letters and notes, and the photograph of her on his desk served to remind him daily of the beauty, wit, allure and excitement of the girl he had fallen in love with all those years ago. He had never allowed a word critical of her to pass his lips even in the aftermath of divorce; and as time passed, he viewed their marriage through ever-rosier spectacles.

*

Along with the complications of his private life, there were financial ones as well. With a wife now living separately, their daughter, and his son by another woman to support, Tony's expenses were mounting. As well as an annual payment to Lucy, plus the rent of her flat, there was money for Melanie, Jasper's school fees at Jordans Nursery School in Holy Innocents Church, Hammersmith, then those for Hawkesdown House in Kensington that autumn, where fees were from £2,375 a term. Accountancy fees ran at over £13,000 a year: his accountant handled everything from his business accounts and butcher, laundry and other household bills down to the minutest petty cash transaction.

His long-time friend and lawyer, John Humphries, had refused to act for him in the (near) divorce from Lucy, saying that he knew them both too well, and the sizeable bill of £10,000-plus from the leading divorce solicitors Withers and Co. was not only a shock to one who had never had to pay legal fees but also a considerable item. There were reminders from the gas, electricity and telephone services, bills from Berry Bros, Council Tax of £1,377 on Launceston Place and expenses for Old House, even though it was classified as empty, such as the £700-odd Council Tax. As he had said earlier: 'I worry about money permanently – all the time. The upkeep of things, the cost of things.'*

He was still a big earner, with a Snowdon portrait charged at £2,500, five-figure sales from reproductions of the Snowdon photographs held at Camera Press and fees coming in from editorial work, as well as from the sale of photographs from various Snowdon retrospective exhibitions which were becoming ever more popular. His annual earnings were between £250,000 and £300,000 but certain savings would have to be made.

The most obvious one was the most painful. With a heavy heart, he came to the conclusion that his beloved Old House would have to be sold. As he was no longer able to drive, he was dependent on others if he wished to go down there; once there, the former projects and activities that he had so much enjoyed were but a memory. 'Neither of my wives much liked it,' he once said and this was true, if only because both suspected – rightly – that Old

---

* In an interview with Lynn Barber on 30 October 1995.

House was the setting for many of the affairs he had conducted with other women. In May 1999 he had offered it to David and Serena Linley ('it's yours as long as you want it'), but they had other plans. Nor was it wanted by Sarah, whose life was full with her small children and her painting – she had had an extremely successful exhibition at the end of November 1999 at the prestigious Redfern Gallery in Cork Street.

Once he had made the decision, he lost little time implementing it. Old House was put on sale through the estate agents Savills in May 2002. In early June 2002 he made a last, sentimental journey there, with Clive Aslett, the editor of *Country Life*. Old House, magnet and playground for some of the best-known names of the sixties, where painters, actors, writers, models, hairdressers and royalty ate, drank, played and partied, a mixture invited, orchestrated and entertained by Tony, its charismatic focus, was put on the market for £1.5 million and sold within three weeks. Its sale was followed by the auction, at Sotheby's, of its contents, miscellanea that included everything from the wrought-iron kitchen stove to one of the few paintings done by Tony himself, 'Still Life with Lemons'.

Tony never went back. To revisit somewhere he had been so happy, as a mere guest of someone else, would have been unbearable. With its sale the last link with his childhood snapped.

In September 2002 Tony set off on a gruelling five-week trek across Siberia, to take the photographs for a 200-page coffee-table book on Russia for Mikhail Khodorkovsky,* the billionaire boss of the Russian oil firm Yukos. From Khodorkovsky's point of view, the book would add a gloss of respectability to his name in Russia and, possibly, also aid him should he decide on ventures in Britain (as had his compatriots Roman Abramovich and Boris Berezovsky). The trip had been organised by an old friend and work colleague, Victoria Charlton, who had reappeared in his life. They had first met when she and her then husband had approached him to take photographs of the Russian dancers they were bringing to the UK.

---

* On 25 October 2003 Khodorkovsky was arrested at a Siberian airport by the Russian prosecutor general's office on charges of fraud and tax evasion. On 31 May 2005 he was found guilty of fraud and sentenced to ten years in prison. Prior to his arrest, Khodorkovsky had funded a opposition political party.

She was the daughter of Warwick Charlton, an Englishman who had served with the World War II American Forces from 1941 to 1945 as a public relations officer. After the war ended, he came up with the idea of making a goodwill gesture to America from the people of England. He wanted to build a reproduction of the *Mayflower* and sail it across the Atlantic. There it would be presented to the American people. It took 'Project Mayflower' the next ten years to plan, develop and accomplish this dream.

Victoria had inherited all her father's enterprise and zest and also, it has to be said, his somewhat bumpy marital track record – when she resurfaced in Tony's life she had been married four times. Energetic, enterprising and greatly admiring of Tony's talents, she was determined to get him work. She had always been entre-preneurial; now she had specific goals. Working with Tony, she and he together could produce prestige, coffee-table books that her richest clients could use in their corporate businesses or, like that other upmarket, highly desired corporate publication, the Pirelli Calendar, as gifts for important clients.

It was a lucrative market and for Tony, who had always relied on being commissioned by others rather than seeking out work for himself, a tempting chance to do what he was so good at while earning sizeable sums of money. The Siberian trip, during which Tony, Victoria and his assistant Simon Warren criss-crossed 6,000 miles of country, continually traversing time zones, was the first of a number. On his return, he noted in satisfied tones that the rigours of the trip should put paid to the maddening rumour that he was 'frail'.

Simultaneously, there was an exhibition of his portrait photo-graphs, 'Interior Personalities', at his son David's shop, Linley, at 60 Pimlico Road. It included the dramatic and beautiful picture of Margaret, all white profile, neck and shoulders, with huge dark eyes and chandelier earring, that visitors to his studio see on his desk, a tormented-looking Francis Bacon and a photo-graph of Somerset Maugham, his face lined with wrinkles like crevasses, of which Tony had remarked: 'Someone once said that if a fly walked across Willie Maugham's face it would break its legs.'

*

On 19 March 2003 Tony made his annual presentation of the Snowdon Awards at the House of Commons. It was the European Year of Disabled People. As he recalled in his speech, 1981 (when he was UK President) was the International Year of the Disabled – 'a dehumanising title I hated. But some things do happily change in twenty-two years. This year, 2003, is the European Year of Disabled People. So in just two decades "the disabled" have become recognised as people. About time too!'

It was also worth saying, he added, that Britain was the only country in the EU where the rights of disabled people are enforceable, and constantly reviewed by the Disability Rights Commission, always assisted by the Parliamentary All-Party Disability Group. But as he pointed out, even the most well-meaning legislation can only do so much and one didn't have to go very far to experience discrimination. He cited his own experience of parking outside the Royal College of Art (which is in the Borough of Westminster) on a disabled bay, showing his disabled badge to a traffic warden and receiving the response: 'You may be disabled in Kensington, mate, but you're not here,' accompanied by a fine.

He was still as fervent in attacking real-life examples of prejudice or unfairness as ever. When he went with his half-brother Peregrine to Caernarvon Castle, where Prince Charles was to open a museum, he spotted a sign on the wall that said 'Disabled Exit' and went over to see what it involved. What he saw was stone steps, down which only the relatively fit could walk, leading to an outside door. At once he called over the administrators of the Castle to ask: 'Why is this sign up? Nobody in a wheelchair could possibly use this exit.' 'It's the only exit for the disabled,' came the answer. 'It's not a disabled exit, so take the sign down,' said Tony, becoming crosser by the minute. 'We can't because it's drilled to the wall and there are no tools around,' came the triumphant response.

'I have tools,' said Tony. 'I take them wherever I go – you can use my tools.' 'But the sign is too rusted in.' It was too much for Tony. 'The Prince of Wales arrives in forty minutes,' he told them, 'and if this sign isn't down in ten the Prince of Wales will not come and open your museum. So you choose. If the sign isn't down we'll shut the Castle and I'll tell him why.' Within minutes, three burly men appeared and wrested the sign from the wall. After the Prince had concluded the opening ceremony Tony told the organisers that the exit must be established as a proper disabled exit – 'it is insulting to people who are disabled to be told to walk down steps'.

The Snowdon Award Scheme was a powerful and ongoing way of helping others in the community. But another, into which he had put enormous voluntary time and effort, was coming to an end when his fixed tenure as Provost of the Royal College of Art ended. For the past eight years it had been a central strand of his life. Not only was it a post that could have been designed exactly to his specifications, focusing on the subjects that were of interest to him; he found the surging energy and creativity within its walls revitalising and inspiring. He knew it would leave a large gap in his life – how large, he did not yet realise.

His leave-taking from the College, at the Convocation of 2003, was highly emotional, both on his part and on that of the students. As Provost, he played his usual role; this year with the addition of a short speech, received with applause. At the end of the ceremony, according to his usual custom, he remained behind until the Fellows and the honorands had processed out. Then, as one of the College staff came to help him from the platform back to his dressing room, there was an outburst of noise. The entire student body had risen to their feet and were clapping and cheering him to the rafters – a scene impossible to watch without a lump in the throat. Tony himself, overwhelmed, was in tears. 'I have never seen anything like it,' said Helen Robinson, vice-chairman of the College Council.

As for Tony, the end of his term of office as Provost left a gaping void in his life. He missed the College dreadfully. 'I don't want to go in there again – I don't know what I'm going to do without it,' he told Helen sadly.

Surprise, Surprise . . .

At the beginning of 2004 there were three further twists to Tony's ever-colourful private life. The first was the implant of a pacemaker to regulate his heartbeat – a drama that started when he went to visit his doctor for a different, minor complaint and a regulation ECG test discovered its irregularity (many of his friends, knowing his romantic track record, commented that it was hardly surprising that there was a weakness in this particular organ). The second was a new affair and the third the discovery of another daughter.

Early in 2004 Tony was contacted by Polly, one of the five children of Jeremy and Camilla Fry, two of the people Tony had loved most in his life. Polly had known Tony all her life: he had been a frequent visitor to Widcombe throughout her childhood, often with Princess Margaret, and he was godfather to one of the Fry children. Jeremy Fry, in turn, was godfather to Tony's son David Linley, who as a teenager had spent a lot of time in the Fry household when he was learning cabinet-making. Linley and Polly, the closest in age of the Fry children to Linley, had become close friends, living next door to each other in Bath (to which Jeremy had moved when he sold Widcombe after his divorce). To all appearances Tony was and had been one of the closest of the Fry family friends and an uncle-figure to their children. Yet from the age of eighteen Polly, born on 28 May 1960, just three weeks after Tony's marriage to Princess Margaret, had heard rumours from other family friends that Tony, not Jeremy, was her father. She began to ask questions of these friends, who hastily backtracked, telling the pretty, blonde young woman that there was no truth in such gossip.

Polly, satisfied, continued with her life. She married businessman

Barnaby Higson, with whom she lived in an old rectory on the outskirts of the market town of Frome, Somerset, had five children, began to decorate houses professionally and soon became known for the beauty of the results. She was, as she had always known, very like her mother Camilla but as the years passed and the paternity rumours cropped up again and again, she began to wonder if certain characteristics in herself were not, after all, more like Tony than her presumed father.

Like Tony, she was fair-haired (Jeremy was dark), had a gift for mimicry, a long upper lip and an eye for objects. She knew that he had 'really adored' her mother; she remembered talking to him when she was eighteen about photography – one of her interests – and the testing game he had set her. 'Shut your eyes,' he said as they talked, 'and tell me everything that's in this room.' This variant of 'Kim's game'* was to show her that he regarded memory and an awareness of one's surroundings and what is going on around one as a key element in photography.

When she was forty-four she decided that she wanted, indeed needed, to know the answer, one way or another. Her mother, who might have been hurt by such an enquiry, was no longer alive; Jeremy had been living in India for a long time† and in any case was far less paternal than most fathers. As she put it to herself: 'When you reach a certain stage in your life, you just want to *know* ... who you are, where this or that comes from, what made you.' She wrote to Tony and asked if she could come and see him.

That June, over the traditional light lunch in the Launceston Place kitchen, she nervously broached the subject that had been preoccupying her. 'Could we', she asked, 'have a DNA test to settle things one way or another?' At first Tony demurred. Nat-

---

* In Rudyard Kipling's *Kim* the young boy Kim is shown a tray of objects for a few moments and then asked to recall as many as he can remember.

† Jeremy had bought Pallam Palace, former home of a Rajah, in 1995, after spotting it rotting away in Kottayam – dating from the eighteenth century, it was in a dilapidated state. When he became fed-up with the bureaucracy in Kerala, he carefully dismantled the entire structure and transported it over the border to Rajakkad in Tamil Nadu state, where it was restored and reassembled. He also restored the surrounding plantations of cardamoms and coffee, irrigating them with a network of waterways.

urally enough, he did not want to alter what seemed a perfectly satisfactory status quo, he did not want his old friend Jeremy upset and he needed no further potential complications in his own life. But, honourably, he agreed to do what Polly wished, and take a DNA test. After their lunch she wrote to him to say that whatever answer the test threw up, the last people she wanted to hurt were Tony or his children. She simply wanted to discover her own roots.

The test, jointly funded by each of them and done by the same doctor who had conducted the DNA test that had decided Jasper's paternity, took place that summer of 2004, at Launceston Place, with swabs of saliva taken from both their mouths. It proved conclusively that what Polly had suspected was true: Tony was indeed her father. It was something both of them found difficult to come to terms with. On Tony's side, there was no wish to disturb the tenor of his life – he would, after all, shortly be seventy-four, an age at which few men expect an addition to their family. He and Polly already had an affectionate relationship – was this not enough? Polly, for her part, felt a mixture of relief and guilt. At last the niggling question that had troubled her for years was answered; and she knew, finally, who she really was. She also felt a heavy burden of guilt: she was the one who had forced the issue, she was the one who had uncovered something that possibly, after all these years, might have been best left undisturbed, and in doing so upset various members of Tony's family. But just as adopted children often have an atavistic desire to know who their real parents are, so she had felt that knowing for certain was important to her. Once she had discovered, she wanted nothing more from Tony than acceptance and recognition.

To her great distress, the story broke in the newspapers that December – leaked, probably, by a friend. She had not wanted her siblings to know in case it altered the emotional dynamic between them and she certainly did not want such news to reach Jeremy, now eighty and increasingly frail. Jeremy, when contacted by the press, responded vigorously that the 'allegation' that he was not Polly's father was 'utter nonsense'. Tony at first neither confirmed nor denied the allegation, saying: 'I don't know anything about it. It has nothing to do with me.' Later he said that he had no knowledge of any rumours or of a DNA test, adding that the story did not bother him – 'Not upsetting at all – good luck with it,' he remarked jokingly. His somewhat mixed reactions were largely due to the fact that Polly, who had not known the story would appear, had therefore not been able to contact him in advance, so that there was no combined 'plan of action', though both of them knew they did not want Jeremy upset. Polly's own reaction was to say 'No comment' when telephoned by the press, a fact she confirmed to Tony by postcard on 22 December.

After a while the story died, thanks largely to Jeremy's denial, Tony's stonewalling and Polly's silence. But her hope that they could forge a new father–daughter relationship foundered; the old affection remained exactly as before but it was too late in the day for Tony to readjust his emotional perspective, especially as Polly was physically distant. Nor did he particularly want to take on board five new grandchildren.

The third change, the affair, given Tony's tendency for 'moving on' was perhaps inevitable. Discussing work possibilities, lunching together and arranging plans, he and Victoria Charlton had drawn closer. He was always attracted by energy and enterprise, qualities Victoria possessed in spades. Her presence held another powerful allure: the promise of work, all his life a motivating force. ('I hate August,' he once said, 'there's never any work around.') Victoria, as a professional woman with a successful career, fully understood this attitude. A further point in common was that both were half-Jewish.

One weekend in the spring of 2004 when Emmy was away they began an affair, something that suited them both. For a long time Emmy was unaware of it. Tony had explained that exhibitions and a trip to India that would result in a book were in the offing and that to discuss these he was seeing Victoria Charlton, but he had not disclosed the new development in their relationship. Early in October 2004, after they had lunched together, Victoria drove him back to Launceston Place in her left-hand-drive sports car. Together they walked up the steps to the front door where they shared a passionate kiss. It was recorded by a *Daily Mail* photographer and featured in that paper's gossip column along with a five-paragraph biography of Victoria. Emmy, well aware that Tony invariably used the ground-level side door coming and going from his house, felt sure the kiss had been stage-managed – the front steps gave a much better view of the embrace – and wondered if it was to alert her to the fact that Tony's affections were wandering. But he reassured her that it was a mere harmless farewell and that they had been discussing their forthcoming trip to India.

Tony's trip to India took place in November 2004 (he made three more visits before the project was finished). The photographs he took, largely portraits of Indian notables – writers, scientists, artists, film directors, actors and politicians – were for a book sponsored by Sun Capital, an investment company owned by the Khemka family which had interests in hotels, pharmaceutical companies, hospitals, trading companies and IT in India, Russia, the UK and America. It was destined for the company's charitable arm and would be used to illustrate India as it is today at events the Khemka family chaired and ran.

For Tony the trips were a breath of fresh air, a return to the golden days when he flew all over the world on exciting commissions. He went, naturally, with Victoria, and his current assistant Dylan Thomas. He relied on them both for everything, from checking that bathroom floors were non-slip – his inability to use his legs was now such that falling was a constant threat – to finding restaurants that would serve smoked salmon and scrambled eggs, the only food he would eat in the subcontinent. Victoria got him ready every morning and Dylan acted as confidential aide as well as photographic assistant, ensuring that he could ring up Emmy and Lucy without Victoria's knowledge. The trip was extremely strenuous but he adored it, refusing to be ruffled by heat, exhaustion or the distances travelled. It was also lucrative, bringing him £60,000 (Dylan earned £150 a day).

Emmy, knowing Tony, had naturally been suspicious over the India trip. So when he said he would take her to St Petersburg for Christmas she was delighted. To spend time together in such a beautiful place, with its superb buildings, away from the routine of everyday life was, she felt, both romantic and a reassuring sign that their relationship was still on track – and seeing St Petersburg for the first time would in any case be a wonderful experience.

It did not prove so. Tony had issued the invitation and assured her that he was looking forward to it, but everything from his general approach to his body language suggested the reverse. From the start there were difficulties: he forgot to take not only his hat and coat but also his credit card. Emmy had to pay for everything with her debit card, or by cash (naturally, she was repaid later). Sightseeing, for Emmy one of the reasons for the trip, was limited, as he wanted a drink after two hours and had a rest in the afternoon. She had the embarrassing task of ringing the hotel management to say: 'Lord Snowdon wants the adult TV channel.' In England such a choice would quite likely have made all the gossip columns but in St Petersburg it passed unnoticed, a small example of a general lack of recognition that depressed him, as when Emmy took him to the Mariinsky Theatre – and no manager came rushing up to offer them one of the blue-velvet-hung boxes.

With hindsight, it was not too difficult to see why this trip to one of the most beautiful cities in the world was, to put it bluntly, rather a fiasco. Holidays did not mean as much to Tony as to most people: he had already visited an extraordinary number of places all over the world, usually (though not always) in conditions of great comfort and in any case he much preferred work to any holiday. 'I hate holidays – they're a waste of time,' he had said earlier. 'I've travelled enough through work.' There was, too, the question of Victoria. He was deeply fond of Emmy, he knew that to hear he was being unfaithful would devastate her, and the sensation of guilt must have played a part in his generally resentful attitude.

There began to be signs Emmy could not ignore. The crunch came in spring 2005 when she asked him what their plans were for that weekend, only to be told he was going to Bath. When she discovered he was taking Victoria it was too much. The suspicions and difficulties of the past months crystallised; she herself had been completely faithful and she did not see why she should put up with infidelity from someone for whom she had done so much. She decided to withdraw, dignity intact. When she told him she was leaving him, he protested, but she said quietly: 'I'm into caring – but not into sharing.' There followed a bombardment of telephone calls but Emmy was adamant. They had known each other too long, however, to break off all contact, so that occasionally she would agree to his frequent suggestions that they meet for lunch.

Amid all these emotional complications, Lucy was still very much part of his life. If a newspaper paragraph showing them lunching or dining together commented in surprised tones on what excellent terms they were on, Tony would respond by saying, 'Well, she *is* my wife.' Lucy, for her part, often came in and out of Launceston Place – while flat-hunting she kept many of her clothes there – establishing communication on good terms first with Emmy and then Victoria.

What neither Lucy, Emmy nor Victoria knew at that time was that another of Tony's friends had also become his lover. Marjorie Wallace's close friendship with Tony through the years had recently deepened until, as she recounted to the author, they became lovers. Marjorie felt herself free: her husband, Count Skarbek, by whom she had had three children, had left her twenty years earlier; and her long-standing partner, Tom Margerison, co-founder with David Frost of London Weekend Television, was so incapacitated with Parkinson's Disease that he needed round-the-clock care. And Tony, she reflected, was virtually a single man again.

In February 2005 there was a nostalgic reminder of his youth. He began coxing again, at Teddington, near Hampton Court. Victoria's sister, Caroline Charlton, rowed for East Molesey, sometimes with a cox and four, sometimes a cox and eight. Tony preferred the eight but arrangements were easier with a four as it was their own boat. Although by now able to walk only if he had something like a railing to pull himself along with or an arm to lean on – and then only for a short distance – he was able to take his seat in the boat's stern without help, by sitting on the riverbank and sliding in. It was enjoyable once again to direct, in a voice that carried effortlessly without a megaphone: 'Are you ready ... *Row!*'

For Tony, June 2005 was a bad month. First, he learned of a downmarket film to be screened later in the year on Channel 4, called *The Queen's Sister.** Among its wilder claims was the portrayal of Margaret having a lesbian affair that was condoned by the Palace Household as it would keep her away from Peter

---

* It was televised on Sunday 27 November at 9 p.m.

Townsend and obviate any risk of pregnancy. It was described as 'part fact, part fiction'. Tony, who had not been consulted or approached over any part of it, sprang once again to the defence of his former wife.

On the 18th his dearest friend, Jeremy Fry, died. It was another link severed with the golden, carefree past, but it was not a surprise. Jeremy had been ill for some time and Tony, who had been to stay with him the previous year at Grand Banc in Provence when Jeremy made his annual pilgrimage to Europe, had returned shattered by Jeremy's gaunt appearance and frequent withdrawals from the general company owing to illness.

His own health had begun to give further problems. His blood pressure was up and his doctor had warned him to cut down on his high consumption of alcohol or he could not be responsible for the consequences. For a brief spell – it lasted mere weeks – he went on the wagon. A fortnight after this great renunciation, Victoria drove him with his nephew Tom de Vesci to Wimbledon to see his lawyer and friend John Humphries. On the way back he suddenly said: 'I don't feel very well.' Such a remark was so unlike him that when he repeated it Victoria realised that something was very wrong. They returned to Launceston Place as fast as she could drive, where she rang first his doctor and then called an ambulance. As it was the evening, she was able to ring her brother, a doctor at the renowned US Mayo Clinic, who told her to keep Tony's feet elevated, keep him talking and turn his face a little to the side until the arrival of the ambulance.

He was taken to the Chelsea and Westminster Hospital in the Fulham Road, with a suspected stroke. Once in hospital, the old Tony reasserted himself with teasing answers to routine questions to test his level of concentration and lucidity. 'Who is the Prime Minister?' 'Oh, that terrible little twerp.' 'What is the Queen's name?' 'Lilibet.' 'Tony – *please*,' said Tom. His illness proved not to be a stroke but a TIA (transient ischaemic attack)* which passed quickly. Immense efforts were made by Lucy, David and

---

* A condition caused by a temporary reduction in blood and oxygen supply to part of the brain. Symptoms can include loss of vision, leg and arm weakness, slurring of speech and loss of consciousness, resembling those of a stroke but fortunately clearing up within twenty-four hours.

Sarah, who all visited him in hospital, to avoid any publicity but these were stymied by Tony, who himself informed the *Daily Mail* diary – in all, he spent £30 on phonecards during his three days in the hospital.

His health went on being a bother. In December he felt nausea and was sick a number of times. As he and Victoria planned to spend Christmas in Egypt, he consulted his doctor, who confirmed him as fit to go – but five days into their visit, the sickness returned. They came home and Tony went into the Chelsea and Westminster again on 3 January 2006, where a heart test proved satisfactory but he was found to have an ulcer. As usual, he made light of it, though when Victoria had to undergo a serious operation he was deeply worried about her and made no secret of his concern.

In early February 2006 Tony suggested to the Queen that he take her photograph to mark her eightieth birthday. She was delighted by the idea and – a signal mark of honour – instead of summoning Tony to Windsor or Buckingham Palace, came to the Launceston Place studio for her sitting. Her visit, on 22 March, was made with the minimum of fuss and in great secrecy.

In June that year Tony's children Sarah and David put many of their mother's possessions up for sale through the auction house Christie's. The reason given was to raise sufficient money to pay the death duties, estimated at around £3 million, on Princess Margaret's £7.7 million estate. It was a two-day sale, preceded by four days when the general public, admitted by ticket, could view the collection. Tony was both perturbed and worried by the idea, partly because he had known so little about it, partly because he felt that many of the items should not have been included.

The jewellery alone made a stunning exhibition. Among the 200-odd pieces was the ruby and diamond brooch from Cartier that Margaret's father George VI had given her when she was twelve, with the matching ruby and diamond earclips she later bought, the five-strand pearl necklace given her on her eighteenth birthday by her grandmother Queen Mary, an Art Deco sapphire and diamond brooch (also given by Queen Mary) and, the most valuable of all, the Poltimore tiara, which she had bought for and worn on her wedding day.

Her Art Deco sapphire and diamond bow brooch fetched over £40,000 (ten times more than the estimate); one of her jewel cases, in blue leather with her 'M' monogram, went for £4,650 instead of the expected £300–500. In all, the sale of the jewellery raised almost £5.5 million, with a delicate Fabergé clock given to her by Queen Mary fetching the highest price, £1,240,000.

The second day of the sale, which took place on 14 June, involved furniture, *objets d'art*, silver and paintings. Tony was furious about some of the items included in this part, as he believed they either belonged to him or should have been retained in the family, so much so that he wrote to the Chairman of Christie's UK, Dermot Chichester, pointing out that he believed several items were not actually David's to sell. 'David sells *everything*,' he remarked mournfully at the time (one abiding complaint was that David had sold Tony's beloved blue Aston Martin, given to him by Tony when he found it too much to drive). Fortunately, these disagreements were resolved before they became too exposed.

In the eyes of the public, the most controversial item was the Pietro Annigoni portrait of Princess Margaret, painted in 1957 as a companion to his most famous work, that of the young Queen Elizabeth II in a deep blue cloak that hangs in the National Gallery. In Kensington Palace it had faced all those who walked in through the mahogany-panelled double doors. Most people felt it should either have been retained in the family or presented to the National Portrait Gallery.

The sale was a huge success financially, raising around four times the expected sum – a total of £13.6 million instead of the estimated £3 million. David, bowing gracefully to opinion, himself bought the Annigoni portrait of his mother for £680,000 – more than three times the original estimate. Six months later, to his father's delighted pride, David, whose success had been growing steadily through the years, was appointed Chairman of Christie's, a post for which his taste, flair, energy and business acumen well fitted him.

In July 2006 Melanie and Jasper left London as she felt a country upbringing would be best for him. She selected Castle Cary in

Somerset as it was only thirty minutes' drive away from her mother and stepfather, one of her best friends lived there and it was near Jasper's new school – he was now eight.

Tony was not so busy now: there was a new wave of young, thrusting, hungry photographers with a different approach, few of whom used anything but digital cameras – Tony had always set his face resolutely against new technological developments – and to the outside world he appeared less than robust. A widely used photograph of him being pushed in a wheelchair by Melanie appeared to underline this, nor had it helped when he himself informed the press about his pacemaker. But the work that he did was prestigious. In 2006 he shot the autumn advertising campaign for Bottega Veneta, the chic, expensive Italian luxury brand. As the firm's focus was on monotones – shades of black, grey and brown – Tony chose to shoot all the images in black and white. It was a handsome commission, bringing in $40,000, plus expenses – the shoots took place in Milan.

There were more portraits: the Prime Minister had been so pleased with Tony's earlier photograph of him that he was asked to photograph both the Blairs at Chequers, a sitting that took place on 30 August 2006. 'You were the first one to take my photograph, so I think this is very appropriate, don't you?' said Blair, deeply tanned from a holiday in Barbados. It was the first time Tony had been to Chequers; always sensitive to atmosphere, he found it gloomy, perhaps because the sensation of being in a house where nothing except, figuratively speaking, their tooth-brushes belonged to its inhabitants was alien to him.

In September 2006 Tony had an exhibition of seventy-two of his photographs at the Chris Beetles Gallery in Ryder Street, St James's. One, showing the Princess in the Caribbean soon after their marriage, had never been seen before; Tony had originally given it to Margaret, who had returned it with the words, 'To Darling Tony, All my Love' written on the mount. Other photo-graphs included pictures of Diana, Princess of Wales, the Queen Mother, Noël Coward, Peter Cook, Lord Olivier and Margot Fonteyn, as well as 'ordinary' subjects.

The speech at the private view on 19 September was given by Sir Christopher Frayling, who recalled the 'Snowdon corridor' of

RCA notables at the Royal College of Art – David Hockney, Barbara Hepworth, Ruskin Spear, Peter Blake, Terence Conran – and talked of the unpretentious way Tony had always viewed his work. 'He's said that one must never confuse a medium with an art form. His views on photography resemble Noël Coward's on acting: just try and remember your lines and don't bump into the furniture.'

Many of the photographs were in black and white, images that included the famous – the Queen Mother, Noël Coward and Laurence Olivier – alongside moving and disturbing pictures of subjects such as the inhabitants of a mental institution. All the prints were signed and numbered, from a limited edition of fifty, each priced at around £2,000, half of which went to the Gallery and half to Tony – over a dozen were bought by the singer Elton John. One of the most commented on was the head and shoulders of Princess Margaret in her bath, wearing the Poltimore tiara. The exhibition was a huge success, with Tony making around £300,000 and in March 2007 it was taken to New York.

Also in March he was chosen by the Queen (from a shortlist of four photographers suggested to her by the Royal Mail) for the portraits used on the special stamps issued to mark her and Prince Philip's diamond anniversary in November. The shots of the Queen were taken at his studio, although he went to Buckingham Palace for the double profile shot of the Queen and Prince Philip together. Later in the year there was an unlikely pairing: on 10 September he was asked to photograph all the winners of *Big Brother* – a programme of which he had scarcely heard – for a book to celebrate the twenty-five years of Channel 4's existence, edited by the writer Rosie Boycott and his friend Meredith Etherington-Smith.

September saw the loss of another old and valued friend, Simon Sainsbury, who died of Parkinson's disease on the 27th, aged seventy-six. A notable athlete at Eton, he had become a great philanthropist, supporting various museums and buildings, from the British Museum and the Tate to the original Addenbrooke's Hospital building in Cambridge (now the Cambridge Judge Business School) and Hawksmoor's most famous building, Christ Church Spitalfields. It was hardly surprising that Tony's resolute cheerfulness now sometimes gave way to a grumpiness and angst that he himself summed up as 'General terror – it gets worse with age'. But that winter saw a happy and cheering family event: on 4 December 2006 he and Lucy saw their daughter Frances married to Rodolphe von Hofmannsthal. She was given away by Tony, whose reserves of courage and determination allowed him to walk up the aisle with her.

At the end of September there was another exhibition of his photographs, 'In Camera: Snowdon and the World of British Art', which opened at the Pallant House Gallery in Chichester on 28 September and ran until 27 January 2008. As well as thirty-four portraits from his 1965 book *Private View*, there were more recent portraits – Damien Hirst naked in a fish tank, the potter Grayson Perry in frilly dress and halo bonnet, the first female Turner Prize winner Rachel Whiteread in a white room with white sculptures. The exhibition received respectful reviews in *The Times* and other newspapers and a long, adulatory article in the November 2007 issue of *Vogue*.

In his late seventies, the physical horizons of Tony's life have shrunk. Because of his inability to walk more than a few steps, he spends most of the daylight hours in his studio/workroom in the basement of Launceston Place, sitting in a wheeled chair beside his desk with its massed photographs – a young and exquisite Margaret, a smiling Queen, Prince Charles, portraits of Lucy and a 'rather grand' one of Diana, Princess of Wales in tiara and strapless black evening dress with a necklace of jet and diamonds round her throat and matching bracelet. She sits in an antique gilt chair with Prince of Wales feathers on the top of its high back, lent by the Ministry of Works. 'They said: "You can borrow that so long as nobody sits in it," so of course I sat in it straightaway,' he says. The photograph is inscribed 'Dearest Tony, with love from Diana'; engraved on the top of its frame is a big 'D' under a coronet. 'I was shattered when she died,' he says, 'but no, I cannot remember where I was at the time.'

There is a determined shutting of the mind to unpleasantness that extends to an airbrushing of the past: to listen to him, it was roses, roses all the way. Today this translates into a gloss of optimism over everyday life: a forceful determination to suppress loneliness or sadness and a wholly admirable lack of complaint.

He has never stopped inventing – a silver belt buckle that holds a watch, a knife and fork for a businessman that folds into a neat oblong, a spoon that fell into the waste disposal unit and was crushed interestingly was turned into a brooch. This quicksilver ability to see the outlines of one object within the material boundaries of another – a kind of artistic lateral thinking – illustrates one of the contradictions at the heart of his extraordinarily complex character. Highly intelligent, he never reads a book; yet the same mind that can turn odd scraps of metal into a Gothic dog kennel (as he did for his daughter Frances's puppy) is resolutely set against any kind of modern technology, from digital cameras and dishwashers to mobile phones and computers (only the latter is allowed in the house and that for his PA).

As his friend Carl Toms pointed out:* 'People meeting Tony for the first time have to undergo a disconcerting critical scrutiny' as he tries 'to discover what makes them tick and whether he should bother with them at all ... he is a modern eccentric with an eccentric's absolute determination to have his own way, which can goad people to the brink of assassination only held back by a charm that could halt a ravening beast in its tracks.'

He loves a party but friends are kept resolutely apart, 'each of us in our separate little box,' as one told me, and he flirts constantly, with everyone from women to waiters. Or as Gyles Brandreth once put it: 'To be candid, he flirts with the letterbox as we pass.' He has been the focus of eyes countless times, performing his public appearances with relaxed ease and charm, yet he still shakes with nerves before making a speech. He is completely democratic, with a hatred of pomposity, yet dislikes people not recognising his status.

He is enormously conventional in one sense, writing thank-you letters almost on leaving the lunch table, yet (in his youth) constantly pushing at the boundaries of convention. His manners

---

* In his introduction to *Photographs by Snowdon*, published by the National Portrait Gallery in 2000.

are exquisite and yet at times few can be ruder. He is completely sure in what he is doing and although basically he does not care what people think, he needs instant affirmation that a photograph (or design) has 'worked' – preferably in the form of lavish praise. Few of his intimates have come away without bruises, yet to anyone handicapped, or hit by personal disaster or sorrow he is kind, thoughtful and compassionate. He is impeccably neat – every one of the exquisite objects in his house must be in its rightful place to a millimetre – yet no one could call his life tidy. As for the constant procession of women – few men in their late seventies have two regular mistresses – one possible answer is the remark made of the great psychiatrist Carl Gustav Jung by Anthony Stevens, himself a Jungian analyst: 'It was as if the early separation from his mother had taught him that he could never trust the love of one woman and must always seek safety in numbers.'

What will he be remembered for, apart from marriage to the Queen's sister? He is, above all, an innovator. Asked (by the author) what he believed in most deeply, he replied unhesitatingly: 'Work. And change.' His life is a testimony to both.

Professionally, his photography, with its grainy realism and immediacy, changed the face of theatrical photography for ever and his informal portraits of royalty and others are at the opposite end of the spectrum from the earlier posed, Beatonesque glamour. Yet perhaps his true genius lies in the field of photo-reportage, where his combination of sharp-edged visual perceptiveness and respect for the dignity of human life gives a creative empathy that can sum up whole interior landscapes in one unforgettable image – as in his features for the *Sunday Times* and the *Telegraph Magazine*. There is no striving for effect, simply a recognition of what exists beyond most people's vision. 'His work is instantly recognisable,' says the well-known photographer Terry O'Neill. 'His range is incredible, studio, outdoor, reportage – he can do anything.' Or as the late Lord Lichfield, fellow photographer and Princess Margaret's cousin commented, 'He is in a class of his own.'

In his voluntary work, his insistence on a meld of functionalism, simplicity and elegance meant that his contribution to British design (through the Design Centre) was immense. In his role as

Provost of the Royal College of Art, there was the same total involvement and hands-on professionalism. 'Quite simply, he was the best Provost we have ever had,' says Sir Christopher Frayling.

His marriage broke the mould of royal pairings, not simply because he did not come from the kind of rich, landed background into which a princess was then expected to marry. Although he gave Princess Margaret unstinting and effective back-up on the royal tours and visits they did, judged by the standards of the day their private life was amazingly free of protocol. Together they were icons of the sixties, in the vanguard of all that was new and exciting, effortlessly mingling the arts and the Establishment in their blue drawing room. Long before Buckingham Palace entertained them, writers, painters, journalists and dancers poured through the doors of Kensington Palace.

The same sense of originality and innovation characterises the two enterprises of which he is most proud. The Snowdon Aviary, with its filmy pyramids that contrast so spectacularly with the concrete dwellings of most of the Zoo's inhabitants, could not be less like the wire cages in which most birds are confined. Entrusted with designing a setting for the Investiture of Prince Charles as Prince of Wales, his immediate grasp of the importance of television and the necessity of a setting in keeping with an ancient tradition and yet televisual – often in the teeth of objections from the more hidebound officials concerned – produced a spectacle that was at once dignified, moving, beautiful and comprehensible to the millions who watched it.

Yet perhaps his greatest legacy is the largely unsung work he has done for the men and women unfortunate enough to have been born handicapped, or to have acquired a disability. The Snowdon Award Scheme, begun with money he set aside soon after his marriage, the Survey it commissioned, and his unrelenting campaigning to improve conditions for disabled people were a powerful force in the enlightenment of public and official perceptions that eventually resulted in the Disability Discrimination Act of 1995. To have helped others is perhaps the greatest monument any man could have.

Source Notes

Most of the material in this book, unless otherwise stated, comes from Tony himself, as the result of hours of taped interviews and of the access to his files that he generously gave me. Thanks to his introductions, I spoke to most of his close friends, and many of those of the Princess. I have not indicated in these notes every point they made, as it is usually obvious from the context who told me what. Letters quoted come from the files. Tony's engagement diary, kept from his earliest days, provided an accurate record of engagements, times and places.

Every conversation and interview used in compiling this book was taped, with the full consent of the person involved, both for purposes of record and to ensure accuracy.

CHAPTER 1: The Other Son

Ronnie Armstrong-Jones's friend and fellow barrister Robert Carey-Evans, who was in the same chambers, provided an overall view of Ronnie, and described the house in First Street and the break-up from his second wife. Much of Tony's childhood is from his own description of it. Tom Parr recalled the photograph of small boys where Tony's hands are behind his back. Lord de Vesci, the son of Tony's sister Susan, described the depth and closeness of the bond between the two, talked of some of the pranks Tony got up to as a child and confirmed Tony's closeness to Oliver, repeated later by Francis Wyndham. Both he and Tony confirmed the bitterness of the break-up between Tony's parents. Richard Rhodes provided a vivid description of Sandroyd, the prep school he attended at the same time as Tony, as well as his memories of Tony there. When I stayed with Lord Rosse he kindly told me much about Birr Castle and the life he and his brother and Tony and Susan led with Lord and Lady Rosse, and of his memories of Tony and their childhood there. Kenneth Rose, who had taught Tony at Eton, and Simon Sainsbury, his contemporary there, supplied details of Tony as an Eton schoolboy. Lord McColl described the onset of polio and its effects.

CHAPTER 2: On His Way

Anthony Barton, Andy Garnett, Robert Belton, Simon Sainsbury, Justin de Blank, Peter Saunders and others recalled Tony's time at Cambridge and his life in the 1950s, also confirming the 'wild parties' and 'goings on' at Widcombe. Tom Stacey was helpful about London parties; Peregrine Armstrong-Jones was very informative about their father's attitude to homosexuality. An obituary of Anne Rosse written by Lady Meyer, a great friend, talks of her designing and sewing her daughter Susan's wedding dress.

CHAPTER 3: Pimlico Road

Frank Tait remembered Tony leaving dinner and saying 'Mind your own business'. Tom Parr, Angela Huth, Bob Belton and several others confirmed that Tony hated to make plans ahead. Veronica Keeling, who also worked for Tony in the studio, was another who saw him kiss men on the lips; she also remembered Tony's bruised and battered appearance at Ascot after he had been beaten up at a party and the incident with the Kabaka of Buganda. John Timbers was illuminating about Oliver Messel and Vagn, and their relationship with Tony. Tony confirmed, to the author, that several men had been in love with him and his love affair with Camilla Grinling. Andy Garnett recalled the motorbike games. Robin Banks and John Timbers described life in the studio. Robin Banks confirmed that Tony was a good shot before he ever went to Balmoral. Lady Airlie, whose mother was a great friend of Oliver Messel, talked of Oliver's house and the atmosphere there. Robert Belton and Peter Saunders described Tony's weekend disappearances when he was courting Princess Margaret. Tony's comment about illusion was made in an interview with Gyles Brandreth in February 2000. Lady Reading was among many who talked of Tony's relationship with his mother. Candida Crewe's article on 12 November 2005 on Jeremy Fry in the *Daily Telegraph* was illuminating. Bob Belton provided details of the room at Rotherhithe and early days at Old House. Thomas Messel described Tony's 'rejected childhood' and how 'he could never do anything right in his mother's eyes'.

CHAPTER 4: 'Tony Snapshot'

Gina Ward told me of her love affair with Tony. John Timbers and Anthony Barton had a ringside view of the girls who passed through Tony's life; John Timbers, as his assistant, described studio life. Much of the description of the Rotherhithe room can be found in Bill Glenton's book *Tony's Room*. Dr Frank Tait, a great friend of Lady Elizabeth Cavendish and also of John Cranko, was kind enough to supply eyewitness accounts and anecdotes; both he and Bob Belton saw a lot of Jacqui Chan and confirmed that she was the resident girlfriend. Lady Glenconner recalled Tony taking their wedding photographs; Lady Grade described a party at their penthouse. The anecdote of Cecil Beaton and the lilies came from Anthony Powell, then working for Oliver Messel. The story of Tony leaving Kingsley Amis and Elizabeth Jane Howard at a pub to find their own way home is in Kingsley Amis's memoirs. The comment by Tony about Alex Liberman is from *Them: A Memoir of Parents*, by Francine du Plessix Gray.

CHAPTER 5: Margaret

Descriptions of Princess Margaret, of which there are many in her biographies, have also come from those who saw her regularly in Clarence House. I have drawn on my memories of the late Group Captain Peter Townsend, as well as my taped interview with him, for descriptions of his attitude and personality. Lady Glenconner talked of the Princess's despair after the death of her father and of the real start of the Townsend affair in South Africa. Marigold Bridgeman told me about the prayer group to which the Princess belonged, which sometimes met at her family home, Dowdeswell Park. I am indebted to William Tallon for descriptions of the life of Princess Margaret at Clarence House, her relationship with the Queen Mother – confirmed by Dame Frances Campbell-Preston – and her behaviour after her love affair with Group Captain Townsend was over.

Raymond Salisbury-Jones, invited to several of the parties attended by the Princess, was at the buffet-dance where she scorned her host, and was one of those who sometimes drove her home. The information about the violet-tinted lavatory paper in Rotherhithe comes from Bill Glenton's book *Tony's Room*. Christopher Warwick was told by Princess Margaret that she and Tony might never have met again after the first dinner party had not one of her friends wanted Tony to photograph her; it was then she decided she wanted him in her circle. John Timbers, Tony's assistant at the time, would often see the Princess when she arrived at the Pimlico Road studio. Lady Juliet Townsend told me the story of the Queen Mother's remark about education and marriage. Three of Tony's closest confidants told me of the frolics at Widcombe Manor. Robert Carey-Evans described Ronnie's parting with Carol and her meeting with Pepe Lopez. Gina Ward told me of Tony's telephone call to her.

CHAPTER 6: Engagement

Anthony Powell, who was working simultaneously with both Oliver Messel and Cecil Beaton in their adjacent houses ('I would dart from one to the other'), was standing by Beaton's side when the Queen Mother telephoned him about the engagement. Lord Lichfield recalled the 'stuffiness' among older families about the engagement. Anthony Barton recounted the alleged story about the rowing coach who swam out to sea.

Working on the film *Cleopatra* with Messel, Powell described the luncheon party with Beatrice Lillie. Kenneth Rose described the pre-lunch drinks routine at Clarence House. Information about the black Labrador given to Tony by the Queen came from Princess Margaret's chauffeur John Larkin, who looked after it. Information about the wedding presents received and the formalities is in the Royal Archives, as is Tony's letter to the Queen Mother. Malcolm Higgins described Anne Rosse's outfit.

CHAPTER 7: A Glittering Couple

Malcolm Higgins, the Snowdons' butler, described the behaviour of the Princess's dresser, Ruby Gordon, and the routine of the Princess's day. The anecdote about the telescope came from Tony. Malcolm Higgins witnessed the incident of the diamond-stud earring, and Lady Rosse's descent to say goodbye. The Princess's cousins, Lord Lichfield and Lady Elizabeth Anson, confirmed that she had said that the question of children had never been discussed before their marriage. Kenneth Rose supplied background information on Tony's choice of a title. Lady Grade described the party at the Grade penthouse for which Princess Margaret flew down from Scotland. Richard Wood remembered Princess Alice's remark on seeing David Linley as a baby. Malcolm Higgins, as well as Tony himself, confirmed the mutual antipathy between Tony and Nanny Sumner and described how Tony would roll his son over on the lawn. Leslie Field described the Princess's jewels. Kenneth Rose made available his draft letters concerning the state of the Snowdons' house.

James Cousins, as well as Tony, described much of the interior of the house and the work they both did on it. A detailed schedule of the duties of the various domestics and their conditions of service is in Tony's files. John Larkin described the Princess's cars. Richard Wood, the under-butler, described weekends away, and remembered the Princess's comment, 'I was always brought up to respect a soufflé.' Francis Wyndham described working with Tony for the *Sunday Times Colour Magazine*. Descriptions of the parties at Kensington Palace came from Angela Huth – who remembered Anne Scott-James's hand shaking – Lady Airlie, Lord Lichfield and others. Malcolm Higgins heard the Queen Mother's remark about the difficulty of looking 'convincingly happy'.

CHAPTER 8: Married Life

The Docklands Ball story was reported in newspapers on 2 December 1964. William Tallon recorded that the Princess sent her dogs to Windsor; Marigold Bridgeman and Milton Gendel often noticed how good Tony was at remembering small and pleasing details. Letters from the Aga Khan describe the presents the Snowdons brought him and their holiday. Milton Gendel and Janie Stevens talked of the Italian holidays. Colin Miller, an officer in the Gordon Highlanders, one of the regiments that provided a ceremonial bodyguard at Balmoral, provided background information about customs there; William Tallon described Tony casting on the lawn. The episode of the game chips was witnessed by Richard Wood, serving dinner. Lorenzo Berni, owner of the San Lorenzo, described the party of Italian women rising to their feet and Tony's arm- wrestling. Letters about Rotherhithe are in Tony's archive. Christopher Warwick confirmed the Princess's overwhelming possessiveness; Robert Belton viewed it from Tony's side, and noticed the occupations she invented to occupy herself; Richard Wood and James Cousins also witnessed it at close quarters. James Cousins reported on the Council of Industrial Design trips they went on together.

Francis Wyndham recalled the Edith Evans anecdote and Margaret's constant wish to accompany Tony on stories. Mary Gilliatt was very helpful about the trips her neighbour Paul Reilly took with Tony. Anthony Barton described their skiing holidays. Dame Frances Campbell-Preston witnessed disagreements at Royal Lodge. Pamela Lady Harlech and Simon Sainsbury talked of the Snowdons' waterskiing. Details of the Aston Martin are in Britt Ekland's autobiography *True Britt*. Descriptions of the 1965 visit to the United States are in the Royal Archives. Anthony Barton described how his affair with the Princess began – and ended; and his rapprochement with Tony years later. Tony showed me the jewellery box he designed, and its contents. George Melly provided colourful accounts of parties attended by both him and Tony. The Hon. Annabel Whitehead confirmed Margaret's visit to a psychiatrist. Peter Saunders, who knew both Frys intimately, talked of their break-up.

CHAPTER 9: Harsh Words

Sholto Douglas-Home told me much about his father Robin's life and character. Tony showed me the Margot Fonteyn necklet. A long memorandum from the Private Secretary describes the arduous duties and taxing routine of the servants. The Princess's ladies-in-waiting confirmed that Tony was on excellent terms with the royal family and that they knew how difficult Margaret could be. George and Diana Melly and Andy Garnett described some of the parties Tony attended; Diana Melly noticed how uncomfortable the Princess often felt at the more bohemian ones. Kenneth Rose recounted the story of a courtier pushing Tony off his motorbike; Mary Gilliatt was one of those present at the private showing in Kensington Palace of *Don't Count the Candles*. James Cousins was sitting with the Princess when the news of Robin Douglas-Home's suicide appeared on the television news; he heard the Snowdons argue about the Tokyo trip.

CHAPTER 10: Old House and Les Jolies Eaux

Lady Glenconner provided a full description of life on Mustique. Details of shoots at Balmoral, Sandringham and Windsor are in Tony's files. Princess Margaret described the unkind notes Tony left for her to her biographer Christopher Warwick and to Lady Glenconner. Pamela Harlech, Lady Airlie, Patrick Lichfield, Lady Elizabeth Anson and the servants were among the many who witnessed the Snowdons' quarrels; John Larkin would often hear them fighting in the car. Lady Juliet Smith described the visit to Cambodia. Hugo Vickers supplied the story about the ambassador and dancing. Richard Wood would hear the Princess tell her children they were not royal.

Frank Tait was present at the barbecue where Tony brought presents for everyone except Margaret and witnessed the episode of the ballgown; he was also present when Tony shouted 'I'm not your chauffeur!' Annabel Whitehead had a ringside view of Nanny Sumner's 'grandness' and Tony's running battles with her; Malcolm Higgins was present at the incident of the London bus. Numerous people, including Tony himself, recalled Margaret's dislike of Old House; Lady Glenconner was one of those to whom she described the ghost she had seen there. Robert Belton remembered how difficult Margaret found visiting it. Frank Tait remembered the 'buttered eggs' story. Many of those working at Kensington Palace witnessed the Monday morning scenes when food was found missing.

Details of the Investiture are in a file bulging with congratulatory letters in Tony's archive. Dame Gillian Wagner (whose husband, Sir Anthony Wagner, was Garter King-of-Arms) provided much background material. Hugo Vickers told the story of the Sandie Shaw song.

CHAPTER 11: Feeling Trapped

Lady Reading and Lady Jacqueline Rufus-Isaacs talked to me at length about their friendship with Tony; Janet Goodwin, whose friend worked with Jackie at the Yves St Laurent boutique, recalled the 'Doctor Ricketts' subterfuge. Lady Jacqueline described the breaking of the story about their affair and the arrival of the press in Switzerland; Sir Dai Llewellyn told me of the visit he and his brother Roddy made to her there. Sir Edward Cazalet described the episode of Tony throwing wine over his uncle Peter (as did Tony). There is a complete file on *Born to be Small* in Tony's archive. The comment from Princess Margaret to the actor Gordon Jackson is noted in Kenneth Williams's letters. The invitation to join the Central Council for Integration of the Disabled came in a letter from Lord Goodman. Lt-Col. Freddy Burnaby-Atkins told me of his difficulties in running the Princess's household; he was among those who noticed her advances to the Air Commodore on the flight back from Western Australia and heard her remarks about Lucy. William Tallon described the rows in front of the Queen Mother. Frances Donaldson recalls her husband Lord Donaldson's anecdote in her book *A Twentieth-Century Life*.

CHAPTER 12: Lucy

The Countess of Snowdon told me that she and Tony first met at the house of Colin Clark. Tony's engagement diary, as fully kept as ever, lists his movements. Princess Caracciolo described the holiday the Snowdons took with her in Italy, and Margaret's flirtation with Luigi d'Orso. Lord Napier described the running of the Princess's household during that difficult period and the housekeeper finding Tony's stocking footprints on the hall floor. Dame Gillian Wagner (former Chairman of Barnardo's) talked of the need to keep the Snowdons apart at the Barnardo exhibition. There is a file on *Happy being Happy* in Tony's archive. Lady Glenconner supplied a full description of the Princess's visit to Glen and her meeting there with Roddy Llewellyn. Nicholas Haslam also talked of Roddy. Letters from the BBC as well as Tony's diary confirm the dates he was away. Mary Gilliatt described Margaret's hurt at finding Lucy at his bedside in hospital. Lady Glenconner confirmed the Snowdons' ongoing sexual closeness; Mrs Greenfield (Margaret's dresser) witnessed Tony's ability to persuade Margaret out of her reluctance to keep engagements.

CHAPTER 13: 'Tell Your Friend to Keep Out of My House'

Lady Glenconner not only saw the romance between the Princess and Roddy Llewellyn at close quarters but was one of the Princess's confidantes. Lord Napier, travelling with the Snowdons, witnessed Tony's delayed entrance to the convention hall and conveyed Tony's refusal to move out of Kensington Palace to the Princess. Lady Penn and Lady Glenconner witnessed Margaret's distraught state after Roddy's flight to Turkey. Everyone who knew both Snowdons and the Queen described how Tony remained on good terms with both the Queen and the Queen Mother. John Rendall, a founder-member of Surrendell, described the life there, and Margaret's visit to the house. Lord Napier recalled the difficulty of telling Tony he could not accompany the Princess to Australia, and how he eventually told her when Tony was leaving Kensington Palace. He also witnessed the scene with Nanny Sumner. Letters to the National Fund for Research into Crippling Diseases for the Snowdon Survey are in the Fund's archives.

CHAPTER 14: Separation

Princess Margaret's ladies-in-waiting and confidantes like Lady Elizabeth Anson told me of her deep misery at the separation from Tony. Lord Napier talked of Roddy's proposed and actual statement to the press, which appeared in virtually every newspaper. There is a description of

Colin Tennant's gold-themed party in an article by his son Charlie. Details of Oliver Messel's Barbados house are from Thomas Messel. There are details of the Launceston Place house in the Local History archives at Kensington and Chelsea Central Library. Ann Hills' father Dr Elliott Philipp and her close friends Tim Symonds and Derek Jackson provided a description of her character, flat, attitude to sex and her relationship with Tony. Christopher Warwick – to whom the Princess had told it – recounted the story of her arriving at Launceston Place believing that Tony wanted to ask her for a divorce. Lady Glenconner related the story of Princess Margaret's rebuttal of the suggestion that Tony might spend Christmas with her and the Queen Mother.

CHAPTER 15: Remarriage

Kenneth Rose reported the story about the Castle of Mey. Tony's archives contained a diary of alterations and improvements to his house as well as a list of what came from Kensington Palace. Lord Napier described the amicable way this was arranged. Tony's half-brother Peregrine Armstrong-Jones remembered Tony's helpfulness over the Plas Dinas plans. Ann Hills' state of mind was known to her father, to Tim Symonds and to Derek Jackson among others. Hugo Vickers remembered lunching with Lady Rosse at Nymans. Christopher Warwick heard the story of Roddy's reaction to her pink dress from the Princess. Lady Glenconner charted the shift in Margaret's relationship with Roddy from love to friendship.

CHAPTER 16: Campaigning

Stephen Bradshaw was particularly helpful describing the problems suffered by disabled train-users and Tony's response to these. Details of the Snowdon Award Scheme are in Tony's archives and in those of the Scheme; his engagement diary gives details of his movements. Andrew Farquhar recalled Tony's speech-making to Rotarians and others. Lady Glenconner told of Princess Margaret's visits to the Lighthouse. Victoria Charlton described the trips to Russia with Tony.

CHAPTER 17: Working Ever Harder

Sue Odell described working with Tony and his effect on art directors. Details of Tony's contracts with the *Sunday Times* and the *Telegraph Weekend Magazine* are in his archives, as is the correspondence about Anthony Freeman. Andy Garnett recalled one of the occasions on which Anne Rosse got drunk. Lord Rosse confirmed the sale of the Womersley diamond stars. Lady Penn described the luncheon at Kensington Palace with Peter Townsend. Professor Sir Christopher Frayling spent much time telling me about Tony's work at the Royal College of Art as Provost and his role in the Convocations. The eminent professor Lord McColl of

Dulwich gave me a description of post-polio syndrome. Andrew Farquhar remembered meeting Ann Hills several times at Tony's house. Graham Pigott, who assisted Tony, described the photographing for *Vanity Fair*.

CHAPTER 18: 'I Need to Speak Urgently to Lord Snowdon'
Tim Symonds, Dr Philipp and Derek Jackson told me much about the last stages of Ann Hills' life; Margaret Purcell told of Ann Hills' repeated emphasis on the need for discretion in her 'mystery' affair; Anthony Powell remembered Lucy's departure for India. The story was also fully covered in newspapers. Other details were filled in by Tony. Particulars of the Snowdon Award Scheme meeting and of the launch of the Survey are in Tony's archives. Details of the department Designing for Disabilities started by Tony at the Royal College are in his archives. Sir Christopher Frayling described the 'Provostial breakfasts' and Tony's contribution to the College, fleshing out details that are in Tony's archives.

CHAPTER 19: Melanie
Melanie Cable-Alexander told me in detail about her love affair and relationship with Tony, including the story of their first meeting (also recounted by John Rendall). Peregrine Armstrong-Jones, who saw much of Tony and Melanie together at Old House and witnessed their empathy, described the affection he and his wife had for Melanie, also his own closeness to Jasper. Tony told me of his christening present to Jasper. Meredith Etherington-Smith talked of the decision made to use Mario Testino's photographs of Diana, Princess of Wales rather than Tony's. Details of the Queen's visit to the Royal College of Art are in Tony's files. Lady Airlie mentioned her surprise at Tony's horror of public speaking. Peregrine Armstrong-Jones described their visit to the Dome together. Melanie described the gradual break-up of her love affair with Tony. Pamela Lady Harlech described the 21st birthday party she gave for Frances.

CHAPTER 20: Battling On
Tony showed me letters from women who were still in love with him. Conversations with Tony and Lucy Snowdon respectively indicated their attitude to the altered state of their marriage. Emmy Hirst talked of her friendship with Tony. Lady Glenconner supplied a full description of Princess Margaret's illness. Dame Frances Campbell-Preston witnessed the wheelchair episodes. Angela Huth talked of the Princess's attitude to seeing friends. Lady Elizabeth Anson, Lady Glenconner and Angela Huth confirmed that she did not want to see Tony, or any man, after her second stroke. David Griffin described Tony's constant and deep concern for his former wife; Hugo Vickers recalled how depressed Tony was for several

months after Margaret's death. Evelyn Humphries confirmed that her father never charged Tony. There is a vivid description of Old House and its contents by Clive Aslet in the *Daily Mail* Weekend Magazine of 8 June 2002. Tony and Victoria Charlton described the trip to Russia. Peregrine Armstrong-Jones was present at the incident at Caernarvon Castle. Helen Robinson recalled Tony's leave-taking in the Albert Hall. Andy Garnett, Marjorie Wallace, Emmy Hirst, Graham Pigott and a number of others described his enjoyment of lunches out and at being recognised.

CHAPTER 21: Surprise, Surprise ...

Polly Higson described the events leading up to her request that her relationship with Tony be clarified, confirmed the DNA test that did so and told me of her feelings on learning that Tony was her father. The kiss with Victoria Charlton, at the top of Tony's front-door steps, was featured in the *Daily Mail* together with a full account of Victoria Charlton's background. Victoria told me about her relationship with Tony, and Emmy Hirst of the alteration in hers. Marjorie Wallace told me of the mutation in kind of her deep friendship with Tony. Dylan Thomas told me about the trip to India. Tony and Victoria described his visit to the Chelsea and Westminster Hospital.

Select Bibliography

※

Amis, Kingsley, *Memoirs* (Hutchinson, 1991)

Aronson, Theo, *Princess Margaret: A Biography* (Michael O'Mara Books, 1997)

Austin, Tony, *Aberfan: The Story of a Disaster* (Hutchinson, 1967)

Beaton, Cecil, *Beaton in the Sixties: More Unexpurgated Diaries*, ed. Hugo Vickers (Weidenfeld and Nicolson, 2003)

Botham, Noel, *Margaret: The Untold Story* (Blake Publishing, 1994)

Bradford, Sarah, *Elizabeth: A Biography of Her Majesty the Queen* (Heinemann, 1996)

Castle, Charles, *Oliver Messel* (Thames and Hudson, 1986)

Cathcart, Helen, *Lord Snowdon* (W.H. Allen, 1968)

Cooper, Duff, *The Duff Cooper Diaries*, ed. John Julius Norwich (Weidenfeld and Nicolson, 2005)

Coward, Noël, *The Noël Coward Diaries*, ed. Graham Payn and Sheridan Morley (Weidenfeld and Nicolson, 1982)

Crewe, Quentin, *Well, I Forget the Rest: The Autobiography of an Optimist* (Hutchinson, 1991)

Dimbleby, Jonathan, *The Prince of Wales: A Biography* (Little, Brown, 1994)

Donaldson, Frances, *A Twentieth-Century Life* (Weidenfeld and Nicolson, 1992)

Ekland, Britt, *True Britt* (Sphere, 1980)

Field, Leslie, *The Queen's Jewels* (Harry Abrams Inc., 1987)

Fleming, Ann, *The Letters of Ann Fleming*, ed. Mark Amory (Collins Harvill, 1985)

Gladwyn, Cynthia, *The Diaries of Cynthia Gladwyn*, ed. Miles Jebb (Constable, 1995)

Glenton, William, *Tony's Room: The Secret Love Story of Princess Margaret* (Pocket Books Inc., 1965)

Hamilton, William, *My Queen and I* (Quartet, 1975)

Heald, Tim, *Princess Margaret: A Life Unravelled* (Weidenfeld and Nicolson, 2006)

Hoey, Brian, *Invitation to the Palace: How the Royal Family Entertains* (Grafton Books, 1989)

Hoey, Brian, *Snowdon: Public Figure, Private Man* (Sutton, 2005)

Hunting, Guy, *Adventures of a Gentleman's Gentleman: The Queen, Noël Coward and I* (John Blake, 2002)

Keay, Douglas, *Elizabeth II: Portrait of a Monarch* (Century, 1991)

Kenward, Betty, *Jennifer's Memoirs: Eighty-Five Years of Fun and Functions* (HarperCollins, 1992)

Lacey, Robert, *Royal: Her Majesty Queen Elizabeth II* (Little, Brown, 2002)

Lake, Tony and Hills, Ann, *Affairs: How to Deal with Extra-Marital Relationships* (Open Books Publishing, 1979)

Lees-Milne, James, *A Mingled Measure: Diaries 1953–1972* (John Murray, 1994)

Lees-Milne, James, *Ancient as the Hills: Diaries 1973–1974* (John Murray, 1997)

Lees-Milne, James, *Through Wood and Dale: Diaries 1975–1978* (John Murray, 1998)

Lees-Milne, James, *Deep Romantic Chasm: Diaries 1979–1981*, ed. Michael Bloch (John Murray, 2000)

Lees-Milne, James, *Ceaseless Turmoil: Diaries 1988–1992*, ed. Michael Bloch (John Murray, 2004)

Lewis, Jeremy, *Cyril Connolly: A Life* (Jonathan Cape, 1997)

Lewis, Roger, *The Life and Death of Peter Sellers* (Century, 1994)

MacCarthy, Fiona, *Last Curtsey: The End of the Debutantes* (Faber and Faber, 2006)

Pimlott, Ben, *The Queen: A Biography of Elizabeth II* (HarperCollins, 1996)

Strong, Roy, *The Roy Strong Diaries 1967–1987* (Weidenfeld and Nicolson, 1997)

Thornton, Michael, *Royal Feud: The Queen Mother and the Duchess of Windsor* (Michael Joseph, 1985)

Tynan, Kenneth, *The Diaries of Kenneth Tynan*, ed. John Lahr (Bloomsbury, 2001)

Vickers, Hugo, *Elizabeth, the Queen Mother* (Hutchinson, 2005)

Vidal, Gore, *Point to Point Navigation: A Memoir* (Little, Brown, 2005)

Warwick, Christopher, *Princess Margaret: A Life of Contrasts* (André Deutsch, 2002)

Waterman, Ivan, *Helen Mirren: The Biography of Britain's Greatest Actress* (John Blake, 2007)

Williams, Kenneth, *The Kenneth Williams Letters*, ed. Russell Davies (Harper Collins, 1994)

Wilson, Harold, *The Labour Government 1964–1970: A Personal Record* (Weidenfeld and Nicolson with Michael Joseph, 1971)

Wyatt, Woodrow, *The Journals of Woodrow Wyatt*, vol. 1, ed. Sarah Curtis (Macmillan, 1998)

Index